PRESIDENTS WITHOUT PARTIES

the pennsylvania state university press | university park, pennsylvania

PRESIDENTS WITHOUT PARTIES

the politics of

economic reform

in argentina

and

venezuela

in the 1990s

JAVIER CORRALES

Library of Congress Cataloging-in-Publication Data

Corrales, Javier, 1966–
    Presidents without parties : the politics of economic reform in
Argentina and Venezuela in the 1990s / Javier Corrales.
        p.   cm.
    Includes bibliographical references (p.   ) and index.
    ISBN 0-271-02194-2 (cloth : alk. paper)
    1. Argentina—Economic policy. 2. Venezuela—Economic policy.
3. Executive power—Argentina. 4. Executive power—Venezuela.
5. Political parties—Argentina. 6. Political parties—Venezuela.
I. Title.
HC175.C6684 2002
338.982—dc21   2001055951

It is the policy of The Pennsylvania State University Press to use
acid-free paper. Publications on uncoated stock satisfy the minimum
requirements of American National Standard for Information
Sciences—Permanence of Paper for Printed Library Materials,
ANSI Z39.48-1992.

contents

Part One: Introduction

Part Two: Background to the Reforms

Part Three: Executive–Ruling Party Relations

Part Four: The State-Without-Party Condition in Latin America

list of figures and tables

Figures

Tables

preface and acknowledgments

One of the most enduring trends in Latin American politics since the transition to democracy in the 1980s is the low public esteem for political parties. A public opinion poll conducted by Chile's Latinobarómetro in 2001 revealed that less than five percent of Latin Americans express having "much confidence" in political parties. In some countries, political parties are among the least trusted institutions, often ranking lower than the military. Both citizens and state leaders alike seem to have developed an incurable aversion to all things partisan. Citizens are cynical of traditional parties, and office seekers enjoy flaunting their independence from parties. Parties are often blamed for the worst evils of the nation. Latin Americans are simply scornful of political parties.

The primary objective of *Presidents Without Parties* is to show why the discrediting of political parties has harmed this region. Often, this discrediting has translated into deliberate efforts by citizens and state leaders to repudiate parties. And yet, for better or for worse, political parties play an irreplaceable role not just as instruments of representation but also as instruments of governance. States must, I contend, form strong partnerships with political parties and, most important, with the ruling party in order to manage their economies effectively. Rather than eschewing political parties, good governance requires cultivating strong links with them.

To demonstrate the importance of political parties for economic governance, or more specifically, of a harmonious relationship between the Executive branch and the members of the ruling party, *Presidents Without Parties* carefully examines the politics of market reforms in Argentina and Venezuela over the last two decades. In the mid-1980s, Argentina and Venezuela were favorite cases in Latin American studies classrooms: Argentina because it represented Latin America at its worst, and Venezuela because it represented Latin America at its most promising. Argentina was the quintessential case of "reversal of development" (Waisman 1987): it had squandered its wealth and fallen deep into debt. It had lost control of its currency and fallen prey to noncooperative business and labor sectors. Neither civilian nor military governments had succeeded in ending the chaos that reigned in the political arena. And under the last military government, the state had waged one pointless and expensive war against its own citizens ("the Dirty War") and another against the United Kingdom over a chain of windswept treeless islands populated for the most part by sheep. Venezuela, while never really a paradise, was nonetheless considered an effective "manager of dependence" (Tugwell 1975). It established a stable democracy, characterized by intra-elite cooperation and stable macroeconomic conditions.

In the 1990s, these images were suddenly reversed. Argentina emerged as a paragon of resolve, and Venezuela as the epitome of economic decay. Argentina implemented one of the furthest-reaching market-oriented reform programs in the region, whereas Venezuela stumbled at the effort. Since then, no Venezuelan government has been able to reverse the steady contraction of the economy that began in the late 1970s, let alone introduce deep market forces. All the while, political conflict has reached new heights. In 2001, Venezuela was arguably one of the most polarized, undemocratic, and economically stagnant countries in the region.

By 2001, Argentina, on the other hand, seemed to have reverted to its old self. The governmental resoluteness that characterized the 1991–97 period turned to wavering. The formidable economic growth rates of the 1990s gave way to a severe recession, starting in 1998. A series of policy shocks failed to prevent this recession from turning into a financial collapse in 2001 that was so catastrophic that Argentines reacted much the same way they had reacted to hyperinflation in 1989: with riots and looting. On December 19, 2001, dozens of supermarkets and many retail stores were ransacked. Rioters set parts of the Ministry of the Economy on fire. The country plunged into its worst political crisis since 1989, compelling the president to resign the following day. His successor, Adolfo Rodríguez Saá, who had been appointed by Congress, resigned a week later amid continuing riots. A new president was appointed in the first week of 2002, the Peronist Eduardo Duhalde, who promised to put an end to the worst political and economic crisis that Argentina had seen since the early 1980s. The collapse of 2001 seems all the more inexplicable, given the achievements of the 1990s.

Why has the Venezuelan state failed to govern the economy? Why did the Argentine state through most of the 1990s manage to escape the economic woes of the 1980s, only to succumb to similar ailments in the opening years of the new century?

Answering these questions provides an opportunity to tell a story about the factors that shape state capacity. In this version of the story, there are two main characters—the Executive and the ruling party—and the plot revolves around the different relationships established between them in each country. These different relationships, I argue, help explain why some states manage transitions to the market more effectively than others.

The question of what determines the outcome of market-oriented reforms became irresistible to economists and political scientists alike in the 1990s. For economists, cases of reform attempts provided a laboratory for testing policy prescriptions—which economic measures are more likely to bring about which economic results. For political scientists, the study of market-oriented reforms provided an opportunity to revisit old themes in comparative politics.

The first is the question of change—what explains profound transformations in societies. Most political scientists agree that when adopted in full, market reforms are nothing less than an effort to move from an old to a new model of economic development. The second question is the issue of cost imposition. Although market reforms do generate winners, they also entail the "distribution of sacrifices over time and across groups" (Williamson and Haggard 1994, 531). And yet, viewed as a question of change and cost imposition, market reforms emerge as nothing new in history or in the social sciences. Societies have always undergone changes and sacrifices, and political scientists have always studied these processes.

What is new about the study of market reforms is the optimism among those who implement these reforms and those who study them that these changes and sacrifices can take place while avoiding two also-ancient vices— authoritarianism and rebellion. Societies have always been capable of great transformations, and states have always been capable of imposing costs. But they have less often been able to accomplish both and still remain democratic and at peace. That, however, is what is expected of market reformers today.

Presidents Without Parties strives to make two contributions to the debate on the conditions that generate economic change. The first is to argue that, indeed, great transformations that involve sacrifice can occur without significant compromises in levels of political stability. The second is to suggest that the key to maintaining political stability during moments of major, top-down transformation corresponds directly to whether or not the Executive can obtain the consent of the ruling party. Ruling-party support is a necessary condition for deep economic transformations from above. Without it, Executives lose credibility and political fortitude to neutralize the opposition from skeptical as well as cost-bearing sectors of society. An Executive who fails to rally the ruling party behind the reforms will stumble politically. However, states that obtain the support of their ruling parties become resilient. They can establish links with interest groups (which is necessary for state-society cooperation), without creating the conditions for interest groups to capture the state (which is necessary for autonomous policymaking).

This conclusion is nothing more than a revival of the old argument that political parties are indispensable for democratic governability (see Schattschneider 1942). It is reminiscent of Huntington's (1968) argument that the "no-party state" is a fragile one. And it is consistent with Offe's (1984) argument that parties make democracy and markets compatible. And yet the notion that parties matter for governance is somewhat revolutionary among political economists of development in the mid-1990s. Insofar as political parties matter, many theorists would say, their importance has to do with their programmatic orientation (whether left or right) or self-restraint (whether they stay out of economic policymaking). These factors are no doubt important, but not as important, I will argue, as the capacity of parties to adapt to new circumstances, embrace the risk of change, and form a solid working relationship with the Executive branch.

Writing this book entailed extensive fieldwork—a source of personal and professional joy. The opportunity to live in and learn about societies previously unknown to me has been thrilling. And yet conducting field work was also the root of a moral dilemma. As a U.S.-based scholar, I come from institutions that are fairly well endowed. But when abroad, I have no option but to use the resources of countries and institutions that are significantly poorer than my own. Every day of my research time abroad, I was overwhelmed by the thought that I was always gaining more from my hosts than they were gaining in return.

Two institutions in particular went out of their way to facilitate my research abroad. The first is the Center for Public Policy at the Instituto de Estudios Superiores de Administración (IESA) in Caracas, Venezuela, where I was a visiting researcher in the spring of 1994 and a visiting professor in the summer of 1998. The other was the Instituto Torcuato di Tella in Buenos Aires, which hosted my stay during the fall of 1994. Despite their limited resources, these institutions showered me with privileges: office space, computer and Internet access, clerical services, contacts with local elites, library borrowing privileges, and most important, a forum for debating my ideas. I am eternally grateful for their disinterested generosity.

I am also grateful to those who agreed to be interviewed for this project (see Appendix 4) and to a long list of individuals who have offered comments on this book at different stages of its development. Jorge I. Domínguez, Jeanne K. Giraldo, Janet Kelly, Steven Levitsky, M. Victoria Murillo, Robert

D. Putnam, William C. Smith, Carol Wise, Deborah J. Yashar, and various anonymous reviewers exhibited exemplary collegiality by agreeing to read the bulk of this work. Other scholars read only individual chapters or short segments of this book, but their comments were equally valuable: Carlos H. Acuña, Robert Bottome, Katrina Burgess, Imelda Cisneros, Michael Coppedge, Margaret Crahan, Rut Diamant, Rodolfo A. Díaz, Peter Evans, Gustavo Ferrari, Peter Kingstone, Scott Mainwaring, James W. McGuire, James Mahon, Moisés Naím, Joan M. Nelson, Michael Penfold, Aníbal Romero, Mariano Tommasi, Juan Carlos Torre, Joseph S. Tulchin, and Kurt Weyland. I am eternally grateful for their help and I hope that they accept my apologies for every suggestion that I was unable to incorporate into the final manuscript. I am also grateful to my colleagues at Amherst College—Hadley Arkes, Amrita Basu, Kristin Bumiller, Tom Dumm, Victoria Farrington, Pavel Machala, Lisa Raskin, Austin Sarat, Donna Simpter, William Taubman, and Ronald Tiersky—for supporting my work. My wonderful friend James Martel has always been an example of how to be an academic without losing touch with reality.

I have also been fortunate to count on the help of first-rate research assistants. Javier Biardeau helped with my research in Venezuela, Anthony Spanakos with Chapter 12, and Patricia Del Grosso and James Hart in finalizing the manuscript. Without these four, I would have never completed this project.

I would also like to express my gratitude to four institutions in the United States. The Weatherhead Center for International Affairs and the David Rockefeller Center for Latin American Affairs, both at Harvard University, hosted me while I was a graduate student in the Department of Government, where the idea for this book was born. Amherst College, where I have been Assistant Professor of Political Science since 1996, has provided the intellectual space and the necessary funding to develop this project. And the Woodrow Wilson International Center for Scholars in Washington, D.C., where I was a fellow in the 2000–2001 academic year, offered me the necessary serenity and resources to finalize this project.

Last, Robert A. Hemmer, who has known me better than anyone else for more than sixteen years, has always been there whenever I have needed encouragement or simply someone to talk to.

To all these friends, colleagues, and institutions, I am eternally grateful.

acronyms

Argentina

B&B	Bunge & Born (private firm)
CGT	Confederación General del Trabajo (leading labor federation)
DNU	Decrees of Necessity and Urgency
ENTel	Empresa Nacional de Telecomunicaciones (pre-privatization telephone company)
FREPASO	Frente País Solidario (center-left party)
MODIN	Movimiento por la Dignidad y la Independencia (right-wing party)
PJ	Partido Justicialista, or Peronist Party
SRA	Sociedad Rural Argentina (association of agricultural producers)
Ucedé	Unión de Centro Democrático (center-right party, Argentina)
UCR	Unión Cívica Radical (center-left party)
UIA	Unión Industrial Argentina (peak association of industrialists)
YPF	Yacimientos Petrolíferos Fiscales (oil company)

Venezuela

AD	Acción Democrática
CANTV	C.A. Nacional Teléfonos de Venezuela (telephone company)
CEN	Comité Ejecutivo Nacional (the governing body of AD)
COPEI	Comité de Organización Política Electoral Independiente (Social-Christian Democratic party)
COPRE	Comisión Presidencial para la Reforma del Estado (state agency)
CTV	Confederación de Trabajadores de Venezuela (peak labor confederation)
CVG	Corporación Venezolana de Guayana (large industrial complex)
Fedecámaras	Federación de Cámaras y Asociaciones de Comercio y Producción (peak business association)
FIV	Fondo de Inversiones de Venezuela (cabinet-level agency in charge of investments)
IESA	Instituto de Estudios Superiores de Administración (graduate school of business and public administration)
MAS	Movimiento al Socialismo (leftist party)
MVR	Movimiento Quinta República (center-left, military-based party)
PDVSA	Petróleos de Venezuela, S.A. (state-owned oil company)

| RECADI | Régimen de Cambios Diferenciales (system of exchange rate controls in the 1980s) |
| VIASA | Venezolana Internacional de Aviación, S.A. (Venezuela's national flag carrier) |

Other

APRA	Alianza Popular Revolucionaria Americana (Peru)
IMF	International Monetary Fund
LPO	Lavalas Political Organization (Haiti)
PAN	Partido Acción Nacional (Mexico)
PFL	Partido da Frente Liberal (Brazil)
PMDB	Partido do Movimento Democrático Brasileiro (Brazil)
PPB	Partido Progressista Brasileiro (Brazil)
PRD	Partido de la Revolución Democrática (Mexico)
PRI	Partido Revolucionario Institucional (Mexico)
PSC	Partido Social Cristiano (Ecuador)
PSDB	Partido da Social Democracia Brasileira (Brazil)
PTB	Partido Trabalhista Brasileira (Brazil)
SOE	State-Owned Enterprise
VAT	Value-Added Tax

PART ONE

introduction

1

unlikely

reformers,

unlikely

results

In the early 1990s, no nation could claim to be immune from the pressure to liberalize its economy. Everywhere state leaders turned, they were bound to feel this pressure. If they looked outside their countries, they encountered a battery of international scholars, policy advisers, financiers, and investors who demanded market-oriented reforms as a condition for extending their blessing.[1] If they looked to their own regions, they were likely to find

1. For discussions of international pressures on behalf of economic liberalization, see Williamson 1994, Kahler 1992 and 1994, Frenkel and O'Donnell 1994, and Stallings 1992.

a neighboring country already engaged in economic liberalization, and thus, winning a better seat at the negotiating table with international actors.[2] And if state leaders looked to their own countries, they found a growing number of local scholars, elites, technical experts, social movements, and citizens also clamoring for greater economic freedom.[3] Thus, the pressure to liberalize in the early 1990s was ubiquitous.

This is not to say that the political enemies and institutional obstacles to economic liberalization had vanished; in many countries, the defenders of statism remained as entrenched and determined as ever. But the context of their struggle had changed. By the late 1980s, they could no longer claim to be free of rivals.

Few state leaders, therefore, have been able to ignore this three-tiered pressure to liberalize economically. By the late 1980s most state leaders had begun to open or at least seriously considered opening their economies to market forces. This opening, in general terms, consisted of a combination of economic stabilization and structural adjustment reforms.[4] After spending decades intervening in their economies to correct or compensate for market failures, states were now intervening (or thinking of intervening) in their economies to make room for the market. By any standard, this has been the most significant redirection of state policies since the Great Depression.

It is even more remarkable that this "revolution" in state policies has occurred without a corresponding wholesale replacement of state elites.[5] Indeed, the transition to the market in many countries was often launched by

2. For a discussion of regional determinants of domestic economic trends, see Stallings 1995. On regionalism more generally, see Gamble and Payne 1996 and Fawcett and Hurrell 1995.

3. For a discussion of the strengthening of pro-liberalizing domestic actors in Latin America in the 1980s, see, for example, Domínguez 1997, Silva 1997, Biersteker 1995, Edwards 1995, and Remmer 1991b.

4. "Economic stabilization" refers to government-implemented measures that seek to restore some balance in macroeconomic variables such as inflation, exchange rates, balance of payment, and fiscal deficits. "Structural adjustment" refers to government-implemented changes in how the economy is organized to make room for private competition in the production and exchange of goods and services (e.g., trade opening, privatizations, tax reforms, deregulation, decentralization, export promotion). For different versions of these definitions, see Edwards 1995, Haggard and Kaufman 1992 and 1995, Williamson 1990 and 1994, Bates and Krueger 1993, Bresser Pereira 1993, Krueger 1992, and Przeworski 1991.

5. Political scientists agree that major redirections of state policies often occur with a concomitant change in state elites. The authors in Hall 1989, for instance, show that the revolutionary adoption of Keynesianism in Western Europe after the 1930s was strongly correlated with the accession to power of new political entrants—parties with strong ties to labor groups—which displaced more conservative political rivals.

the very same political forces that not too long ago were busy demonizing markets and inflating state bureaucracies. The communists of Eastern Europe and Asia, the socialists of Western Europe, and the populists of the developing countries are not identical political forces, but during the postwar period, they shared a historical disdain for markets and a penchant for interventionist economic policies, which they often justified through a proworker, anti-oligarchic rhetoric. And yet it was these very same statist political forces, from China to Italy, from the Kyrgyzstan to New Zealand, that led the transition to the market in the 1990s.

Not all these efforts proved politically viable. While some parties have managed to take market transitions very far, others have experienced setbacks, ranging from mere paralysis to outright societal upheaval. Likewise, while some statist parties have succeeded in transforming themselves into effective deliverers of market forces, other statist parties have failed. The transition to the market, whether carried out by old-time believers or new converts, has produced cases of both accomplishments as well as setbacks.

Recall the differences in performance of Mikhail Gorbachev in the Soviet Union and Deng Xiaoping in China. Both leaders came from quintessentially statist political parties. In the 1980s both leaders decided to reduce the role of the state in the economy and embrace market reforms. Deng Xiaoping carried through without jeopardizing his political regime. Mikhail Gorbachev, on the other hand, provoked a political backlash that brought him down.

On a somewhat more modest scale, in Argentina and Venezuela, two quintessentially statist political parties—Acción Democrática (AD) in Venezuela and the Partido Justicialista (the PJ, or Peronist Party) in Argentina—decided to embark on a transition to the market in 1989. As in China and Russia, the transition entailed a complete abandonment of a model of economic development that had been in place since at least the 1940s, inflicting heavy costs on key constituents of these parties. Five years later, the outcomes could not have been more different. In Argentina, the reforms were accepted and extended, most political forces accepted the new economic regime, and the reformers were reelected in 1995. In Venezuela, however, the reforms were rejected, the reformers were thrown out of office in 1993, and the country plunged into an economic and political crisis that lasted throughout the 1990s.

Argentina and Venezuela are part of a wider constellation of market-oriented reforms by statist political forces that culminated in either implementation or interruption. Statist, labor-based parties managed to implement reform without provoking major political unrest in Australia, Bolivia, Colombia, Costa Rica, Chile, France, Hungary, Jamaica, New Zealand, Poland,

Spain, and Vietnam in the 1980s and 1990s. In many other cases, similar efforts failed. In Brazil, for example, between 1985 and 1994, presidents from statist-populist political forces (José Sarney, Fernando Collor de Mello, and Itamar Franco until 1994) continuously failed to tame hyperinflation, let alone undertake deep structural reforms. In Peru, Zambia, Greece, and the Dominican Republic in the 1980s, statist political forces tried to introduce market reforms, but quickly gave up. In India, prime minister P.V. Narasimha Rao from the statist-populist Indian National Congress announced an ambitious market reform program in 1991. Five years later, the reforms had made only negligible progress, and the highly fractured ruling party suffered a resounding defeat at the polls. In Colombia, the very same ex-statist party that had carried out deep economic reforms in the early 1990s (the Liberal Party under César Gaviria) had serious difficulties sustaining the reform process under the subsequent administration (Ernesto Samper). And in Paraguay, Ecuador, Haiti, Uruguay, and Jamaica the economic reforms presented by statist parties either went nowhere or proceeded very slowly.

Thus, some leaders from statist-populist forces have gone far in implementing antistatist reforms, while others have stumbled. This defies two important arguments. One is the "populists-make-bad-reformers" argument that statist forces cannot be expected to deliver market reforms because they lack the conviction, autonomy, and commitment to push for sound reforms. The second is the "Nixon-in-China" argument that it is precisely the statist forces that have the best chance at reforming because market reforms (like the process of embracing an enemy nation such as China) is a risky affair, and thus, the most mistrusting political force is more likely to undertake this process effectively (see Cukierman and Tommasi 1998 and Rodrik 1994 and 1996).

In short, it is not clear why some former statist political forces attempting to implement antistatist policies succeed, like the PJ in Argentina, and why some, like AD in Venezuela, fail. By focusing on two dichotomous cases in detail, Argentina and Venezuela in the 1990s, and several other cases in more general terms, this study seeks to discover the reason for these outcomes.

Why Study Market Reforms

Studying the conditions under which states prevail at market reform is more than just a simple exercise in policy analysis. Instead, it is an inquiry into two larger topics in comparative politics. One concerns the issue of the relationship between markets and democracy. The other has to do with the sources of "stateness," that is to say, what is it that allows states to govern economies. Scholars studying these questions have come to realize, rather recently, the importance of third variables. That is, for markets and democracy to thrive jointly, and for states and economies to reinforce each other, some third, intermediate variable must be present. Scholars disagree, however, over what this third variable might be—a certain legal order, levels of trust, richness of civil society, class structure, levels of development, and so on. I contend that this third variable is political parties.

The Debate About the Relationship Between Markets and Democracy

In the 1950s, a consensus existed among non-Marxist social scientists that the relationship between democracy and capitalism was symbiotic. Both systems were presumed to share the same logic: democracy is about competitive politics, and the market is about competitive firms (Schumpeter 1950). Efforts to seek political liberty inevitably engender economic liberty and decentralization of power; likewise, deepening markets create demands for political liberties (Friedman 1962). Market expansion leads to more wealth and more wealth-holders, who, in turn, tend to be political (in that they place demands on the political system), democratic (in that they demand decentralized liberties), power-checkers (in that they constrain abuses of power), and moderate (in that they limit their demands to modest change).

In the 1960s, scholars began to question these views, seeing the relationship instead as involving a tradeoff between political liberty and economic liberty: pressing for one necessarily undermines the other. For instance, by encouraging markets, capitalism creates a privileged and disproportionately powerful group (the business sector), on whom the rest of the population depends for its livelihood (Lindblom 1977). Markets are not voluntary, as neoclassical theory contends, but choice-constraining. They create a system of "private government" where important public decisions rest in the hands of corporations (Katznelson and Kesselman 1987). Markets thus "imprison" democracies (Lindblom 1982).

One problem with these arguments was that democracy and markets were defined in either utopian or mutually exclusive terms. For example, Katznelson and Kesselman explicitly reject procedural or representational standards of democracy in favor of a "substantive"—and arguably, unrealistic—one, "in which all citizens have relatively equal chances to influence and control the making of decisions that affect them" (1987, 13). And Lindblom (1982) argues: "For minimal democracy, we require a market system. For fuller democracy, we require its elimination. But its elimination might pose more obstacles to a fuller democracy than does its continuing imprisoning of policy making. It may therefore be that a fuller democracy is never to be ours" (1982, 332). This type of judgment, however, cannot be proven or disproven and thus does not lead to researchable insights.[6]

If democracies and markets are enemies, it follows that capitalists and authoritarians are allies. In the early 1970s, this hypothesis became more accepted, supported by the extent to which relatively developed Third World countries succumbed to pro-market authoritarian regimes.

However, in the 1980s, the market-authoritarian equation was challenged.[7] As new democracies in Southern Europe and South America emerged, and old democracies in the West (presumably plagued with Olson's distributional coalitions) began to prosper again, scholars recognized that markets and democracy can coexist, and even thrive jointly. Markets might not need (or engender) democracy, but democracies have not arisen without markets (see Dahl 1998, 166). Democracies may spoil markets, and maybe even hinder development (see Bardhan 1999), but no more than authoritarian regimes (Bhagwati 1995; Alesina and Perotti 1993; Kohli 1986). Thus Almond (1991) concludes: "We have to recognize . . . that democracy and capitalism are both positively and negatively related, that they both support and subvert each other" (473). Dahl calls this complicated relationship "an antagonistic symbiosis" (1998, 166).

In explaining the experience of the Western world (high levels of political liberties and wealth), scholars have recently made a theoretical correction to

6. The affinity of democracy and markets was also challenged with economic arguments. Olson (1965, 1982), for example, argues that democratic freedom can atrophy the market. As individuals organize politically, they form "distributional coalitions." Rather than work toward the provision of collective goods (e.g., a larger economic pie), these coalitions engage in selfish exploitation (i.e., a larger share of the pie). Interest groups are self-serving and consequently growth-constraining (Tullock 1990).

7. Hirschman (1979) was an early dissenter, asserting that these arguments were too functionalist (i.e., authoritarianism is explained on the basis of a presumed economic need, such as the need to industrialize or to carry out orthodox reforms). He criticized O'Donnell (1978a, 1978b) for failing to demonstrate that authoritarians were aware of (and motivated by) the exigencies of deepening rather than just the motivation to restore social order. And he refuted the idea that orthodoxy required authoritarianism by invoking the Colombian case, which adopted market-oriented policies without establishing authoritarianism. For a discussion of how democratic states might escape the predicament that "government is systematically shaped by forces beyond those generated by popular control," see Benjamin and Elkin 1985.

the liberal consensus of the 1950s. Markets and democracies can prosper simultaneously, not because they need or encourage each other, but because they both depend on a third variable. If that third variable is present, then democracies and markets will thrive simultaneously. The relationship between democracies and markets then seems to be spurious rather than symbiotic.

One of the first to make this point was Offe (1983). Acknowledging that "there is a lot of evidence *against*" his own original position that markets and democracy are incompatible, Offe argued that the surprising coexistence of capitalism and democracy in the West is explained by two institutions—competitive party systems and the welfare state. These political institutions alleviated the inherent tension between pure Smithean capitalism and pure Rousseaunian democracy. It follows, therefore, that in the absence of these institutions, democracy should falter. Putnam (1993) took a different route. In his study on the performance of local governments in Italy, Putnam concluded that effective governance is instead a function of an "environmental institution": horizontal modes of organization and civic traditions. These institutions create "social capital," that is to say, "features of social organization, such as trust, norms, and networks, that can improve the efficiency of society by facilitating coordinated actions" (1993, 167). Trust is the key component of social capital, and trust lubricates cooperation (1993, 171). For Putnam, social capital is the *sine qua non* of democratic performance (no trust, no democracy), but also of market performance (no trust, no markets).[8]

Putnam recognizes that his conclusion challenges Olson (1982): rather than a constraint on markets and democracies, group life is a source of vitality because it generates social capital. Even distributional coalitions can be an asset for capitalist democracies because they can generate social capital.[9] A few months after the publication of Putnam's book, Olson (1993) implicitly conceded Putnam's point: "The conditions that are needed to have the individual rights needed for maximum economic development are exactly the same conditions that are needed to have a *lasting* democracy. . . . Thus the *same* court system, independent judiciary, and respect for law and individual rights that

8. For Putnam, the institution of credit, which is a principal fuel of market growth, is enormously trust-dependent, as highlighted by the etymology of the word.

9. In some sense, however, Olson and Putnam discuss different types of groups: distributional coalitions differ in organization, size, and goals from Putnam's soccer clubs. Thus Putnam's challenge is somewhat misplaced. Nevertheless, Putnam would argue that even selfish distributional coalitions generate a positive externality: interaction in horizontally based groups makes individuals develop expectations of trust. It remains to be determined which type of groups are more trust-generating than others.

are needed for a lasting democracy are also required for security of property and contract rights" (572; italics in original). Olson's logic here is almost identical to Putnam's: democracies and markets are compatible not because their relation is symbiotic but because they both depend on a third factor.[10]

A weakness in Olson's argument is that his key explanatory variables are exogenous (e.g., where does "respect for law" come from?). A weakness in Putnam's argument is his inability to distinguish trust-creating from trust-constraining associations. This led others to argue that the emergence of democracy requires not just societal pressures on its behalf but also the spread of certain "norms" (such as "fairness") (see Levi 1999). However, the overall premise stands—the mutual prosperity of democracy and markets is contingent on the presence of trust-based institutions and norms.

In short, there is ample theoretical and empirical evidence to support Almond's assertion that democracies and markets can either help or hurt each other. They can prosper together, provided additional variables are present. Two likely candidates for this third variable are parties (as theorized by Offe 1983) and the emergence of trust, or credible commitments (as theorized by Putnam 1993). The argument that I propose in this book rests heavily on these precepts.

Market Reforms as a Test of Stateness

The second issue concerns the conditions under which states are able to govern the economy—that is to say, what is the source of "stateness." Theorists of state-formation often point out that a major measurement of state strength is whether states manage to obtain the cooperation, or compliance, of societal groups on behalf of policies that contradict societal preferences (see Migdal 1987, Tilly 1985, and Nordlinger 1981). Market reforms impart

10. Olson (1993, 2000) also makes a theoretical correction to the Weberian tradition. Unchecked monopolies of violence (what he calls the victory of the "stationary bandit" over "roving bandits") serve capitalist interest only in the short run. In the long run, authoritarian rule (the stationary bandit) has diminishing returns: the ruler becomes too insecure about his or her political future and responds to this uncertainty with irrational forms of economic intervention (taxation and arbitrary expropriations) in order to finance the increasingly expensive coercive apparatus that is necessary to stay in power. Thus the authoritarian state initially provides a public good (order), but inevitably creates a public evil (arbitrariness and distortive economic interventions). Here, Olson disagrees with Putnam, for whom authoritarianism can become a stable equilibrium where social capital is scarce. In short, Olson came to believe that authoritarian regimes (not democracies) are more prone to rise and decline. Almost twenty years earlier, Tilly (1975) made a similar point: while the early European capitalists welcomed the public order brought about by the coercive state, organized coercion was a mixed blessing, especially for the aspiring capitalist, because it was arbitrary and costly.

enormous costs across society and thus elicit societal resistance. Thus, when countries decide to liberalize their economies, they confront a major test of stateness (Corrales and Cisneros 1999, 2100). Discerning the conditions under which states survive and overturn this resistance to reforms is thus an inquiry into the sources of state strength in modern societies.

Theorists tend to provide two sets of answers to the question of the sources of stateness. One set of answers focuses on internal characteristics of states: their degree of technocratic competence, internal cohesion, presidential commitment, insulation from clientelistic pressures, and so on. Another set of answers focuses on characteristics of the interaction between the state and society, for instance, whether states manage to establish fluid relations with the very same societal groups they seek to govern. In isolation, however, these two approaches are problematic. States that focus exclusively on enhancing their internal features with disregard for connections with society risk becoming alien creatures—so completely detached from society that eliciting societal loyalty becomes impossible. States that focus on establishing close links with society risk being colonized by particularistic groups. Until the early 1990s, Argentina was an excellent example of the first error; Venezuela is an excellent example of the second. Argentine presidents often believed that the key to sustained reform was to maximize technicism; Venezuelan presidents focused on societal links.

States With and Without Parties

In developing markets, how then can states solve this dilemma of stateness? How can states reconcile the need for technical competence shielded from interest groups and the need for connections with the very same interest groups targeted for reform? Is there some mechanism that can mediate between these two seemingly irreconcilable necessities?

In the early 1990s, the Argentine state discovered this mechanism—political parties, or more specifically, a strong alliance between the Executive and the ruling political party. As this book will show, the main difference between the Argentine and Venezuelan reform experiences, and the one that best explains the observed outcomes, is that the Argentine Executive managed to establish a cooperative relationship with the ruling party, whereas the Venezuelan Executive did not.[11] Cooperative relations between the Executive and the ruling party, more so than other variables typically associated with

11. Throughout this book, "Executive" refers to the president of the republic and those cabinet officials who enjoy great leverage (i.e., "executive authority") over economic affairs.

reform success, enabled the state to deliver the deepest economic transformation that Argentina ever saw and, more important, overturn societal resistance to change.

Most political scientists agree that parties are a fundamental, sometimes even an "indispensable" pillar of *democratic* governance (Lipset 2000). However, few scholars of economic development—either neoliberal or neostructuralist—ever think of parties as equally indispensable for *economic* governance. Insofar as parties matter, they would tell you, it has to do with their programmatic orientation (that is to say, whether left-wing or right-wing; see Boix 1998). Yet parties matter for more than that. In fact, their programmatic orientation, in many ways, may be secondary. Parties matter for economic governance because of the political grounding they provide. Parties bring to the state the capacity to shield it from interest group pressures while simultaneously linking it to civil society. Parties therefore help the state solve the problem of stateness.

To govern the economy, states need a solid relationship with a strong ruling party. This conclusion proves that governance is the product of both historic-institutional variables and political management variables. It is the product of historic-institutional variables because, for a state to govern with a party, there must first *be* a strong party in existence. It is a product of political management because having strong parties is not enough. As this book shows, strong parties tend to react adversely to market reforms. Presidents need to find ways to temper those reactions. Otherwise, they will confront the "state without party" condition, which is lethal for governability.

This book thus brings political parties, or more specifically, ruling political parties, back into discussions of economic governance. It takes seriously the insight developed by theorists of markets and democracies—that both of these require an intermediate variable, which is often political parties—and applies it to the theories of state governance and development. Parties are more than just instruments of aggregation of interests. They are pivotal for economic governance. They can block economic change, or usher it in, even if it is an economic order that they once despised.

2

bringing

(ruling)

parties

back in

the

argument

The key to reform sustainability, and hence economic governance, is the nature of the relationship between the Executive and the ruling party. If the president manages to get the ruling party to cooperate with the reform process, the state's capacity to govern the economy will increase. The Executive is more likely to carry out reforms and, more important, survive the frictions in state-society relations that these reforms engender. If, however, the relationship is noncooperative, the reform process will be imperiled. This chapter elaborates on this argument.

To make the point that ruling parties matter for economic governance, this chapter offers a brief review of the literature. The purpose of this review is not simply to highlight the existence of an empirical puzzle, but to make a larger theoretical claim. The key political challenge of every reforming state is to achieve some degree of insulation from vested interest groups, which is necessary for policy coherence, but simultaneously retain links to society, which is necessary for eliciting societal cooperation with the state. States need to be both shielded from, and connected to, society. The institution that best allows states to achieve this is political parties, and more specifically, ruling parties. Executives can develop different relationships with ruling parties. The chapter concludes with some hypotheses about the expected causal effects of different types of Executive–ruling party relationships.

Variations in Reform Sustainability

In 1989 the newly elected administrations of Carlos Andrés Pérez in Venezuela and Carlos S. Menem in Argentina launched similar market reform programs. Both presidents belonged to dominant,[1] statist-populist, labor-linked[2] political parties (AD and the PJ).[3] The first years of the reforms were quite difficult. Reformers accomplished important objectives, but they also faced numerous political and economic obstacles.

Soon after, the reform processes took divergent paths. Venezuela under Pérez plunged into its most serious political crisis since the 1960s, including an explosion of civic protests, two military coup attempts in 1992, continual cabinet changes, interruption of most reforms, a doubling of murder rates, an outburst of political terrorism, a deepening of political polarization, the resignation of President Pérez in 1993, and a devastating financial collapse at the end of 1993. In the December 1993 elections, Venezuelans voted AD out of office, electing instead an anti-reform candidate, Rafael Caldera. For the next two years, Caldera kept his promise to undo many of the implemented reforms. After two years of economic hell, he decided in 1996 to try market reforms (the so-called Agenda Venezuela), but to no avail. By the end of 1998,

1. According to Sartori, a dominant party is one that generally "outdistances all the others" (1976).

2. Przeworski defines a labor-linked party as one that has a strong penetration of labor unions and thus "poder convocatorio" (power to summon), including "the power to discipline the behavior of their constituents" (1991, 181).

3. "Adeco" and "Peronist" are used to signify relation to either AD or the PJ. They are also used to refer to members of these parties.

Venezuela trailed most of Latin America. Its political system was unstable, and its economy was in ruins. Its per capita GDP contracted while that of the rest of the region grew.[4] Its inflation rate remained among the highest in the region. Venezuela became even more dependent on oil and unable to reduce its public sector deficits. It became one of the few Latin American countries to experience not one but two lost decades—the 1980s and the 1990s.

The Menem administration of Argentina, however, thrived between 1991 and 1996. Unlike his predecessors, Menem managed to control the gigantic fiscal deficit and—miracle of miracles—wipe out inflation. Thereafter, almost every large state-owned enterprise (SOE) at the federal level was privatized, including the oil company (YPF). Most markets were deregulated. Most urban services were outsourced to private operators. Most social services, including secondary education and health, were decentralized. Argentina's market transition was so speedy and profound that scholars called it nothing less than a "revolution" (Acuña 1994), a period during which "history seems to have quickened its pace" (Palermo and Novaro 1996). Even more astounding than Menem's policy changes were the political accomplishments. After two decades of resisting reforms, the majority of business, labor, military, and opposition leaders gradually came to accept the new economic model. By 1994, Menem even got the opposition to agree to one of his long-standing dreams—to rewrite the constitution to allow for his reelection. And in June 1995, in the middle of a recession, and after implementing one of the most severe economic adjustment programs in the history of Latin America, Menem was reelected by a huge margin (the largest for any Argentine ruling party since the early 1960s). In sum, approximately four years after the launch of similar reform programs, the Venezuelan reform team was "dethroned" while the Argentine team was "crowned."

The different political outcomes of these two administrations represent one of the most dramatic reversals of fortune in South America in the 1990s, to borrow Navarro's (1994) label. Table 2.1 provides additional indicators of this reversal. In less than five years Argentina rose from being one of the sickest macroeconomic performers in the region to one of the most robust. Its famous 1991 stabilization program—a strict currency board known as the "Convertibility"—became one of the most frequently discussed and often copied stabilization policies worldwide. Although the country suffered a serious recession in 1995, Argentina's historically more volatile variables—

---

4. Between 1981 and 1990, the annual growth rate of GDP per capita for Argentina, Venezuela, and Latin America as a whole was −2.1, −3.2, and −0.9. Between 1991 and 2000, the rates were 2.9, -0.1, and 1.5 (ECLAC, various years).

inflation, exchange rates, deficits—remained in check. Argentina, until 1997, while not free of economic troubles, sustained one of the highest growth rates in the region, the lowest inflation in the region, and the greatest jump in rankings of economic freedom in the world.[5]

At the start of these reforms Argentina and Venezuela were quite similar in a number of variables; they both had middle-income economies and highly democratic, bipartisan political systems with strong non-Marxist political parties and labor unions. In addition, the presidents who launched the reforms came from statist parties. Why, then, did seemingly similar reform experiences in similar contexts yield such dissimilar outcomes?

Rival Explanations

Most theories about the determinants of market reform implementation fare poorly when applied to these cases. Especially problematic are theories that posit that reform outcomes are somewhat determined by economics. In this section I review these and other arguments with two goals in mind: to identify valuable insights from each theory that might serve to construct a more powerful new theory of reform sustainability; and to show that the Argentina and Venezuela outcomes were not preordained.

Economic Crisis

One of the most frequently invoked arguments about the determinants of reform sustainability is that economic crises work to the advantage of the reformers.[6] Crises, some scholars contend, make states and citizens more likely to embrace deep economic change (Stallings and Peres 2000; Weyland 1996b; Tornell 1995; Drazen and Grilli 1993; Krueger 1993; Keeler 1993; Alesina and Drazen 1991; Gourevitch 1986). Many scholars explain Argentina's reform sustainability as a result of its harrowing crisis, which included no fewer than three hyperinflations in a three-year span (1989–91). Yet the

---

5. Menem's reform record until 1997 impressed both supporters (e.g., Castro 2000) and detractors (e.g., Novaro 1999b). Far less impressive are Menem's last two years in office (1998–99), during which the public debt and fiscal deficits escalated, the pace of structural reforms declined, the exporting sector lost dynamism and diversification, and little was done to address unemployment and inequality. This has elicited criticisms at home (Curia 1999) and abroad (Pastor and Wise 1999b). Chapter 10 discusses this turnaround.

6. This section draws from Corrales 1997–98.

Table 2.1   Argentina and Venezuela: Reversal of Fortune at a Glance, 1988–1995

Regional Ranking in Macroeconomic Performance

Inflation
(Variations in Consumer Price Indices, December–December)

1988		1994	
1. Peru	1,722.6	1. Brazil	929.3
2. Brazil	993.3	LAC	337.3
LAC	776.8	**2. Venezuela**	**70.8**
3. Argentina	**387.7**	3. Uruguay	44.1
4. Ecuador	85.7	4. Ecuador	25.4
5. Uruguay	69.0	5. Colombia	22.6
6. Mexico	51.7	6. Paraguay	18.3
7. Venezuela	**35.5**	7. Peru	15.4
8. Colombia	28.2	8. Chile	8.9
9. Bolivia	21.5	9. Bolivia	8.5
10. Paraguay	16.9	10. Mexico	7.1
11. Chile	12.7	**11. Argentina**	**3.9**

Public-Sector Deficit or Surplus
at Current Prices[a]
(Nonfinancial, percentage of GNP)

1989		1994	
1. Brazil[b]	−6.9	**1. Venezuela**	**−13.8**
2. Peru	−6.9	2. Bolivia	−3.0
3. Uruguay[c]	−6.1	2. Uruguay[c]	−3.0
4. Mexico[c]	−5.0	4. Paraguay[d]	−0.8
5. Bolivia	−4.8	5. Mexico[c]	−0.3
6. Argentina	**−3.2**	6. Ecuador	−0.2
7. Colombia	−1.9	**7. Argentina**	**−0.1**
8. Ecuador	−1.4	8. Brazil[b]	1.2
9. Venezuela	**−1.1**	9. Chile	2.0
10. Chile	2.8	10. Peru	2.4
11. Paraguay[d]	5.2	11. Colombia	2.6

[a] Calculated on the basis of figures in local currency at current prices.
[b] Operational consolidated public sector.
[c] Consolidated public sector.
[d] Central Government.
LAC: Average for Latin America and the Caribbean

Source: ECLAC (1995).

argument that economic crises contribute to reform implementation is problematic for a number of reasons.

1. Cooperation versus Defection. The crisis hypothesis assumes that actors will adopt cooperative responses to economic crisis—they will band together,

in alignment with state preferences, to make necessary sacrifices. Yet it is difficult to predict beforehand how actors will respond to economic calamity. In the context of an emergency, cooperation is plausible, but not inevitable. Defection, in game-theoretical terms, is equally plausible. Actors can eschew cooperation if they fear that others will not do their part, at which point, self-help behaviors prevail. Cooperation is thus the result of existing mediating circumstances, rather than simply the natural response to an emergency.

2. Diachronic Relativity. Crisis arguments often ignore issues of diachronic relativity. Venezuela's pre-reform crisis might have seemed "mild" relative to Argentina's, but it was in fact record-breaking in relation to Venezuela's own history. Venezuela in the 1980s experienced its most severe economic crisis since the 1930s, including accelerating inflation and consumer good scarcity in 1988 for the first time ever. Furthermore, crisis scholars tend to privilege indicators of crisis such as growth rates and inflation rates. If one picks alternative indicators of crisis—for instance, GNP per capita or real wages—then Venezuela emerges worse off than Argentina. Venezuela's GNP per capita declined by 22.6 percent between 1980 and 1988—whereas Argentina actually experienced a gain of 31.5 percent in this indicator at the same time (see Fig. 1). Both countries experienced a comparably severe drop in GDP per capita between 1988 and 1989 (around 20.5 points). Venezuela's real wages in the 1980s shrank in half—also one of the worse erosions in Latin America, twice as large as that of Argentina.

3. Where Is the Bottom? Crisis arguments assume that once a country hits bottom, it automatically rebounds. In reality, however, no one knows for sure where the bottom lies. For all intents and purposes, Argentina reached new bottoms in 1976, 1980, 1981, 1982, 1983, 1985, 1987, 1989, and 1990. And yet these bottoms were not followed by long-lasting turnarounds. For some political economists, the bottom is hyperinflation—a situation in which the monthly inflation rate exceeds 35 percent. However, the evidence that hyperinflation is an automatic generator of reform sustainability is inconclusive. It is hard to find a correlation between runaway inflation and subsequent reform implementation. Although most countries stabilized inflation in the 1990s, possibly reflecting a worldwide trend against inflation, few actually became deep reformers.[7]

When applied to Argentina, the hyperinflation argument can only account for the first three months of the Menem administration, when the exorbitant weekly inflation rate of 50 percent led to an outburst of state-society

7. Between 1988 and 1996, five Latin American nations (Argentina, Brazil, Nicaragua, Peru, and Surinam) and fifteen "transition economies" (Belarus, Latvia, Lithuania, Moldova,

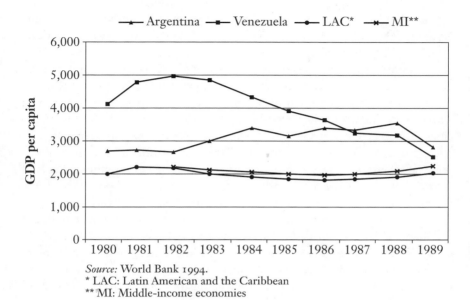

Source: World Bank 1994.
* LAC: Latin American and the Caribbean
** MI: Middle-income economies

Fig. 1   Argentina and Venezuela: GDP per capita, 1980–1989 (U.S.$ Atlas methodology)

cooperation and congressional support at Menem's inauguration time. However, this honeymoon proved short-lived. Pressures against the reforms soon exploded (the UCR voted against most reform initiatives, and business groups rebelled against fiscal reform), plunging Argentina into a second round of hyperinflation (December 1989 to February 1990). In the midst of this second hyperinflation, more serious episodes of noncooperation took place: a faction of the ruling party defected (the Group of Eight), Peronist labor unions protested against privatizations, and the leading opposition figure, Eduardo Angeloz, declined Menem's invitation to join the government. The government responded by enacting seven stabilization packages throughout 1990. All failed. A financial panic in February 1991, followed by yet another run on the dollar in March 1991, signaled that Argentina teetered on the brink of a third hyperinflation. In April 1991, the state

---

Romania, Ukraine, Russia, Armenia, Azerbaijan, Georgia, Kazakstan, Kyrgyzstan, Tajikistan, Turkmenistan, and Uzbekistan) experienced triple-digit or higher annual inflation rates for at least three, sometimes five, consecutive years (IMF 1996). Yet only five (Argentina, Peru, Latvia, Lithuania, and Kyrgyzstan) achieved the status of deep market reformers, according to the World Bank (1996). The fact that these high levels of inflation endured in so many countries for so long casts doubts on arguments which stress that high inflation immediately produces rebounds.

remained isolated, with very few political actors willing to support the administration. The 1989 hyperinflation did not induce state-society cooperation.

4. The Vagueness of Risk-Taking. Relying on prospect theory, Kurt Weyland (1996b) argues that economic crises make both reformers and citizens less risk-averse and more tolerant of harsh policies (see also O'Donnell 1992). The central argument of prospect theory is that people tolerate risk when facing threats to their well-being, but are cautious when facing auspicious prospects. Crises trigger boldness, whereas the expectation of gain produces timidity. Whether or not,this is true, it is difficult to classify many political events as either risk-taking or risk-averse. For instance, Weyland (1996b, 192) treats the presidential elections of 1989 and 1990 of Argentina, Brazil, and Peru as examples of risk-taking because voters rejected incumbents in favor of political outsiders. The problem is that two of the elected presidents (Menem and Collor) were not real outsiders—both were governors with proven records as populists. In addition, the choices for Menem, Fujimori, Collor, and Pérez were similar in that all four promised old-fashioned populist relief. One may debate whether this was risk aversion or not, but the point is that the electoral behavior seems similar in all four cases. In Venezuela, voters sympathized with coup plotters in February 1992 and supported the premature departure of Pérez in 1993, suggesting a degree of comfort with risk that Weyland would not easily predict. Moreover, the expulsion of Pérez in 1993 is identical to what happened in Brazil under Collor, and yet the economic conditions (using Weyland's indicator of high inflation) were worse in the latter. Risk-taking is thus hard to define a priori. Extreme circumstances do push actors to intrepid choices, but it is not clear that supporting reform is riskier than rejecting it.

5. Public Opinion versus Interest Group Behavior. Finally, the crisis hypothesis places too much emphasis on public opinion. Even if one were to accept that economic crises render the public more accepting of change, other obstacles to sustainability remain—namely, the behavior of interest groups. The political preferences of interest groups do not always coincide with public opinion. For instance, in Argentina and Venezuela, even while public opinion clamored that "something be done," interest groups continued to oppose specific reforms. Whether interest groups decide to relinquish their defense of entrenched interests depends on factors other than the general mood of the country—e.g., the availability of allies, their degree of influence over decision-making authorities, the political fortitude of reformers, etc.

In sum, the explanatory power of the crisis hypothesis varies depending on the dependent variable. If the dependent variable is the likelihood that authorities will adopt draconian measures, the explanatory power is high (see also Remmer 1998). If the question is reform sustainability, the explanatory power is considerably lower. The response of actors to crisis depends on intervening variables.

Economic Success

Economics-based explanations of reform sustainability are not restricted to the crisis hypothesis. An alternative route is to argue the mirror-image—that economic gains lead to reform sustainability. This argument also comes in different versions, none of which, however, does a very good job of explaining the Argentine and Venezuelan outcomes.

  1. The Political-Business Cycle. Political-business cycle theories posit that voters are likely to support incumbents who produce satisfactory economic results (see Lewis-Beck and Stegmaier 2000). Accordingly, support for the incumbent, and hence reform sustainability, should move in the same direction as economic indicators.[8] Yet the evidence from Venezuela and Argentina challenges this argument. Pérez's reforms collapsed in the wake of two consecutive years of impressive economic growth (1990–91) and declining unemployment (from 9.6 percent in 1989 to 8.7 percent prior to the February coup and to 7.2 percent by the end of 1992).[9] Furthermore, polls revealed that Venezuelans were beginning to feel more optimistic about their "personal economic situation" and less concerned with "economic problems" in 1991 right before the collapse of the reform program.[10] In Argentina, however, unemployment increased continually after 1991, reaching 9.9 percent

8. Remmer 1991b and Nelson 1992 have corroborated that incumbent governments have not necessarily been punished electorally for undertaking reforms per se, but only when they have failed to introduce lasting correctives.

9. Unemployment declined in all but two regions (Guayana and the Central Western Region). It declined even in Caracas, where the situation was politically more explosive (*El Universal*, May 17, 1993, 2). Food consumption and real wages increased (Naím 1993b). Poverty levels declined from their peak of 41 percent in 1989 to 35 percent at the end of 1991 (Márquez 1993; Márquez et al. 1993). In Caracas (as in Greater Buenos Aires) income inequality increased between 1990 and 1992, but poverty levels declined by 4.1 percent (CEPAL 1994).

10. An index of "perception of personal situation" was positive (+16 points) by the third quarter of 1991 (Consultores 21). In addition, the number of respondents who considered "economic problems" to be the principal problem of the country declined from 66 percent at the start of the reforms to 40 percent in the fourth quarter of 1991 (36 percent thought that the principal problem was "political" and "social," up from 14 at the start of the reforms). The economic problems mentioned in this survey were the cost of living, the external debt, the economy (in general), unemployment, and the VAT. The political problems were corruption, bad government, and the political system or situation. Social problems included crime, hunger, misery, and marginalization.

by the October 1993 elections and 18 percent in 1995. Also unlike Venezuela, real earned salaries in Argentina declined every year during the reforms, and poverty levels remained high for historical averages (Powers 1995). And yet the reform program continued.

2. Empowering Winners. Another version of the economic-gain argument focuses not so much on macroeconomic results but on channeling economic gains to strategic political actors, what Schamis (1999) labels "empowering winners." These new beneficiaries, usually business groups, can then become the pillars of newly recast pro-government "policy coalitions" (Gibson 1997). For many scholars, this explains Menem's political success (see also Palermo 1999, Starr 1997, and Palermo and Novaro 1996). There is no doubt that Menem came to enjoy the support of business and conservative groups. The problem is that it is not clear that the formation of this new coalition was the cause, rather than the effect, of renewed state capacity (see Corrales 1999b). Coalitions are either carefully crafted by states (which presumes the prior existence of capacity) or come into being once actors perceive that the state is a formidable political entity. In other words, actors might decide to bandwagon with the state (rather than defect) once they realize that the state is creditworthy. New coalitions could simply be the outcomes, rather than the source, of state fortitude.

3. Compensating Losers. A final version of the economic-gain argument focuses instead on compensating losers. Przeworski (1993), for instance, argues that market reforms in Spain in the 1980s were sustained because they were accompanied by broad social policies that included compensation for those hurt by the reforms and low levels of unemployment. This argument is also problematic. Specialized compensation can soften opposition in some sectors, but might stimulate resentment in others. Actors who receive less compensation than they expected will feel cheated. Compensation can give rise to controversies surrounding the asymmetry of distribution of gains. At the empirical level, this hypothesis cannot explain Venezuela. In addition to lowering the unemployment rate, Pérez actually deployed direct compensatory mechanisms. Generalized subsidies were replaced with social programs specifically targeted at lower-income groups.[11] The share of the national budget allocated for social spending increased from 32.5 percent in 1989 to 37.1 percent in 1991 (Maingón 1993). The middle class also got a special

---

11. Social programs included (1) a nutritional grant program consisting of direct cash subsidies to families of school children in low-income areas (*beca alimentaria*); (2) a maternal-child health care and feeding program aimed at expanding primary health coverage and improving health service delivery through food distribution to vulnerable groups; (3) a community-based day-care program directed at children of working mothers in low-income neighborhoods (*hoga-*

mortgage subsidy law after interest liberalization in 1989. Laid-off public sector workers were compensated more generously than was merited by their legal claim. In 1991, the government launched the "Social Megaproject": an umbrella project covering new and ongoing programs ranging from day care and nutrition to health and education, absorbing almost 9.7 percent of the national budget.

In short, some economic differences (e.g., crises) were not that significant; other differences (e.g., economic gains) did not yield the political results predicted by theory. Invoking economics-based arguments to explain differences in reform sustainability in Argentina and Venezuela misses the point. Those arguments fare poorly mostly because effective governance is not just a matter of getting the economics right but rather of developing institutions that align societal preferences with state preferences.

Looking at the Past

Is history the answer? Does historical experience play a role in influencing reform sustainability? Theorists who look at historical antecedents, paradoxically, can derive opposite conclusions from the very same historical data. Some theorists conclude that a history of repeated failures at reforms can be advantageous for reform sustainability; others argue the opposite.

1. The Advantages of Repeated Failure. A history of repeated failures can be advantageous for reform sustainability because of "political learning." Scholars of this tradition would not find the Venezuelan and Argentine outcomes surprising. Argentina had more experience with shock stabilization programs than almost any other country in Latin America. At least one major stabilization effort was launched every decade (see Table 2.2), and no fewer than eight in the 1980s. It is no surprise, some would argue, that the country finally managed to get it right in the 1990s. Another version of the "experience helps" argument is Alesina and Drazen's (1991) famous "war of attrition" hypothesis. Accordingly, reform implementation is less dependent on "technical correctness" and learning than on endurance. As long as the reformers persevere, their enemies will accumulate costs until they finally cave in.[12] One could hypothesize that Argentina's 1990 experience reflects the

---

res de cuidado diario); (4) a preschool expansion program targeting poor rural and urban areas; and (5) a cereal bonus for low-income children (*beca de cereales*) (World Bank 1993).

12. At one level, the Alesina-Drazen model is inapplicable to the question at hand. This model seeks to explain "rational delay" of reform adoption and not reform sustainability. The model assumes that, once adopted, a reform policy is accepted for good. However, the model

caving in of reform enemies after a long history of severe beatings: the military repression of 1976–82 and the severe economic collapse of 1986–89.

And yet both the "learn-from-experience" and the "attrition" hypotheses are also problematic. Learning arguments seldom specify the timing of "graduation." Why was Argentina wiser in 1991 than in 1989? Why did it take so many "lessons" for Argentina to finally learn? Learning arguments assume that the root of societal resistance to reforms is some form of cognitive handicap—the inability of actors to comprehend the reforms. However, resistance to reform is more often the result not of ignorance but of full knowledge of who the cost-bearers will be. The attrition hypothesis itself lacks specificity about the conditions under which the opposition caves in. The model simply hints that the balance of forces must somehow shift in the direction of the reformers (e.g., usually by means of an electoral victory). But both Pérez and Menem came to office in 1989 with landslide victories, and neither experienced a long honeymoon. Moreover, the turnaround in Argentina occurred in 1991, a time when the government was not especially strong politically, besieged by low popularity and less-than-landslide electoral victories in midterm elections.

2. The Disadvantage of Greater Experience. An alternative conclusion from history is that greater experience prior to the reforms is actually a disadvantage: the more a country fails in the past, the more it is likely to fail again. One reason is "path dependence": the notion that politicians, after making certain choices, become "locked in" a given path (see Pierson 2000). Actors learn from experience, but rather than learning to avoid previous mistakes, they learn to expect them again, setting the stage for self-fulfilling prophecies.[13]

Even this version of the "history-repeats-itself" argument would mispredict the Argentine and Venezuelan outcomes, since these are cases of complete breaks with the past. Argentina broke with a long history of economic ungovernability, and Venezuela broke with a history of bipartisan consensus on economic policy and military subordination.[14] Nevertheless, these arguments

---

could be reformulated: reforms become consolidated insofar as reform enemies become politically weak. This is similar to Bresser Pereira's (1993) notion that reform is adopted when the cost of resisting exceeds the cost of the status quo.

13. Game theorists use the concept of expectations based on "repeated interaction" to explain the incidence or absence of cooperation. Likewise, economists invoke "inflationary expectations" to explain the persistence of inflationary pressures despite the relaxation of "economic" sources of inflation. This explains why IMF (1996) found that the higher the inflation rate of a country, the higher the probability that its inflation rate will be higher the next year.

14. For a review of this bipartisan consensus, see Oropeza (1983). For a somewhat dissenting view, see Coppedge (1994b), which argues that political cooperation was more infrequent than is often claimed.

Table 2.2 Repeated Failures: Argentina's Famous Stabilization Programs

Minister (launching stabilization and year of launch)	Administration	Evolution of Annual Inflation	Outcome
Alfredo Gómez Morales (1952)	Juan Domingo Perón (1951–55)	1952–38.8 1953–4.0 1954–3.8 1955–12.3	Escalation of political unrest, followed by coup and interruption of adjustment program (1955)
Adalberto Krieger Vasena (1967)	Juan Carlos Onganía (1966–70)	1967–29.2 1968–16.2 1969–7.6 1970–13.6	Massive riots (the 1969 Cordobazo) and interruption of stabilization program
Celestino Rodrigo/Antonio Cafiero (1975)	María Estela (Isabel) Martínez de Perón (1974–76)	1975–335.0 1976–347.5	Major unrest (the 1975 "rodrigazo") including rising terrorism, followed by a coup
José Martínez de Hoz (1977)	Jorge Rafael Videla (1976–81)*	1977–160.4 1978–169.8 1979–139.7 1980–87.6 1981–131.3	Capital flight, increase in unemployment, massive banking crisis in 1981, interruption of reforms
Juan Sourrouille (1985)	Raúl Alfonsín (1983–89)**	1985–385.4 1986–81.9 1987–174.8 1988–387.7	Hyperinflation and capital flight in 1988–89, premature presidential resignation

Notes:
* Videla's successor, Roberto Viola, implemented a shock program under Minister Roberto Alemann in December 1981, but it ended quickly—in April 1982—as a consequence of the Falklands War.
** Toward the end of his tenure, Alfonsín's first minister of the Economy, Bernardo Grinspun, reluctantly accepted to implement an IMF-endorsed austerity package in September 1984. The plan was of short duration; Grinspun resigned in February 1985. Six stabilization packages were implemented under Sourrouille: the Austral Plan (June 1985), the "second shock" (April 1986), the "Australito" (February 1987), the "fourth shock" (July 1987), the "fifth shock" (October 1987), and the "Spring Plan" (April 1988).

Sources: Smith (1991); Guerchunoff and Llach (1998) for 1953–55 and 1967–69; INDEC for 1976–81 and 1985–88.

are useful because they suggest that a crucial challenge in the politics of economic reform is to defeat the expectations of failure of economic agents. Any powerful argument about economic change must offer an account of how these expectations are overturned.

Looking at the Future

Altering the expectations of societal actors is not easy, or at least, not realizable through policies that the affected groups will find easy to accept. Most governments that launch market reforms start out with serious credibility problems. These reforms are so politically risky and these governments have such long histories of unfulfilled commitments that few actors believe that the Executive will carry through (Sachs 1995; Calvo 1989). For some scholars, the only way to close this credibility gap is through "shock policies," or what Rodrik calls "overshooting," that is to say, adopting "a *larger* policy reform than would have been dictated in the absence of the credibility problem" (1989, 769, italics in original; see also Åslund 1994 and Krueger 1992). However, the idea that shock policies are enough is also problematic. As Chapter 3 argues, the reform packages of Argentina and Venezuela differed little in terms of their level of overshooting. In addition, policy shocks do not necessarily neutralize resistance to reform that has little to do with skepticism, such as, for example, the expectation of actual losses. More important, reformers must convey credibility continually, but policy shocks have a short-term, one-time-only impact. Stabilization packages and reforms in general tend to collapse, not at the beginning of the program, but some time well into the reforms and usually after some degree of economic improvement is attained, when actors become more insistent on compensation, less willing to continue to make sacrifices, and more capable of blocking further reforms (see Hellman 1998; Corrales 1997; Waterbury 1992, 217; and Smith 1991, 267–97). Economic improvement can thus bring a rise, rather than a decline, in sociopolitical unrest (Smith and Acuña 1994, 2), a scenario that Argentina exemplified prior to 1991. Each stabilization package in Argentina worked briefly and then collapsed amid intense political unrest (see Table 2.2). A good theory of reform sustainability must account for mechanisms of conveying credibility over time, rather than one time only.

Incorporation versus Concentration

Power sharing—that is to say, whether the Executive includes actors from civil society or centralizes power—is said to shape reform sustainability. Yet there is no consensus as to which style is more conducive to which outcome.

Power concentration can enhance implementation because it allows the Executive to preserve the technical correctness of the program and to convey more resoluteness, but it can also alienate societal actors, thus destabilizing state-society relations. Consultation can encourage societal cooperation, but it could also be a recipe for policy paralysis (see Bresser Pereira 1993, 9). These theoretical ambiguities aside, it is difficult to explain the Argentina-Venezuela dichotomy with either argument because it is not easy to separate these cases according to differences in levels of power-sharing.

For instance, numerous scholars (e.g., Acuña 1994, O'Donnell 1992, Novaro 1994, McGuire 1997, and Niño 1996) link Argentina's reform outcomes with the concentration of power on the Executive (hyperpresidentialism, Hobbesian strategies, delegative democracy, declining institutionalization, societal clamor for messianic leadership, etc.). Yet it is hard to disqualify the Pérez administration on this basis, for it has also been described as employing unilateral attempts "to impose new rules . . . through Hobbesian stratagems" (McCoy and Smith 1995, 264). A closer look, however, reveals that political styles were more nuanced in both countries, or at least equally mixed: sometimes the Executives negotiated some policies with some groups; other times, they imposed policies. Sometimes consultation worked; sometimes it did not. Moreover, arguments about style are excessively state-centric. It may very well be that society is so polarized, so mistrusting, and so anti-reform that consultations with societal actors need not produce cooperation.

A more promising approach is to look at "networks of state-society connections" as Evans (1995, 1992) does. Rather than maximizing autonomy (as in Evans et al. 1985), Evans now argues that the transformative capacity of states requires a combination of "internal coherence" and "external connectedness," what he calls "embedded autonomy." Similarly, Migdal et al. (1994) argue that effective governance is contingent on deepening state-society connections. "State power and social forces in low-income settings may, under certain circumstances, enter into relationships that are mutually reinforcing (or mutually empowering)" (Kohli and Shue 1994, 319). And this mutual reinforcement "lies at the core of the developmental state's success" (Evans 1995, 228). The transformative state needs to cultivate "networks of connection" with the actors whose behavior it seeks to transform.

The problem is that these works are not that specific about which networks of connection are more appropriate than others. Evans seems to stress connections with business groups. He argues that even rent-seeking firms will welcome the chance to compete, for instance, if the state connects with them by meeting some of their needs: "information, advice and occasional strategically applied succor in order to survive" (1992, 180). And yet the

Argentina-Venezuela dichotomy cannot be explained as a result of differences in embedded autonomy. The vague concept of "connectedness" could easily describe the relationship that existed between Argentina's military junta and the business sector in the late 1970s, or during Menem's first failed stabilization attempt (1989), which was designed under a minister of the economy who came directly from the private sector.

The "state-in-society approach" and the concept of "embedded autonomy" are nevertheless useful because they suggest that reformers must somehow establish connections with the targeted groups (rather than maximize autonomy). Any theory of reform sustainability must incorporate this insight. But these approaches cannot explain how to prevent such connections from becoming bridges through which interest groups can capture the state. As both Evans and Migdal et al. recognize, states and society can reinforce each other, but they can also corrode each other. How then can states connect with society without falling prey to interest groups?

Political Parties and Economic Governance

The concluding chapters of Migdal et al. (1994) and Evans (1995) suggest a clue. Almost in passing, these chapters mention that the key to state-society connectedness might lie in strong political parties: "The phenomenon of mutual empowerment . . . depends on the viability of institutions that can link state power with social forces. And in a competitive democracy . . . , this must mean political parties—well-organized, disciplined parties that can generate and offer to the electorate alternative social goals embodied in coherent policy programs" (Kohli and Shue 1994, 320). Evans also argues that for states to succeed "they will need party organizations capable of providing coherent support for long-term collective aims" (1995, 246). He recognizes that proposing "strong parties" as a key to effective governance is controversial because, in developing countries, parties are associated "with clientelism and the capture of the state," the antithesis of what development is all about. Yet both Evans (1995) and Kohli and Shue (1994) recognize that without strong parties that share a "joint project" uniting the state and society, the governing capacity of states will falter.

In the 1990s, two of the most important works to focus on the role of political parties in economic reform in Latin America were Haggard and Kaufman (1995) and Geddes (1994). In both works, the key determinant of reform implementation is the interplay between the incumbent and the opposition parties. Haggard and Kaufman argue that when reformers confront a polarized or fragmented party system, the prospects of reform implementation decline. Polarized party systems, by definition, render all opposition averse to cooperation with incumbents; fragmented party systems render the parties more prone to advance the interests of particularistic pressure groups. Likewise, Geddes (1994) argues that when opposition parties achieve parity with the incumbent party, apprehension toward efficiency-enhancing reforms declines. If the ruling party and the opposition achieve a comparable share of the vote, both forces will estimate that they will suffer the political costs of the reforms more or less equally, and this makes implementation of efficiency-enhancing reforms more likely.

But it is difficult to make the case that Argentina and Venezuela differed significantly in terms of the level of party system fragmentation. Table 2.3 shows that prior to the reforms (circa 1989) these were unambiguously bipartisan countries in which the two leading parties captured more than 80 percent of the vote. Haggard and Kaufman (1995) do suggest that Argentina's party system was polarized in the 1980s, which explains its reform difficulties during this period. However, even if we accept this interpretation,[15] it is unclear that the Argentine party system changed significantly between the 1980s and early 1990s. If anything, the tendency was toward continued polarization until 1995, measured by the propensity of the opposition to cooperate with the reforms. Furthermore, reforms collapsed in Venezuela and consolidated in Argentina when the distance between the parties was actually decreasing in the former and increasing in the latter, as measured by party-controlled votes in Congress and in local elections (see Table 2.3), showing problems with Geddes's party-parity hypothesis. Contrary to Geddes, parity might actually act as an inducement for reform avoidance. Precisely because they are becoming close electorally to their competition, parties might be disinclined to do anything that will cause them to lose even a small margin of votes.

Executive–Ruling Party Cooperation and Reform Sustainability

Clearly the determining factor in Argentina and Venezuela was not interparty relations. Instead, I will argue, it was the relationship between the ruling party and the Executive. We know from Kohli and Shue (1994) and Evans

---

15. The literature on Argentina's historical polarization resulting from an irreconcilable Peronist/anti-Peronist (or populist/liberal) cleavage is vast. Examples include Halperín Donghi 1994, Cheresky 1991, Smith 1991, Schoultz 1983, and O'Donnell 1973.

Table 2.3 Argentina and Venezuela: Electoral Results of the Main Parties (Percentage of Valid Votes)

Venezuela

	1963	1968	1973	1978	1983	1988	Second Pérez Administration				
							1989	1992a	1992b	1993	1995
AD	32.8	28.2	48.7	43.4	57.7	52.7	39.7	32.3	31.1	23.6	34.5
Copei	20.2	29.1	36.7	46.7	35.1	40.0	32.8	32.3	38.4	22.7	21.3
Convergencia-MAS										30.9	19.1
Causa R										21.9	12.7
Distance*	12.6	0.9	12.0	3.3	22.6	12.7	6.9	0.0	-7.3	7.3	-15.4

Argentina

	1946	1951	1973a	1973b	1983a	1983b	1985	1987
PJ	52.4	62.5	49.5	61.9	39.9	38.4	34.9	41.5
UCR		31.8	21.3	24.4	51.8	47.8	43.6	37.2
Distance*		30.7	28.2	37.5	11.9	9.4	8.7	-4.3

Notes:

1989 and 1992a are elections for mayors; 1992b and 1995 represent elections of governors.

Table 2.3 *(cont'd)*

	Menem's First Administration							
	1989a	1989b	1991	1993	1994	1995a	1995b
PJ	47.5	44.8	40.7	42.3	38.8	49.9	43.0
UCR	32.5	28.8	29.0	30.0	20.5	17.0	21.8
Ucedé	7.8	9.9	5.3	2.6	1.5	2.6	3.1
Modín			3.5	5.8	9.3	1.7	1.7
Frepaso				2.5	12.7	28.2	21.2
Distance	15.0	16.0	11.7	12.3	18.3	21.7	21.2

Notes:
*Distance between the ruling party and the main opposition party.
The PJ did not participate in the 1958 and 1963 elections.
1973a: March
1973b: September
1983a, 1989a 1995a: Presidential elections
1983b, 1989b, 1991, 1993, 1995b: Chamber of Deputies elections
1994: Constitutional Assembly

Sources: OCEI (various years); Fraga (1989); INDEC (various years).

(1995) that the key challenge is to get the ruling party to act as a facilitator of governance, to embrace "joint programs" with the state, and to offer "cohesive policy programs" to the electorate, rather than to act as a colonizer of state sinecures. This book focuses on this line of thinking. Presidents must build a cooperative relationship with the ruling party. It is not common for ruling parties to turn against their own administrations—but it does occur, and it is quite recurrent in the politics of economic reform (Chapter 5). This is precisely what happened in Venezuela, and the consequences for governability were lethal.

Obtaining the endorsement of the ruling party is crucial (Chapters 6–9). In Argentina, where this happened, the benefits for reform sustainability were extraordinary. Executive–ruling party cooperation, or what I call the "state-with-party" condition (Chapter 11), solves two of the most important political challenges in the process of market reform discussed thus far.

The first is the challenge of neutralizing societal resistance. Political economists tend to think of market reforms as a type of political war between pro-reform forces (namely, the Executive together with a few international and domestic allies) and a battery of reform enemies and skeptics within the state and across society (e.g., bureaucrats, interest groups, opposition political forces, students, social movements, the military, the media, religious groups, and so on; see, for example, Nelson 1989 and 1990 and Haggard and Webb 1994). These groups can have diverse and often overlapping reasons to oppose the reforms. For reforms to succeed politically, therefore, the state must neutralize the actions of these cost-bearing groups (Haggard and Webb 1994).

The second challenge is building credibility. Reform implementation is not just a matter of neutralizing cost-bearers but of gaining societal trust as well. For economic agents to cooperate with the reforms, they must be persuaded that the state is truly committed to carrying through with them. This credibility problem is even more serious if the Executive comes from a statist-populist party. When actors are unsure about the intentions of the reformers, that is to say, when they anticipate a future reversal of reforms, they are hesitant to cooperate, not because they fear losing, but because they fear being cheated by other players who fail to do their part. Players are trapped in a prisoner's dilemma: they can gain from reform, but they fear receiving the sucker's payoff. To overcome this skepticism, reformers need to deliver assurances of commitment.

Obtaining the endorsement of ruling parties allows states to address the challenges posed by both cost-bearers and reform skeptics. A harmonious

Executive–ruling party relationship creates, first, a credibility boost. It allows the state to convey that the populist forces of the country are siding with the Executive (that is to say, less likely to defect). Rodrik's credibility problem softens.

Gaining credibility is a good start, but it is not enough. Although some authors think that gaining credibility is all that is needed for reform sustainability (if states manage to persuade actors that the reform program will be implemented, then noncooperative interest groups will drop their resistance) (see World Bank 1996d, 94; Sachs 1995; Rodrik 1989), I contend instead that the effect of credibility on state-society relations is more complex. This is because not all enemies of reform will react to the credibility boost the same way.

On the one hand, those groups that oppose the reforms because of skepticism will respond favorably to credibility boosts. Harmonious Executive–ruling party relations soften the opposition of skeptics. It gives them fewer reasons to suspect that the state (or the populist forces) will defect. On the other hand, cost-bearing groups will not respond as favorably. The certainty that the state will move forward with the reforms alarms these groups. The rise of a more credible reform team will thus heighten the opposition of cost-bearing groups. In Argentina, for instance, almost every government that showed a serious commitment to reform (the Peronist government in 1975, the military junta in 1978–81, the Alfonsín government after 1985) provoked the ire of cost-bearing groups. The Menem administration was no exception.

The reason that Menem survived these pressures was the new institutional arrangement that emerged as a result of the alliance between the Executive and the ruling party. By siding with the Executive, the ruling party shielded the state from the sabotaging effects of these activated cost-bearing groups. Unable to count on the statist-populist party, and thus, to defeat the Executive, many cost-bearing groups had no option but to abdicate. They reconsidered their resistance and gradually adopted more cooperative stands. Thus, by 1994, there remained few cost-bearing groups intent on derailing the reform in Argentina.

The exact opposite transpired in Venezuela. By mid-1991, Executive–ruling party relations collapsed. This left the Executive in political limbo while simultaneously providing reform enemies with a new political ally—the ruling party itself, now more eager than ever before to embrace anti-reform grievances. Consequently, skeptics had even more reasons to distrust the Executive, and cost-bearers had more resources with which to challenge the state. Estrangement in Executive–ruling party relations thus undermines the state's ability to command the credibility of reform skeptics and to neutralize the mobilization of reform enemies. As Hobbes would say, the inability of the state to convey "awe" leads to rebellion.

Table 2.4 summarizes the hypothesized causal effect of the nature of Executive–ruling party relations on reform sustainability. Where this relationship is disharmonious, reform sustainability ought to be mixed. The Executive is able to push for some reforms, but still lacks the political capital to cope with societal resistance. If the relationship turns completely hostile, reform sustainability ought to collapse completely. The ruling party abandons the Executive, aggravating the Executive's credibility, siding instead with cost-bearing sectors and reaffirming the fears of reform skeptics. If the relationship turns harmonious, reform sustainability ought to improve. The government is able to generate a credibility boost. This turns reform skeptics into reform supporters, but

Table 2.4   Hypotheses About the Causal Effects of Executive–Ruling Party Relations

Executive–Ruling Party Relations	Impact on Reform Sustainability
Disharmonious (Argentina and Venezuela, 1989–91)	Mixed Sustainability: • The ruling party begins to behave like an opposition party, thereby increasing the transaction cost of the reforms. • Eroding cooperation on the part of the Congress and the Cabinet. • "Corruption" of the reform program: emergence of measures to rescue the reforms and win allies, which compromise the reform process.
Hostile (Venezuela, 1991–93)	Low Sustainability: • Information gap and credibility gap expand. • Black hole in the political system: – Mistrusting sectors end their cooperation with the state. – Cost-bearing sectors find allies for their plight to challenge the state. – Anti-establishment sectors find that the time is right to take center stage.
Harmonious (Argentina, 1991–97)	High Sustainability: • Reforms advance (together with economic growth and stability). • Boost in credibility. • Ruling party delegitimizes or ignores societal claims and ceases to be available as a political ally of antireform interest groups.

it also irritates cost-bearing sectors. However, cost-bearers will not prevail because they will be deprived of a crucial ally—the ruling party.

This argument builds on, but is nonetheless different from, those of Haggard and Kaufman (1995) and Geddes (1994), because it places less emphasis on interparty politics and more on intraparty politics. There is no question that the role of opposition political parties was crucial. It played a particular role in shaping whether the ruling party would cooperate with the Executive (see Chapter 10). However, I contend that the only way that Executives will muster the political capital necessary to survive the pressures from the opposition is to forge a strong alliance with the ruling party. This requires attending to the dislocations that the reforms produce within the ruling party itself. It requires leaders to spend more time building parties than they usually do.

Once I establish that a key determinant of reform sustainability is the nature of the Executive–ruling party relationship, the follow-up question is: why did Executive–ruling party relations become harmonious in Argentina, but not in Venezuela? This question goes to the heart of the growing debate in political science about the determinants of political party adaptability.

In Chapter 10, I probe three possible answers. First, the nature of the party system matters. Where interparty collaboration is less frequent, the ruling party is more likely to align with the Executive. Dissenting members of the ruling party would be disinclined to challenge the Executive in fear of siding too closely with the opposition. In essence, a polarized party system places limits on the "voice" and "exit" possibilities, to borrow from Hirschman (1970), of dissenting ruling party leaders, resulting in a lesser propensity to challenge the Executive. This finding questions the conventional thinking that nonpolarized party systems are more conducive to governance.

Second, internal party features matter. One such feature is the party's level of dependence on state resources (measured, among other things, by the frequency of past electoral victories and the extent of party penetration of the bureaucracy). Higher dependence makes ruling parties less likely to accept the reforms and thus cooperate with the Executive. Another internal feature is the level of cartelization. Ruling parties with a history of restricted internal or external contestation will have a harder time embracing reforms because these deficits in contestation cause leadership structures and ideology to become entrenched. Both conditions—dependence on state resources and low internal and external contestation—were salient in AD prior to the reforms, but not in the PJ.

The third and ultimately much more decisive factor is the response of the Executive to the dislocation with the ruling party. Executives can adopt three different responses. The first is what I call a "party-neglecting" approach: the Executive simply neglects the political concerns of the party and attempts to implement the reforms by circumventing the ruling party. The second approach is what I label "party yielding": the Executive gives in completely to the anti-reform preferences of the party, in essence abandoning the reform program. And finally, the Executive can adopt a "party-accommodating" strategy, that is to say, negotiate some compromise with the party, where the Executive grants certain concessions that are important to the interests of the party in return for the party's consent to the reforms. Under party accommodation, presidents find a way to make room for, rather than displace, the orthodox sectors of the party.

I argue that, of all these approaches, party accommodation has the highest chance of abating Executive–ruling party frictions. This is true even if the environmental context (that is to say, the party system and internal party features) are not entirely conducive to party adaptation.

Because reform sustainability depends on ruling party endorsement of the reforms, reform outcomes will naturally reflect some of the concerns of the ruling parties. In order to consent to the reforms, the ruling party, especially its most reform-resistant sectors, will demand certain concessions. Executives will need to accommodate some of these demands. The result is less-than-neoliberal reforms. Executives will be able to implement reforms to a greater degree, going further than interest groups would have allowed, but never as far as neoliberal technocrats would have preferred, because they will have to accommodate party-based concerns.

Despite this trade-off, there is no question that a state-with-party condition is more conducive to economic governance than a state-without-party condition. Under the latter, not only will reforms lag, but the political system will experience serious strains, including heightened instability and democratic erosion. This argument is demonstrated by looking not just at Argentina and Venezuela, but also at the reform experiences of other Latin American administrations in the 1990s (Chapter 11).

To summarize, there is a causal relationship between the nature of Executive–ruling party relations and the nature of state-society relations in the act of governing economic change. Whenever the Executive succeeds at establishing a cooperative relationship with the ruling party, reforms will deepen. A cooperative Executive–ruling party relation helps the state resolve fundamental problems typical of economic reforms: (1) it bridges the credibility gap, which is necessary for societal actors to cooperate with the reforms; and (2) it shields the state from reform enemies, which is necessary for policy cohesiveness. It allows the state to strike the right balance between the need to obtain some autonomy from anti-reform interest groups as well as "connectedness" with societal actors.

However, in contrast to Huntington (1968), who hardly discussed the possibility that a strong party could harm governance, strong parties can pose serious dangers for reform sustainability. The decision of a strong ruling party to sabotage its own administration could very well be one of the most destabilizing developments to take place in any political system. This decision, I argue, is always a possibility in any reform effort. Preventing it must be the first order of business of state leaders.

The conclusion that economic governance is contingent on the emergence of harmonious Executive–ruling party relations validates the importance of theoretical approaches that combine historic-institutionalism and strategic choices. Historic-institutionalism matters because countries that inherit strong institutions in the form of strong parties stand a better chance of managing economic change. Yet this institutional legacy is not enough. The way presidents respond to their own parties is equally crucial. Presidents who choose to disregard their own parties, perhaps in favor of alliances with non-party actors, jeopardize their chances of becoming great reformers.

PART TWO

background
to the
reforms

3

the concept of
reform sustainability
and the cases
in detail

Scholars who study economic reforms raise three different sets of questions about their subject. One is whether the reforms produce the intended results. Scholars in this tradition ask whether the chosen policy is the right policy, technically speaking, to generate the intended economic objectives (e.g., whether fixing the exchange rate stabilizes inflation, or whether trade liberalization stimulates economic growth).[1] Typically, this is a highly economicist

---

1. Examples include Llach 1997 and Fanelli and Frenkel 1994 in reference to Argentina, and Hausmann 1995 in reference to Venezuela.

approach, insofar as the focus is on assessing the impact of economic variables (policy measures) on economic outcomes.

A second mode of inquiry is concerned not so much with the technical merits of policy, but rather with its desirability. These scholars wonder whether the objectives pursued by neoliberal policies (e.g., efficiency, competitiveness, nonsubsidization of the economy) are valuable in their own right or at least compatible with other democratic goals such as redistributing income or boosting civil society.[2]

Yet a third approach is concerned not so much with whether or not the reforms deliver what they promise or whether or not the promise itself is valuable, but rather with whether or not the outcome has a demonstrable cause.[3] Typically, scholars in this tradition want to identify the factors that bring about the results, regardless of whether such results were intended or not, or valuable or not. Its central mode of inquiry is to isolate causal factors, or determinants, of outcomes.

Most scholarship on economic reform in Latin America has specialized in the first two modes of inquiry. This book focuses on the third. It asks: why do certain states manage to sustain reforms over time, while others do not? Fundamentally, this is a question about the capacity of states to produce change.

Scholars in the 1980s showed that state leaders can have preferences that are independent of those of other domestic political actors, and that states can be classified according to their capacity to carry out those preferences (e.g., Krasner 1978, Nordlinger 1981, Evans et al. 1985, and Waisman 1987). Market reforms constitute a particular kind of state preference—the risky bearing of short-term political and economic costs in the hope of obtaining future benefits, such as economic efficiency, macroeconomic stability, renewed growth, and competitiveness. Scholars have long argued that state leaders have an almost insatiable tendency to pursue control of society, often by way of state expansion (Tilly 1985; 1992), and more so if they happen to be populists (Kaufman and Stallings 1991). When states embrace market reforms, they are still interested in state assertiveness, but through a different route: by shrinking rather than expanding state intervention (Glade 1986). State actors realize that the only hope of restoring governability, and hence, reasserting state authority, is to get the state to withdraw from owning and running productive assets. The problem is that state shrinking is inherently a process of

2. Examples include Borón 1996 in reference to Argentina, and Valecillos 1992 in reference to Venezuela.

3. For books on Argentina and Venezuela that combine all three approaches, see Palermo and Novaro 1996 and Naím 1993b.

distributing costs across society, hurting directly those who benefited the most from state intervention (see Pierson 1994; Williamson and Haggard 1994, 531; and Nelson 1988). For these reasons, when state leaders decide to embark on reforms, they are expressing a preference for taking risks and inflicting costs (see Weyland 1996b).

Before discussing why the Argentine state sustained the reform effort, whereas Venezuela did not, it is important to define the concept of reform sustainability. This chapter does that. It also shows that the first Menem and second Pérez administrations represent three different cases of reform sustainability.

The Reforms

Soon after taking office—and within less than six months of each other—Pérez and Menem announced a comprehensive set of economic reforms. In Argentina, this was not the first time that market reforms had been attempted, but these represented the most market-oriented reforms ever launched. The reforms in Argentina and Venezuela were not carbon copies of each other, but the similarities were striking. First, they were "internationally correct," that is to say, they conformed to the classic IMF formula of economic stabilization and structural adjustment.[4] In fact, unknown perhaps to their respective designers, both programs fit closely with the prescriptions of the "Washington consensus," a phrase that was coined almost a year after the announcement of the Argentina and Venezuela reforms (see Table 3.1).[5]

To call these programs mere reform packages, however, is to miss the point. These programs represented dramatic about-faces in economic development strategy.[6] The inward-oriented, state-dependent pattern of economic development was to be jettisoned in favor of a new outward-oriented, market-friendly,

4. See Krueger 1992 for a historical overview of this IMF prescription.

5. Williamson (1990) coined the phrase "Washington consensus" to describe the policy initiatives that were being urged on Latin America by multilateral and international advisers throughout the 1980s. This phrase quickly became polemical. Critics essentially argued that the term was a misnomer: these policies did not stem from Washington (but rather, from some economics departments of U.S. universities), and there was never much of a consensus (even market advocates disagreed about the right pace, degree, and style of implementation). Williamson (1994) acknowledges that he should have been more explicit about these points, but he still advocates the use of the term.

6. A development strategy consists of government policies that "shape a country's relationship to the global economy and that affect the domestic allocation of resources among industries and major social groups" (Gereffi 1990, 23).

Table 3.1. The Venezuelan (January 1989) and Argentine (July 1989) Reform
Packages (According to the "Washington Consensus")

"Washington Consensus"	Venezuela	Argentina
Fiscal Discipline	Significant real reductions in public spending, aiming toward a year-end fiscal deficit below 4 percent of GNP. One-time general increase in public-sector wages, followed by a freeze in public-sector employment.	Significant real reductions in public spending. One-time general increase in public wages, followed by wage and employment freezes. The Treasury (rather than the Central Bank) would manage the deficit.
Rationalizing Public Expenditures	Spending would be redirected away from megaprojects, focusing instead on infrastructure and social spending. Gradual increase in prices of SOE goods and services, including annual increases for the first three years in the domestic prices of approximately 14 oil-based products (an initial 100 percent increase in the price of oil and a 30 percent increase in the price of public transportation).	Increase in public service tariffs (oil, electricity, transport, communications), including a 600 percent increase in the price of oil (average rate increased by 500 percent). Law of Economic Emergency suspends 50 percent (approximately U.S.$200M annually) of industrial subsidies and tax-breaks, renewable every 6 months. "Buy national" laws are abrogated. Tariff increases to be used to finance the deficit.
Tax Reform	Government commits to reform the tax code and the tax collection system.	Taxation of titles on domestic debt, adjustable deposits, and Argentine assets held abroad.
Financial Liberalization	Interest rates liberalized up to a ceiling set at around 30 percent. Commitment to reform the financial sector and the Central Bank charter by 1990.	Commitment to overhaul the financial sector (including an interest rate reduction) and reform the Central Bank charter.

Table 3.1 *(cont'd)*

"Washington Consensus"	Venezuela	Argentina
Exchange Rates	Devaluation followed by exchange-rate unification; replacement of preferential exchange rates with a floating regime.	Devaluation followed by exchange-rate unification (the Central Bank would set the exchange rate).*
Trade Liberalization	5-year plan of rationalization of tariffs and import prohibitions (with the exception of a few luxury items).	5-point tariff reduction and deepening of trade liberalization with neighboring countries.
Foreign Direct Investment (FDI)	Negotiations with the IMF for new credits. Indiscriminate treatment of foreign direct investment in several sectors.	Further flexibilization of FDI; foreign and domestic capital would be treated similarly. Payments on the foreign debt to commercial banks (suspended since April 1988) were not reinstated, but negotiations with IMF for credit approval were initiated.
Privatizations	Privatizations announced in February 1990.	Law of State Reform grants the Executive prerogative to privatize, by decree if necessary.
Deregulation	Price liberalization (except in 18 items); deregulation of capital, labor, and goods markets.	Commitment to deregulate markets.
Property Rights	Government agrees to create stable and transparent rules of property rights, along with regulatory state agencies.	Government agrees to create stable and transparent rules of property rights.

Note:
* The most well known aspect of Menem's reform—the Convertibility Law, which fixed the exchange rate and banned the Central Bank from printing money—was not part of the original package of reforms.

Sources: Venezuela: *Veneconomía* (various issues), Hausmann (1990), Kornblith (1989), *Memorando Relacionado . . .* ; Argentina: Feletti and Lozano (1994), Bouzas (1993), *Carta Económica* (various issues).

fiscally sound model of development. The reformers were seeking what Przeworski et al. (1995, 3) labeled "modernization via internationalization"—that is to say, they were pursuing integration into the world economy and imitation of Western policies in order to embark on the passage to the First World. In Venezuela, the reforms were baptized "the Great Turnaround" (*el Gran Viraje*), aptly signifying the far-reaching intentions of the authorities.

Both programs were similar in that they were quintessential "shock therapies" on at least three counts. First, the shift toward the new economic model was to occur immediately.[7] Second, the reforms were shocking because they entailed deep (and painful) austerity measures. In the words of Menem, they entailed "surgery without anesthesia." These were "orthodox" packages (that is to say, stabilization through fiscal and monetary restrictions) rather than the until-then regional-favorite "heterodox" approach (that is to say, stabilization through wage and income policies) (see Stallings 1990).[8] From business tycoons to retired pensioners, every sector of society was bound to feel the pinch. Third, the reforms were shocking because they went far beyond what everyone expected. This is not to say that the reforms came as a total surprise. Although Menem and Pérez campaigned on populist platforms, during the transfer-of-power period they revealed a lot about their intentions. Rumors that "something serious is coming" were widespread prior to inauguration day. The surprise lay instead in the depth of the reforms, which exceeded the expectations of even the minority of citizens who hoped for neoliberal solutions.

There were, nevertheless, key differences. First, international support for the Venezuelan package was much stronger than for the Argentine. While the World Bank provided technical support, it did not approve any loans for Argentina from October 1988 (the collapse of the Primavera Plan) to December 1990. The Bank was also "slow in providing financial support" in the 1989–92 period (World Bank 1996a), mostly due to the Bank's disenchantment with Argentina's repeated failures. The Venezuelan reformers, however, enjoyed immediate support from abroad.

Another difference was that in Venezuela the centerpiece of the program was price and interest rate liberalization, whereas in Argentina the emphasis

7. In a gradualist approach, reformers adopt a long time-horizon and proceed step by step, addressing a few sectors of the economy at a time; in a big-bang approach, by contrast, they adopt a shorter time-horizon and tackle the greatest number of fronts at once. See Åslund 1994 and Krueger 1992 for a defense of the shock approach and Bhagwati 1994 for a critique. Today, there is increasing recognition that the gradualist versus big-bang debate is possibly a false dichotomy. When the economic situation is in freefall, gradualism is impossible. After stabilization, reforms are almost always implemented gradually.

8. Although initially there were some heterodox traces in both packages (e.g., efforts to control prices through agreements), most of these traces were gradually abandoned.

was on price anchoring. This difference stemmed from the different economic contexts of the reforms. Venezuela's long history of price controls had
led to repressed inflation, severe consumer good shortages, and rising black
markets (especially for foreign exchange). Argentina, on the other hand, was
experiencing runaway inflation. Thus, the immediate tasks were different:
Pérez needed to liberalize prices first; Menem needed to stabilize prices. As a
result, the immediate impact of the reforms in Venezuela was an abrupt rise
in inflation (from a monthly inflation rate of 6.8 in December 1988 to 23
percent in March). In Argentina, it was a dramatic decline of price instability
(from a monthly inflation rate of 196.6 percent in July 1989 to 9.4 percent in
September). Not surprisingly, the initial societal reaction was quite positive
in Argentina, but quite negative in Venezuela. Although inflation and consumer shortages declined rapidly by August 1989, Venezuelans associated the
reforms with higher prices.[9]

But even in Argentina, public enthusiasm for the reforms fizzled as the
country plunged into a second hyperinflation in December 1989. By then,
Argentines considered the reforms as one more episode of failed stabilization.
Thus, six months into the reforms, both governments faced growing societal
disenchantment.

Sustainability

To what extent were the Argentine and Venezuelan states able to sustain the
reform process? Answering this question requires coming up with indicators
of sustainability. A good starting point is to look at agenda implementation:
the extent to which the government carried out its announced reforms.

To evaluate agenda implementation, some authors recommend looking at
macroeconomic results (e.g., Przeworski et al. 1995 and Bresser Pereira
1993). However, focusing on macroeconomic results exclusively is an insufficient and probably misleading indicator of reform sustainability. For example, whether there is economic growth or contraction says little about
whether a neoliberal policy is being implemented or not. Growth can result
from any number of policies, not just market-oriented ones. The key question is whether or not the government perseveres in implementing a given
reform agenda, regardless of whether the agenda is generating the intended

9. Another initial difference was that the Venezuelan team started with a focus on exchange
rate reform and trade liberalization, whereas the Argentine team focused on privatizations. Not
long after, however, this difference would disappear. Venezuela would discover by 1990 the need
to carry out privatizations, and Argentina, the need to focus on the exchange rate regime.

economic result. In the case of Menem until 1996, the government sustained a program of privatizations, liberalization, and austerity, even when the evidence that the reforms were generating their intended objectives was inconclusive. This capacity to persevere is worth explaining.

Thus, following Nelson (1990), I complement the discussion of macroeconomic results with a comparative description of the implementation record.[10] Ideally, one would like to be able to say that at a given moment, a certain percentage of the reform program had been implemented in each country. This, however, is not so easy, given the comprehensive and often intangible scope of the reforms. In addition, numerical indicators of reform implementation do not convey political transaction costs: that is to say, the political frictions generated by the reforms and the capacity of the state to absorb such friction.

Analysts distinguish between implementation and consolidation of reforms, arguing that each involves different political challenges (e.g., World Bank 1996d, Haggard and Kaufman 1992 and 1995, and Nelson 1988). The key challenge at the implementation phase, for example, is to overturn the expectations of economic agents, that is to say, to convince them that the old economic rules no longer apply. Implementation is thus contingent on the ability of the state to introduce uncertainty—or shock—throughout the population. Consolidation, alternatively, involves the creation of predictability. Actors must come to expect that the new rules of the game will not be easily overturned (Haggard and Kaufman 1995, 9–10).

While it is not difficult for governments to complete initial implementation stages (almost every government can easily shock its population), it is harder to achieve consolidation. Stabilization programs encounter most political difficulties months after they are implemented. The passage of time allows reform enemies the opportunity to organize strategies to undermine the reform process. For all of these reasons, sustaining the reforms for more than a few years is a necessary test of reform consolidation.

Sustainability and the Weberian Dilemma

To some extent, sustainability is related to the issue of "political order"—always a controversial subject in political science. The controversy hinges on how to tell whether the rise of political order is the result of societal acceptance of the changes, rather than the result of higher levels of state coerciveness. This

---

10. Bresser Pereira (1993) and Przeworski et al. (1995) argue that to focus on "continued implementation of reforms" ignores the possibility that the measures might be inappropriate or mistaken. This criticism is normative, concerned with the extent to which the reforms produce socially desirable goods (in this case, material welfare improvements).

dilemma is at the heart of Max Weber's theory of the state. For Weber, a crucial aim of states is "pacification" (1968, 908). The problem is that this pacification can be the result of either the "monopolization of violence" by the state or, simply, the rise of legitimacy (that is to say, societal acceptance of authority), or what is even more complicated, of both processes simultaneously (1968, 54, 901–10).[11]

In the late 1960s, the study of political order became fashionable (e.g., Binder et al. 1971). For Huntington, disorder, or to use his term, "political decay," is clearly undesirable because it is symptomatic of a "gap" between socioeconomic development and institutional development (1968, 53–56). Thus he calls for institutional reform as a way of generating order. Nevertheless, he still fails to solve the Weberian dilemma: how can one tell whether the rise of order is really the result of societal acceptance and not of state coercion and the suffocation of civil society (see Kesselman 1973)?

I do not pretend to have a solution to a dilemma that not even Weber solved; however, there are ways of discerning the extent to which sustainability might have more to do with rising acceptance rather than coercion. First, a reliable assessment of sustainability ought to take into consideration the political response of societal actors to the reforms. Clearly, some level of societal acceptance, or "consent," must exist to conclude that there is reform sustainability (see Rose 1980). However, it is unrealistic to expect perfect societal consent. Market reforms are enormously painful. Society is unlikely to react cheerfully. Episodes of societal upheaval are to be expected. Thus a true measure of sustainability is not the absence of state-society conflict, but as Skocpol (1985) would argue, whether or not the state meets its goals over the objections of social groups and under adverse conditions. A reform process that survives episodes of societal protests, and maybe even succeeds in neutralizing them, can be said to score high on sustainability.

To assess societal reaction in Argentina and Venezuela, I examine the following:

1. *Public opinion* (as revealed by polls) *and societal unrest* (as revealed by strikes, protests, or general turmoil). Not all protests and strikes in Argentina and Venezuela in the early 1990s were explicitly against market reforms—other

---

11. This complication is captured in this quotation: "Thus, the political community monopolizes the legitimate application of violence for its coercive apparatus and is gradually transformed into an institution for the protection of rights. In so doing it obtains a powerful and decisive support from all those groups which have a direct or indirect economic interest in the expansion of the market community, as well as from the religious authorities. . . . Economically, however, the groups most interested in pacification are those guided by market interests" (Weber 1968, 908).

issues such as human rights, public security, and educational reforms were important—and not all economic-related protests (e.g., wage disputes) are necessarily indicative of overall economic policy rejection. Nevertheless, strikes and protests are a thermometer of political climate, more so in countries where reforms are affecting almost every aspect of daily life. Moreover, regardless of their motives, strikes and protests complicate the task of governing and, therefore, are appropriate indicators of sustainability.

2. *Interest groups and political institutions.* The political preferences and reactions of pressure groups (business, labor, the military, the press, etc.) need not match those of "public opinion." In both Argentina and Venezuela, for instance, surveys showed that labor organizations at first tended to be more opposed to reforms than "the public." In addition, the role of key political institutions such as Congress must also be considered, since many market reforms in democratic contexts must pass congressional approval.

3. *Opposition parties.* The response of opposition parties is an important component of sustainability. If opposition parties reject policies, citizens often follow suit (Kavanagh 1980). In addition, the type of response by opposition parties can reveal whether sustainability has to do more with the rise of societal legitimacy than with state suffocation of civil society (the Weberian dilemma). If opposition parties respond by upholding outright repudiation of the reforms, then clearly we would be unable to speak of sustainability. If opposition parties, however, become more accepting of the reforms, without necessarily losing their dynamism (that is to say, if party life remains vigorous), then this would be a sign of reform sustainability, but one that is not entirely the result of rising state coerciveness. In a country where the state is achieving "order" through suffocation of civil society, one would never expect to find a vibrant opposition party. Thus opposition parties that soften their criticism of reforms without softening their activism are indicators of reform sustainability.

4. *Elections.* The electoral performance of government forces is another indicator of the nature of state-society relations. In the early 1990s, Venezuela and Argentina experienced a series of nonpresidential elections at the national and local levels. The economic reforms were not always an explicit issue in these elections. Nevertheless, given the centrality of the reforms in the political agenda, these elections served as *de facto* plebiscites on the reforms—at least, that is how domestic political actors and analysts interpreted them.

To summarize, a working definition of reform sustainability is the presence of a high degree of agenda implementation together with a fair degree of state-society cooperation, or at least, an ability on the part of the state to survive and overturn episodes of societal challenge. Ultimately, as Weber argues, the rise of order can never be completely free of some element of state preponderance. It is thus impossible to rule out the possibility that sustainability is somewhat related to strengthening the state's ability to dominate society. But by getting a better idea of societal response, especially the response of opposition forces to both the reforms and the government, one can better assess whether some element of true societal acceptance lies behind sustainability.

Mixed Sustainability: The Early Years of the Pérez and Menem Administrations

Applying this definition of sustainability to Argentina and Venezuela reveals four different cases: two cases of mixed sustainability (Menem, 1989–mid-1991; Pérez, 1989–late 1991), one case of low sustainability (Pérez, late 1991–93), and one case of high sustainability (Menem, 1991–96). This section discusses the cases of mixed sustainability.

Reform Implementation

In both Argentina and Venezuela, the key characteristic of the reform process in the early stages was the coexistence of impressive accomplishments and daunting setbacks. Several weeks after the announcement of the reforms, Venezuela experienced dramatic urban riots, the so-called Caracazo,[12] followed by a dramatic doubling in inflation. These were severe stumbling blocks. Nevertheless, they did not succeed in halting the reform process. On the contrary, the government persevered. In April 1989, for instance, Pérez declared: "We will not vacillate in implementing the adjustment measures, knowing as we do that they will have a negative impact in the short term" (quoted in Beroes 1990, 163). By the middle of 1989, Venezuela's accomplishments were impressive. Almost every reform that could be implemented by Executive order was smoothly implemented. A prominent example was

12. The riots occurred on February 27–28, 1989, shortly after the announcement of price liberalization, including the doubling of gasoline prices (from about U.S. $0.12 per gallon to about U.S.$0.24). This announcement led bus drivers to double their fares, far exceeding the government-stipulated limit of a 30-percent increase in bus fares. In addition, bus drivers began to disregard student prices. The timing of these incidents (at the end of the month, when the budgets of fixed-income families are at their lowest levels) exacerbated the shock of the population. To contain the riots, Pérez mobilized military units, resulting in one of the bloodiest episodes in Venezuela since the 1960s.

trade liberalization. A five-year plan of reductions in tariffs and trade barriers was announced in early 1989. The government anticipated enormous resistance. But by mid-1989, most industrialists had acquiesced, and trade liberalization proceeded on schedule (Corrales and Cisneros 1999).

By early 1990, the reforms began to produce impressive economic results, including declines in fiscal and balance-of-payment deficits. Encouraged by these trends, the government announced a massive privatization drive (more than sixty SOEs were put up for sale).[13] In February 1991, the government announced that oil exploration would be opened to private investment. This was a dramatic turnaround for a country (and a president) that sixteen years prior had proudly sealed off this sector. The government announced yet another set of reforms by mid-1991: the enactment of a VAT, a bill to make the Central Bank more independent, and more privatizations. In July 1991, Pérez took the symbolic step of restoring the "economic guarantees," the clause in the constitution protecting economic freedom, which had been suspended for decades.

The speed and fruits of Venezuela's reforms mesmerized even World Bank officials (Zermeño, interview). Venezuela's 9.7 percent growth rate in 1991 was one of the highest in the world. That year, investment rose by 81 percent (World Bank 1996c). Foreign reserves peaked at U.S.$14.1 billion in December, more than twice the level of reserves at the start of the reforms. By the third quarter of 1991, a monthly average of 6,590 cars were being sold domestically, almost three times more than in 1989. Venezuela was creating an ever-growing number of trade liberalization agreements. By the end of 1991, two commercial banks, the country's major airline (VIASA), and the telephone company (CANTV) were privatized. All of Venezuela's external commercial debt (U.S.$19.7 billion) was restructured. Venezuela seemed to be a case of "reform success." And in every international forum, government officials flaunted their accomplishments to invariably impressed audiences.

Not everything, however, was picture-perfect. Some reforms were simply neglected by the government (e.g., banking sector liberalization). Other reforms were either shelved or distorted by the cabinet (e.g., the privatization of the huge industrial complex, the Corporación Venezolana de Guayana, CVG) or by Congress (e.g., tax reform). Still others were proving to be too controversial. In 1991, for instance, there was a major protest against agricultural liberalization, the so-called Cherokee protest. Moreover, the government

---

13. Gerver Torres, president of the government's privatization commission, announced that two hundred of the four hundred or so SOEs were suitable for privatization (*Latin American Regional Report, Andean Group*, March 8, 1990, 4).

embarked on a dramatic fiscal expansion at the end of 1990 that contradicted the austerity goals of the reforms and prevented further declines in inflation (below 30 percent annually). The government was also unable to impede the emergence of reform-contradicting laws (e.g., the Caldera Law).[14]

Menem's reform scenario was equally mixed at first. The reforms began on a stronger footing. The hyperinflation and food riots that preceded his inauguration were followed by an outburst of state-society cooperation of an order that had not been seen in Argentina since Alfonsín's honeymoon in the first half of 1984. Menem obtained an alliance with two unlikely partners— the business conglomerate Bunge & Born (B&B) and the conservative party, Unión de Centro Democrático (Ucedé), both of which were emblematic of anti-Peronism.[15] Menem also obtained from Congress, which was not yet controlled by his party,[16] the "Law of State Reform," mandating the privatizations of several hundred SOEs, and the "Law of Economic Emergency," which froze all state subsidies and grants for a period of 180 days.

On the positive side, the government restored the external equilibrium, reduced fiscal expenditures, ameliorated the internal debt problem, privatized several SOEs, and replenished the foreign reserve stock by March 1991. But none of this occurred effortlessly or conclusively. There were ten stabilization packages, each with serious implementation problems. Unable to secure a fiscal reform package, the country plunged into yet another round of hyperinflation in December 1989. The government was forced to adopt increasingly severe monetarist measures, such as the January 1990 Plan Bónex, which replaced the government's short-term internal debt and time-deposits with ten-year bonds. But rather than kill inflation, this severe plan caused a steep drop in exchange rates and a steep rise in interest rates, which only exacerbated price instability. In March 1990, new and more severe fiscal adjustments had to be announced. The new package ameliorated price instability,

14. The Caldera Law (November 1990) was a labor-reform bill that introduced a number of labor-protecting clauses that contradicted the spirit of the reforms (see Chapter 7).

15. B&B had always been seen as the nemesis of Peronism. In 1974, during the second Peronist administration (1973–76), Peronist guerrillas kidnapped two top B&B executives in what became one of the most notorious (and folkloric) episodes in Peronist-business animosity ever. Likewise, the Ucedé comprised the most anti-Peronist sectors of Argentina, including military sympathizers. Thus most Argentines were shocked to learn that Menem invited B&B executives Jorge Roig and then Néstor Rapanelli to become ministers of the economy, and Ucedé president Álvaro Alsogaray to become main adviser on foreign debt issues.

16. The new Congress was scheduled to start in December 1989. The PJ was the largest minority in the Senate, two seats short of a majority. It was the second minority in the Chamber of Deputies. The UCR, however, cooperated by providing the necessary quorum for Congress to do business.

but it failed to bring monthly inflation below 10 percent. The government began to focus on the management of public sector balances and the regulation of liquidity via announced interventions in the exchange market. Its main objective was to instill the belief that reforms were not going to be stopped. However, by September 1990, the reforms appeared to be advancing very slowly, if at all. The privatization program was facing one hurdle after another. Despite increasingly tighter monetary and fiscal controls, inflation went haywire again in January 1991. That same month, the government experienced its most severe cabinet crisis ever. Between July 1989 and April 1991, there were six severe foreign exchange crises (*corridas cambiarias*).[17] A new stabilization plan was introduced in April 1991 (the Convertibility Law), which produced immediate results, but as with previous stabilization packages, doubts about its durability soon surfaced.

One should not underestimate the magnitude of these accomplishments or the travails associated with them. The completion of these early privatizations, for instance, defied everyone's expectations.[18] In Venezuela, privatization proceeds by the end of 1991 (U.S.$2.3 billion) exceeded original estimates (U.S.$150 million) (Torres, interview). Yet, these accomplishments did not come easily. The privatizations of Argentina's ENTel (November 1990) and Venezuela's CANTV (November 1991), for instance, were the most politically contentious projects of the reform agenda. Both projects tested the waters and tested wills. They tested the waters because they revealed the extent of societal opposition to the reforms (on the part of labor, Congress, business, and even the ruling party). Menem even threatened to mobilize the military to quell labor opposition to ENTel's privatization. These privatizations were also a test of will because each was considered by local analysts as the ultimate battle that would decide whether the overall reforms would proceed.

The privatization programs thus epitomized everything that was positive and negative about reform sustainability during the initial years. In both

17. There were two such crises in December 1989, one in February 1990, one in December 1990, one in January 1991, and one in March 1991 (Llach 1997, 125–26).

18. The implementation of privatizations is a good barometer of reform sustainability for several reasons. First, privatizations in democratic contexts cannot be done at the stroke of a pen, as is the case with trade liberalization, exchange and interest rate reform, price-setting for SOE products and services, and social policy design. Privatizations require intensive negotiation with multiple constituencies (e.g., Congress, labor, management, interested buyers, jurists, bureaucrats, international actors, the military, public opinion, etc.), which makes them more dependent on, and hence better barometers of, the mood of state-society relations in general. For more on the political difficulties posed by privatizations, see Corrales 1998, Armijo 1998, and Molano 1997.

cases, the governments were forced to tone down their ambitions (e.g., Venezuelan authorities were unable to add the CVG to the list of companies for sale). By mid-1991, the privatization program remained uncertain, perhaps more so in Argentina than Venezuela. The privatization of ENTel was riddled with so many improprieties (*desprolijidades*) that its popularity declined considerably. The privatization of CANTV, however, was more transparent, which actually helped increase the number of privatization sympathizers in Venezuela. Thus Venezuelan privatizing officials were more upbeat after the sale of CANTV than their Argentine counterparts were after the sale of ENTel; they even began to reconsider the possibility of privatizing the CVG (Torres, interview).

Societal Reactions

Polls and Protests   Although the reforms in Venezuela had an inauspicious beginning in terms of societal reaction, the government was able to recover quickly. Five months after the Caracazo, Pérez's approval rating improved (Fig. 2). Between 1989 and mid-1991, the government never became extraordinarily popular, but it was not entirely unpopular either. Some indicators of positive attitudes toward the government and the reforms were actually high and stable until 1991. In fact, the number of people who wished the government to persevere with the reforms actually increased from 29 percent in the first quarter of 1989 to 45 percent in the first quarter of 1991.

In terms of labor conflicts, Venezuela was no social paradise. However, after the Caracazo, the level of societal protests stabilized and probably returned to historically medium levels. Although the evidence is mixed, some indicators of social unrest were moving downward between 1989 and early 1991. In May 1989 the AD-dominated CTV carried out its first-ever general strike against an AD government.[19] Thereafter labor's propensity to take the streets declined until the second half of 1991. While the number of labor disputes (*pliegos conflictivos*) increased steadily between 1988 and 1991, actual strikes (authorized and otherwise) declined (Table 3.2). Noticing this trend, one analyst described the year 1990 as "a breath of fresh air in the desert" (Quirós Corradi 1992, 166).

Societal quiescence during the first two years in Argentina was also mixed. The popularity of the reforms and the reformers, quite robust in the beginning,

19. CTV leaders claimed to have shut down 90 percent of business activities (*Latin American Regional Report, Andean Report*, June 22, 1989). Pérez characterized these actions as a "self-suicide [*sic*]" (*Economía Hoy*, February 2, 1994, 5).

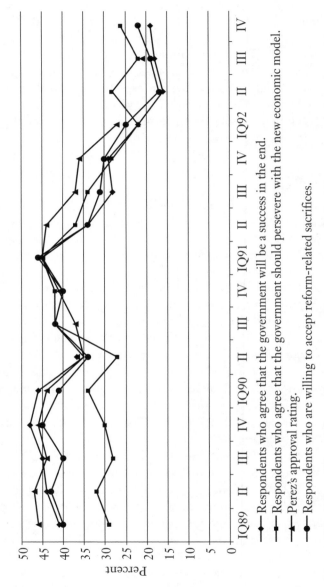

Respondents who agree that the government will be a success in the end.

Respondents who agree that the government should persevere with the new economic model.

Perez's approval rating.

Respondents who are willing to accept reform-related sacrifices.

Fig. 2   Venezuela: public opinion polls

Table 3.2   Venezuela: Labor Tensions, 1988–1991

	1988	1989	1990	1991
Disputes*	69	95	134	159
Strikes**	37	23	19	10

* Labor disputes (*pliegos conflictivos*) filed with the Ministry of Labor.
** Authorized and nonauthorized strikes.

Source: Ministry of Labor (various years).

declined thereafter.[20] Approval of the reforms among PJ voters declined even more: a poll by the firm Lynch, Menéndez, Nivel y Asoc. showed that by March 1991, only 14 percent of those who voted for Menem in the 1989 presidential elections supported the economic program, down from 70 percent in September 1989, shortly after the reforms were announced. While there were no general strikes during this period (in sharp contrast to Venezuela and to the three general strikes that took place during the first two years of the Alfonsín administration in Argentina), labor conflicts remained high (an average of 58.7 per month; see McGuire 1997). In short, some of Menem's strongest initial political allies—public opinion, his rank-and-file, and the labor unions—were abandoning him.[21]

Political Institutions and Interest Groups   Relations between the government and opposition parties deteriorated in both countries, as the main opposition parties, COPEI and UCR, intensified their opposition to the reforms. This was significant, since both parties had called for market-oriented reforms during the presidential campaigns and, after the elections, had promised to cooperate. Both COPEI and the UCR split into two factions, one more critical of the reforms than the other.[22] In both parties, the most critical faction was led by former presidents (Rafael Caldera in COPEI and Raúl Alfonsín in the UCR) and gradually became dominant. In Argentina, Executive-opposition hostility peaked in February 1990 when in the middle of Argentina's second

20. A poll in *Carta Económica* (June 1991) indicated that Menem's positive image in May 1991 dropped to 21 percent.

21. Despite these trends, Menem was by no means politically isolated. In April 1990, he obtained a significant show of support in a progovernment rally that took place in the Plaza de Mayo. This so-called Plaza del Sí was endorsed by various media personalities, business leaders, and Menemistas.

22. One faction, led by Eduardo Fernández, did not criticize the reforms *per se*, but rather pointed out their internal inconsistencies, decried their lack of "social concern," and expressed fear of a "useless sacrifice" (Fernández 1989). The other faction, led by Rafael Caldera, was harsher, calling for an outright termination of the reforms.

hyperinflation, the former UCR presidential candidate, Eduardo Angeloz, declined Menem's invitation to join the cabinet. Menem's alliance with the smaller, pro-reform Ucedé also suffered a setback in January 1991 when Ucedé president, Álvaro Alsogaray, decided to quit the government.

State-business cooperation differed in both countries. Despite government efforts in Argentina to maintain close relations with business groups (Palermo and Novaro 1996, 134–46), business sectors behaved quite disruptively during the first year and a half. In Venezuela, in contrast, business behavior was more tame. As Naím (1993b) argues, these potential "minotaurs" behaved more like quiescent "paper tigers" (see also Corrales and Cisneros 1999). Nevertheless, state-business relations in Venezuela were not devoid of tension. For example, business sectors rejected most tax reform proposals. The banking sector successfully lobbied against the liberalization of its sector, thereby provoking conflicts with the retail and industrial sectors, which were liberalized. By mid-1991, large media conglomerates (e.g., the Granier Group) became highly critical of the government. In its July 1991 annual meeting, Fedecámaras issued a document harshly critical of the reforms. The government, however, was able to get Fedecámaras to retract the document and even to apologize, suggesting a lingering capacity by the government to contain business opposition.

Another key group is the military. In Venezuela, military involvement in politics was rare after 1958 (Burggraaff and Millet 1995; Agüero 1993), in contrast to Argentina, where the military had a long history of political involvement (see Diamant 2000 and Norden 1996) and animosity toward state reforms (see Fontana 1986). This did not change during the first years of the reforms. The military remained relatively disengaged in Venezuela and highly engaged in Argentina. Menem began his administration with an effort to appease the military through an amnesty to many of the military officers convicted of human rights violations. This, however, failed to deter military unrest, and a coup attempt took place in December 1990.

Electoral Performance   From the point of view of the Executive, there is possibly no greater standard of political success than electoral triumph. In 1989, neither Pérez nor Menem was constitutionally permitted to seek reelection. The most that Pérez could hope for was to generate victories for his followers. Menem, however, was keen on reforming Argentina's constitution to allow for his reelection.

Prior to 1992, Pérez's and Menem's electoral performances, while not catastrophic, raised doubts about the prospects of fulfilling these electoral ambitions. In Venezuela, the first-ever elections for governors and local offices occurred in

December 1989, less than a year after the launch of the reforms. AD's performance was ambiguous. AD came out ahead, but its lead over the runner-up was significantly smaller than in 1988 (see Table 2.3). Those Adecos who were expecting severe "vote flight" during the first and presumably harshest years of the reforms were not terribly surprised; they also took comfort in the fact that the opposition had lost votes. However, the majority of Adecos, who were hoping to retain AD's electoral hegemony, were dismayed.

In Argentina, there were no major elections during this period, but rather a series of isolated elections for governorships and provincial party primaries. The electoral performance of Menemist forces was mixed. They won some elections, but lost others, such as the internal primaries of Mendoza, Formosa, and Entre Ríos. The PJ also suffered an astounding defeat in the high-profile August 1990 plebiscite in the province of Buenos Aires on the question of whether or not to change the provincial constitution to allow for the reelection of the governor, who at the time also happened to be the president of the PJ, Antonio Cafiero.[23] As with AD, the PJ's electoral performance during the first years in office is thus open to various interpretations. What was not open to interpretation, however, was that both incumbents were far from realizing their electoral dreams.

The reforms were taking a heavy toll, not just on state-society relations, but also inside the government. High instability in the cabinet suggests low internal coherence (see Huber 1998), which is usually lethal for reform implementation (Evans 1995, Williamson 1994, and Waterbury 1992). Both the Menem and Pérez administrations suffered from this (Table 3.3). Menem changed ministers twenty-one times between July 1989 and July 1991, an average of 2.1 changes per post in twenty-four months. Two key posts— Central Bank and Economy—were especially volatile (six and four changes, respectively). Pérez's record was better, but far from shining: twenty-three ministerial changes between January 1989 and September 1991, an average of 1.0 change per post in thirty-two months.[24] Argentina's cabinet volatility was high compared not only to that of Venezuela but also to that of Argentina under Alfonsín: the number of cabinet members and Central Bank presidents

---

23. The reform was strongly endorsed by the leading political figures at the time: Cafiero, Menem, and even the UCR. Its defeat, therefore, came as a total surprise. Analysts speculated whether or not this defeat represented a setback for Menem's intentions. While Menem endorsed the plebiscite, he was also at odds with the plebiscite craftsman, Antonio Cafiero. Thus, many analysts regarded this as a win-win situation for Menem. If the plebiscite passed, Menem could capitalize on the victory. If the plebiscite was defeated, Menem would benefit politically from the fall of his most serious rival within the party.

24. Pérez's cabinet (sixteen positions plus five reform-crucial, nonministerial positions) was larger than that of Menem (ten positions plus the Central Bank). The key reform-crucial nonministerial

Table 3.3   Argentina and Venezuela: Cabinet Changes

	Venezuela		Argentina	
	Jan 89 to Sept 91	Oct 91 to May 93	Jul 89 to Jul 91	Aug 91 to Dec 93
Total cabinet changes	23	29	21	9
Number of months	32	20	24	30
Number of posts	22	22	10	9
Changes per month	0.72	1.45	0.88	0.30
Changes per number of posts	1.00	1.31	2.10	1.00
Reform-crucial posts	11	11	5	4
Changes in reform-crucial posts	11	13	12	2
Changes per month	0.34	0.65	0.50	0.07
Changes per number of posts	1.00	1.18	2.4	0.50

Source: Author's estimates.

during Menem's first two years in office (twenty-eight) was almost the same as for the entire Alfonsín administration (thirty-one in 66 months).[25]

To summarize, Argentina and Venezuela during the first years of the reforms were cases of "muddling through," achieving important goals, omitting others, and surrendering some. Each accomplishment took a heavy toll in state-society relations. Both Argentina and Venezuela were, therefore, cases of mixed reform sustainability. If anything, Argentina seemed in worse shape politically and economically. There was no basis to expect in 1991 that Argentina would go further in consolidating the reform than Venezuela, which is exactly what happened next.

The Fork in the Path

Venezuela—From Triumphalism to Collapse

Implementation   When CANTV was sold in November 1991, Venezuelan government officials were jubilant. Their ability to privatize CANTV

---

positions in Venezuela were Cordiplan (the central economic ministry, in charge of designing and coordinating overall economic policy); COPRE (Commission for the Reform of the State, in charge of studying and recommending reforms); the FIV (Venezuela's Investment Fund, in charge of privatizations); and the CVG (Venezuelan Corporation in Guayana, in charge of the huge industrial complex in the state of Bolívar). Most cabinet changes in Argentina occurred during two cabinet crises: December 1989 (six changes) and January 1991 (eight changes).

  25. Based on data from *Carta Económica* and the Central Bank.

instilled in them a sense that the worst was over. Less than three months later (February 1992), a violent military coup attempt led by Hugo Chávez Frías killed that triumphalism. Although the government survived militarily, the country plunged into a severe political crisis. Almost every political sector, even those that had cooperated with the state until then, turned against the government with varying degrees of disruptiveness. Reforms such as privatizations, the recently announced financial and tax reforms, the price adjustments of SOE goods and services, the creation of a Macroeconomic Stabilization Fund, the liberalization and reform of the agricultural sector, the restructuring of the Social Security Institute, and increases in domestic petroleum product prices had to be forgone (based on Torres 1993). Essentially, after February 1992, reforms were either not implemented or were implemented in a manner that contradicted the spirit of the reforms.[26]

Paradoxically, 1992 was not a bad economic year. Even as social discontent was rising and the reform program was dying, key macroeconomic indicators remained healthy until the end of 1992 (see Table 3.4). The political crisis, therefore, is not attributable to economic woes. But by the end of 1992, the political turmoil and policy incoherences began to take a toll on the economy. Economic variables began to decline for the first time since late 1989. To combat the reemerging deficit, inflation, and capital flight, the Central Bank tightened monetary policy (interest rates during the first half of 1993 were 40 points higher than the inflation rate), exacerbating a recession that was to last several more years.

Pérez was forced to resign in May 1993. An interim president, the Adeco Octavio Lepage, was appointed and replaced eleven days later by another Adeco, Ramón J. Velásquez. There was an instant improvement in the relations between the Executive and Congress led by AD: Congress granted Velásquez an "Enabling Law" to impose economic reforms by decree, often the very same reforms denied to Pérez. In one week in August 1992, Congress

---

26. Venezuela's privatization program experienced the same drawn-out death that the government experienced. The government completed only fifteen privatizations between 1992 and 1993—all minor. The most important privatizations were shelved. Privatization revenues reached a meager U.S.$30 million, considerably short of the government's first-quarter estimate in 1993 of U.S.$2.3 billion. Given that Pérez's successor had ample power to privatize, this shortfall is all the more revealing of reform unsustainability. FIV president Carlos Hernández Delfino declared that the opposition to privatization became so radicalized in 1992 that the sale of CANTV would have been impossible if it had been attempted that year (in Wade 1993). In some cases, the privatizations failed because the government could not find interested buyers (e.g., for state-held shares of VIASA); in most cases, because Congress, labor, and business leaders refused to cooperate.

Table 3.4   Argentina and Venezuela: Key Macroeconomic Indicators, 1989–1993

Indicator	Country	1989	1990	1991	1992	1993
GNP growth (at constant	Venezuela	−7.8	6.8	9.7	5.8	−0.2
market prices)	Argentina	−6.2	−0.1	8.9	8.7	6.0
GNP growth per capita	Venezuela	−10.2	4.2	7.1	3.4	−2.4
(at constant market prices)	Argentina	−7.5	−1.4	7.5	7.3	4.8
Private consumption	Venezuela	−14.4	0.5	4.6	6.1	−4.1
growth	Argentina	−6.1	−3.4	11.6	9.6	4.4
Fiscal balance (% of GNP)	Venezuela	−2.3	−2.1	2.7	-3.6	−5.0
	Argentina	−16.2	−2.7	−1.3	0.6	1.9
Inflation (annual)	Venezuela	81.0	36.5	31.0	31.9	45.3
	Argentina	4,923.6	1344.9	84.0	14.1	6.5
Unemployment (urban)	Venezuela	9.7	11.0	10.1	8.0	6.6
	Argentina	7.6	7.5	6.5	7.0	9.6

Sources: ECLAC (1995); *Economía Hoy* (February 12, 1994, pp. 16–17); Ministry of the Economy and Public Works and Services (1994).

approved more bills (twenty-six) than it had in the entire previous year. The fact that the political sector was so eager to grant the new president reform prerogatives that it had denied to Pérez suggests that the quarrel with Pérez was not about the desirability of the reforms.

Societal Reaction   The deterioration in state-society relations in Venezuela actually began before the February 1992 coup attempt. The real turning point was circa October 1991 (see Fig. 3). This was followed by a successful strike by the CTV in November that virtually paralyzed Greater Caracas. Unrest surged after the February coup. Legislators condemned the government more harshly than they had condemned the coup plotters. The leaders of COPEI (Rafael Caldera), Causa R (Aristóbulo Istúriz), and the Communist Party (Ricardo Gutiérrez) delivered apologetic defenses of the motives for the coup, blaming the reforms and the government's corruption for creating conditions that made social unrest "understandable." Except for one AD senator (David Morales Bello), who criticized Caldera and called for "Death to the coup plotters," most legislators refrained from challenging these coup apologetics (Sonntag and Maingón 1992). These pronouncements were broadcast on national television and radio, achieving the highest ratings in viewership in Venezuela's history (ibid.).

Public support for the coup plotters and animosity toward the government and the reforms were huge. A poll shortly after the coup revealed that 84 percent of Venezuelans blamed the president and AD for the country's crisis (in

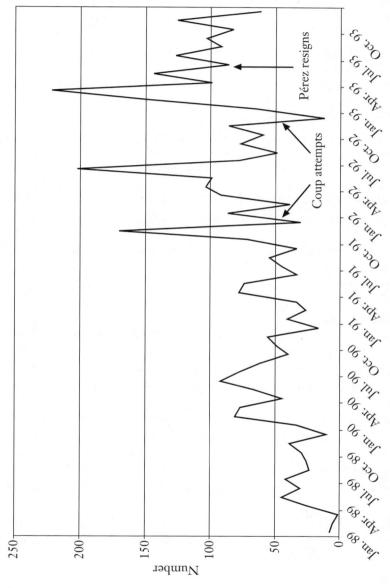

Fig. 3 Venezuela: demonstrations and protests, 1989–1993

Source: Author's calculations based on data from PROVEA (various years).
Notes: Protests include rioting, marches, traffic interruptions, looting, hunger strikes, seizures of establishments, acts of civil disobedience, etc. Data for 1989 exclude riots and protests outside Caracas, and protests related to the Caracazo.

Romero 1997). During the spring 1992 carnival season, one of the most popular costumes among children was the military fatigues worn by Hugo Chávez. On March 10, *caraqueños* took to the streets, banging pots, chanting "Viva Chávez," and calling for Pérez's resignation (the "Cacerolazo").[27] The government was bombarded with accusations of corruption and incompetence. Pérez was forced to appoint an advisory council to evaluate the reforms and make recommendations for changes.

Government efforts to reach agreements with societal groups and parties during this period failed. For instance, an agreement with COPEI shortly after the February coup attempt to "save the constitutional order" (which stipulated granting COPEI two cabinet posts) collapsed in June 1992. Interparty cooperation, the hallmark of Venezuela's political regime since 1958, ended. Intrasocietal relations were equally tumultuous. Business-labor relations disintegrated, mostly over salary issues. In addition, the two largest parties experienced severe internal divisions. AD was divided between those who wanted to break completely with Pérez and those who wanted to "hang on." COPEI suffered its first division ever when Caldera left in 1993 in protest of the chosen presidential candidate and platform. Societal turmoil in general—including street protests, organized strikes, terrorist attacks, street violence, attempts at political assassination, and crime—reached an all-time high (*Revista SIC*, August 1992, 338).[28]

Pérez had no option but to turn the cabinet into a gigantic bargaining chip. Bowing to pressure from every sector, he reshuffled his cabinet, sacrificing ministers in the hope of reducing societal discontent. The rates of cabinet changes per month and per post skyrocketed (see Table 3.3). Turnover rates in key economic posts virtually doubled between October 1991 and May 1993.

And yet nothing worked. A second, more ferocious coup attempt led by navy and air force officers took place on November 27, 1992, little more than a week prior to the December 6 gubernatorial and municipal elections. While public sympathy for this coup attempt was lower,[29] the electorate delivered to AD its most embarrassing defeat ever. AD's control of governorships declined

---

27. Protesters chanted: "Hoy es 10, son las 10, vete ya Carlos Andrés" [It's the 10th, it's 10 p.m., leave now Carlos Andrés].

28. Crime-related property damage in 1992 was 59.7 percent higher (in nominal terms) than in 1991 (OCEI 1992). Protests in Caracas were 52 percent higher than in 1991 (Metro Caracas Police Department in *El Diario de Caracas*, February 2, 1994, 14–15).

29. The fact that the turnout for the December 6 elections was respectable (50 percent) indicates some societal desire for regime preservation.

from 13 to 7 of 22. Even the internally divided COPEI managed to increase its governorships from 7 to 10, and leftist parties won 5 (MAS obtained 4, including the AD-bastion province of Delta Amaruco, and newcomer Causa-R obtained 1). AD's control of the municipalities declined from 157 to 124 of 282 mayoralties (a near-tie with COPEI, which advanced from 110 to 123). AD also lost the mayoralty of Caracas to Causa-R. For the first time, AD failed to achieve a net increase in votes and was forced to share control of the state apparatus with nontraditional parties.

By early 1993, Pérez was virtually unable to make a public appearance without being confronted by public protests. In his annual speech to Congress in early 1993 (which he almost could not deliver because of disruptions caused by MAS and Causa-R legislators), Pérez captured the climate of the nation: "We are coming out of the crisis with a crisis. . . . In 1992, my administration has been the most difficult that any president in the democratic history of the country has ever faced" (Pérez 1993).

The year 1993 would turn out to be worse than he expected. The same day he delivered this speech, his attorney general, Ramón Escovar Salom, asked the Supreme Court to examine whether or not there were sufficient grounds for trying the president for corruption. From that moment on, cries for Pérez's resignation escalated, coming from all sectors of society, including AD. Overwhelmed, Pérez resigned in May 19, 1993, stating: "I would have preferred a different death."[30] The following day, the Supreme Court ruled that there were sufficient grounds to charge him with corruption.

For the next several months, Venezuela experienced one of the most uncertain political periods ever. "We never knew whether we would make it to the end," said one of President Velásquez's ministers. The interim government did make it to the December 1993 elections, but AD obtained the lowest share of the vote ever. Its distance from the divided COPEI and the newcomer Causa-R was negligible. The combined votes of the two leading anti-reform parties, Convergencia-MAS and Causa-R, was 52.8 percent, showing the extent of the anti-reform sentiment. The most prominent enemy of reform in the country, Rafael Caldera, took power in 1994, vowing to dismantle Venezuela's "naive economic opening." The day of his inauguration, shortly after placing a floral wreath by the tomb of Simón Bolívar in the Panteón Nacional, Caldera confirmed that he would eliminate the VAT, offer relief to industrialists, and liberate the participants of the 1992 coup, including Hugo Chávez.

30. This was the first presidential resignation since the 1958 resignation of the successor of ex-dictator Marcos Pérez Jiménez.

Argentina—From Uncertainty to Unstoppability

Implementation   The reforms and the reformers collapsed in Venezuela, but they thrived in Argentina. Between 1991 and 1996, the Menem administration implemented and consolidated one of the most far-reaching market programs in the history of Latin America.

The turnaround in sustainability began with the April 1, 1991, approval of the Convertibility Law.[31] This was the first significant reform-related law approved by the Congress since September 1989. Ten additional reform-crucial laws followed in 1991. As a consequence, there was a spectacular abatement of inflation, from 27 percent in February 1991 to 0.4 percent in November 1991, which generated a spectacular boom in aggregate demand.

The reform program acquired unexpected momentum. By the end of 1993, most of the goals set in 1989 had been attained. Most sectors of the economy were deregulated (e.g., pharmacy, freight, agricultural markets, and professional services), and other sectors were re-regulated (e.g., capital markets). All price controls were abolished. Tax collection rose dramatically, despite a net decrease in distorting taxes, mostly due to increases in the VAT (from 15.6 percent to 16 percent in February 1991, to 18 percent in March 1992, to 21 percent in April 1995) and a restructuring of the tax-collection bureaucracy (Table 3.5).[32] Subsidies for industrial promotion were substantially cut, while trade opening with Brazil, Uruguay, and Paraguay (Mercosur) was deepened.[33] The federal civil service staff shrank from 671,000 to 284,000. Employment in privatized firms went from 302,000 to 138,000 by 1994. Deadweight fiscal spending decreased by 7.9 percent of GDP (21.8 percent if one includes the quasi-fiscal deficit). In October 1993, the state carried out the partial privatization of the pension system, one of the first of

31. The Convertibility Law established a currency board, required the Central Bank to uphold a fixed exchange rate, barred the Central Bank from printing money, eliminated contract indexation, and mandated that 100 percent of the monetary base be backed by gold, foreign exchange, or other external assets. Chapters 7 and 8 discuss this law further.

32. Some twenty-one federal taxes, levies, and exemptions on the VAT, all of which yielded about 3 percent of GDP, were abolished. As of January 1994, employer payroll tax rates were reduced by 30 to 80 percent, mostly in the traded goods sectors. The new tax bureaucracy invested heavily in equipment and staff, expanding its processing capacity to about 600,000 tax returns from business firms annually. This improvement was not long-lasting. VAT revenues as a percentage of GDP declined after 1993. Evasion of the VAT remained high (see IMF 1995).

33. In 1993, concern about alleged unfair trade practices and macroeconomic instability in Brazil led to temporary increases in trade barriers. However, in August 1994, Argentina agreed with its Mercosur partners to establish a common external tariff, moving closer to the establishment of a regional common market.

Table 3.5   Argentina: Tax Revenues (percentage of GDP)

	Efficient Taxes				Taxes on Work	Distorting Taxes	Total
	VAT	Direct	Other	Total			
1980–83	3.1	1.7	3.5	8.3	2.4	1.3	12.0
1984–88	2.2	1.4	4.1	7.7	3.4	2.3	13.4
1989–90	2.0	1.5	3.1	6.6	3.2	3.2	13.0
1991–95	5.6	1.9	2.8	10.3	4.7	1.0	16.0

Source: Llach (1997, 157).

its kind under a democratic regime in Latin America. Despite protectionist pressures by industrialists and devaluationist pressures by exporters, the fixed exchange rate regime remained intact.

Whereas Venezuela experienced serious cabinet turmoil, Argentina experienced unprecedented cabinet stability, especially at the two key economic posts. There were cabinet battles during this period, but these struggles exacted a lesser toll on the cabinet than ever before. The minister of the economy, Domingo F. Cavallo, stayed in office until July 1996—the longest tenure for any minister of the economy in Argentina in recent memory.

Argentina became a champion of privatizations between 1991 and 1995 (Table 3.6). Nearly 90 percent of national-level entities were privatized—from the most deficit-ridden sectors (e.g., railroads) to the most profitable (e.g., YPF), from the most tied to national security (e.g., nuclear power plants) to the most inconsequential for national security (e.g., sanitation services). There was substantial opposition to privatization throughout this period, but the impressive number of privatized companies and the impressive amount of privatization revenue stand as testimonies of the government's political victory. Argentina's privatization stampede was accompanied by an increase in commitments on the part of new owners to make direct investments and efficiency improvements, suggesting a strong state capacity to elicit business cooperation.

This is not to say that everything worked out as planned for the government. The government had to yield on some reforms. For example, labor-flexibilization remained timid. The government acquiesced to congressional demand for a public component in the privatized pension system. The August 1993 Pacto Fiscal with the provinces, whereby the government agreed to forgo U.S.$0.9 billion in provincial debt, increase transfers, and take over responsibility for provincial social security systems, was riddled with obstacles. Nonetheless, the degree of reform implementation defied the expectation of

Table 3.6   Latin America's Leading Privatizers, 1990–1995

	Number of transactions	Privatization revenue as % of GDP
Argentina	123	1.21
Venezuela	29	0.61
Mexico	174	2.00
Nicaragua	75	1.52
Peru	72	1.58
Brazil	45	0.27
Honduras	32	0.45
Bolivia	28	2.03
Colombia	16	0.24

Source: Inter-American Development Bank (1996).

almost every observer. Argentina switched from being a case of uncertain muddling through to one of political determination.

Societal Reactions   Once it became evident that the government would deepen, rather than abandon, the reforms (end of 1991), the reaction of many economic agents was not necessarily supportive. To be sure, there were some solace areas in state-society relations. For instance, "public opinion" support continued to be high (albeit never as high as during the initial honeymoon). The approval ratings of the minister of the economy often surpassed that of the president (unprecedented in Argentina). And despite greater labor assertiveness, overall labor conflicts (as measured by strikes) declined (see Fig. 4).

Nevertheless, state-society relations were not optimal, especially at the level of political parties and crucial interest groups. The UCR adopted a more anti-reform attitude, at times choosing to deny quorums in Congress. Peronist labor unions, internally divided in the early stages of reform, reunited and carried out the first general strike in November 1992 against the government and the reforms. After electing in 1991 the most openly protectionist and anti-reform leadership in decades, the UIA began to clamor for reform reversals, such as trade protection, subsidies, and devaluation. Financial sectors, never confident that the exchange rate regime would endure, staged a major run on the dollar in November 1992. Riots broke out in the provinces of Corrientes and Santiago del Estero during 1992–93, prompting the federal government to intervene. And as in Venezuela, the government was continually bombarded with accusations of corruption, favoritism, incompetence, and disregard of constitutional procedures.

But unlike in Venezuela after 1991 and in Argentina itself prior to 1991, these societal pressures failed to derail the reforms. For the most part, the

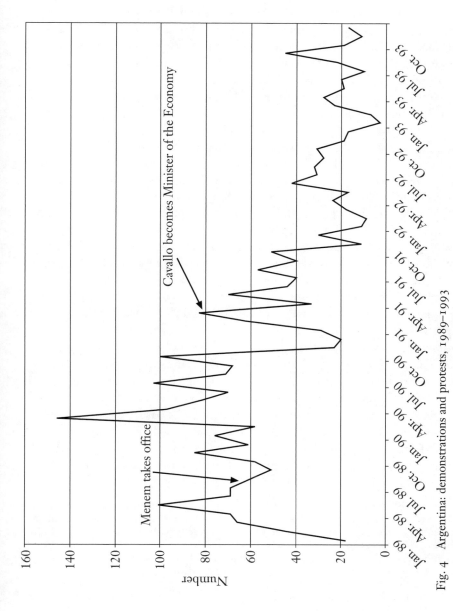

Fig. 4   Argentina: demonstrations and protests, 1989–1993

Source: Centro de Estudios Unión para la Nueva Mayoría (various years).

government won almost every battle. By 1994, group-based demands against the reforms softened considerably. Most opposition parties toned down their anti-reform positions, the UIA elected a more conciliatory leadership, financial sectors restrained their calls for a devaluation, and so on. By late 1993, the most salient political issue was no longer whether the new economic model was the right one, but whether to call for a plebiscite to reform the constitution to allow for Menem's reelection.

Even here, the government prevailed. The electoral advance of the government, although slow at first,[34] was overwhelming by October 1993. The 1993 legislative elections were the most pivotal of Menem's first administration.[35] The government billed them as a plebiscite on the overall performance of the government and on the desirability of a constitutional reform to allow for Menem's reelection in 1995. To leave no doubt about its intentions, the government filled the streets of Buenos Aires with posters reading "Menem 1995." The triumph of the PJ far exceeded the expectations of even the most optimistic observers. Numerically speaking, the advance of the incumbent relative to the 1991 elections was not outstanding (less than 2 points), but the context of this election made this victory all the more significant. No president since World War II, except Perón in 1952, had ever won midterm elections in the fourth year in office.

In fact, no president since Perón had ever won elections after implementing market reforms. No president had ever won societal approval for constitutional reform, including the possibility of incumbent reelection. Menem demoralized the up-and-coming Ucedé and the vociferous UCR. He obtained 50 percent of seats in Congress, coming very close to obtaining two thirds of Congress (necessary for passage of congressional reform). The PJ also won control of the capital, traditionally a UCR bastion. A new political alternative emerged, the Frente Grande, but its growth was fed by defecting voters from the opposition rather than from Peronism. In both chambers of Congress, PJ seats increased continually from 1991 to 1997 (see Table 3.7).

34. In the first midterm elections under Menem (second half of 1991), the PJ's overall share of the votes was 40.7 percent. How savory this victory was for the Peronists depended on the standard of comparison. Compared to the PJ's 1983 and 1985 performances, the 1991 results were encouraging, but compared to 1987 and 1989, they were disappointing. The PJ obtained significant inroads in the Senate (from 56 to 65 percent of the seats), a negligible increase in Deputies (from 45 percent to 46 percent), and a noticeable decline in governorships (from 17 to 14 governorships).

35. Half of the seats in the Chamber of Deputies and one-third of the seats in the Senate were up for grabs in the 1993 elections.

Table 3.7   Argentina: Distribution of Seats in Congress

	Total Number of Seats	PJ Seats (percent)	UCR Seats (percent)
	Chamber of Deputies		
Jul 89–Dec 89	254	97 (38.2)	114 (44.9)
Dec 89–Dec 91	254	120 (47.2)	90 (35.4)
Dec 91–Dec 93	257[a]	116 (45.1)	84 (32.7)
Dec 93–Dec 95	257	127 (49.4)	84 (32.7)
Dec 95–Dec 97	257	131 (51.0)	68 (26.5)
Dec 97–Dec 99	257	119 (46.3)	66 (25.7)
	Senate		
Jul 89–Dec 89	46	21 (45.7)	18 (39.1)
Dec 89–Dec 92	46	26 (54.2)	14 (29.2)
Dec 92–Dec 95	48[a]	29 (60.5)	10 (20.8)
Dec 95–Dec 98	72[b]	37 (52.8)	18 (25.7)

Notes:
Half of the seats of the Chamber of Deputies are renewed every two years. One-third of the seats of the Senate are renewed every three years.
[a] Increase in seats due to creation of new province: Tierra del Fuego.
[b] 1994 Constitution increased the number of seats per district from 2 to 3.

Source: Molinelli, Palanza, Sin (1999).

As a result, UCR leader Raúl Alfonsín felt compelled to sign a pact with Menem agreeing to reform the Constitution to allow Menem to run for reelection (the Olivos Pact). This was Menem's finest electoral moment—his political coronation and his ticket to a ten-year tenure in office. It also constituted the turnaround in the behavior of the opposition: from recalcitrant opposition to a more subdued criticism of the reform without relaxing pressure on the government. The opposition began to focus on issues of "horizontal accountability": that is to say, the extent to which Menem violated and weakened institutional mechanisms for controlling and monitoring the actions of the Executive.[36]

The Reform Program During Bad Economic Times (1995–96)   Argentina's reform process survived both the good times as well as the bad. The collapse of the Mexican peso in December 1994 produced waves of panic throughout Latin America. Many observers predicted that Argentina was next in line—

36. The UCR focused on issues such as corruption in privatizations, excessive use of decrees, the undermining of the independence of the Supreme Court, protection of mafias, clientelism in social programs, illegal sale of arms to Ecuador and Croatia, etc.

Table 3.8 Four Cases of Reform Sustainability

	Mixed Sustainability		High Sustainability	Low Sustainability
	Venezuela (January 1989–September 1991)	Argentina (July 1989–mid-1991)	Argentina (mid-1991–1996)	Venezuela (October 1991–December 1993)
Implementation	Some accomplishments (e.g., price and trade liberalization) and some setbacks (e.g., fiscal reform)	Some accomplishments (e.g., replenishing of foreign reserves), but some setbacks (few structural reforms, price instability)	Most reforms are accomplished, including the unexpected privatization of YPF	Most reforms are slowed downed, halted, or reversed
Societal Reaction: A. Polls and Protests	After an initial upsurge (the Caracazo), protests return to historical levels	Initially robust public support steadily deteriorates, and labor conflicts increase	Some increase in protests followed by gradual decline; reforms and reformers remain popular	Public opinion turns strongly against government and reforms, highest level of sustained societal conflicts since the early 1960s
B. Interest Groups and Political Institutions	Some cooperation (e.g., business sectors regarding trade liberalization) and some noncooperation (e.g., financiers oppose finance reform)	Considerable reluctance to cooperate with reforms	After some reluctance (1991–1992), most groups acquiesce to the reforms by 1994	All business and labor groups refuse to endorse the reforms; two coup attempts

Table 3.8 (cont'd)

	Mixed Sustainability		High Sustainability	Low Sustainability
	Venezuela (January 1989–September 1991)	Argentina (July 1989–mid-1991)	Argentina (mid-1991–1996)	Venezuela (October 1991–December 1993)
C. Opposition Parties	High levels of activism against the reforms and the government	High levels of activism against the reforms and the government	Declining criticisms of the reforms, active criticism of the government; opposition parties shift focus to issues of horizontal accountability	High levels of criticisms against the reforms and the government; cooperation attempt with COPEI collapses; anti-reform parties strengthened and radicalized
D. Elections	AD wins December 1989 elections, but with small margin of victory	The PJ obtains some favorable, some ambiguous, and some adverse results	The PJ wins second mid-term elections and the presidential elections of 1995	AD suffers worst-ever electoral defeats

with a growing trade deficit and an overvalued currency, it seemed the perfect candidate for a sharp devaluation. Liquid international reserves declined by 30 percent (U.S.$4.8 billion) and more than 17 percent of banking deposits (U.S.$8 billion) were lost (World Bank 1996a; 1996b). By the second quarter of 1995, a severe recession had set in that lasted until 1996, producing a decline in fixed investment of 16 percent and a severe banking crisis (The Economist Intelligence Unit). Unemployment and poverty rates soared.

Comparable external shocks in the past would have decimated any stabilization package in Argentina. This time, however, the program survived. A new Central Bank reform, a financial sector restructuring, a bankruptcy law, and a labor-flexibility law for small and medium-sized enterprises were enacted. In addition, the president won the May 1995 presidential elections (with almost 50 percent of the vote, the highest share for the PJ in recent memory) on a platform of more austerity. True to his promise, the reelected Menem tightened liquidity (even if this meant exacerbating the recession). Although the government was unable to secure every measure sought, it managed to sustain reform momentum until early 1997, despite enormous societal opposition between 1991 and 1993, several macroeconomic problems, a severe external shock in 1995, and well-founded accusations of violations of horizontal accountability. In 1997, Menem could claim to be one of the most resilient reformers in the world.

Conclusion

In 1989, Venezuela and Argentina launched sets of market reforms that were remarkably similar in the extent to which they were internationally correct, risk-taking, and shocking. More than mere reforms, these were foundational acts—deliberate state attempts to replace a decade-old, inward-oriented economic model with a market-friendly, externally oriented, fiscally sound alternative.

Judged in terms of the two main components of reform sustainability—agenda implementation and societal response—the reform process underwent two separate phases in each country (Table 3.8). The initial years were characterized by mixed sustainability in both countries: many reforms were accomplished, many others were omitted and still others were surrendered. Both Executives shared similar trophies (e.g., economic recovery, some privatizations) and similar embarrassments (e.g., incomplete structural adjust-ments), similar allies (e.g., international actors) and similar enemies (e.g., sec-tors of the bureaucracy, the ruling party, the opposition, labor and business), similar positive reputations (e.g., charismatic appeal) and similar negative images (corruption, favoritism, constitutional disregard).

By the end of 1991, however, the reform programs took separate routes. Venezuela plunged into its most serious political crisis since the 1960s, killing the reform process and the government. The reform program in Argentina, however, acquired unprecedented momentum. Menem, unlike Pérez, sur-vived all forms of societal poundings. The most stable political regime of the continent came close to perishing, whereas the most renowned economic and political basket case of the region became a paragon of reform sustainability. The following chapters show why these outcomes defy some of the most important theories in political science.

4

the

fog-like

state

argentina and venezuela
as windows
on latin america's
populist-corporatism

A study of the political determinants of reform sustainability might have chosen any number of cases. The
1990s are replete with examples of reform sustainability
and reform collapse. So why choose Argentina and
Venezuela? The answer is, first, because prior to the
reforms, they were "very Latin American," that is, they
were emblematic of a syndrome that was endemic to the
region—the populist-corporatist tradition. The legacy of
this tradition was a state that was highly preponderant,
simultaneously omnipotent and impotent. It was a fog-like
state: pervasive, distortive, dense, and yet easily penetrable.

Understanding the contours of this state is important to understanding why these reforms were necessary and politically difficult.

Another reason for selecting Argentina and Venezuela is that, in other respects, they resembled each other more than either resembled the other countries in the region. This is not to deny that there were differences between them. For instance, Argentina was the epitome of political instability and military involvement—and Venezuela after 1958 was one of the most stable democracies in Latin America, the exact opposite of Argentina. Nevertheless, at the start of the reforms, Argentina and Venezuela shared a number of similarities in areas posited by scholars to matter in the politics of economic reform. Other Latin American countries shared some of these similarities, but not as many of them or to the same extent. Thus, Argentina and Venezuela, despite their representativeness, were similarly distinct.

The result of choosing Argentina and Venezuela is a research design based on "similar contexts, divergent outcomes." This design carries a number of methodological advantages. Comparing matching cases—that is to say, cases that are alike in as many ways as possible except for the observed outcome and, presumably, the hypothesized explanatory variable—allows researchers to control some variables, which is an efficient way of achieving unit homogeneity in small-n studies. Researchers can then rule out the common factors and focus instead on differences between the cases as potential explanations (Przeworski and Teune 1970). The task is to isolate the factor or a limited number of factors that appear to produce changes in the dependent variable (Peters 1998).[1] This chapter discusses commonalities between the cases and in the process provides a historical background to the reforms.

Argentina and Venezuela as Very Latin American Cases:
The Populist-Corporatist Tradition

One of the most salient features of Latin America's development since World War II was an overexpanded state that intervened in almost every aspect of the economy. Gerschenkron (1962) would explain this as the expected economic outcome of joining the industrialization race late in history. For others, the rationale for state expansion in Latin America was more political than

---

1. This research design is vulnerable to overdetermination, i.e., the inability to eliminate rival explanations (Przeworski and Teune 1970), and to omitted variable bias, i.e., the inability to ensure that all the potential biasing factors have been accounted for (King et al. 1994).

economic-functional. The state expanded to carry out populism—that is to say, to mobilize support within organized labor, lower-middle-class groups, and domestically oriented businesses (Kaufman and Stallings, 1991). In mid-century, mobilizing these groups was necessary to counterbalance the agricultural exporters, which until then had dominated Latin American politics.[2]

In the annals of Latin American history, Argentina and Venezuela emerge as extreme examples of populism. Both countries experienced two "classical" populist episodes almost simultaneously. The first occurred right after World War II (the first Peronist and Adeco administrations, 1946–55 and 1946–48), and the second in the 1970s, during the second Peronist (1973–76) and the first Pérez (1974–79) administrations. Despite various interruptions in the political regime (three "revolutions" in Argentina between 1955 and 1973, and an authoritarian regime in Venezuela between 1948 and 1958), the basic populist imprint survived in both countries. As Schvarzer (1993) argued in reference to Argentina, the goal of the state remained to "culminate but not modify" the industrial policies of the late 1940s. In the 1970s, Perón resorted to the old populist formula of disregarding fiscal and monetary discipline.[3] And Pérez, enjoying a formidable oil boom, invested in gigantic, capital-intensive industrial megaprojects (Hausmann and Márquez 1983; Rodríguez 1991). Statism was embraced even by the political challengers of the original statist-populists: the first elected non-Adeco administration (the 1969–74 Caldera administration) turned out to be Venezuela's nationalization pioneer (see Romero 1986).

Populism tends to go hand-in-hand with corporatism (Malloy 1977), which is commonly defined as state attempts to (1) "structure" interest representations (by sanctioning some groups and stigmatizing others); (2) "subsidize" official associations; and (3) "control" the leadership, demand-making, and internal governance of these associations (Collier and Collier 1977, 493; Schmitter 1974). Argentina and Venezuela epitomized these

2. See Roberts (1995) for a more expansive definition of populism that includes, in addition to economic distribution, the creation of a multiclass coalition, a type of discourse, and a pattern of top-down mobilization by personalist leaders that bypasses institutional forms of political mediation. This fits Argentina and Venezuela well. Although populism in Venezuela was not characterized by disregard of existing institutions, the role of "personalist leaders" remained significant. For instance, most of AD's leadership in 1988 was composed of the very same elites who participated in the founding of the regime in 1958, and COPEI remained extremely dependent on the "paternalistic role" of its founding leader, Rafael Caldera.

3. From 1972 to 1975, public sector outlays rose from 37 percent to 46 percent of GNP (most of which went to finance public sector employment and wage increases) and the fiscal deficit skyrocketed from 5.1 percent to 14.4 percent of GNP (FIEL 1990).

three conditions. Since the rise of Peronism in the 1940s, every Argentine Executive had been obsessed with tinkering with the political loyalties of societal associations:[4] Peronist governments privileged Peronist associations; non-Peronist governments disfavored Peronist associations, an obsession that O'Donnell (1973) labeled an "impossible game."[5] Venezuela's corporatism differed from that of Argentina mostly in the extent to which the state pursued exclusion and repression, not in the extent to which it sought to structure, subsidize, and control interest groups.[6] When the Adecos returned to power in 1958, they opted for a softer formula of corporatism: the state would refrain from monopolizing the political space, but certain groups would continue to be subsidized (the main labor union, CTV, and the main business federation, Fedecámaras), and state control over labor would be deepened (the state reestablished and expanded labor unions).[7] The rules of Venezuela's softer version of corporatism were encoded in the famous Punto Fijo Pact of 1958 (see Kornblith and Levine 1995, López Maya et al. 1989, and McCoy 1989).

Did the hyper-populist-corporatist tradition in Argentina and Venezuela lead to enhanced state capacity? The answer is yes and no. The paradoxical idea that states can exhibit capacity and incapacity simultaneously was developed in 1987—through separate undertakings—by political scientist Joel S. Migdal (1987) and economist Deepak Lal (1987). They argued that state efforts at self-strengthening can become self-defeating. For Migdal, trying to accommodate an entire fragmented society eventually leads to an erosion of state capacity. For Lal, when governments intervene heavily in the economy to control economic agents, a point is reached after which this control actually diminishes (the "Laffer curve of government intervention"). Cavarozzi

4. Peronism was essentially the successful attempt of a state bureaucrat (Juan D. Perón, before becoming president) to tinker with the loyalties of existing socialist and anarcho-syndicalist labor unions (Torre 1989).

5. Even Alfonsín succumbed to this: he attempted unsuccessfully to de-Peronize labor unions through a 1985 reform of labor electoral laws (Gaudio and Thompson 1990) and create a "third-historical" movement under his party. Like many of his predecessors, Alfonsín's tinkering efforts tarnished state-opposition relations throughout his tenure.

6. The first Adeco administration (the Trienio, 1946–48), like the first Peronist administration, also flirted with semi-authoritarian attempts to monopolize societal representation, leading to the alienation of sectors of civil society and the collapse of the regime (Blank 1973; Levine 1978).

7. AD allowed opposition parties (except Marxists) to have access to state office and influence over labor unions and Fedecámaras to remain independent. The state also incorporated the CTV and Fedecámaras in decision-making to the exclusion of most other societal groups (Crisp 1994, 2000; Oropeza 1983; Gil Yepes 1981). For Collier and Collier (1991), this level of inclusion is the main difference between corporatism in Argentina and in Venezuela, and the main explanation for regime instability in the former and stability in the latter.

(1994) called this the state-centric matrix, and O'Donnell (1994, 174) called it the impotent omnipotence of states. Argentina and Venezuela were clear examples of this paradox.

State Impotence: International and Domestic Incapacity

Argentina and Venezuela experienced substantial erosion of state capacity in the 1980s—both internationally and domestically. The Argentine state began the 1980s as an international pariah (Escudé 1992; Tulchin 1990), repudiated by the international community for having conducted two senseless bloody wars—against the British for the Falklands and against its own citizenry for domestic order. Argentina's international political standing improved a bit after the 1983 democratic transition, but its economic standing plummeted. As one of the most dismal cases of economic insolvency, Argentina lost, one by one, all of its international economic allies, culminating with the 1989 refusal by the World Bank to support Alfonsín's last stabilization attempt. An unusually high international achiever during the 1970s (see Domínguez 1985), Venezuela also saw its external leverage dissipate throughout the 1980s. One of its sources of international leverage—oil export revenues—declined by half in the 1980s (from U.S.$20 billion in 1981 to barely U.S.$10 billion in 1989). This was both a cause and an effect of Venezuela's international decline. It reflected secular trends (oil prices declined from approximately U.S.$30 per barrel in 1981 to U.S.$14.15 in 1988), but also Venezuela's declining leverage (Venezuela could not avoid obtaining successively smaller allocations of oil export quotas from the Organization of Petroleum Exporting Countries).

A good indicator of the discredited international images of Argentina and Venezuela prior to the reforms is the decline in the price of each country's external debt paper on secondary markets. Between 1986 and 1989, the accumulated loss in the original values of the debt, low to begin with, was 87 percent in Argentina and 63 percent in Venezuela.

The erosion of state capacity was even more evident domestically. Scholars of state-building (e.g., Cohen et al. 1981 and Tilly 1985 and 1992) consider the ability to tax a defining feature of domestic state capacity. According to this standard, Argentina and Venezuela were very "stateless" societies. The Venezuelan state essentially abdicated its prerogative to tax the population in the 1940s. Deeming it "unthinkable" that citizens from an oil-rich country should pay taxes, the first Adeco government reduced indirect taxes, domestic oil-consumption taxes, and taxes on the middle sectors to the minimum level possible (Betancourt 1979). Venezuela in 1988 remained the only Latin American country without a VAT, and it charged domestically one of the lowest prices for oil in the world. Domestic prices of oil-derived products were 44 percent lower than their exporting opportunity cost (Torres 1993, 249). Not an oil-rich state, Argentina could not afford the luxury of Venezuela's tax laxity. Yet it managed to set up quite an inept tax system, which was economically distortive, since it penalized the most dynamic sector—agricultural exports.[8] It was also highly contentious because it pitted the agricultural export sector against almost every other sector. More important, it was insufficient—from the 1970s on, public revenues fell consistently short of public expenditures, creating a structurally permanent demand for more debt and deficit spending (see Llach 1997, 63–69, and Cortés Conde 1992). Tax codes in both countries were full of low-yielding, inefficient, loophole-ridden and regressive taxes.[9] Consequently, opportunities for tax evasion were high, which, in turn, fueled institutional decay.[10]

These countries, therefore, faced what Harberger (1993) calls a "demoralized tax system": taxpayers felt cheated by the state because state services were dismal. Taxpayers were thus ill-disposed to pay taxes, which made raising taxes, always politically unpalatable, all the more repulsive. These countries faced an urgent need to rebuild state capacity, at a time when the public was less willing than ever to pay for it.

State Omnipotence: Suffocating Markets

On another dimension, there was too much state. Although central government expenditures in Argentina and Venezuela never surpassed 35 percent of GNP, which is not particularly high by world standards, the degree of state control over the commanding heights of the economy was astounding, as

---

8. The World Bank (1987) ranked Argentina as one of the most anti-export economies in the world.

9. As the economy deteriorated in the 1980s, so did the state's tax-collecting capacity. Inflation eroded the real value of tax receipts; capital flight reduced the direct tax base; economic slowdown and informal markets affected the resources of the social security system; and the rationing of financial markets encouraged tax evasion (Chisari et al. 1993).

10. In Venezuela, only 6.4 percent of firms were effective taxpayers in 1991 (García 1993). The remainder declared losses, no income, or no profits. Of these taxpaying firms, less than half declared taxable income above Bs 2 million. The average tax paid was Bs 2.4 million (U.S.$23,657). Thus the total average for Venezuela was Bs 151,000 (U.S.$1,514). In Argentina, the failure to reform the tax system was perhaps the principal explanation why stabilization did not succeed during the Alfonsín government (Machinea 1993, 131). Direct taxes paid by the private sector never exceeded 1.5 percent of GDP in the 1980s, and the VAT never yielded more than 3 points of GDP.

revealed by the proliferation of SOEs in both countries, approximately 430 in Venezuela, and more than 500 in Argentina (see Appendix 1).[11] These states were heavily involved in—and often, ineptly running—almost every sector of the economy. In Venezuela, the state even owned the primary sources of foreign currency—oil, iron ore, and aluminum. With some exceptions (mostly PDVSA and Metro de Caracas in Venezuela), these SOEs suffered from colossal ailments (e.g., nonaccountable managers, low labor productivity, and nonaudited balance sheets), magnified by the "buy nationally" laws in each country.[12] Discontent with SOEs was pervasive among the population,[13] exacerbating Harberger's tax dilemma: the tariff structures of SOEs needed to be raised, but no one was prepared to pay more, given the poor quality of the goods and services they provided.

State preponderance meant the suffocation of markets. The Venezuelan state, in fact, was not even ashamed of its desire to suffocate markets. In 1961, the Articles of the Constitution that guarantee economic freedoms were suspended (Decree 455), opening the legal door for arbitrary state intervention in the economy. State interventions in the economy generated huge catastrophes, such as the financial crash of 1983[14] and the exchange rate scandals of the late 1980s.[15] Price controls proliferated in the 1980s, leading

11. The Argentine state was minority shareholder in 222 of these 500 firms (Minsburg 1991).

12. SOEs were economic vampires, accounting for much of the fiscal and debt crisis that afflicted Argentina and Venezuela. Yet their savings rates and, hence, investment rates were negligible. Argentina's public sector savings rate in the 1980s never surpassed a meager 1.0 percent of GNP (ECLAC 1992). The Venezuelan SOE savings rate declined to 2.4 percent of GNP in 1988 (down from 7.5 in 1980), coming close to Argentina's dangerous levels. From 1980 to 1988, real public investment declined 20 percent and 38 percent in Argentina and Venezuela respectively (ibid., 227). Guerchunoff (1992) estimated that the financing requirements of Argentine SOEs exceeded U.S.$50 billion between 1965–87, equivalent to the entire stock of the foreign debt. The overall deficit of the Venezuelan SOEs reached 2.0 percent of GNP in 1989 (World Bank 1993, 3). Argentine SOEs accounted for about half of the nonfinancial sector's overall deficit in the 1980s (Alexander and Corti 1993, 2). In 1989, the thirteen largest Argentine SOEs showed a combined operating deficit of U.S.$3.8 billion (ibid.). They also held U.S.$16.4 billion in external debt (Pirker 1991, 82), representing almost 25 percent of Argentina's total external debt. Thus, while the financial requirements of the increasingly obsolete SOEs expanded, their ability to meet those requirements became increasingly insufficient.

13. An indicator of public discontent with SOE services in Argentina was the dramatic decline of 25 percent in ridership in urban and suburban train services between 1980 and 1988 (*Anuario estadístico de la República Argentina*).

14. State policies of overvalued exchange rates and artificially low nominal interest rates generated stagflation (the non-oil domestic product failed to expand between 1978 and 1982). This is remarkable, given Venezuela's handsome profits from the second oil boom of 1979. Stagflation led to a severe capital flight (more than U.S.$11 billion in the 1980–81 period) and debt accumulation (Hausmann and Márquez 1983; Larraín 1990, 348).

15. The Venezuelan state responded to the 1983 crisis by establishing price and exchange-rate controls, which came to be known as RECADI (*Registro de Cambios Diferenciales*). Under RECADI,

to a perverse dynamic in state-business relations. Producers pressured for release of controls (through lobbying, plant shutdowns, hoarding, corruption, etc.), while the government tried to resist (stimulating black markets), but ultimately yielded, either devaluing the currency (as in 1986) or renegotiating controls (as in 1987). In the second half of 1988, the government again faced intense pressure to lift price controls, but resisted for electoral reasons. The result again was catastrophic: supply declined, speculation expanded, and consumers began to buy everything in sight, exacerbating shortages. At the end of 1988, Venezuela was thus in the midst of one of its most severe state-made economic collapses in history.

The Argentine state was another champion of market suffocation. The conventional economic instruments used to induce growth (market prices to signal resource allocation and fiscal policy to achieve more equitable income distribution) were inverted. The state used distorted prices to achieve income distribution, and fiscal policy to influence resource allocation (Cavallo et al. 1989). As in Venezuela, prices were set for an impressive list of products and services.[16] Almost every stabilization attempt since the 1970s involved some price-control mechanism.

In short, the state was both overbearingly present, and at the same time, conspicuously inconsequential. The perverse effects of this fog-like state on the economy were seen in almost every economic sector. Markets were plagued with a list of strong administrative controls and bans on competition. At the same time, however, the state was noticeably absent in the area of antitrust regulation. The result was what Bhagwati (1978) labels "chaotic incentives," giving rise to informal markets, financial speculation, illegal awarding of licenses, faked invoicing, smuggling, allocative inefficiencies, and capital flight.

Patronage-Dependent, Rent-Seeking Societies

The Argentine and Venezuelan states did not suffocate all types of markets. In fact, like their regional counterparts, they were quite adept at stimulating

---

the government purchased foreign exchange at the low official rate of Bs 14.50, and sold it domestically at a higher rate, in essence imposing a tax on foreign exchange transactions (Rodríguez Balza 1993). Only those sectors deemed to be importers of "priority goods" were allowed to buy cheap dollars from the state. In practice, RECADI became the source of enormous corruption. Every Venezuelan economic agent jockeyed for the largest possible quota of foreign currency (Naím 1993a, 45). Collusion occurred between state officials and economic agents falsely claiming to qualify for cheap exchange rates. Approximately U.S.$40 billion were disbursed to 26,000 "importers" between 1983 and 1988, mostly without any records (Beroes 1990, 60). And yet RECADI actually aggravated capital flight, the very same malady that it was supposed to resolve.

16. Thirty-two percent of Argentina's production was subject to licensing (Ministry of the Economy 1994, 97).

one special market—the market for political favors among unequals, also known as patronage. One variation of patronage is rent-seeking: "the collusive pursuit by producers of restrictions on competition that transfer consumer surplus into producer surplus" (Tullock 1990, 199). As elsewhere in Latin America, rent-seeking in Argentina and Venezuela encompassed more than just producers and more than just restrictions on competition. Almost every economic agent or sector devoted the bulk of its time to figuring out how to extract privileges from the state and block reforms.[17] Rent-granting fulfilled key political purposes, but, in line with Migdal (1987) and Lal (1987), it also accelerated state decomposition. The state's primary clients became the state's primary parasites. The most favored beneficiaries of this system—sheltered business and organized labor—came to develop an ever-increasing appetite for rents. They also developed institutional means to control policymaking and to veto policy reforms (see Merkx 1969 and Crisp 1994 and 2000).

If the state was the cow to be milked, then SOEs were the cow's udders—the principal arena for the trading of rents (e.g., work relief for part of the labor force, sheltered markets and subsidized inputs for national firms, economic opportunities for lagging regions, and sinecures for the well-connected) (Glade 1986). SOEs existed to correct deficiencies not just in the economic market but also in the political markets (see Cavarozzi 1984). As engines of economic development, SOEs left much to be desired, but as instruments for the exchange of political favors, they were quite functional.

In both Argentina and Venezuela, interest groups operated under the impression that the supply of rents was inexhaustible. In Venezuela, oil was responsible for this perception (Coronil 1997; Karl 1987 and 1997), but it was not the only culprit (Romero 1986). When oil proved insufficient, the state found alternatives (e.g., external borrowing as in the late 1970s, foreign exchange controls [RECADI] as in 1983–88, reserve-burning as in 1985–88). All of these were policies common to the region. For this reason, it is an error to assume that oil made Venezuela that unique. Argentina's monetary and fiscal

---

17. The Venezuelan private sector virtually ransacked the state through financial and foreign exchange speculation in the 1980s. Lobbying government officials for trade exemptions, for instance, was endemic (e.g., tariff payment exonerations were approximately two-and-a-half times greater than tariff receipts and amounted to 3.2 percent of GNP in 1988). The celebration of Secretary's Day in the Ministry of Development, which was responsible for price setting and tariff exonerations, was an amazing feast with private funding, in which corporations typically showered the administrative staff with handsome gifts (e.g., cases of beer, family trips to Orlando, yearly supplies of baby food) (*Veneconomía*, September 1990). Comparable lobbying occurred in Argentina. An analyst described a typical business day like this: "The morning hours are devoted to meeting with bureaucrats, followed by working lunches with high government officials or with 'competitors.' Then it is back to the office for still more news on the radio. The typical Argentine entrepreneur is too busy to work!" (de Pablo 1990, 123).

laxity fulfilled the same function of rent-sourcing as Venezuela's oil. The Argentine state's seemingly infinite capacity to create money—thus inflation—to cover fiscal deficits generated the perception that the state had an infinite capacity to dispense rents. Public sector subsidies to the private economy (excluding tax incentives) amounted to 5 percent of GNP in the 1980s (Cortés Conde 1992).

Tilly (1985) has argued that by creating an imaginary threat, states also create the demand for protection from this threat, which ultimately translates into more demand for state intervention. This "racket" was customary in hyper-populist-corporatist states such as Argentina and Venezuela. States were quite willing to rescue actors from reckless economic decisions, giving rise to a chronic moral hazard. In times of hardship, economic agents could easily cajole the state to come to their rescue (Cortés Conde 1992). In Argentina, going out of business was half-jokingly described as the best business, because the state always stood ready to take over. In Venezuela, the state's refusal to create stabilization funds to moderate oil "boom-bust" cycles burdened the country with volatility. And every time a downturn occurred, the state intervened to provide relief. In line with Tilly, this cycle of recklessness followed by relief led to societal demand for statism. Polls in Argentina and Venezuela showed that despite all the economic troubles of the 1980s, many citizens remained highly supportive of statism.[18]

The End of Credibility: Macroeconomic and Political Unrest

The combination of the state's ever-increasing weight in the economy, ever-declining revenues, ill-conceived economic policies, unfavorable international circumstances, and unruly domestic economic actors culminated in macroeconomic instability. In Argentina, macroeconomic instability was not new. What was new after 1988 was that it spiraled out of control. The then-in-place Primavera Plan[19] began to collapse as news spread that the government's negotiations with multilateral organizations were in trouble. Doubts spread that the government would be able to defend the exchange rate. Fears were fueled by the increasing prospects that the unpredictable Menem would win the upcoming May 14 presidential elections (the "fear-my-contender" campaign launched by the UCR candidate did little to reduce this anxiety). A

18. See Catterberg (1989, 32) for Argentina. In Venezuela circa 1989, 52 percent of those surveyed by a public opinion poll taken at the start of the Pérez administration (first quarter of 1989) preferred a return to the old statist model (Consultores 21, 1994).

19. This was a stabilization plan based on dual exchange rates and an implicit tax on exports, which initially lowered monthly inflation to less than 10 percent.

financial panic struck at the end of January 1989. People began to "flock" to the dollar *en masse*. The Central Bank, which was selling nearly U.S.$500 million per week in a futile attempt to defend the currency, decided on February 6 to suspend foreign-exchange interventions. From then on, inflation grew exponentially, leading to Argentina's severest hyperinflation.

The Argentine state virtually went into a prolonged holiday. Having lost every instrument of governance, the government decreed sporadic shutdowns (mandatory holidays, withdrawal restrictions, exchange-rate controls) of financial and foreign-exchange markets—these markets were closed 20 percent of all working days between April and July 1989 (based on Fernández 1991). Between the beginning of the new year and Menem's inauguration, the government tried to defend six exchange rate regimes (Guerchunoff and Llach 1998, 418). All failed. In the meantime, unrest escalated: between May and July, there were 676 acts of looting, in which 52,000 people participated, 3,201 were arrested, 198 wounded, and 16 killed (*Carta Económica*, August 1989). The government lost the May 1989 elections, and the chaos continued. During the following weeks, no one, not even the government, knew what the value of the currency was. In June 1989, foreign reserves barely reached U.S.$200 million, which is functionally equivalent to zero (Llach 1997, 64). In what has been labeled as a market coup, the economic and political crisis forced Alfonsín to resign five months ahead of schedule (Epstein 1992a).[20]

In Venezuela, the macroeconomic instability that began after 1987 was a novelty.[21] Previously, inflation had been moderate and stable (albeit repressed), averaging 11 percent per year in the 1974–86 period. But by the second half of 1988, the rate of consumer-price inflation reached 60 percent annually. This too was the result of erosion of the government's credibility. The state lost its ability to persuade economic agents of its capacity to uphold the foreign exchange and price-control regimes. Consequently, people flocked to the dollar, producers hoarded products, and consumers rushed to the stores to rid themselves of bolivars. The results were widespread scarcity, a rapid appreciation of the real exchange rate (the black market exchange rate jumped to Bs40 to the dollar), a deterioration of balance of payments (extraordinarily unusual for an oil-exporting country), a current account deficit (reaching 10 percent of GDP), and a sharp decline of foreign-exchange reserves (from U.S.$11 billion at the end of 1987 to approximately U.S.$6 billion in early 1989; net reserves were U.S.$3 billion). Social unrest,

20. Even close allies of the president participated in this "coup." The UCR's candidate, Eduardo Angeloz, called for the resignation of the minister of the economy, Juan Sourrouille. Alfonsín complied, exacerbating the panic.

21. These data are derived from World Bank 1993 and "Memorando relacionado. . . ."

which was increasing in the 1980s (Hillman 1994), peaked in 1988. Looting of retail stores, especially supermarkets, proliferated.

To conclude, Argentina and Venezuela were representative—and in some dimensions, exemplary—of Latin America's populist-corporatist tradition. Economic actors spent most of their productive time figuring out how to take advantage of, or circumvent, the overexpanded state. These efforts normally succeeded because these states, despite their preponderance, were extremely porous and incompetent. Argentina and Venezuela were cases, therefore, of too much state and too little state at once. The dilemma of implementing market reforms in these hyper-populist-corporatist settings is that they entailed addressing this mutually contradictory set of problems, that is to say, shrinking and reviving the state simultaneously. In addition, reforms were bound to produce opposition from the privileged offsprings of populism—bureaucrats, politicians, and business and labor groups—all of whom enjoyed important power positions—and hence, veto opportunities. As Nelson (1988, 105) explains, where government relies extensively on patronage, stringent budget discipline "cuts not merely at a government's general popularity, but at the resources needed for it to maintain its support base." To succeed, market reforms require combating the preferences of these interest groups. But in these countries, no government ever stayed in office by battling or excluding labor and business (Bergquist 1986, 185; Schvarzer 1993, 386; Crisp 2000). That is why austerity measures were, sooner or later, relaxed. It was now Menem's and Pérez's turns to do what no one else had managed.

Argentina and Venezuela as "Matching Cases"

Despite being very "Latin American," Argentina and Venezuela were similar in ways that set them apart from the other countries in the region. That similarity influenced the politics of economic reform in special ways.

Upper-Middle-Income Democracies (in Distress)

Scholars have argued that the more middle-income and democratic a country is, the greater the handicaps for implementing market reforms.[22] At the start of the

22. Middle-income countries tend to have larger urbanized middle-income groups, which suffer higher "relative costs" from adjustment policies than other income groups (Nelson 1992; 1988). In addition, democratic regimes maximize the means through which disaffected groups can exercise pressure (e.g., strikes, protests, voting) and dilute power concentration at the Executive, who must contend with other powers (e.g., the Congress, the Judiciary, the press).

Table 4.1   Freedom House Ranking of Political and Civil Rights, 1989[a]
(20 countries in Latin America)

Rank	Political Rights	Civil Rights
1	**Venezuela**, Costa Rica, Dominican Republic	**Argentina**, Costa Rica
2	**Argentina**, Bolivia, Brazil, Colombia, Ecuador, Honduras, Peru, Uruguay	**Venezuela**, Ecuador, Uruguay
3	El Salvador, Guatemala, Mexico	Bolivia, Brazil, Colombia, Dominican Republic, El Salvador, Guatemala, Honduras, Peru
4		Chile, Mexico, Nicaragua
5	Chile, Nicaragua	Haiti, Panama
6	Panama, Paraguay	Cuba, Paraguay
7	Cuba, Haiti	

[a] This annual survey defines freedom in terms of both civil and political freedoms as these have been traditionally understood in the constitutional democratic states. 1 is the best score and 7 is the worst.

Source: Freedom House.

reforms, Argentina and Venezuela were two of the wealthiest democracies in the Third World—two of the only four Latin American and Caribbean countries listed by the World Bank as upper-middle-income countries in 1988 (World Bank 1990b). They scored above the regional median in levels of literacy, education, urbanization, unionization, energy consumption, medical services, and survivability. In addition, Argentina and Venezuela were highly democratic by mid-1980s Latin American standards, second only to Costa Rica (see Table 4.1), and even by world standards (see Coppedge and Reinicke 1990).

However impressive, the political and economic institutions of Argentina and Venezuela were showing signs of atrophy. Institutional decay is inimical to reform sustainability because it undermines the system's ability to regulate and contain conflict. One of the casualties of this decay was the welfare system and public spending on social policies (CEPAL 1994). Poverty levels almost doubled in Venezuela between 1981 and 1987 (see Márquez et al. 1993, 155) and tripled in Argentina between 1980 and 1989 (Llach 1997, 71). Until the late 1970s, most non-Marxist scholars marveled at Venezuela's democratic achievements. By the 1980s, most were appalled at Venezuela's democratic deficits (e.g., Naím and Piñango 1985, Romero 1986, Stempel París 1981, and Gil Yepes 1981).[23] Argentina's democratic institutions were besieged by intense labor instability, continual military upheavals, civic disappointment

23. See Abente (1987) for a more optimistic view.

with the settlement of human rights abuses under the military, and mistrust of parties and politicians.

Strength of Organized Labor

Venezuela and Argentina were also similar in that organized labor occupied a salient political position,[24] which in the politics of market reform can be both a liability and an asset. It is a liability because organized labor is a key target of the reforms, and because it is organized, it can mount a formidable challenge. However, organized labor can be an asset because it can obtain the cooperation of its membership for reforms.

Argentina's and Venezuela's workers enjoyed uncommon privileges. Economically, for instance, union members' standard of living was middle class. Vacationing in Mar del Plata or Córdoba (for Argentines) and Margarita or Orlando (for Venezuelans) was not unusual. Politically, unions enjoyed participation in decision making at the government- and firm-level, and hefty economic subsidies. Furthermore, unions were highly militant (unlike their counterparts in Mexico), but they were not socialist (unlike their counterparts in Chile). Peronist unions were strong enough to undermine almost every government, including Peronist governments. In Venezuela, although unions lost their ideological passion in favor of "bread and butter" issues (Bergquist 1986, 16), they still created trouble for non-Adeco governments (Coppedge 1994a). And yet, these unions were not Marxist: Venezuelan unions supported the government's war against Marxist guerrillas in the 1960s, and Argentine union members, to this day, sign petitions to the pope asking for the canonization of Evita. Finally, although union members often marched alongside students, they had a long tradition of distrusting intellectuals-turned-politicians.[25] Argentine and Venezuelan unions, therefore, were not programmatically rigid, but rather, politically privileged.[26] Their political ideologies and loyalties did not automatically dispose them against market

24. Unionization rates in Argentina and Venezuela in the 1980s had declined since the heydays of the 1970s. Yet they still hovered around 30 percent in 1988, among the highest in Latin America (see U.S. Department of Labor 1991).

25. In Venezuela, the rift between intellectuals and workers dates to the insurrection of the 1960s, which attracted numerous AD students and intellectuals, but was repudiated by AD labor. And in Argentina, a favorite Peronist labor slogan was "Alpargatas sí, libros no" [Shoes yes, books no].

26. Despite these similarities, Argentine and Venezuelan labor unions were not identical. A crucial difference was the level of internal political pluralism. In Argentina, unions were dominated by one party (the PJ), whereas in Venezuela, other political parties were present. This explains why Venezuelan labor leaders displayed less willingness to cooperate with the reforms. They were hesitant to impose internal discipline in fear that their constituents would switch political allegiances to other parties (Murillo 2000).

reforms. Their anti-Marxist tradition liberated them from a visceral rejection of the market. What they were likely to resent was any type of reform that undermined their privileged political positions, and even more so if the initiative originated from highly schooled technocrats, as happened under Pérez and Menem.[27]

Political Parties and Party Systems

Mainwaring and Scully (1995) argue that governability is enhanced under institutionalized party systems, that is to say, where parties obtain reasonably stable shares of the vote, experience low electoral volatility, have strong roots in society, and exhibit independence on choice of leaders. According to these criteria, Argentina and Venezuela should have experienced an easier time implementing the reforms than many of their regional counterparts. Institutionalized bipartisanism had been a fixture in Argentina since the late 1940s and in Venezuela since 1973 (see Chapter 2).[28] Mainwaring and Scully (1995) rank the party systems of Argentina and Venezuela as moderately institutionalized (more institutionalized than Mexico, Paraguay, Bolivia, Ecuador, Brazil, and Peru, but less so than Costa Rica, Chile, and Uruguay). If anything, since Venezuela scores higher than Argentina, one should have expected Venezuela to have had an easier time than Argentina.

Reforms by the Least Expected

Argentina and Venezuela are also cases of reforms initiated by the least expected movements and leaders. The parties that elected Menem and Pérez considered themselves to be the founders of the very same populist-corporatist institutions that the reforms sought to dismantle. Both parties had a long tradition of

---

27. For an explanation of why market reforms generally give rise to intellectuals-turned-politicians, so-called technopols, see Grindle 1996, Domínguez 1997, Montesinos 1997, and Williamson 1994.

28. Haggard and Kaufman (1992) suggest that Argentina qualifies more as a fragmented party system than a bipartisan case because the two strongest parties have been internally divided since the 1940s. The problem with this classification is that both parties have run for elections as unified entities since the 1970s. A stronger argument against Argentina's bipartisanship would invoke the role played by conservative forces (i.e., military and civilian sectors, with strong ties to the agro sector, and strong aversion to populism in general, and Peronism in particular). The *gorilismo*, as this sector is locally known, has played a decisive role in politics, albeit through extra-partisan and nondemocratic means. In the post-1983 democratic period, the Ucedé attempted to represent this conservative sector, with minor electoral success. But even accepting this as evidence that Argentina is not bipartisan, those who defend the theory that bipartisanship contributes to market reforms would be at a loss in trying to explain the Venezuelan outcome.

statism, reinforced further in the 1980s. Lusinchi and his party basically ignored COPRE's recommendations for state reform,[29] and the PJ killed (in Congress and in the streets) most market reforms proposed by Alfonsín.

Menem and Pérez themselves had unmistakable records of statist-populism. As governor of the province of La Rioja (1983–89), Menem ruled like a typical Latin American populist caudillo. He increased public employment by 200 percent in his first two years as governor, leaving a huge deficit and a heavily indebted local lottery. As president (1974–79), Pérez embarked on one of the largest state expansions in Venezuela's history. In addition, both leaders went out of their way to proclaim their populist credentials in the late 1980s. In 1987, for instance, Pérez told some reporters: "Write it in capital letters, I am a populist" (in Romero 1994, 70). In 1986, during the most successful moments of the Austral Plan, Menem disparaged the "new ideas in vogue of state shrinking," as serving only to "shrink the nation" (Cerruti 1993, 201). Menem called for a huge wage increase (*salariazo*) and proclaimed that the solution to recession was to produce more arms.

Closer to election time, both Pérez and Menem were a bit more ambiguous (see Palermo and Novaro 1996 and Naím 1993b). For instance, Menem campaigned alongside free-market economists such as Domingo Cavallo. Pérez called for some mixture of market reforms and populist principles.[30] However, there was no ambiguity as to which candidates were more serious about reforms—the candidates from the opposition, Eduardo Fernández (COPEI) and Eduardo Angeloz (UCR).

The final and most important parallel between Menem and Pérez is that they won their party's nomination through a type of assault against their party's leadership. In the primaries, neither of them enjoyed the support of their party's machinery, which was controlled by the *Lusinchista* faction in Venezuela and by the *Renovación* faction in Argentina. Both Pérez and Menem were founding members of these factions. But these factions—which included most of the party leadership, legislators, and governors—supported

29. The COPRE (Comisión para la Reforma del Estado) was a state agency created by President Lusinchi to explore possible solutions to the economic crisis of 1983. It became Lusinchi's "Frankenstein," proposing reforms that went far beyond what AD ever deemed pertinent, e.g., political decentralization, the restitution of economic guarantees, gubernatorial elections, and the democratization of political parties (Kelly 1986; Gómez Calcaño and López Maya 1990).

30. An example of Pérez's ambiguity can be found in an interview with a business magazine shortly before the elections. Pérez declared: "Venezuela is ripe for undertaking a profound change in the orientation of our economy. . . . I have combined the position for and commitment to the reform of the economy together with the reform of the State" (*Gerente Venezuela*, November 1988, 8, 16–26). A few paragraphs later: "I do not agree with these neoliberal theories which advocate sending more people into unemployment and more sectors of the population into hunger as shields against inflationary policies."

other candidates: Octavio Lepage (hand-picked by Lusinchi) and Antonio Cafiero (president of the PJ). To overcome this formidable internal opposition, Pérez and Menem employed similar tactics: mobilizing the marginal sectors of the rank-and-file and the more traditional labor unions. This was tantamount to carrying out a pseudo coup d'etat against the party establishment, which naturally gave rise to tensions within the party leadership.

This tactic was electorally successful. But for the process of reforming the economy, it was a mixed blessing. Being traditional, caudillo-style politicians with broad appeal among the marginal masses gave these leaders somewhat of an advantage—they enjoyed the trust of the very same sectors that would feel the cost of reforms the most. Nevertheless, having to appeal to the marginal sectors forced Pérez and Menem to incur a political debt with voting groups that were very likely to be hurt by the reforms. It also exacerbated the credibility problem: few economic actors believed that these leaders were at liberty to pursue market reforms. Consequently, in addition to the difficult challenges associated with reforming their fog-like states, both Pérez and Menem had to deal with the issues of party resentment and lack of credibility.

Conclusion

Latin America's populist-corporatist tradition, epitomized by Argentina and Venezuela, explains both the urgent need for market reforms and the political complexities faced by the reformers. Argentina and Venezuela were representative of Latin America prior to the reforms. Populist-corporatism left a legacy of a fog-like state—pervasive, intrusive, distortive, and capable of great density. In terms of international and domestic capacity, these states were ethereal. They had a weak presence and were incapable of fulfilling some of the most rudimentary functions of a state, such as collecting taxes. These states were simultaneously overbearing and escapable. Reforming them, however, would require addressing both sides of their contradictory natures.

Reforming statist-populism would also mean tinkering with well-entrenched patronage networks. These states typically showered the spoiled offspring of this populist-corporatist tradition—bureaucrats, politicians, organized business, and labor—with sinecures. Political parties in these societies served as brokers of favors between these actors and the state. Thus, societal actions, not to mention party leaders, had compelling reasons to dislike the reforms.

The amount of rent available became insufficient in the 1980s, but the appetites of rent-seeking groups remained insatiable. Like termites on a log,

Table 4.2   Argentina and Venezuela in the Latin American Context (circa 1989):
More Similar to Each Other Than to Regional Counterparts

Argentina and Venezuela	Brazil	Peru	Colombia	Cuba	Mexico	Chile	Bolivia	Paraguay
Upper-middle income (in distress)								
Below regional median (2.7 percent) of growth rates of GNP per capita, 1950–80	•	•		N/A			•	•
Below regional median (-0.8 percent) of growth rates of GNP per capita, 1981–89	•			N/A	•		•	
Top two in Freedom House ranking of political and civil rights (1989)								
Strong, anti-Marxist, privileged labor unions	•				•			
Reforms by the least expected movements or leaders	•	•			•	•		•
Reforms by "traditional" politicians			•	•			•	

state clients succeeded in wasting the state away. And the most serious loss experienced by these states was not so much their rent-making capacity, but their credibility, leading to the worst economic crisis ever experienced by either country since the 1930s.

Comparing Argentina and Venezuela also makes sense because, despite their representativeness, they were more similar to each other than to other Latin American cases in terms of a number of variables that matter for economic governance. Table 4.2 shows this and compares features that might negatively affect reform sustainability. These two countries had a large contingency of people who stood to lose by reform (because they were middle-income) with enormous capacity to challenge the state (because they were democratic, with strong parties and strong unions). These states had a declining capacity to moderate conflict (because they were experiencing institutional decay). Political parties had multiple reasons to oppose the reforms (not just because they were statist, but also because they were brokers among rent-seeking groups). The ruling-party leadership also harbored resentment against the newly elected presidents (because these presidents had staged intraparty coups in order to obtain their respective nominations).

Precisely because they are common to both cases, none of the issues discussed in this chapter can be invoked as explanations for the reform outcome of each case. One cannot explain reform outcomes on the basis of preexisting crises, institutional decay, strength of unions, affliction for rent-seeking, presidential betrayal, etc., as many do. The answers must lie elsewhere.

PART THREE

executive–ruling party
relations

5

market reforms and
the dislocation in
executive–ruling party
relations

Market reforms constitute a special kind of state policy. They are examples of policies that impart costs across society. Almost every economic agent and economic activity is disrupted when an effort is made to reform a fog-like state. And no domain suffers a more severe disruption than the ruling party itself. Market reforms impose significant costs and risks on ruling parties, more so if the ruling party happens to be statist in character. This triggers a political crisis within the party. The result is tension between the Executive, who wants to deepen the reforms, and sectors of the ruling party, which hesitate. Market reforms, consequently, can jeopardize the natural tendency of ruling parties to cooperate with the Executive. In and of itself, this dislocation in Executive–ruling party relations is not serious. But if left unattended, it can escalate to the point of jeopardizing reform sustainability.

This initial dislocation is not irreparable. Ruling parties are not necessarily predisposed to reject market reforms in toto. Some features of market reforms are quite compatible with some of the political preferences and institutional objectives of ruling parties, including statist parties. Market reforms threaten some but not all interests of ruling parties. The possibility that a ruling party will embrace reforms is not out of the question.

This chapter discusses these points. At the start of the reforms, relations between the Executive and the ruling party were mixed in Argentina and Venezuela: sectors of the ruling parties had reservations about the reforms, but still went along with them. I argue that this initially mixed reaction is a predictable starting point in Executive–ruling party relations in any process of market reform.

However, this initial reaction is not a stable equilibrium—over time, the dislocation must be solved one way or another. Either the ruling party sheds its apprehensions toward the Executive, or it revolts. The former took place in Argentina; the latter, in Venezuela. These outcomes were neither preordained nor historically common (at no other time have these parties responded to their Executives this way). How exactly did the initial dislocation in Executive–ruling party relations turn into outright hostility in Venezuela and harmony in Argentina is the subject of other chapters. For now, I focus on the complexities of this dislocation.

Ruling Parties and Market Reforms

When political parties assume office, they do not cease to exist as separate entities. Not all party leaders join the state and not all party structures mesh with the state apparatus. At a minimum, ruling parties preserve their hierarchy, which typically includes a central committee in charge of running party affairs, setting party policies, influencing the voting pattern of the legislature, and conducting relations with outside organs such as the state. Not all members of these committees are necessarily state officials (that is to say, there are party notables, provincial officeholders, legislators, financiers, labor bosses, technical experts, etc.). In addition, ruling parties preserve a set of internal organizations and committees (e.g., secretariats, legislative blocs, labor groups, internal factions, civic associations, and regional-level units), which preserve some degree of autonomy.[1] The political opinions, preferences, and actions of party leaders and organizations, therefore, need not coincide with the opinions, preferences, and actions of the Executive.

Any explanation for the different evolution of Executive–ruling party relations must begin with a map of the initial preferences of ruling parties regarding market-oriented reforms. Geddes (1994) demonstrated that incumbent presidents have reservations about efficiency-oriented reforms because they bear the political costs of these reforms more intensely than nonincumbents. This creates a dilemma for presidents, who realize that efficiency is necessary for effective governance, but it can also undermine the very same system of patronage that sustains him or her in office. Two factors tend to solve or soften this dilemma for presidents. One is international constraints such as a debt crisis, a balance-of-payment deficit, the need to attract investment, and loan conditionalities. The other is a domestic governability crisis such as when the state finds itself unable to assert itself. Both conditions tend to compel Executives to prefer reform over the status quo.

Like the Executives, ruling parties face their own dilemma: they recognize that reforms can hurt them politically, but they also understand that not cooperating with the Executive can be costly. Ruling parties are simultaneously repelled by and attracted to market reforms. For Geddes (1994), the solution to this dilemma is simple: ruling parties become more favorable toward reform when their electoral distance from other parties shrinks, allowing them to share the cost of reforms with others. In reality, however, this dilemma is more complicated and harder to resolve.

Points of Repulsion

The Problem of Being a "Ruling" Political Party

Being a "ruling" party as opposed to an "opposition" political party significantly shapes the response of the party toward market-oriented reforms. Neoliberal reforms contradict the expectation of victorious parties to exploit the advantages of office-holding. As Max Weber argued: "The party following, above all the party official and party entrepreneur, naturally expect personal compensation from the victory of their leader—that is, offices or other advantages." Ruling party leaders, therefore, reach office with the expectation of entitlement to the spoils of office. Access to state resources give ruling

---

1. See Coppedge (1994b) for a description of the internal structures of AD, and McGuire (1997) and Levitsky (1999a) for the PJ.

parties ample opportunities to derive economic gains, reward political friends, and penalize disloyal groups. The call to roll back the state challenges these expectations, regardless of the party's ideology.[2] In highly clientelistic states, the impact of the reforms on ruling parties can be more severe. In Nelson's words, "Patron bosses who rely on distribution of rents as a way to buy political support will be loath to relinquish such controls to price mechanisms that do not distinguish supporter from opponent" (1988, 106). Fear of losing this most coveted means of rewarding and punishing friends is a crucial reason that ruling parties dislike market reforms.

Different Electoral Arenas, Different Electoral Timings

Another source of Executive–ruling party friction stems from the fact that Executives face electoral competition at different times and in different arenas than do ruling party leaders. Executives run for reelection at the end of their terms, which usually last four years or longer. The party, however, faces more frequent electoral contests: mid-term congressional elections, municipal and local elections, gubernatorial elections, etc. Because market reforms tend to produce economic hardship in the near term (de Melo et al. 1996; Przeworski 1991), they appear riskiest to those actors who face electoral competition in the near term. Executives worry less about these intermediate electoral costs because they do not apply to them directly.

In addition, presidents and party officials compete in different electoral arenas. Presidents get elected by nationwide constituencies; party leaders, for the most part, compete in narrower districts. Given that market reforms tend to produce concentrated losers (e.g., the liquidation of an SOE can create a surge of unemployment in a particular locality; liberalization can result in the contraction of employment opportunities in specific regions of the country), politicians who depend heavily on the votes from narrow constituencies (mayors, governors, legislators) are likely to be less enthusiastic about reforms. In short, differences in the timing and incidence of elections explain why ruling-party officials adopt more risk-averse positions than Executives.

The Clash Between Statism and Neoliberalism

Executive–ruling party dislocation is likely to be even more acute if the ruling party happens to be a statist-populist party. Various elements of these parties clash directly with neoliberalism:

2. Pierson (1994, 178–82) discusses how even conservative ruling parties in the United States and England in the 1980s lost enthusiasm for welfare cuts once they came to office.

1. Market-Correctors. Statist-populist parties consider themselves to be in the business of "correcting" market failures. They mistrust the capacity of markets to address social and economic needs. In the words of a leading Adeco: "What we have always advanced is that the market suffers from a 'social blindness' that requires state action and correction" (Canache Mata 1991, 344). These parties understand that by safeguarding the preeminence of the state over other societal spheres, they create opportunities for politicians to be preeminent as well. Consequently, the notion of "state shrinking" places statist-ruling parties in a political quandary. If the state shrinks, what other resources will exist to carry out political projects?

2. Brokers. Often, statist parties serve as "brokers" in the distribution of rents among these corporatist groups, specializing in assigning rents and screening rent-demanders (e.g., recommending individuals for public office or public sector employment, deciding which groups obtain special privileges). These brokerage functions make parties averse to market reforms. Ruling parties fear that the reforms will diminish the rents that they broker and weaken the groups that use their services.

In the 1970s, Kaufman (1977) described Argentina's and Venezuela's parties as "group-based," meaning that these parties coexisted with, and derived support from, strong workers' and employers' associations (in contrast to Colombia and Uruguay, where employers' associations are weak, and Mexico and Brazil, where both workers' and employers' associations are weak). One of the most important clientelistic ties of these parties was not so much that with the rank-and-file, but with their financiers—large industrialists, which tended to be highly protected and state-dependent. In exchange for funding and other favors, statist-populist parties traditionally acted as "brokers" of rents for these clients. The PJ and AD enjoyed a bargaining advantage vis-à-vis business groups because they had control over a "commodity" that was highly coveted by business groups—labor peace and, when in office, access to state rents. Large industrialists and populist-laborist parties clashed on a number of issues, but they also understood that they needed each other. Business needed labor cooperation and state contracts, parties needed funding, and labor needed jobs. AD and the PJ thus exploited these interests by acting as brokers between labor, the state, and business. Because market reforms threaten these activities, these parties naturally feared the reforms.

3. Custodianship. Statist-populist parties often consider themselves founders—and thus, custodians—of the postwar political and economic institutions of their nations, the very same institutions that economic reforms seek to change. As custodians, these parties expect to be consulted about the fate of these institutions. Given that much of the success of stabilization packages

depends on designing shock policies in secrecy, Executives are tempted to implement these reforms without much prior consultation with the political establishment. Nobody likes political exclusion, but politicians who come from parties that self-identify as custodians of the status quo resent this exclusion even more.

4. Third-Position Nationalism. Statist parties are usually intensely nationalist, not in the sense of being isolationists (Peronist and Adeco governments always advocated activist foreign policies), but in the sense of not selling out to foreign interests (*vendepatrias*). They pride themselves in having resolved their country's underdevelopment by discovering a "third position" between Western capitalism and Soviet socialism. Market reforms, which require conformity with foreign conditionalities, often stemming from the very same international institutions that these parties once demonized (e.g., the IMF, the Paris Club, the U.S. Treasury, multinationals, foreign investors), embarrass this "third-position" nationalism. Thus many AD leaders considered the Letter of Intent with the IMF that Pérez secretly signed committing Venezuela to pursue market reforms a "genuflection before the IMF" (Hernández 1990). Third-position nationalism makes these parties feel that economic opening not only denies them an effective vote-catching banner, but also makes them appear rhetorically inconsistent. Insofar as parties worry about reliability,[3] this inconsistency is troublesome for party leaders. Whereas the Executive construes the reforms as a rational strategy of self-fortification—since it secures much-needed international allies—"third-position" nationalist parties see them instead as a sure path toward self-weakening and embarrassment.

5. War Veterans. Many statist-ruling parties achieved political salience as a result of a fierce political struggle, if not an actual war, against domestic adversaries. Peronists, for instance, considered themselves winners in a national war waged upon them by *gorilismo*—anti-Peronist military sectors—and economic liberals, who, since 1955, had tried to eradicate the PJ from the political scene. AD saw itself as the winner of a war against the extreme right, which AD defeated by overthrowing Pérez Jiménez in 1958, and the extreme left, which AD defeated by quelling the leftist insurrection of the 1960s.

Parties that see themselves as war veterans have a hard time with market reforms because market reforms often require "sleeping with the enemy."

---

3. Relaxation of party reliability (i.e., the idea that policy statements at the beginning of an election period should accurately predict the party's behavior during that period) leads to voter defection (Downs 1957).

That is, reforms require the state to seek an alliance or entente with the historical enemies of statist-ruling parties. One of Menem's first acts as president was to invite economic liberals from B&B and the Ucedé to join the government and to grant amnesty to the military. Pérez not only made overtures to opposition parties, including COPEI and the conservative Nueva Generación Democrática (inviting one of its leaders, Vladimir Gessen, to become minister of tourism in 1990), but he also appointed technical experts with strong anti-Adeco backgrounds. Executives look forward to these alliances, not just because they welcome all the support they can muster (and in the case of economic liberals, their endorsement enhances the credibility of the reformers), but also because these are the sectors with the strongest interest in and ideas about reforming the status quo. In Venezuela in 1989, most social scientists interested in changing the status quo had, almost by definition, an anti-Adeco background, sometimes even a leftist or student-oriented background (e.g., Miguel Rodríguez, Carlos Blanco, and Ricardo Hausmann).[4]

While "sleeping with the enemy" might be tactically necessary for the state (and in Venezuela, the only possible way to recruit reformers), it is intensely irritating for ruling parties that see themselves as victorious veterans of a war against these forces. Party leaders interpret this as evidence that the Executive is intent on hurting the party. Thus, making overtures to these actors becomes a major point of contention in Executive–ruling party relations.

This analysis now permits drawing the map of preferences of Executives and ruling parties. Each actor holds quite opposite primary preferences vis-à-vis two variables: (1) the depth of market reform implementation; and (2) the degree of party inclusion in policy-making (Fig. 5). Point A in Figure 5 represents the Executive's primary preferences: the Executive prefers to pursue deep reform and exclude the ruling party as much as possible from decision making. The Executive correctly perceives the ruling party as being apprehensive about the reforms. Points $B_1, \ldots, B_n$ represent the possible initial preferences of the ruling party. Compared to the Executive, the ruling party certainly prefers less reform implementation and more inclusion in policy-making. However, depending on how many of the previously discussed points

4. Miguel Rodríguez and Ricardo Hausmann, for instance, applied Marxist theory in their graduate work. Carlos Blanco collaborated with leftist student movements in the 1960s. In explaining his conversion to market economics, Blanco argued on behalf of the commonality of his position in the late 1980s and early 1960s: "We were always concerned about the cartelization of Venezuela's economy, and it became clear in the 1980s that these reforms offered the best antidote against cartels" (Blanco, interview).

these parties share, ruling parties might allow more flexibility. For instance, some parties, such as AD, have a history of granting great autonomy to the Executive (closer to point B_1). Other parties know that some reforms are desirable, but never to the extent that Executives intend. Alternatively, different party wings can occupy different positions within the dotted oval. Thus the range of preferences within and among ruling parties can vary, although in general these parties are far more averse to reform implementation than Executives are.

Points of Attraction

Despite all these points of conflict, one should not conclude that ruling parties are bound to reject economic reforms automatically. Many institutional, political, and ideological features of ruling parties, even statist-populist parties, are compatible with the political objectives of market reform, which creates the possibility of ruling-party cooperation.

The Costs of Abandoning Governments

Ruling parties understand that nothing is worse for their electoral future than a failed administration. Voters who penalize incumbent presidents tend to penalize the ruling party as well. Thus ruling parties will think twice about sabotaging the actions of their own governments.

Moreover, ruling parties also understand that an image of inertia—that is to say, of doing nothing in the face of economic crisis—can be harmful at election time. In Argentina, for instance, the PJ discovered in the 1989 elections that they were able to extract significant capital by denouncing the UCR's incapacity to deal with the crisis. Once in office, Peronists were keen on preventing the opposition from making the same points. In Venezuela, the issue was a bit more complicated, given that AD was the incumbent ruling party in the 1988 elections, and thus AD avoided making government inaction a campaign issue. However, even AD recognized that there was a premium to be derived from appearing to be pro-reform. In the late 1980s, for instance, a series of groups (civic leaders, opposition leaders, neighborhood associations, COPRE) began to pressure the candidates to embrace political reforms, such as the direct election of governors and mayors. AD adamantly opposed the reforms (Gómez Calcaño and López Maya 1990). Nevertheless,

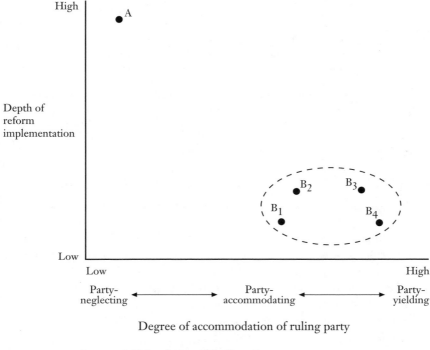

Fig. 5   Preferences regarding reform implementation and degree of party accommodation

candidate Pérez repeatedly told AD leaders that, given the "popular clamor" for reform, failing to embrace reform could be electorally costly. In June 1988, AD finally agreed to the reforms, indicating that it understood the political costs of portraying *immobilisme*.

In short, ruling parties have built-in incentives to cooperate with their own governments and portray themselves as "pro-change," even if they fear the changes announced. While Executives and ruling parties disagree regarding their first order of preference, their second order of preference is actually mutually compatible (Table 5.1). Although Executives prefer full reform implementation and little accommodation with the ruling party, they nonetheless prefer "some" implementation and "some" party inclusion over the third alternative—no reform at all. Likewise, although ruling parties

Table 5.1   Starting Preferences of Executives and Ruling Parties

Preference Ranking	Executives	Ruling Parties
First	Full reform implementation; low party inclusion	Low reform implementation; full party inclusion
Second	Some reform implementation; some party inclusion	Some reform implementation; less than full party inclusion
Third	No reform implementation	Full reform implementation; low party inclusion

would prefer little reform with total inclusion in the government, they still would prefer "some" reform with "some" exclusion over the alternative— the complete failure of their government. Thus the ranking of preferences of a reformist Executive is, first, full implementation without modification; second, implementation with modification; and third, no implementation. For the ruling party, the ranking of preferences is, first, full incorporation; second, some reform with less incorporation; and last, the failure of the government. Thus, at the start of the game, the first preferences of the Executive and the ruling party are incompatible, but the second preferences are not (Corrales 2000a). Cooperation is possible, as long as both the Executive and the ruling party are willing to settle for their second preferences.

The Congruence Between Statist-Populism and Neoliberalism

Despite their apparent historical aversion to neoliberalism, even statist ruling parties are not predisposed to reject market reforms entirely. Political scientists have highlighted affinities between statist-populism and neoliberalism (Gibson 1997; Weyland 1996a; Roberts 1995; Kay 1996; Gamarra 1994). Like populism, neoliberalism provides utopian visions of the future (a more plentiful world), as well as clear enemies (privileged interest groups that capture the nation's resources). Both ideologies allow for the mobilization of actors that have been "hurt" by the existing model of economic development, including both masses and business elites. More could be added to this list:

1. Foundationalism. Statist-populist parties see themselves as the movements that brought modernity to their nations—that is to say, the ones who adapted nineteenth-century ideologies (Marxism and liberalism) to twentieth-century developing-country realities and introduced a model of development that was quite "avant-garde" for its time (e.g., nationalizations, anti-oligarchic and distributive policies, labor incorporation, and agrarian

reform).[5] Betancourt once called AD a party that "was born to make history." Skillful reformers could portray the reforms as precisely "foundational" and "vanguard" acts: as efforts to re-create the domestic order by adapting, rather than copying indiscriminately, the best international ideas of the time.

2. Nonprogrammatic. Statist-populist parties tend to have strong ideological orientations, but they often lack strong programmatic traditions. Latin American political parties operate in extraordinarily presidential systems, where one of the prerogatives accorded to the Executives, even by ruling parties, is significant autonomy in policymaking (see Cansino 1995). At most, these parties only require the Executive to implement policies based on "the philosophical and doctrinal principles of the party," to quote directly from AD's statutes (Acción Democrática 1993). But these principles are vague (e.g., preserve the sovereignty of the people) and flexible (e.g., promote social justice). In fact, some doctrinal components (e.g., the contempt for privileges and cartels) were not incompatible with the anti–rent-seeking objectives of market-oriented economic reforms. Moreover, these parties seldom propose alternative programs during the implementation of the reforms. In short, a nonprogrammatic tradition, vague philosophical parameters, and deficit of ideas create an opportunity for suasion. Skillful reformers at the state level could exploit this opportunity to mobilize the party on their behalf.

3. Change Is Not New. Few statist parties have been frozen in time. Statist-nationalist parties are accustomed to change. As Eduardo Duhalde, Menem's first vice president, explained: "Peronism has two characteristics: acceptance of leadership and adaptation to changes" (*Página/12*, October 4, 1992, 6). This is not just rhetoric. For instance, not all PJ governments were alike in terms of economic policy, some changing even while in office (e.g., interrupting populism in favor of austerity, improving relations with the opposition and other interest groups, normalizing relations with England or the United States).[6] These parties were thus quite capable of self-transformation. Being asked to change—even to surrender old banners—was not a new experience to them.

4. Strong Links with Societal Groups (especially Labor). Statist parties tend to have strong links to labor, which, at one level, is an obstacle to economic

---

5. Martz (1966), for instance, describes AD as one of Latin America's first "modern" political parties and a "national revolutionary" party. By this he meant, among other things, that "from its inception the party advocated a set of basic reforms that might well be characterized as revolutionary" (376). In the case of Argentina, Cheresky (1991) prefers the term "re-foundation" to describe the role played by Peronism in transforming Argentina in the mid-twentieth century.

6. For the evolutionary changes of the PJ, see Iturrieta 1994; for AD, see Aznar 1990.

reform because organized labor is one of the privileged sectors "affected" by the reforms. However, at another level, these labor links are also assets because they give these parties a comparative advantage in an area that escapes most other democratic parties—mobilizing and disciplining labor groups. Rueschemeyer et al. (1992) even consider this labor-disciplining capacity of labor-based parties a crucial explanation for the ability of democracy and capitalism to coexist in Western Europe. In Latin America, labor-based parties did not necessarily lead to democracy in all countries. Nevertheless, labor-based parties enjoy a comparative advantage in shaping the behavior of unions, which in turn, is a useful instrument for any anti-inflation policy. Unions that are large enough to represent most of the labor force (as was the case in Argentina and Venezuela) and capable of centralized strategic action (which links with parties facilitate) have a higher chance of inducing members to moderate their wage demands and, hence, reduce inflation (see Crouch 1985). This is not to say that labor groups in Argentina and Venezuela were completely nonautonomous. The point is that both AD and the PJ, as a result of labor-penetration and historic loyalties (Burgess 1999), had a fair degree of capacity to obtain labor acquiescence to specific policies.

5. Electoral Dominance. Another characteristic that could conceivably encourage ruling-party cooperation with reforms is electoral dominance. Since their founding, AD and the PJ have enjoyed electoral dominance. When Pérez and Menem were inaugurated, AD had won five of the seven presidential elections held since 1958, and the PJ had won all but one of the six presidential elections in which it had been allowed to participate since 1946.[7] The "organizational density" of each party, that is to say, the ratio of party members to the total number of voters, was among the highest in the world.[8]

On the one hand, dominance could have been a point of repulsion between parties and the Executives. Given that market reforms entail unpopular measures, and hence the possibility of voter defection, dominant parties

7. Argentina held presidential elections in 1946, 1951, 1958, 1963, May 1973, September 1973, 1983, and 1989. The PJ was proscribed in the 1958 and 1963 elections. In 1958, the elected president (Arturo Frondizi) owed his victory to the support of the PJ. In 1963, the "blank ballot" (presumably the Peronist vote) obtained the second-largest number of votes.

8. According to Levitsky (1999a, 84), the organizational density scores were 58 percent for AD (in 1988), 54 percent for the PJ (in 1992), 38 percent for the Swedish Social Democratic Party (1966–65), 32 percent for the Austrian Social Democratic Party (1966–85), 29 percent for the Chilean Communist Party (in 1969), 21 percent for the Italian Communist Party (in 1963), 6 percent for the British Labor Party (1966–85), and 3 percent for the Spanish Socialist Party (in 1983).

might see market reforms as a threat to their hegemony, which these parties were naturally reluctant to give up. This hegemonic status is what allowed AD and the PJ to describe themselves as parties "of the people," often even as the "natural" parties of their nations, and to treat their enemies with comfortable disdain.[9] Because hegemony was therefore a major source of collective identity, these parties naturally cherished this dominance and were keen on preserving it, a mindset that could render the party risk-averse.

On the other hand, hegemony could just as easily have made these parties more willing to take risks. Precisely because these parties controlled such large shares of the votes, they had a lot of votes to spare. More than any other party, dominant parties such as AD and the PJ had the structural cushion to withstand short-term electoral declines stemming from market reforms without losing their tickets to political power. In this sense, hegemony could have encouraged these parties to cooperate with the reforms.

To summarize, market reforms produce a dislocation in Executive–ruling party relations. This dislocation, however, is not impossible to overcome. Ruling parties, even statist, nationalist, populist, and laborist parties, share certain characteristics that open the possibility of some kind of rapprochement with a reform-minded Executive. Although the first preferences of each entity are mutually incompatible, the second preferences of each are quite compatible. In addition, even statist-nationalist parties can end up embracing reforms because some features of statist-nationalist parties are amenable to neoliberalism (vanguard foundationalism, adaptiveness, utopic orientations, and a desire to appear to be anti-status quo), create vulnerabilities that could easily be exploited by skillful Executives (nonprogrammatic histories), or encourage the party to take greater risks (e.g., labor penetration, votes to spare). Thus Executive–ruling party cooperation on behalf of market reforms is difficult, but not impossible.

Executive–Ruling Party Relations in Argentina and Venezuela

What then was the evolution of Executive–ruling party relations in Argentina and Venezuela? How did this initial dislocation evolve in each case? To assess the opinions, preferences, and actions of ruling parties in Argentina and

9. In Argentina, even the most democratically oriented sectors of Peronism (the Renovators) succumbed to these vanities in the 1980s. For instance, a leading renovator, José Manuel de la Sota, said, "The Peronist ideology could never change because it is *the natural ideology of the argentines*" (in de Ípola 1987, 343).

Venezuela, I employed various research strategies. First, I conducted a conventional review of primary and secondary materials, including an exhaustive review of the press, which in both countries frequently reported on the politics within ruling parties. I also reviewed the speeches and writings of party leaders. Second, I conducted open-ended interviews. More than 150 political actors and observers in each country were interviewed in the course of almost five years. Third, I interviewed the top leadership of each ruling party. At the end of each interview, I asked each party leader to respond to a fixed questionnaire. The list of all interviewees, a copy of the questionnaire, and a brief description of the interview methodology appears in the appendix (see Appendixes 2 and 3, and Table 5.2).

The questionnaire was presented to twelve CEN members of AD and ten Executive Board members of the PJ (see Appendix 2 and Table 5.2). The main advantage of the questionnaire is that it provides quantifiable and thus comparison-friendly answers. The main disadvantage is that, at best, the answers apply mostly to the situation at the moment of the interview (1994).[10] In combination with other sources, these interviews provided a clear view of Executive–ruling party relations in Argentina and Venezuela.

Hostility in Venezuela, Harmony in Argentina

My research unambiguously revealed two clear results. First, at the start of the reforms, Executive–ruling party relations were predictably mixed in both countries in conformance with the previous analysis. Both the PJ and AD exhibited a mixture of willingness to collaborate with the reforms and an apprehension of them. Party leaders wanted to collaborate with the newly elected presidents, even though they were disturbed by a program of reforms that few understood, desired, or helped formulate. For instance, the PJ approved Menem's "Law of State Reform," authorizing widespread privatiza-

10. One variable that might have influenced the results of this survey was the fact that the PJ was in office at the time of the survey. Insofar as interviewees are concerned about exhibiting a facade of loyalty toward the government, the timing of the interview might have biased the results from Argentina in the direction of more positive attitudes toward the government. In Venezuela, where Pérez was out of office (and soon to be arrested and expelled from the party), the need to display this loyalty was lower. This difference, however, does not contradict the main conclusion: if PJ interviewees lied in their answers in order to maintain a facade of loyalty, this would confirm the finding that Executive–ruling party relations are harmonious (at least insofar as party members are interested in preserving the image of unity). Asking Adecos how they felt about Pérez at a time when Pérez was in need was a good test of true sympathies. Had the party felt positive about Pérez, these sympathies would have surfaced.

Table 5.2   Executive–Ruling Party Relations: Results of Questionnaire (N = 12 for Venezuela, 10 for Argentina)

Please state whether you: (1) agree with the following statements; (2) disagree with the following statements; or (3) have a neutral/intermediate position.

Question	Country	Disagree (%)	Agree (%)	In Between (%)
1. As a member and leader of AD/PJ, you felt represented in the government of Pérez/Menem.	Venezuela	8 (67.0)	2 (17.0)	2 (17.0)
	Argentina	1 (10.0)	9 (90.0)	0 (0.0)
2. The government of Pérez/Menem took into account many opinions on economic matters of AD's/PJ's leadership.	Venezuela	10 (83.3)	1 (8.3)	1 (8.3)
	Argentina	5 (50.0)	3 (30.0)	2 (20.0)
3. Miguel Rodríguez/Domingo Cavallo made a great effort to enter into dialogue with AD/PJ.	Venezuela	5 (41.7)	4 (33.3)	3 (25.0)
	Argentina	2 (20.0)	8 (80.0)	0 (0.0)
4. Pérez's/Menem's economic advisers were loyal to the basic principles of AD/PJ.	Venezuela	7 (58.3)	1 (8.3)	4 (33.3)
	Argentina	4 (40.0)	2 (20.0)	4 (40.0)
5. In general, you agreed with the economic reforms proposed by Perez's/Menem's government more than you disagreed.	Venezuela	2 (16.7)	6 (50.0)	4 (33.3)
	Argentina	0 (0.0)	10 (100)	0 (0.0)
6. AD's/PJ's leadership did everything possible to convince the other party affiliates to back the economic package.	Venezuela	10 (67.0)	0 (0.0)	2 (17.0)
	Argentina	1 (10.0)	7 (70.0)	2 (20.0)
7. In general, the conflicts between AD/PJ and the Pérez/Menem administration were the main cause for the delay of important economic reforms.	Venezuela	0 (0.0)	11 (91.7)	1 (8.3)
	Argentina	10 (100)	0 (0.0)	0 (0.0)

tions, and the "Law of Economic Emergency," freezing all state subsidies and grants for a period of 180 days. Yet PJ leaders continually criticized the depth of the reforms. In Venezuela, AD legislators demanded the disclosure of the "Letter of Intent to the IMF." Yet AD's "father figure," Gonzalo Barrios, issued a strong defense of the reforms and the international agreements in Congress after the February 1989 Caracazo, and in late March 1989, the CEN endorsed the government and the reforms once again, albeit with some reservations (indeed, COPEI's endorsement was more enthusiastic).

The second finding is that halfway into the reform process, this initially mixed reaction turned into outright hostility in Venezuela and fluid cooperation in Argentina. This divergence of reactions is clear from the answers to several questions in the questionnaire (Table 5.2).

Question 1 asked whether the interviewee felt represented in the Pérez/Menem administration. No definition of "represented" was offered (that is to say, its meaning could range from ideological affinity to assessment of personal leverage within the administration). Most AD respondents (67 percent) felt unrepresented, whereas most PJ respondents (90 percent) felt represented.

Question 5 asked interviewees whether, for the most part, they agreed with the administration's economic objectives. All PJ respondents and, surprisingly, half of AD respondents expressed agreement. Only two AD respondents expressed economic disagreements with the government, suggesting that the party's sense of alienation from the Pérez administration cannot be attributed to disagreements about economic policies.[11]

Question 2 asked interviewees if they thought that the Executive had taken into account the party's opinions regarding economic matters. The majority of AD leaders disagreed, suggesting that the lack of consultation in Executive–ruling party relations was part of the problem. The replies from PJ leaders are surprising. Thirty percent of respondents felt that the party was consulted on economic matters, revealing that Menem was able to make party leaders feel represented in his government despite some disregard for the leadership's opinions on economic matters.

Question 7 asked interviewees whether they believed that Executive–ruling party conflicts affected the reform process. The purpose of this question was

11. Indeed, the evidence that Executive–ruling party divorce under Pérez had little to do with economic policy differences is strong. Soon after Pérez's departure from office (May 1993), AD granted the new Executive (Ramón Velásquez, AD) extraordinary powers to implement economic reforms, often the very same powers that they had denied Pérez. Moreover, AD's presidential candidate for the 1993 elections, Claudio Fermín, campaigned on a pro-reform platform.

to assess how aware interviewees were of the status of Executive–ruling party relations and the consequences of this relationship. Adecos responded with remarkable candor: the vast majority acknowledged that Executive–ruling party relations were not only conflictive, but also the culprit of the program's shortcomings. Peronists disagreed unanimously. They might have been underestimating the conflicts that existed in Executive–ruling party relations. However insincere, these answers still demonstrate that PJ leaders preferred to portray themselves as close allies of the government. Subsequent chapters show how this posture was crucial for the success of reforms.[12]

This divergence in Executive–ruling party relations in Argentina and Venezuela is difficult to explain. Both parties shared a similar starting point (mixed reaction), yet with time, they developed opposing attitudes toward the Executive. AD's rebellion against the Executive intensified in 1991, when its distance from the opposition was declining, thus challenging Geddes's argument that parties support reforms as they approach conditions of parity with other parties. Many Venezuelanists actually make the opposite argument, attributing AD's discontent to its decline in the share of the vote under Pérez.[13] However, the PJ in Argentina also experienced a decline by 1991 (albeit a less significant one, 6.8 points), and yet that is the year that the PJ began to cooperate with the Executive. In addition, Executive–ruling party relations did not follow economic achievements. In Venezuela, ruling party rebellion intensified during the healthiest macroeconomic year of the administration, and in Argentina, the ruling party began to cooperate in mid-1991, when most economic actors and gurus (including the IMF) had serious doubts about Argentina's new round of stability. The PJ thus began to cooperate with the Executive before there were real assurances that the economic situation would stabilize—a true act of faith.

Hostile Executive–ruling party relations in Venezuela and harmonious relations in Argentina constituted unprecedented events in the history of these parties. While factionalism was recurrent inside AD historically

---

12. Levitsky (1999a) conducted a more extensive survey of Peronist leaders in 1997, including thirty-nine National Council members and eighty-seven national legislators, and found a similar outcome: most PJ leaders accepted Menem's reforms, few of them opposed them outright, and yet few of them considered themselves to be neoliberal (218–24).

13. Venezuelanists often explain Pérez's conflict with AD as a result of the way that Pérez became the presidential candidate—in total defiance of the preferences of AD's leadership, which supported Octavio Lepage. The problem is that this variable is present in Argentina as well (see Chapter 4).

(Coppedge 1994b), the revolt of AD under Pérez after 1991 was qualitatively different from anything seen previously. The factionalism that Coppedge observed prior to the 1990s never affected the policy arena. At most, factionalism arose over disagreements over the Executive's choice of successor. Even in the 1960s, when AD suffered three splits (1960, 1961, and 1967), only the first split was over ideology. The 1961 and 1967 splits concerned candidate selection. In the 1980s AD did not resent austerity that much. Coppedge (1988, 174–75) conducted a survey of seventy-seven AD leaders in the mid-1980s, including twenty-one of the twenty-eight members of the CEN during the 1984–85 period, and found that 55 percent of respondents agreed with the statement "In the long run, austerity is positive for the country." Only 1 percent agreed with the statement "Austerity is not the solution to the economic crisis that the country is currently undergoing." Coppedge concluded by arguing that "an economic crisis and the adoption of unpopular programs, by themselves, are not enough to transform the party into an obstacle for the government." In the 1990s, the very intentions and thus policies of the Executive were seriously questioned and challenged by the triumphant "outs." The ultimate goal of these "outs" went beyond controlling the succession process; they wanted the complete reversal of government policies. This was total mistrust, total defiance, total sabotage.

No one reflected this turnaround better than party leader Humberto Celli. During the Lusinchi administration, Celli frequently warned fellow party leaders not to "give in to the temptation to practice opposition proselytism around the government's failings and omissions" (in Coppedge 1994b, 151). Under Pérez, Celli transformed himself into one of the most vociferous critics of the administration. He traveled the country repeating "Éste no es un gobierno adeco, ni en sus hombres ni en sus ideas" [This is not an Adeco government; neither its men nor its ideas are Adeco] (Celli, interview). He actively lobbied for removal of cabinet ministers and was at the helm of the group of Adecos pushing Pérez to leave office prematurely.

Likewise, the level of harmony in Executive–ruling party relations achieved after 1991 was unprecedented in Argentina. Unlike AD's internal divisions prior to 1988, the divisions within Peronism did affect the policy realm, quite often resulting in violent conflicts. During the first Peronist administration (1946–55), internal bickering plagued the movement. When the government was compelled to implement austerity in 1952, the PJ rank-and-file rebelled, leading to a rise in labor unrest, strikes, slowdowns, sit-down strikes, ousting of labor bosses, etc. (McGuire 1997, 68–75).

Internal conflicts within Peronism became even more serious during the second Peronist administration (1973–76). The PJ split into two strands. One was composed of corporatist elements, including among their number top labor bosses, who preferred labor peace and cooperation with the state. The other more numerous wing was composed of radical laborists. It grouped the youth and workers. They wanted nothing less than leftist policies similar to those implemented by Salvador Allende (1970–73) in Chile. The conflicts between these wings, and within them, overwhelmed the second Peronist administration, almost from its very first day. When the government announced an austerity "shock" package, labor unions, party leaders, Peronist youth and student groups, and Montonero terrorists escalated their confrontation, prompting the government to respond with repression.[14] In the end, the government had to jettison the reforms and agree to a massive wage hike, leading to hyperinflation (Smith 1991, 230).[15] At the last meeting that President Isabel Perón held with party leaders in March 6, 1976, she declared: "There are many among us who tell me: 'Madame, or Isabelita, we love you very much,' but they stab me in the back" (*Gente* 1976). In mid-March 1976, as inflation and violence spiraled out of control, the CGT directive voted down a proposal to issue a statement supporting the Peronist government (McGuire 1997, 170). The party had abandoned the president. A few days later, the Peronist government was overthrown in a military coup.

In short, prior to the 1990s, AD had a history of consistent support for its administrations, even during periods of austerity, whereas the PJ had a history of disarray, internal bickering, and conflict with the Executive, even during Peronist administrations. These histories were completely reversed under Pérez and Menem. Menem not only avoided a severe confrontation with the party, but actually obtained the party's endorsement for a set of economic reforms that struck at the heart of Peronism. No other Argentine government ever achieved this type of political endorsement. This could very well be the most remarkable political feat of this administration, and not simply because it was unexpected, but because it transformed forever the politics of economic reform in Argentina.

14. On the day of Perón's return to Argentina (June 20, 1973), confrontations between both sides of Perón's supporters, who had gathered to greet Perón, led to a violent massacre in which thirteen died and hundreds were left injured. This incident became known as the "matanza de Ezeiza" (the Ezeiza massacre).

15. In total, there were six ministers of the economy during this three-year administration. These were José B. Gelbard, Alfredo Gómez Morales, Celestino Rodríguez, Antonio Cafiero, Emilio Mondelli, and Pedro Bonanni.

Conclusion

This chapter made three major points. First, the opinions, preferences, and actions of ruling parties need not be the same as those of the Executive. Political parties retain institutional and organizational autonomy. In processes of market reforms, ruling parties can adopt very different kinds of responses to the reform process.

Second, the initial reaction of ruling parties to the reforms, for the most part, is predictably mixed. Most ruling parties begin by harboring serious reservations, but still show willingness to cooperate. This was true in Argentina and Venezuela, contradicting arguments that predict an automatic honeymoon between the Executive and the ruling party or an automatic repudiation of market reforms by statist-populist parties.

The reason behind this initial mixed response is that market reforms confront ruling parties with a difficult dilemma. Parties either cooperate with the reforms and risk portraying an image of heartless neoliberalism, programmatic inconsistency, clientelistic treason, and ideological hypocrisy, or instead reject the reforms and risk abandoning their own government. This dilemma, however, is only the tip of the iceberg of a very complex relationship between ruling parties and market reforms. Market reforms clash with some of the institutional and political features of ruling parties. If the ruling party happens to be statist-nationalist, the clash is even more severe, since market reforms contradict institutional, ideological, historical, clientelistic, and functional features of statist parties. Nevertheless, ruling parties have a built-in tendency to prefer the success of their own governments and to avoid an image of inertia, which is precisely what holds them back from breaking completely with the government despite this initial clash. Moreover, not all features of statist-nationalist parties clash directly with neoliberalism. Thus, even statist-ruling parties have the capacity to assimilate market reforms.

The key challenge of any reform-minded Executive is thus to resolve this initial dislocation in Executive–ruling party relations. At the very least, Executives must prevent this dislocation from deteriorating to the point where the ruling party loses interest in cooperating with the Executive. Better yet, Executives should strive to turn this dislocation around and secure the party's full blessing.

Finally, this chapter showed that Menem was far more successful in obtaining this blessing. Halfway into the reforms, the PJ turned cooperative toward the Executive, whereas AD turned hostile. The obvious question is how exactly Menem managed to obtain this cooperation and what impact it had on reform sustainability. One additional advantage of analyzing the points of conflict and points of compatibility between market reforms and ruling parties is that it provides hints about the ways in which this blessing might come about. Insofar as Executives manage to (1) address the points of conflict (electoral concerns, custodianship, protagonism, brokerage, ideology, etc.); (2) capitalize on the points of compatibility (the ruling party's interest in seeing the administration succeed and avoiding an image of inertia); and (3) exploit the party's vulnerabilities (nonprogrammatic traditions, dependence on leaders, flexible ideologies), then the chances of overcoming the initial dislocation in Executive–ruling party relations increases.

6

the

spiral

of

rejection

executive–ruling party

relations in

venezuela and

argentina, 1989–1991

In the earliest stages of the reforms, when the Executive discloses his or her intentions of launching market reforms, leaders from the ruling party will not hesitate to express their mixed feelings. Not everyone in the party, perhaps not even a majority, will object to the reforms, but signals will be sent that the reforms generate concerns within the party. The emergence of this dislocation in Executive–ruling party relations confronts the Executive with a political choice: either attempt to win over the party or ignore these concerns, maybe even ignore the party altogether, hoping that the party, like the rest of society, will eventually come around.

Most Executives will choose the latter response, at least initially. There are several reasons for this. First, reforms are usually launched in a context of economic crisis, which commands most of the attention of the Executive. The Executive estimates that there is no time to spend on internal party affairs. Second, Executives assume that these reforms are unpopular only in the short term. They are confident that once the reforms start to yield positive economic results, support for them will expand (Stokes 1999). Third, Executives feel that they have a significant political cushion. As a result of their recent electoral victory and hence mandate, Executives feel that they can forgo the support of the party because they have an alternative source of support—public opinion. Finally, shortly after every presidential election, there are no major elections in the horizon, and hence the incentives to take care of party affairs decline. For all of these reasons, Executives easily conclude that the initial dislocation in Executive–ruling party relations is temporary and unworthy of much attention.

Executives soon discover what a mistake this conclusion is. The party's discontent will increase to the point where it will begin to interfere with the government's reform agenda, triggering a vicious cycle. Feeling increasingly excluded, the ruling party will begin to feel that it has little at stake in the success of the government. A ruling party that ceases to feel invested in the presidency will feel disinclined to work on its behalf. As the party turns uncooperative, the Executive becomes more and more frustrated and, naturally, less inclined to make overtures to the party. A spiral of rejection is unleashed. This is precisely what happened in Argentina and Venezuela between 1989 and 1991.

This spiral of rejection undermines reform sustainability. The dislocation in Executive–ruling party relations "corrupts" the Congress and the Cabinet, causing the reform program to experience delays and setbacks. In desperation the Executive will resort to "rescue" measures to salvage the reforms. These rescue measures themselves can turn out to be counterproductive. They can alienate, rather than rekindle, societal support. Thus, a party-neglecting policy, although seemingly rational at first, can be devastating for a reform program.

Two causal arguments underlie the above scenario. The first is that a party-neglecting strategy causes Executive–ruling party relations to deteriorate. The second is that the deterioration of Executive–ruling party relations causes reform sustainability to decline. This chapter discusses these propositions.

Party-Neglecting Approaches

To the utter dismay of the officials of their respective parties, both Pérez and Menem adopted party-neglecting strategies during the early stages of their administrations. Neither president believed that his ruling party had the wisdom, courage, or expertise to contribute to the reform process. In Venezuela, Pérez believed from the start that AD would be a source of difficulty.[1] In Argentina, Menem thought that he needed to deemphasize his links to the PJ for the sake of credibility—that is to say, to demonstrate that he was not attached to old populist formulas. In both cases, the consequences were identical: a deterioration in Executive–ruling party relations, leading to a severe crisis within the party and an intensification of opposition to the reforms.

Venezuela: "Éste no es un gobierno adeco"

Pérez's party-neglecting approach was evident in many ways. First, Pérez bypassed the "comisión de enlace" (transition commission) established after the 1988 elections in order to coordinate the transfer of power from Lusinchi to himself. He and his advisers only met once with the commission (Lauría, interview). Furthermore, he negotiated the reforms with the IMF during the transition period without consulting AD.

Second, Pérez appointed a very non-Adeco cabinet, composed mostly of political friends (e.g., Pedro Tinoco, Central Bank) and highly trained, non-partisan, market-oriented social scientists (e.g., Miguel Rodríguez, Cordiplan; Moisés Naím, Development; Carlos Blanco, COPRE; and Eduardo Quintero, FIV). Even the Ministry of Health and Social Assistance, historically a bastion of the ruling party, was given to non-Adecos (Felipe Bello, Marisela Padrón). In addition, Pérez often encouraged ministers to recruit non-Adeco staffs, even when the ministers themselves preferred otherwise (Coles, interview; Lauría, interview). In time, therefore, the Adeco presence in the cabinet declined further. For a country where political parties traditionally staffed most governments, the low number of AD cabinet members was an enormous gaffe.

Third, the background of several of Pérez's social scientists irritated most AD leaders. These social scientists were locally baptized the "IESA Boys," in reference to the preeminent graduate business and public administration school where three cabinet members either taught or conducted graduate work. Some observers believe that what AD resented was this elitist, technocratic "IESA background." However, what truly bothered AD leaders was instead their "COPRE background" (see Chapter 4). For most traditionalist Adecos, the COPRE staff were a bunch of anti-Adeco extremists, who pushed

1. Pérez was fully aware of AD's troubles: "One of the current calamities of our nations, especially Venezuela, is the obsolescence of traditional parties. Unless reformed, our parties are unsuitable to address the contemporary needs of our peoples" (Pérez, interview).

for political reforms in the 1980s as an effort to weaken AD. Their presence in the cabinet was an irritant.

Fourth, Pérez's discourse—both his public statements and his private remarks to the CEN—were terribly disconcerting for AD. In public, Pérez frequently disparaged, or allowed his ministers to disparage, almost everything related to the "old regime." A favorite phrase of Pérez was "Nationalism is out of style" (*Revista SIC*, September–October 1992). Pérez and his ministers were eager to criticize the past to justify the reforms. The problem was that, by default, criticizing the old regime inculpated AD. Miguel Rodríguez went even further: he constantly criticized and often insulted AD. Reform enemies were labeled "dinosaurs," "unadapted," "cowards," and "unschooled." Pérez did little to restrain Rodríguez's declarations. Pérez believed that given the strong anti-politician sentiment of the population, as revealed by most public opinion polls, criticizing traditional politicians would allow him to gain popularity. As the self-conceived custodians and war veterans of the old regime, Adecos had every reason to feel under attack.

In private meetings with the CEN, Pérez's discourse was less dismissive, but still unpersuasive. Pérez explained the reforms to the CEN as a necessary evil—measures that are anathema to social democratic values, but which are unavoidable because of international and domestic exigencies. Rather than defend the program outright, Pérez talked about "the inescapable need for doing this," "that he is not a neoliberal, but a true social democrat who has no other option." This rhetorical tactic was intended to reassure the party, but instead it confirmed AD's impression that the package was ideologically unacceptable and that Pérez had lost both conviction and, more important, international leverage. Party members wondered why Pérez could not get a better deal from the IMF. In short, Pérez's mixed rhetoric alienated AD. His public statements were directly insulting and his private comments were not reassuring.

Finally, Pérez's reaction to the issue of corruption under the Lusinchi administration, which became salient after June 1989, did not help either. Lusinchi concluded his term in office with one of the highest popularity ratings in the history of Venezuela, especially among AD leaders. But by mid-1989, the Pérez administration could not avoid (or as many Adecos would argue, actually triggered) a campaign to investigate acts of corruption committed under Lusinchi.[2] Most Adecos interpreted this investigation as another Executive affront against the party. AD leaders blamed Pérez for this campaign or at least for

---

2. Most accusations of corruption involved Lusinchi tangentially (e.g., the RECADI scam); others involved him directly (e.g., misuse of public funds). Prior to the December 1989 midterm elections, warrants were issued for the arrests of ten high-ranking members of the Lusinchi

doing little to stop it (much as AD leaders did when Pérez was accused of corruption in 1979). Others went so far as charging Pérez with deliberately pursuing a witch hunt against Lusinchi in order to debilitate the party. Whether or not Pérez deliberately pursued the corruption investigation of Lusinchi is less important. What is crucial is that, regardless of the motivations, its effect was to accentuate the feeling of estrangement and the perception of threat that market reforms triggered within AD.

It should be stressed that Pérez's party-neglecting policy was profound for Venezuela's historical standards, but it was not as absolute as many Adecos would argue. Various economy-crucial cabinet positions were originally given to top AD leaders, some of whom had participated in the Lusinchi administration: Eglée Iturbe de Blanco and Roberto Pocaterra (Finance); Eugenio de Armas (Agriculture); Leopoldo Sucre Figarella (CVG), Beatriz Rangel (Presidency), and Celestino Armas (Energy and Mines). In addition, Pérez still left some room for AD excesses and control of state resources. For instance, in June 1989, Pérez granted Sucre Figarella, a preeminent Adeco financier and Lusinchi adviser, total control over the CVG industrial complex (Decree 282), in essence insulating this traditional source of AD rents from the jurisdiction of reform-czar Miguel Rodríguez. The initial package of reforms came with wage increases for government and private sector employees, one of the most important demands of the CTV during the transition period (*Latin American Regional Reports Andean Group*, April 13, 1989, 13; January 26, 1989, 3). Moreover, Pérez adhered to a strict schedule of weekly meetings with the CEN.[3] And throughout 1990 and 1991, Pérez went out of his way to defend AD labor leaders against charges of corruption.

Nevertheless, AD never felt that it had any weight in the formulation of economic policy. As a prominent Adeco leader and former presidential candidate stated it (in his weekly newspaper column): "The CEN of AD feels impotent vis-à-vis Pérez" (Lepage 1991, 61). Pérez's party-distancing policies, attitudes, and discourse frightened AD.

The effect of this neglect was to split the party among three groups: the orthodox sectors, who wanted an immediate halt to the reforms; the balancers

---

administration, including four key ministers. However, the warrants were found to be legally ungrounded. In February 1990, new accusations surfaced that Lusinchi authorized the purchase of sixty-five Jeeps with state funds, which were distributed to AD leaders. AD responded to these corruption scandals by expelling some members accused of corruption, but soon reinstated most of them.

3. AD leaders argued that these meetings were not consultations with the party but mere notifications of policies to be implemented. Government officials argued that, indeed, the meetings were used to inform the party of the reforms; alternative ideas were always solicited from the party, but the party never offered any.

(known as the "ni ni," neither/nor), who wanted a slower-paced reform and more dialogue with the government; and the *Perecistas*, who were historical friends of the president, albeit not completely persuaded by the reforms either.[4] The first sign of dislocation in Executive–ruling party relations was Pérez's failure to obtain "special powers." Congressional granting of special powers was not unusual in Venezuela: Rómulo Betancourt (1961), Pérez (1974), and Lusinchi (1984) obtained this privilege.[5] Most cabinet members wanted Pérez to obtain similar powers. However, AD legislators made it clear to Pérez that they would not do it. Aware that he would never get special powers, Pérez did not even bother to request them. This was the beginning of a spiral of rejection. AD hinted mistrust, which pushed Pérez to seek distance from his party. Pérez felt that the party's growing crisis justified his party-neglecting strategy.

The orthodox groups of AD began to take the upper hand after the December 1989 elections for governors and mayors, the first of its kind in Venezuela. Although AD came out ahead, not an insignificant accomplishment given the preceding Caracazo and the still fragile state of the economy, the party lost a significant number of governorships. AD felt devastated. Long accustomed to Venezuela's winner-takes-it-all system, in which the party who wins the Executive also obtains control of local offices, most AD leaders interpreted these results as a substantial reversal. The elections "opened up a process of internal shake-ups" (Lepage 1991, 5). AD leaders held meetings to analyze the elections in January 1990. The CEN publicly blamed the results on three factors: (1) the reforms; (2) AD's exclusion from policymaking positions; and (3) the anticorruption campaign (ibid.). The implicit culprit behind each of the factors was Pérez, who had forced AD to accept the electoral reform of 1988 and then proceeded to implement a deep austerity program in a crucial election year.

From this moment on, AD transformed itself into a de facto opposition party. Both the *Perecistas* as well as the "ni ni" began to distance themselves from Pérez. This defection away from the Executive manifested itself in the following acts:

4. At the start of the reforms, the orthodox sectors included most *Lusinchistas*, such as Lewis Pérez, Octavio Lepage, Paulina Gamus, and Manuel Peñalver; the "ni ni" included Humberto Celli, Luis Alfaro Ucero, Gonzalo Barrios, Luis Piñerúa Ordaz, Marcos Falcón Briceño, and Reinaldo Leandro Mora; and leading *Perecistas* included Héctor Alonzo López, Antonio Ledezma, David Morales Bello, and Carlos Canache Mata (*Veneconomía*, September 1989; *Revista SIC*, January–February 1990).

5. Pérez's successors—Ramón Velásquez, Rafael Caldera, and Hugo Chávez—received this privilege as well.

1. AD leaders openly and continually questioned Pérez's cabinet. Unable to provide alternative programs of reforms, the CEN focused instead on hunting down cabinet ministers. By January 1990, for instance, AD's secretary-general Humberto Celli was arguing that "it is necessary and urgent that AD, as the organization that assumes the costs of being a ruling party, be incorporated into policymaking positions" (1993, 16). A month later, Lepage stated publicly:

> What [AD] demands is access to the highest government positions. Being a party militant seems to be a disqualifier for access to the government. . . . Suffice it to examine the composition of the current cabinet to verify that AD's participation is minoritarian, which is an absolutely inconceivable practice in the politics of the most advanced democratic countries of the world. . . . What AD is demanding, and hopes to attain, is greater influence in the heart of the government. (1991, 21–22)

By early 1991, almost every cabinet position had come under attack by the CEN (*El Nacional*, January 5, 1991, D2). Surprisingly, reform-czar Miguel Rodríguez (Cordiplan) was not the most targeted minister. Instead, it was the head of Social Action, Marisela Padrón, a proud non-Adeco who frequently talked about the need to rid social programs of traditional clientelism (*Revista SIC*, January–February 1991; Quirós Corradi 1992, 170). This conforms to the idea discussed in Chapter 5 that AD's problem with the Executive was not based on disagreements over economic policy, but rather a resentment over a lack of presidential attention to the party and lack of access to state resources. Social spending was traditionally controlled by the party, allowing the party to fulfill its clientelistic and brokerage roles. Padrón refused to indulge AD.

2. AD relaxed its internal "Leninism." This was perhaps the most significant change in AD. Historically, AD was one of the most strictly disciplinarian and internally undemocratic parties in Latin America, a true paragon of "democratic centralism" (Martz 1998 and 1992; Coppedge 1994a, 1994b, and 1993). Dissent was kept hidden; decisions were made by a small group of elites; and party leaders adhered to the strictest party discipline. The only Adeco exempted from this Leninism was the Executive. AD always granted Adeco Executives an extraordinary degree of autonomy (Coppedge 1994b).

During the second Pérez administration, this Leninist-centralism for the base and autonomy for the Executive were inverted. The CEN began to grant party leaders, union bosses, ancillary organizations, and governors an unusual degree of autonomy to question and criticize the government,[6] while simultaneously denying autonomy to the Executive. In the words of Arístides Hospedales, "AD will first and foremost defend the people and then the government" (*El Nacional*, August 23, 1990, D-2). AD allowed its affiliate labor and agricultural federations to stage public protests and marches. AD legislators were allowed, for the first time in decades, to criticize the government and block reforms. In February 1991, respect for the president had eroded to the point that Gonzalo Barrios declared, "We now have a situation of wrestling [*lucha libre*], that makes it possible for anyone to say whatever comes to mind . . . none of this would have been possible in the past" (in Lepage 1991, 225). AD legislators became the most meticulous scrutinizers of government bills, the most frequent sponsors of reform-contradicting bill amendments, and the most eager solicitors of ministerial depositions.

3. AD activated a counter-information campaign against the government. For every reform achievement flaunted by the government, AD issued negative qualifications such as "the Party would like to be more involved in decision making," "social issues are being neglected," "economic growth is nothing more than an oil-induced financial bubble," "the privatizations are being carried out too carelessly," etc. The few statements in support of the reform turned increasingly colder.

4. AD began to take sides with opposition parties and anti-reform pressure groups. For instance, AD sided with Senator Rafael Caldera (COPEI) to approve the Caldera Law and block the bill creating the much-needed Value Added Tax.[7] Sectors of AD also sided with Causa-R and MAS to challenge various privatizations, to call for investigations regarding corruption within the current administration, and to block bills reforming Social Security, severance payments, and labor market rigidities.[8] AD also sided with the banking lobby to block the reform of the finance sector and with the agricultural lobby to pressure the government against the sector's liberalization.

5. AD governors refused to implement any kind of economic reform within their jurisdiction, in open challenge to the Executive, but conforming

6. There were some limits, however. In May 1990, the CEN expelled labor leader Juan José Delpino for saying that Pérez was a *mafioso*. But other than personal insults, the CEN came close to tolerating almost any form of dissent.

7. Some of the closest Adeco collaborators with Caldera, such as Juan José Delpino (then president of the CTV) and Luis Raúl Matos Azócar (then AD legislator), joined Caldera's government (1994–99).

8. In mid-1990, two AD congressmen, Luis Emilio Rondón and Tábata Guzmán, were trying to have the CEN of AD raise corruption charges against various ministers (Transport and Agriculture), neither of whom was an Adeco (*Revista SIC*, August 1990, 329).

with the party leadership's desire (*Veneconomía*, September 1991). AD governors remained obsequious vis-à-vis party leaders because the latter still retained the right to select candidates for governorships in the next elections (*Veneconomía*, December 1991).

Thus, the foundations for cooperative Executive–ruling party relations were lost by early 1991. Trust, the *sine qua non*—or "lubricant"—of cooperation, disappeared from Executive–ruling party relations. What began as an apprehensive willingness to go along gradually and visibly deteriorated into a determination to deny political victories to the administration. The CEN's list of grievances—and the frequency of its public statements of them—grew over time. By mid-1991, the upheaval within the party was deep, all-encompassing, and out in the open. AD leaders saw the reform-minded, party-neglecting Executive as extraneous and hostile. The incentives to cooperate with the government disappeared. Many AD leaders began to see opposition to Pérez as the only way to save the party from an Executive who was keen on destroying it. A vicious cycle set in: the party's opposition to the reforms further distanced Pérez. Pérez went as far as to declare in mid-1991 that he was willing to govern without the party, seek allies elsewhere, and even resign from the party (*El Nacional*, May 21, 1991, D-1), which only served to reaffirm AD's fears that this was not an Adeco government.

Argentina: Dealing with "Creditors" and "Bandwagoners"

During his first year and a half in office, Menem came to experience similar levels of frustration with his own party. Upon taking office, he did not seek to exclude the ruling party to the same extent as Pérez. For instance, he invited representatives from various sectors of the PJ to join the government, with half-opened arms, so to speak. Nevertheless, his overall attitude toward the PJ was clearly that of neglect. Like AD, the PJ was not given an active role in the reforms. Instead, Menem hoped that an alliance with private and neoliberal sectors would be more effective in solving the government's credibility gap, hence his high-profile alliances with market-oriented business groups (B&B), center-right parties (Ucedé), the military (his policy of military pardoning), and the U.S. Embassy (his pro-Western foreign policy, especially during the Gulf War in the 1989–91 period). In addition, Menem discontinued the very Peronist neocorporatist practice of appointing representatives from Peronist-friendly, middle-level business associations such as the Confederación General Económica and the Confederación General de Industria, and maintaining a confrontational stand vis-à-vis large business associations such as the UIA or large business conglomerates such as B&B (Acuña 1994, 39). As in Venezuela, ruling party leaders saw this as inexcusable. Menem was not only advancing a reform program that was far more radical than the party deemed convenient, but he was also violating other issues important to the party, such as custodianship, protagonism, war-veteran status, and ideological consistency.

As a result, the PJ also split into three camps. One group could be labeled the "bandwagoners": those who decided to align themselves with the strongman (Menem). Another group included the die-hard dissenters, who were simply appalled by Menem's conversion to the right. The third group could be labeled the "creditors": those who were unpersuaded by and resentful of the state's new direction, but who nonetheless extended the government a "credit line" to solve the economic crisis. The creditors were similar to the "ni ni" under Pérez. They were led by Antonio Cafiero, the president of the PJ and governor of the province of Buenos Aires, the largest bastion of Peronist voters. Cafiero had two grievances against Menem: he resented Menem for having successfully run against him in the 1988 Peronist primaries, and he disagreed with the reforms. Cafiero had the incentives, the opportunities, and the political resources to make life very difficult for Menem.[9] Nevertheless, he decided not to defy the government directly, but rather to adopt a policy of "wait-and-see" with "open criticisms."

And yet despite Menem's open-arms policy and Cafiero's self-restraint, the centrifugal forces in Executive–ruling party relations could not be contained. Since the very first days of the administration, PJ legislators and Peronist economists complained about their lack of access in the cabinet (*La Nación*, June 12, 1989, 1) prompting Menem to respond: "I don't want conditions [*condicionamientos*]" (*Cronista Comercial*, June 28, 1989). When the alliance with B&B collapsed in December 1989 and Menem failed to take this opportunity to incorporate more party leaders, appointing instead an independent economic team led by Antonio Erman González,[10] the crisis within the PJ deepened. In January 1990, the dissenters had enough: approximately twenty Peronist legislators, the so-called Group of Eight, quit the party in protest. Cafiero Sr. did not join the Group of Eight, even though he did endorse their criticisms ("If this were my government, I would have never chosen Bunge & Born as my partner," *Ámbito Financiero*, December 18, 1989, 12). Cafiero's

9. Cafiero admitted that he indeed considered adopting a less cooperative stand (Cafiero, interview).

10. Erman González, a Christian Democrat, was an old friend of Menem who served in Menem's cabinet when he was governor of La Rioja.

son, Juan Carlos Cafiero, did join the group. His explanation for defecting was very telling: "Menem gave very clear signals when he allied himself with sectors foreign to Justicialism and now he seeks to amass political forces alien to our doctrine in order to carry his project forward. . . . Menem surrounds himself with anyone, whether Peronist or not, who helps him misconstrue what was promised to the people this past May 14" (*Clarín*, March 19, 1990, 3).[11] His statement summarized the core of PJ's discomfort with Menem. More than the economics, what Cafiero resented was the affront against the party. Interestingly, this defection occurred in the midst of Argentina's second hyperinflation, again contradicting the notion that economic crises produce cooperation.

Throughout 1990, even those Peronists who stayed in the party increased their criticisms and made them even more public. The following are typical of the public statements made by PJ leaders in 1990 and 1991:

> We are paying a lot in social costs and I do not see the benefit. (Jorge Matzkin, president of the PJ faction in Congress, *Página/12*, February 18, 1990)

> If Menem requests it, the PJ will present an alternative economic plan. (Antonio Cafiero, president of the PJ, *Clarín*, February 19, 1990)

> When free markets are not accompanied by social sensibility, the result is perverse. (Cafiero, *Clarín*, March 10, 1990)

> Alsogaray is our enemy. (Cafiero, *Clarín*, June 2, 1990)

> I believe that the PJ ought to have a much more protagonist role in the government. (Cafiero, *Clarín*, February 24, 1991)

> Menem behaves as if he were ashamed of his Peronist past. (Antonio Balcedo, PJ labor leader, *El Informador*, February 22, 1990)

> We must recognize that there are few top party leaders willing to assume as their own the general course chosen by the government. (José María Vernet, first vice president of the PJ, *Clarín*, March 19, 1990)

11. For a manifesto of the grievances of the Group of Eight, see Barcia and Ivancich 1991.

> Do you know what the main preoccupation of the state's intelligence services is? Finding Peronists infiltrated in the government. (Anonymous joke inside the PJ, circa 1990)

Executive–ruling party relations went into total disarray thereafter. The creditors plunged into a crisis, centered on the question: who in the government is a real Peronist? The creditors criticized everything about the government and the reforms—the alliance with conservative sectors, the disregard of social issues, the extreme application of a "foreign economic model," the betrayal of the party's identity, the negligible influence of the party on policymaking, and the potential for civic unrest. When the government, in conjunction with various TV personalities, organized a pro-reform rally in April 1990 (the so-called Plaza del Sí), many PJ leaders either criticized the rally or refused to endorse it.[12] And like AD, the PJ issued reform-endorsing documents with major salvos such as "the adjustment seems to exceed the limits of what is advisable," "the government should take distance from liberals," etc. (*Clarín*, July 14, 1990, 6). In short, the creditors manifested the same symptoms as that of dissenting Adecos. As in AD, even the moderate PJ leaders were turning increasingly away from the Executive.

The creditors were not the only ones in discord. The bandwagoners, themselves split between Celestes and Rojo Punzó, had their own quarrels too, centered on the question: who in the government is a real Menemist?[13] They argued about everything, from which ministers to appoint to which slogans to use at Peronist meetings. They refrained from criticizing Menem publicly, but they spent most of their time causing political intrigues inside the government in order to hurt the other camp.

Menem thus faced discord and criticism from all sectors of the PJ, detractors and supporters alike. His initial response to this duality of conflicts was to seek distance from the party. In mid-1990, Menem declared: "If I have to govern without the party, or if the party splits, so be it," repeating almost verbatim Pérez's own expression of frustration with his party. As in Venezuela, Menem moved closer to a party-neglecting policy. He tried to displace the creditors from the party's hierarchy, a task that was facilitated by the defeat of

12. The most important promoters of this rally were a series of TV journalists of national repute: Bernardo Neustadt and Julio Ramos (Novaro 1999b, 99).

13. The Celestes were those Peronists who were inclined to negotiate with key interest groups and opposition parties. They included leaders like Eduardo Menem, Eduardo Bauzá, and José Luis Manzano. The Rojo Punzó, on the other hand, favored direct appeals to the "masses" over negotiation (*Clarín*, September 2, 1990, 14–15). They included figures like Julio César Aráoz, Luis Barrionuevo, César Arias, Julio Mera Figueroa, and Hugo Anzorregui (see Kohan 1991).

Cafiero Sr. in the August 1990 plebiscite for amending the provincial constitution to allow for the governor's reelection (see Chapter 3). Whatever authority and political power the *Cafieristas* might have had disappeared after this defeat, allowing Menem to colonize the party's top positions (Palermo 1992; Acuña 1994). Regarding the bandwagoners, Menem adopted a nonposition: he simply allowed them to fight among themselves.

Menem's party-neglecting strategy gave free rein to the centrifugal forces in Executive–ruling party relations. Antigovernment Peronists turned increasingly defiant. Newspapers wrote about the "avance de los antimenemistas."[14] Conflict among bandwagoners intensified. In December 1990, Menem again called for an end to this "internal cannibalism" (*Página/12*, December 12, 1990). Soon after his appointment as minister of the economy (February 1, 1991), Domingo Cavallo got a taste of these relations. In his first visit to Congress to explain the need for more severe reforms, the PJ legislators responded with shouts and invective, forcing Cavallo to walk out of the meeting. By mid-1991, the rift between Menem and the party extended beyond the level of party leaders. Public opinion polls showed that support for "the government's economic policies" among those who voted for the PJ in 1989 declined sharply, from 70 percent in September 1989 (shortly after announcing the reforms) to 27.9 percent in June 1991 (see Lynch, Menéndez, Nivel y Asoc., n.d.). In short, as in Venezuela, the initial dislocation in Executive–ruling party relations had turned into complete disharmony.

The Impact of Disharmonious Executive-Ruling Party Relations on Reform Implementation

Corrupting Congress

One of the most important consequences of Executive–ruling party disharmony was the "corruption" of Congress. In both countries, the Congress became one of the most obdurate institutional obstacles to reform, adopting a lackadaisical and often acrimonious attitude toward reform-related work. The Venezuelan Congress, traditionally one of the most party-disciplined and uninvolved congresses in Latin America (Crisp 2000; Coppedge 1994c, 1993),[15] suddenly became highly obstructionist. Almost every reform and

14. In addition to growing dissent, Menemist forces were defeated in the PJ's internal elections of Mendoza, Formosa, and Entre Ríos (*Ámbito Financiero*, December 11, 1990, 15).

15. The Venezuelan Congress was party-disciplined in that legislators voted along party lines almost without exception to the point there was no need to count the votes. It was unproductive in that the number of laws approved in a single year was typically low. However, others

minister were meticulously scrutinized by Congress, quite often led by Adecos. In addition, the Venezuelan Congress did everything to delay as many reform-supportive bills as possible, prompting a leading news magazine to label the Congress "a cemetery of laws" (*Veneconomía*, November 1991, 26). Table 6.1 confirms that the percentage of reform-supportive bills left pending in Congress increased continually between 1989 and 1991. In 1991, the number of pending reform-supportive bills was more than twice the number of approved ones. One of the most serious reforms shelved by Congress was approval of the VAT, which was urgently needed to streamline tax collection and reduce the deficit. In addition, Venezuela's decentralization process was slowed down: not a single transference of administrative responsibilities to the provinces was approved between 1990 and 1992, despite the intense lobbying by the minister of COPRE (see Penfold 1998).

The Venezuelan Congress also approved anti-reform legislation more easily than Executive-sponsored bills. Between 1989 and 1991, for instance, at least seven anti-reform bills were approved by Congress (Table 6.1). Some of these were not trivial. For instance, Congress enacted the Caldera Law (May 1, 1991), a new labor code that defied the overall spirit of the reforms. The Caldera Law granted labor unions new prerogatives and introduced new rigidities into the labor market.[16] Although baptized as the Caldera Law in honor of its principal sponsor, Rafael Caldera, it could just as well have been called the Adeco Law because AD legislators did everything possible to facilitate its approval. Since the Lusinchi years, Caldera had been trying to get this bill passed. Yet AD legislators always kept it dormant. But in 1989, AD legislators began to work with Caldera to resuscitate the bill. AD labor leaders even collaborated in drafting it (Morales Bello, interview; see also *Veneconomía*, May 1990). Humberto Celli declared that AD should follow the wishes of the CTV (an example of inverse Leninism). AD gave the bill a warm welcome in Congress. The president of the Senate, David Morales Bello (AD), decided to give the bill "maximum priority" over other legislative

---

point out that it was not entirely passive. When the Executive did not control Congress, the latter had a capacity to stalemate the former (Coppedge 1994c). And even when the Executive had control of Congress (e.g., during Pérez's first administration, 1974–78), Congress was not entirely submissive (e.g., Congress refused to grant the first Pérez administration special powers to pursue of tax reform) (Abente 1990).

16. For instance, the law reduced the working week from forty-eight to forty-four hours, updated severance benefit systems, created a new "longevity premium" (*prima de antigüedad*), called for the creation of a pension fund, granted women special labor protections, increased pre- and post-natal leave from forty-eight to eighty-four days, mandated firms to increase the profits that they were required to distribute among workers, etc. (*Latin American Regional Reports: Andean Group*, December 20, 1990).

Table 6.1   Venezuela: Congressional Activity, 1989–1993

	No. Bills Approved (%)			No. Bills Not Approved (%)	
Year	Total	Reform-adverse	Reform-supportive	Total	Reform-supportive
1989	16	3 (19.0)	2 (12.5)	13	3 (23.1)
1990	24	2 (8.0)	12 (50.0)	9	3 (33.3)
1991	33	2 (6.0)	6 (18.0)	25	14 (56.0)
1992	52	1 (1.9)	12 (23.1)	22	8 (36.4)
1993*	0	0	0	7	1 (14.3)

Notes:
* Up to May (Pérez's resignation).
Reform-adverse are bills that were adverse to, or contradicted the spirit of, the reforms.
Reform-supportive are bills considered by the government to be essential for the reforms.
Classification was done by the author, in consultation with two officials from the Pérez administration (FIV president Eduardo Quintero and Minster of Industry Imelda Cisneros) and economist Gustavo García.

Source: Congreso de la República.

matters and even authorized its approval with only one debate (*Veneconomía*, May 1990).[17] Most experts, and perhaps even most legislators, knew that this was a bad piece of legislation; nevertheless, few dared to criticize it.

Another anti-reform bill was the 1991 personal income tax law. The original bill drafted by the government reduced tax rates, loopholes, and exemptions. AD legislators, in full compliance with the lobbying efforts of anti-reform societal groups, accepted the reduction of tax rates, but increased the number of loopholes (González 1995). The result was a distorted bill. In addition to reducing tax revenues (affecting the fiscal deficit), the new bill created more exemption possibilities and complicated rules.[18]

In Argentina, the Congress also became an obstacle to reform implementation between September 1989 and mid-1991. As in Venezuela, some of the most serious challenges to the reforms came from PJ legislators. After the sweeping legislation approved at the start of the reforms, only two reform-supportive bills were approved prior to March 1991. In some cases, Congress refused to even discuss government bills. For instance, the PJ-dominated

17. Senator Morales Bello declared this bill "constitutionally urgent." Bills declared "constitutionally urgent" immediately moved to the top of Congress's agenda. Moreover, they could be approved in the span of only one session.

18. The main beneficiaries of these privileges were not the neediest, but rather the better-off sectors of society. For example, one of the approved loopholes was the possibility of declaring a deduction for car repairs and an exemption for capital gains associated with the sale of homes (see González 1995).

Senate refused to approve automatically the government's key antidote against the 1990 hyperinflation, the Plan Bónex. And throughout 1990, Congress also dragged its feet regarding the privatization of ENTel, the most important component of the reform process that year. In February 1990, the government submitted an important bill transferring education services to the provinces, which would have provided fiscal relief, but PJ legislators refused to consider it.

Another key area of confrontation between the Executive and Congress occurred over the issue of union strikes, which were escalating in 1990 (Chapter 3), threatening the reforms. In April 1990, a few weeks after Argentina's second hyperinflation, Menem announced a plan to ban strikes by unions in public services. Initially, Menem wanted to ban strikes by decrees. Peronist legislators objected and promised Menem, instead, to approve the ban in Congress. However, Congress did nothing but debate the issue, forcing Menem to implement the ban by decree in October.

Corrupting the Cabinet

In both Venezuela and Argentina, Executive–ruling party relations contributed to much of the incoherence and instability in the cabinet in the early stages of the reform. In Venezuela, although AD leaders controlled a historically low number of posts, they still controlled reform-crucial ministries such as Finance (Eglée Iturbe de Blanco and Roberto Pocaterra) and the CVG (Leopoldo Sucre Figarella). These Adecos attempted to apply the brakes in the reforms. They blocked the privatization of the CVG and lobbied against eliminating export subsidies, foreign participation in the local banking sector, and joining the General Agreement on Tariffs and Trade.[19] Consequently, Pérez's economic team spent most of its "political" time during the first year and a half in office wrestling with cabinet infighting.[20]

In Argentina, the fight between Celestes and Rojo Punzó led to significant infighting within the government. This dispute had less to do with the content

19. Based on interviews with Cisneros, Rodríguez, Naím, Blanco, and Rangel Mantilla.

20. By mid-1991, the state apparatus was internally divided as follows. Pro-reform forces controlled Cordiplan, FIV, the Central Budgeting Office, VIASA, CANTV, Education, Agriculture, Development, PDVSA, COPRE, Transport and Communications, and the Vice-Ministry of Finance. Reform-hesitant figures controlled the Central Bank, the Ministry of Finance, the Ministry of Energy and Mines, CVG, the Institute of Foreign Trade, the Industrial Bank of Venezuela, the Cadafe National Institute of Ports, and the National Institute of Obras Sanitarias (*El Nacional*, May 5, 1991, Economía 1). In the second half of 1991, Finance became pro-reform with the appointment of Pedro Rosas.

of the reforms than was the case in Venezuela, but it still hurt reform implementation. Its first effect was to paralyze the government. After leaving office, for instance, privatization czar Roberto Dromi was asked whether there was any internal opposition to privatizations. He replied: "More than opposition, there was internal inaction" (*Clarín*, January 19, 1991, 14–15). The disputes distracted the government and were the cause of the inertia. And yet Dromi's diagnosis was an understatement. The internal disputes were actually producing policy incoherence. By January 1991, for instance, infighting among the Peronists in government turned the Swiftgate affair into Menem's most embarrassing public scandal prior to 1995.[21] It also provoked the financial panic of February 1991. Some Peronists took advantage of this opportunity to advocate a complete break in economic policy, arguing that so far, the new economic direction had not paid off. Their arguments were convincing. The economy was plunging into yet another depression; public support for the government was at an all-time low; and even the U.S. Embassy was abandoning the government. A newspaper columnist wrote: "Peronism always collapses . . . experience shows that order and Peronism are contradictory terms" (José Antonio Abruín, *La Prensa*, January 23, 1991, 7).

Corrupting the Reform Program

Unable to elicit the full support of its most natural ally (the ruling party) and facing reform-unfriendly parliaments, the Executives resorted to a series of "rescue" measures: fiscal looseness in Venezuela, and *decretismo* and rushed privatizations in Argentina. These measures were intended to rescue the reforms from the attacks of the ruling party and put a stop to the rapid decline of credibility. In the end, however, they proved self-defeating.

Fiscal Looseness in Venezuela   When Iraq invaded Kuwait in August 1990, the international price of oil rose abruptly.[22] Once again, Venezuela was flooded

21. This scandal was one of the most serious political crises in the first Menem administration, threatening to destabilize the U.S.-Argentine rapprochement that Menem was trying to build. U.S. ambassador Terrence Todman accused government officials of soliciting huge bribes from firms seeking to participate in privatizations. The accusation was presented in a confidential letter to the government, which was leaked to the press. The then minister of foreign relations, Domingo Cavallo, alleged that the leak was done by some "sectors of the government seeking to hurt those who want a good relation with the U.S." (*Clarín*, January 12, 1992, 2). Afterwards, analysts agreed that one of the two factions was responsible for the leak, perhaps seeking to embarrass the government and persuade Menem to reverse some reforms.

22. From an average of U.S.$16.5 per barrel in the first half of 1990, the price of oil reached almost U.S.$21. In addition, Venezuela was allowed to increase its OPEC quota.

Table 6.2 Venezuela: Current Account and Public-Sector Spending, 1985–1995

	1985	1986	1987	1988	1989	1990	1991	1992	1993	1994	1995
Public-Sector Balance (Percent of GDP)	0.0	−7.7	−5.9	−9.9	−1.4	0.9	−3.8	−6.0	−1.4	−13.9	−6.2
Percent change in public spending	5.5	12.2	−2.6	10.3	−15.2	12.4	12.3	−3.8	−11.2	49.2	−23.0

Notes: Public sector includes central government, PDVSA, FIV, nonfinancial SOEs, the IVSS, Fogade, and the Special Mortgage Fund. It does not include privatization revenues.

Source: García et al. (1998: 113).

with petrodollars: oil revenues increased from a monthly average of U.S.$850 million in the first seven months of 1990 to U.S.$1.6 billion in the last five months (*Latin America Regional Reports: Andean Report*, January 31, 1991).

One would have expected that a government facing such a structural fiscal crisis and dominated by such neoliberal technocrats would have employed this oil windfall to stabilize the economy and rationalize public finances. Indeed, the idea of setting up a "stabilization fund" to counteract future fluctuations in the exchange rate and international price of oil was considered by the cabinet (Cisneros, interview). But instead, the government adopted an exaggerated pro-cyclical policy—increased public sector spending on aggregate demand stimulus in 1990 and 1991. In 1990 and 1991, public spending increased by 12.4 and 12.3 percent respectively (Table 6.2).

The main reason for fiscal expansion was the government's political isolation. Deprived of a supportive ruling party, the government was desperate for political allies. Many of the accusations against the government, echoed by AD leaders themselves, claimed that the program neglected investment promotion and social programs. By spending the money on social projects and aggregate demand stimulus, the government sought to answer these criticisms.

The strategy, however, backfired on almost every count. Economically, boosting aggregate demand hampered the fight against inflation. Whereas consumer inflation declined 55 percent between 1989 and 1990, it declined only 15 percent between 1990 and 1991. Even more frustrating for the government was that fiscal profligacy failed to silence AD. After all, what bothered AD was something deeper than the "neglect of social concerns," but rather the neglect of the party. To increase social spending without relaxing the party-neglecting policies was more aggravating for AD than pure austerity. AD resented the fact that funds it felt it was entitled to administer were given to others to distribute. Furthermore, the emergence of fiscal looseness in the midst of the most severe adjustment program in the history of Venezuela gave the government an image that was the exact opposite of the one it wanted to convey. The anti-establishment opposition interpreted this as confirmation that nothing had changed in Venezuela (the customary pork-barrel politics). The cost-bearing opposition felt cheated by the state: at the same time that they were being asked to make sacrifices, the government was rewarding other actors lavishly. And neoliberal sectors concluded that this government could not be trusted to be fiscally conservative. In short, rather than deliver new allies for the government, fiscal looseness ended up exacerbating the suspicions of the already suspicious and intensifying the hostility of the already hostile.

"Decretismo" and Rushed Privatizations in Argentina The Menem administration's response to political isolation was, first, to resort to decrees. The Menem administration issued 178 "Decrees of Necessity and Urgency" (DNUs), most of which were in the area of economics.[23] This was a historic record—only twenty DNUs were issued between 1853 and 1989. Some interpret this *decretismo* as evidence of an authoritarian style on the part of the Executive, a penchant for power concentration. Others see *decretismo* as the only way to implement market reforms. My interpretation is that this *decretismo* was a symptom of another phenomenon—an isolated Executive. Had the Menem administration received the support of the PJ during this period (and consequently, enjoyed greater cooperation from Congress) the incidence of DNUs, or at least the ratio of decrees to laws, would have been lower.

Another instrument of desperation activated by the administration was rushed privatizations.[24] Despite ample powers to privatize granted by Congress, the government faced increasing political obstacles, as legislators and labor groups (led by the PJ) dragged their feet. Menem responded by trying to privatize ENTel rapidly and almost by force. In the process, the government showed little transparency, failed to create a regulatory framework prior to the sale, absorbed most of the company's liabilities with its private suppliers, and permitted unjustified tariff increases surpassing 100 percent (see Corrales 1998).

Decretismo and rushed privatizations were Executive strategies to rescue the reforms and break the government's image of *immobilisme* in the context of growing political isolation and intractable economic crisis. As in Venezuela, these rescue strategies proved to be counterproductive. Economically, Argentina remained as unstable in early 1991 as in the 1980s. The number of structural reforms remained low; inflation and capital flight remained high. *Decretismo* was in fact becoming a reform handicap because it was fueling discontent even among government sympathizers. Most polls at the beginning of 1991 showed intense public opinion disenchantment with privatizations, in part because of the carelessness (*desprolijidades*) of the privatizing authorities.[25] Peronists themselves were getting angrier, rather than

23. DNUs are rules issued by the Executive that regulate matters or adopt measures that are the responsibility of Congress. When the Executive issues a DNU, it is "making laws"; i.e., assuming for itself the authority of Congress (see Ferreira Rubio and Goretti 1998).

24. This was the most visible, but not the only, undemocratic instrument invoked by Menem. Another instrument was his 1990 "packing" of the Supreme Court. To prevent a quorum failure in Congress, Menem filled the empty seats with busboys and clerks.

25. An August 1991 poll showed that only 27.8 percent of those surveyed had a favorable image of privatizations (*Carta Económica*, November 1991).

happier. Far from bringing in new allies, *decretismo* and rushed privatizations further alienated Menem's detractors and, worse yet, created new ones.

Explaining Instances of Reform Success

Despite all of these setbacks, reform implementation did not collapse in either country during this early stage. As argued in Chapter 3, important reform achievements coexisted with important setbacks (trade liberalization and a few privatizations). What explains these pockets of success, especially in Venezuela, where some structural reforms were accomplished far more smoothly than in Argentina?[26]

The Balance of Forces in Executive–Ruling Party Relations

Part of the explanation for the capacity of the Executives to accomplish some reforms during this period is that the anti-reform sectors of the ruling party never quite achieved dominance during this period. In Venezuela, the groups inside AD were weak, which granted the Executive greater policy leeway. The *Lusinchistas* were demoralized as a result of the corruption charges against Lusinchi; the Balancers could not provide a unifying alternative to Pérez. Hence, no group was able to impose its preference upon the other and upon the government.[27] In Argentina, the weakness of the party had two sources. First, the Executive came to office like a true Leviathan, enjoying considerable

---

26. For instance, whereas the telephone privatization in Argentina provoked significant political unrest, the privatization of the telephone company in Venezuela was peacefully negotiated with Congress and labor unions (Francés et al. 1993; Murillo 2000). These negotiations lasted less than ten months and produced one of the most transparent and financially successful privatizations in Latin America at the time.

27. There is also some evidence that in 1990, the "economics" of the reform program was gaining support among party elites. AD senator Carlos R. Hernández (1990), for instance, argues that this was the result of trips abroad by AD leaders, Venezuela's improving macroeconomic conditions, and the realization that Social Democrats abroad were also pursuing similar policies. There is also evidence that the *Perecistas* were gaining momentum inside the party around the same time. In an "estimate of forces" in March 1990 (when AD was choosing its internal electoral system), the Renovators lost by only 80 of 2,000 votes, a far smaller margin than when they were defeated in the 1986 primaries (*Veneconomía*, December 1990). However, the possibility of a greater acceptance of reforms did not translate into an improvement of Pérez-AD relations, since the lack of "understanding of the reforms" was not the main reason for their mutual animosity. That is why the 1990 "momentum" of the Renovators turned out to be brief. By 1991, the Orthodox came to prevail, after absorbing most Balancers and even some *Perecistas* such as Canache Mata.

congressionally conferred prerogatives and enormous popular support (and decretism allowed him to concentrate even more power). Second, the defeat of the 1990 plebiscite for the reelection of Antonio Cafiero as governor of the province of Buenos Aires somewhat restrained Menem's detractors.

Mini-Technopols to the Rescue

Another explanation for the pockets of success in Venezuela is the rise of mini-technopols. Scholars have emphasized that successful implementation of market reforms is contingent on the rise of technopols: highly trained technocrats engaged in shaping politics. Technopols fulfill crucial political tasks. They help explain to political groups—and the nation as a whole—the technical necessity of the reforms (Domínguez 1997; Williamson 1994; Harberger 1993). They allow politicians in government (that is to say, the president) to signal seriousness and technical correctness, thus garnering credibility among skeptical business groups and international actors (Montesinos 1997; Corrales 1997; Silva 1997). Technopols also permit more avenues of "conversation" between the government and the technical sectors of opposition parties, thus opening the possibility for greater state-opposition cooperation (Giraldo 1997).

At the macropolitical level, Venezuela between 1989 and 1991 is a classic case of failure of technopolitics: Pérez was reluctant, and Rodríguez was unable, to build bridges with the ruling party. However, at another level, Venezuela is a case of successful "mini-technopolitics": lower-level reform ministers, aware of the political difficulties besieging their superiors, activated the resources of technopolitics in order to effect changes within their area of jurisdiction.

Elsewhere I have argued that a technopol is more likely to obtain the acquiescence of societal actors if he or she exhibits "linked independence": the technopol must not be fully beholden to the targeted sector, but must have a professional background that is trusted by the targeted sector (Corrales 1997). For example, in a finance ministry, a *técnico* who is respected by business firms, but who does not depend on a business firm for future employment is more likely to elicit the cooperation of the targeted sector. A *técnico* who is completely devoid of links to the targeted sectors will not be trusted; a technopol, however, who is directly involved in the targeted sector, will have a harder time maintaining independence from sectoral pressure.

In Venezuela, the most significant structural reform achievements between 1989 and 1991 are found in areas where the ministers in charge exhibited significant linked independence—the Ministry of Development (in charge of trade reform), the FIV, and after 1990, the Ministry of Transport and Communication (in charge of privatizing CANTV).

The two ministers of development between 1989 and 1992 (Moisés Naím and Imelda Cisneros) had professional backgrounds that were highly respected by, but they themselves were not beholden to, the rent-seeking industrialists, who bore the brunt of trade reform. Naím was a professor at IESA, and Cisneros was a foreign trade expert working for an international organization (Sistema Económico Latinoamericano). Cisneros herself— unlike Rodríguez (Cordiplan), Blanco (COPRE), and Naím (Industry)—had a friendly Adeco background. She had worked closely with Manuel Pérez Guerrero, an Adeco defender of nationalist oil policies who was highly revered by AD leaders. For this reason, AD found her relatively palatable.

Likewise, the ministers in charge of privatizations (Gerver Torres in the FIV, Fernando Martínez Móttola in CANTV, and Roberto Smith in Transport) did not come directly from the sectors targeted for reforms. Enjoying this space, they devoted significant capital to building "trust" among affected sectors—CANTV managers and AD legislators and unions—often spending up to 80 percent of their working hours meeting with these sectors (Torres, interview). Moreover, Torres and Smith decided to have Congress approve the privatization of CANTV, which, legally, they were not required to do.[28] The results of these efforts were stunning: the Torres-Smith team succeeded in persuading the labor unions, first, and the CEN, later on, to support the privatization (Lauría, interview).[29] Considering that 89 percent of CANTV's workers were CTV affiliates, AD's eventual approval of this privatization was all the more remarkable.

And yet not every Adeco was persuaded. The president of the Commission for Privatization in Congress, Luis Raúl Matos Azócar (AD), together with legislators from the opposition (especially MAS), did everything possible to stop CANTV's privatization until the very end. The crucial difference was that once Pérez's mini-technopols succeeded in persuading the CEN to support CANTV's privatization, this congressional opposition came to an end:

28. The existing telecommunications law (1965) explicitly entitled CANTV to decide autonomously what to do with concessions, including granting concessions to private actors.

29. It seems that AD was offered handsome side payments: for instance, part of AD's debt with CANTV was forgiven (Gómez, interview). AD's total debt with CANTV was approximately U.S.$42 million (Torres, interview). However, side payments are not enough to explain why AD accepted these reforms. After all, the Pérez administration offered AD side payments in other policy areas (Rangel Mantilla, interview) without necessarily causing AD to yield.

the CEN accused Matos Azócar of "autonomous militancy" and demanded congressional approval of the reforms (Francés et al. 1993, 67). This episode of democratic centralism—customary in Venezuelan politics prior to 1989 but exceptional after 1989—made CANTV's privatization possible.

The linked independence of these ministers vis-à-vis the two politically relevant groups—targeted economic sectors and the ruling party—allowed them to make significant progress in their respective areas. In addition, these achievements confirm two theoretical points about Executive–ruling party relations. First, AD's reservations about the reforms were not entirely based on programmatic disagreements. AD was willing to support the reform process provided some political conditions were met—participation in decision making, respect for its custodianship role, and ideological consistency. Cisneros, Torres, and Smith addressed all three issues. In talking to AD leaders, for instance, Torres often invoked "leftist" arguments: "We are finally making the public domain public again, carrying out AD's goal of cleansing the national patrimony of vested interests" (Torres, interview). By allowing Congress to enact a privatization law, Torres granted legislators a greater say in each privatization, thereby addressing the custodianship concerns of the party. Second, these cases show that once the ruling party decides to support the reforms, sectoral opposition to the reforms tends to abate, a point developed in the next chapter. In sum, because of their political engagement and background (linked independence), these ministers created zones of cooperation in the middle of an intense war between the Executive and the ruling party.

In contrast, ministries exhibiting lesser degrees of linked independence—Finance (until 1992), the CVG, and the Central Bank—failed to advance reforms in their respective sectors. Finance Minister Pocaterra and the CVG Minister Sucre Figarella were AD supporters, which explains the lack of any serious fiscal and tax reforms and interest in privatizing the CVG. The Central Bank was headed by Pedro Tenoco, the president and main shareholder of Venezuela's largest bank (Banco Latino), rumored by many to be a significant financier for AD. Together with Finance, the Central Bank president was in charge of the reform of the banking sector. Not surprisingly, these reforms were continually delayed at the cabinet level (García et al. 1998).

Because of the activities of the mini-technopols, Venezuela between 1989 and 1991 is a case of islands of reform success in a fairly stormy sea of reform failures. Only those lower-level technocrats who exhibited linked independence and willingness to "negotiate" with politicians, accomplished significant successes within their own areas of competence. Despite these successes,

Pérez's cabinet on the whole failed politically. Reform enemies from society could latch onto reform-resistant cabinet members to block change, and skeptics remained bewildered by a cabinet that showed few signs of consistent commitment to reform.

Conclusion

Executives tend to react to the initial dislocation in Executive–ruling party relations produced by market reforms by neglecting the ruling party. This response exacerbates the dislocation in Executive–ruling party relations. One year after the start of the reforms and the enactment of party-neglecting strategies, Menem and Pérez both confronted a growing crisis inside their parties. The Executive and the ruling party entered a spiral of rejection. Each hinted mistrust toward the other, thereby inviting a negative reaction from the other. Party dissenters, ranging from moderates to outright opponents of the reform, multiplied between 1989 and 1991.

Under these conditions, reform sustainability suffers. An atomized and hesitant ruling party will turn the Congress into a serious obstacle to reform. It also spoils the cabinet. The party will use its few posts inside the government to obstruct reforms, resulting in a cabinet mired in controversy and unable to signal cohesiveness.

Gradually, the political isolation of the Executive intensifies. In order to press on with the reforms and recover much-needed allies, the Executive resorts to "rescue" strategies (fiscal looseness in Venezuela, *decretismo* and rushed privatization in Argentina). These strategies of desperation had a negative impact on reform sustainability, as well. They produced very few positive economic results while generating enormous political costs in terms of tarnished image.

Disharmonious Executive–ruling party relations thus inject instability into the economic reform process. Despite a strong president and strong mini-technopols, the governments of Argentina and Venezuela found it difficult to push forward the reform agenda. In early 1991, the Argentine economy remained volatile and unresponsive to the most severe stabilization and privatization packages ever attempted in Argentina. In Venezuela, despite very encouraging economic signs and the reactivation of the real economy, the government continued to face serious political difficulties eliciting the cooperation of political parties and interest groups.

However inconvenient, this disharmony was not enough to bring about the collapse of the reforms for at least two reasons. First, in the context of political troubles, mini-technopols will rise to try to salvage their own reform agendas at least by carrying out the political jobs that their own bosses are having trouble accomplishing. Those technical ministers who have trusted but independent links (linked independence) with the targeted sector, and who endeavor to negotiate with the affected sectors, have some chance of success. The rise of mini-technopols, in many ways, is the by-product of a politically isolated Executive.

Second, the balance of power between the Executive and the ruling party did not tilt significantly to one side. Dissent in the party was strong, but not overwhelming, at least initially. The Executive was increasingly isolated, but his rivals were no match for him.

For these reasons, disharmonious Executive–ruling party relations constitute an unstable equilibrium. Both sides of the dispute—the Executive and the dissenting ruling party leaders—become increasingly frustrated. At some point, one side will take some bold action. Either the dissenting party leaders rebel, or the Executive begins to accommodate the party's demands. The former transpired in Venezuela, and the latter in Argentina, as the following chapters detail.

7

hostile

executive–ruling party

relations

venezuela,

1991–1993

Halfway into the reform process, Executive–ruling party relations in Venezuela and Argentina were on a collision course. This collision occurred in Venezuela, but was averted in Argentina. Pérez had succumbed to a quasi-coup d'etat by the orthodox faction of AD by late 1991. Menem, however, took a series of preemptive measures that put an end to the spiral of rejection in Executive–ruling party relations.

This chapter examines the political consequences of the Venezuelan outcome; the next two focus on the Argentine outcome. These chapters, like the previous one, make the same point: there is a causal link between the nature of Executive–ruling party relations and reform sustainability. I have already argued that when the ruling party is internally divided and Executive–ruling party relations are disharmonious—neither fully cooperative nor fully hostile—reform sustainability is mixed. This chapter will show that when Executive–ruling party relations turn hostile, reform sustainability collapses completely.

A ruling party that turns its back on the Executive, as happened in Venezuela between 1991 and 1993, leaves the state in a political limbo. Devoid of political grounding, the Executive loses all credibility and political strength. This not only undermines the government's capacity to enact coherent policies, but also stimulates societal unrest.

Party Rebellion in Venezuela

In the first quarter of 1991—the Gran Viraje's second anniversary—the government had a lot to celebrate. The economy was growing phenomenally, inflation was declining, and the fiscal deficit was under control. More important, Venezuelan society was finally showing signs of accepting the reforms. Rent-seeking industrialists were adapting to trade liberalization without much protest. Investors were returning to Venezuela. Nonpetroleum production was regaining strength, especially tradable goods, which rose by 4 percent. Telcel (a consortium of U.S., British, and Venezuelan firms) won a contract for cellular phone services, suggesting that the political system was accepting the idea of privatized services. Labor groups still had reservations about privatizations, but they were beginning to signal a willingness to negotiate the privatization of CANTV. Even public opinion was stable: 45 percent of Venezuelans wanted the government to persevere with the new economic model; 45 percent believed that the government would succeed in the end; 45 percent expressed approval of Pérez; and 46 percent stated a willingness to continue to make sacrifices on behalf of the reforms (see Chapter 2). The honeymoon that the government never had in 1989 seemed to finally arrive in 1991. Things looked so much better that, in his annual speech to Congress, Pérez stated: "I am pleased to bring an optimistic message. . . . We are leaving the crisis behind" (Pérez 1991).

Ten months later, the political climate could not have been more different. A series of protests, led by labor unions, engulfed the country in November and December 1991. The CTV, which early that year was showing interest in cooperating, turned hostile. Oil-sector workers joined forces with the CTV in a twelve-hour general strike that virtually paralyzed the main cities.

The Ministry of Defense reported more than 924 protests between September 1991 and February 1992 (in Sonntag and Maingón 1992, 18). Even business groups turned unusually critical of the government. On New Year's Eve 1991, Fedecámaras delivered a scathing criticism of the Pérez administration on national TV. Public opinion also deteriorated: the percent of Venezuelans who thought that the government should persevere dropped to 28 percent (see Chapter 3). Even more mysterious, this climate change occurred without any deterioration in economic variables.

What then changed between the first quarter and the last quarter of 1991? The most important change was that Executive–ruling party relations went from disharmony to complete hostility. At the end of 1990, the orthodox sectors in AD were furious, but not yet in control of the party. But by mid-1991, the orthodox sectors gained momentum, increasingly persuading the moderate sectors of the party to shift to their side.

AD began to behave like an opposition party of sorts. The less hostile Adecos considered Pérez to be politically inept and brainwashed by modern social scientists who "knew nothing about the realities of the Venezuelan people." They saw Pérez as insensitive to the social costs of reforms and, worse yet, insensitive to the electoral objectives of the party. The harder-line Adecos saw Pérez as insidiously intent on destroying AD and founding a new political movement. For them, the reform of the economy was a pretext to do away with AD. They were determined to prevent this by denying Pérez as many political victories as possible, including, of course, the implementation of the reforms (Hosepedales, interview).

War between Pérez and the orthodox sectors intensified in February 1991, when AD's secretary-general, Humberto Celli, notified Pérez that AD would "scrutinize" the privatization process (Lepage 1991, 235). Celli kept his word: every single step in the privatization of CANTV was closely scrutinized by the privatization commission in the Chamber of Deputies, presided over by the Adeco Luis Raúl Matos Azócar (Francés et al. 1993). AD's attacks were not restricted to the privatization of CANTV; almost every public policy, cabinet member, and pro-Pérez politician was criticized.[1]

Yet no attack against the Executive was more devastating than that which took place in the internal party elections of September (among the rank-and-file for party delegates) and October 1991 (among delegates for CEN offices). In order to increase their chance of defeating the pro-Pérez forces inside the party, the former moderates joined the bandwagon of the most

---

1. Even the president of Congress, the sometimes-*Perecista* David Morales Bello, was shunned by the party. Morales Bello failed to obtain two-thirds of the vote from AD legislators, thus losing his post in early 1991.

recalcitrant party leaders such as Humberto Celli. The strategy worked: the orthodox faction overwhelmingly obtained control of the CEN. Celli obtained the largest number of votes of all AD leaders, thus becoming the party's president. Only one *Perecista* (Antonio Ledezma) made it to the list of the top ten vote-getters, at position number 10. All the top party positions (presidency, secretary-general, organization secretary, and all three vice presidents) and the majority of secretariats went to staunch anti-reform/anti-government leaders (*Revista SIC*, November 1991, 410–11).[2]

At this point, the balance in Executive–ruling party relations shifted decidedly toward the party, now under the control of recalcitrant reform enemies. AD's iron rule, "opposition unites, governing divides" (Coppedge 1994b), changed under Pérez: AD was governing, opposed, and united. Celli's first remarks after these elections was to demand, more forcefully than ever, cabinet changes and "the return to price controls" (in Quirós Corradi 1992, 250). By December 1991, even the Adecos in the cabinet had become targets of AD invective.[3]

Nothing illustrates better this Executive–ruling party estrangement than AD's reaction to the February 4, 1992, coup attempt, just four months after the October 1991 elections. As the military attack was being repelled, Pérez and some of his allies sought refuge in the presidential palace. Most AD leaders refused to rush to the president's side—not out of fear for their lives, but out of apathy over his fate. Even after the end of the hostilities, few Adecos defended the president publicly. The minority who did took a few days to come forward and, for the most part, expressed little more than a need to defend the "constitutional order," avoiding direct references to the administration. In short, the period between September 1991 and February 1992 was the darkest in Executive–ruling party relations in the history of Venezuela.

Market Reforms and State-Society Relations

The shift in Executive–ruling party relations from disharmony to outright hostility in the second half of 1991 shattered the reform effort. It not only

2. The control of the party hierarchy did not reflect the actual voting: although the orthodox took most top positions, as a whole they only got 56 percent of the votes from the rank and file. A group of "Young Renovators" accused the orthodox of rigging the elections, provoking shoot-out with security guards at the CEN's headquarters (October 3, 1991). Thus, although Pérez had succeeded in alienating the majority of the leadership, including former moderates, he still retained some support inside the party.

3. In November 1991, for instance, AD began to attack even the minister of the CVG, the Adeco Sucre Figarella, who had successfully prevented Miguel Rodríguez from privatizing the CVG, because he refused to endorse them in AD's internal elections (*Veneconomía*, November 1991).

affected the capacity of the government to carry out policies, but it completely transformed the society's reaction to the reform process. To understand this, it is important to elaborate first on the nature of societal opposition to market reforms.

Huntington (1968) argued that carrying out reforms in general is harder than carrying out a revolution because the reformer faces a more complex type of opposition. Unlike the revolutionary, who polarizes the political environment and creates a one-front battleground, the reformer "necessarily fights a two-front war against both conservative and revolutionary" (Huntington 1968, 344). Any reform triggers a double critique: it goes too far, and it does not go far enough. And because reforms are necessarily "selective and discriminating" (that is to say, reforms change some things, not others; reforms change some things a lot; others, just a bit), the reformer often finds that "his enemies on one front are his allies on another" (345). On the whole, these enemies can be classified into three groups: cost-bearing sectors, reform skeptics, and anti-establishment sectors.

Cost-Bearing Sectors

Market reforms seek institutional cleansing, in that institutions are to be liberated from "rent-seeking" groups, and societal demobilization, in that societal groups are to lose specific privileges, such as subsidies, sheltered markets, and employment protection. For this reason, market reforms are said to impose costs across society. Examples include business firms that lose subsidies or protected markets, financiers who lose opportunities to make a profit from price and exchange-rate instability, employees who lose protected jobs, consumers who experience a rise in prices for some services, labor unions that lose job stability, and provinces that lose federal transfers. Public choice theories do a good job in explaining why cost-bearing sectors are likely to protest. Actors are only willing to pay for a good (that is to say, absorb the costs of provision) if the benefits of such a good remain sufficiently private (that is to say, the cost-bearer captures most of the benefits). But when the benefits are to be enjoyed by an entire collectivity (that is to say, the benefits are diffused and general), actors have little incentive to accept unilaterally the cost of provision. Many of the promised outcomes of market reforms, such as economic stability, efficiency, rationality, and economic growth, are highly collective goods whose benefits are diffuse, indirect, or detectable only in the medium term. Thus, they are not likely to elicit immediate societal cooperation or exhibit willingness to absorb the cost of provision. The costs, however, fall directly on specific groups (e.g., those who lose state rents, pay higher taxes or tariffs, face foreign competition, lose job security). Cost-bearing groups will resent not only having to bear these costs, but also any asymmetries that may result in their allocation. If one group ends up bearing a greater share of the cost than others, it will feel cheated, and thus more prone to protest. In short, market reforms are expected to generate substantial opposition from cost-bearers, and little support from winners.

Reform Skeptics

A second source of resistance to reform comes from groups that are unwilling to cooperate, not necessarily because they are net losers in this process, but because they mistrust their counterparts—they are trapped in a prisoner's dilemma. These sectors might gain from cooperating with the reforms, but refuse to do so because they fear that their counterparts might not do the same (Kingstone 1999b). For instance, business sectors might agree to accept higher taxes (a cost of adjustment) for the sake of fiscal health, lower inflation, and low interest rates. But if they cooperate and no one else does (e.g., if the government misspends tax revenues or other sectors pay fewer taxes), business sectors end up with the sucker's payoff: they absorb costs, yet receive none of the rewards. Many business leaders, even market-competitive ones, often fall in this category, which also includes taxpayers, price-setters, dollar-buyers, investors, and some labor bosses. Thus, mistrusting sectors will defect if they fear that others might "free ride" or simply renege on their commitments. Without guarantees, mistrusting sectors will defect. These are the sectors that are constantly on the lookout for signs of commitment on the part of the state.

The Anti-Establishment Sectors

A third group will oppose market reforms, not because they dislike them or mistrust the other players, but because they see the reforms as meaningless. Like reform advocates, these are groups that object to the unreformed status quo. But unlike reform advocates, they consider market reforms a waste of time. At a minimum, they regard the reforms as failing to address the aspects of the establishment that they despise (e.g., social injustice, excessive influence of foreign actors, partyarchy, lack of order, demagoguery, corruption by politicians). Other times, they actually see the reforms as deepening, rather than correcting, the country's vices. The anti-establishment opposition to market reforms tends to cut across traditional ideological lines. Both the radical left and the nationalist right can become strange bedfellows in their opposition to reforms. For instance, the radical left can object to privatization on the grounds that it is a sellout to capitalist interest; the nationalist right can object on the grounds that it is an improper tinkering with the national patrimony.

When thinking about societal opposition to reforms, it is therefore more useful to think in terms of cost-bearers, reform skeptics, and anti-establishment categories than in terms of traditional categories such as class/income groups (upper- versus lower-income groups, bourgeoisie versus proletariat) and sectors (industry versus agriculture).[4] Looking exclusively at class and functional groups, and the impact of policy on them, provides insight only into the cost of reform. Yet, as argued, cost is not the only factor that produces resistance to reform. Potential winners can still reject reforms because of issues of uncertainty or ideology.

In addition, it is important to discern among the different types of opposition to reform because each type responds differently to government policies. The factors that might aid the government in neutralizing one type of opponent might actually infuriate another type of opponent. For instance, a reformer that manages to convey great determinacy to pursue austerity might assuage the fears of the mistrusting groups, but simultaneously stimulate the fears of the anti-establishment and cost-bearing sectors. Greater certainty of reform deepening makes these anti-establishment sectors all the more fearful. They come to understand that the dreaded reforms are for real.

The Impact of Hostile Executive–Ruling Party Relations on State-Society Relations

The main effect of hostile Executive–ruling party relations is to exacerbate each of the sources of societal resistance to reform. This is because hostile Executive–ruling party relations widen the information gap, generate a political vacuum, and destroy the credibility of the state. Under these conditions, states find it virtually impossible to survive the different sources of societal resistance to reform.

Widening the Information Gap

The first consequence of the change in Executive–ruling party relations is an aggravation of the information gap. A crucial requirement of every reform effort is to convince the population of the desirability of austerity measures. In countries with long traditions of statism, persuading the population of the

---

4. For a distinction between a class-based versus sectoral-based analysis, see Mamalakis 1969.

need for cutbacks in state spending is difficult. Moreover, some market policies (e.g., fighting inflation by liberalizing prices, or stimulating economic
growth by opening the country to imports) are counterintuitive. Reform sustainability requires addressing the information gap that reforms engender.

Political parties in general have a comparative advantage as agents of
socialization. As a preeminent grassroots organization with deep links to society, AD would have been an effective instrument of public relations and
information dissemination. This was not a new role for the party. In the early
1960s, when an AD president was trying to consolidate a democratic, secular
regime in the face of widespread opposition from both conservative and leftist sectors, AD played the key role in the government's crucial public relations
battle. In the mid-1980s, when Lusinchi was implementing austerity measures, AD also helped by justifying to the public the need for these measures.

However, during the Pérez administration, AD leadership simply refused
to play this role. In my survey of ruling-party leaders, the overwhelming
majority of the interviewees disagreed with the proposition that AD leadership did everything possible to convince the other party affiliates to back the
economic package. The overwhelming majority (83 percent) disagreed, 17
percent were neutral, and no one agreed.[5]

A newspaper column published in 1991, reprinted here, is very revealing of
AD's stand. It shows that AD was actually ready to contradict almost every claim
made by the government. AD simply "did not feel inclined" to use its own
resources to reach and influence public opinion on behalf of the government.

> Another challenge facing AD stems from its status as the ruling party.
> We are the ruling party despite the paradoxical fact that *we have a
> minority position in the Executive cabinet* and that the ministers who play
> a decisive role in economic and social policy have never been party
> militants or party affiliates. Our influence is not evident in the meas-
> ures that the ministers implement. However, the results of these meas-
> ures, especially if they turn out to be negative, will have direct
> repercussions on AD. *We, not they, will be blamed.*
>
> The Government's economic measures, which have hurt the popu-
> lation, especially the middle- and low-income sectors, *will not translate
> into positive economic results in the short term, contrary to what official*

---

5. Even strong *Perecistas* could not find support within the party to campaign on behalf of
the reforms. For instance, Morales Bello attempted to organize a nationwide tour on behalf of
the reforms, much as he did with Lusinchi's austerity measures, but found no support inside the
party leadership (Morales Bello, interview).

spokespersons . . . have frequently reiterated. . . . People must be made aware of this, otherwise we run the risk of entering a phase of social convulsions. . . . In spite of the undeniable effort by the President of the Republic to explain to Venezuelans the reason for these harsh but indispensable economic measures, and in spite of the deep social compensatory measures, this collective awareness will not be shaped or consolidated without AD assuming the responsibility for stimulating it through the . . . utilization of the resources that AD has at its disposal for reaching and influencing public opinion.

The reality is that *the party does not feel inclined to assume that demanding and risky political task*. The reason for this lack of interest is easy to understand. To a certain extent, the party is resentful because of its marginalization by the government. We cannot hide this mood any longer. The government needs to understand this. (Lepage 1991, 196–97; emphasis added)

It was not just a matter of staying quiet. AD leaders became loud critics of the government, always eager to belittle any economic accomplishment the government announced. Whenever the government announced a major accomplishment (e.g., record-level growth in 1991), AD leaders were the first to introduce caveats: "Yes, but it is growth with neither social equity nor investment, and with plenty of corruption." If the government responded to an AD demand, AD criticized the response. (For instance, in May 1991 Pérez decreed a salary increase in response to AD-condoned rural protests; AD declared that "the increase was not large enough.") The following headlines from *El Nacional* indicate how AD's efforts to disparage the government actually peaked toward the end of 1991.

The losses produced by the general strike were due to the stubbornness of the government. (Antonio Ríos, CTV leader, November 8, 1991)

AD rejects the 1992 budget for being insincere. (Carmelo Lauría, November 12, 1991)

AD rejects the government's violence. Repression and violence are not the right way of responding to student petitions. (Luis E. Rondón, November 22, 1991)

AD demanded that the President modify the economic program in order to restore social peace. (Luis E. Rondón, November 23, 1991)

AD supports Celli's criticisms of Pérez's neoliberal policies. (December 6, 1991)

If AD has any dignity left, it should break completely with the government. (Juan J. Delpino, CTV leader, December 15, 1991)

There is no compenetration between AD and the government. (Luis E. Rondón, AD leader, January 8, 1992)

AD remains unsatisfied by the recent cabinet changes. AD's presence remains minimal. (Humberto Celli, AD leader, January 12, 1992)

The effect on state-society relations of this counter-information campaign was devastating. AD dedicated its efforts to widening, rather than closing, the information gap. Not surprisingly, the government's approval ratings declined precipitously at the end of 1991, despite the improvement in economic variables (see Chapter 3). AD's agitation was especially destabilizing among the cost-bearing sectors, many of whom were part of AD's rank-and-file. By criticizing the reforms, AD corroborated the objections and legitimized the resistance of cost-bearers.

The Political Black Hole

A more important consequence of Executive–ruling party estrangement is the rise of a "black hole" in the political system. In astrophysics, black holes are "empty" objects in space whose gravitational pull is so great that nothing can escape from them, not even light. Space around black holes becomes distorted. Black holes swallow light and gas. As the gas spirals in, it is heated to a temperature of several million degrees, causing the black hole to emit vast quantities of radiation. Black holes are thought to form when massive stars shrink or collapse at the end of their lives.

Black holes are the perfect metaphor for hostile Executive–ruling party relations. By breaking with the government completely in October 1991, AD created a situation in which reform opponents perceived the Executive as isolated and defeatable (the hole) and signaled its willingness to side with government enemies (the gravitational pull). This black hole spurred other political actors to take center stage. Anti-reform societal groups began to perceive their enemy (that is to say, the Executive) as intensely weak and its potential ally (AD) as completely available. Labor protesters, agricultural federations, students, pensioners, import-competing firms, protected bankers, intellectuals, nationalists, leftists, and opposition politicians all saw in AD a possible ally, and in Pérez, a collapsing star.[6] And for the most part, AD agreed to become a viable institutional avenue through which cost-bearers could rise to challenge the state.

This political black hole spurred the anti-establishment opposition into action as well. Two major political events are evidence of this: the growing anti-government stand of the Notables and the February 1992 coup attempt.

The Notables were a group of civilians led by Arturo Uslar Pietri, a world-renowned Venezuelan writer who had become disillusioned with Venezuelan politics in the 1980s and called for a restoration of the Punto Fijo pact. The Notables did not criticize Pérez's program originally, perhaps because they welcomed it as an attempt to overturn Venezuela's rent-based political system. But in 1991, the Notables turned against the government, arguing that Pérez had proven ineffective in bringing real change. By September 1991, Uslar Pietri was calling for an "emergency government."

Many analysts found this about-face to be inconsistent. After all, Pérez implemented reforms that most Notables previously advocated. But the Notables had never been neoliberals, simply opponents of the status quo. By late 1991, the government had become so overwhelmed by party politics that it was unable to demonstrate that it constituted a hope for escaping party-archy. In the words of Uslar Pietri: "The country is in a serious emergency because of *the lack of government*" (*Veneconomía*, December 1991, 4; emphasis added). For the Notables, the infighting between the Executive and the ruling party seemed like the culmination of the worse vices of partyarchy: a dominant party internally divided and atomized over the distribution of positions of power. Pérez was seen as the person who exacerbated, rather than reformed, these vices.

The second manifestation of anti-establishment groups seizing the opportunity created by the political vacuum was the coup attempt of February 4, 1992. Much has been written about this coup attempt, but two points are worth reiterating. First, it was an expression of both cost-bearing and anti-establishment oppositions taking center stage. As middle-level military officers, the coup plotters resented the stagnation of their living standards since the mid-1980s, comparable to that of the poorer sectors (Norden 1996, 76–77; Burggraaff and Millet 1995). Moreover, they resented the fact that

---

6. For an explanation of how agricultural federations took advantages of their institutional links to AD to challenge the reforms, see Corrales and Cisneros 1999.

higher-level officers had not been required to make similar sacrifices.[7] The coup was thus a protest against the asymmetrical ways in which costs were being distributed in the armed forces. But more important, the coup plotters shared an intense dislike for all things partisan. For them, the Pérez government, with its excesses and internal intrigues, became the epitome of all the evils of partyarchy—one more example of how traditional political parties can spoil the political system. The goal of their "Bolivarian movement" was to "liberate" Venezuelans from the "corruption and chaos of this bipartisanship," or "*puntofijista* political class," much as Simón Bolívar had liberated the country from the Spanish yoke.

This analysis of the grievances and objectives of the coup plotters helps explain their action, but not their timing. After his release from jail in 1994, the leader of the coup, Lieutenant Colonel Hugo Chávez Frías, declared that he was part of a lodge of military officers who had been planning this coup since 1983 (*El Nacional*, April 3, 1994: Información 2; see also *Globo*, October 14, 1997, 10).[8] Why, then, was the coup attempt carried out in February 1992 and not before? Barring issues of logistics, the answer is the political vacuum created after September 1991 (see also Zago 1998, 57, 93–94). The opportunities for this risky enterprise were never as inviting. Not since the 1960s had there been a more isolated Executive. Societal unrest was on the rise. All sectors of the political establishment, starting with AD, turned their backs against the government. That the coup plotters had even imagined that some AD leaders would accept an invitation to join their post-coup government suggests that they were aware of (and encouraged by) the estrangement in Executive–ruling party relations.[9]

From Party Neglect to Party Yielding: The End of Credibility

The final consequence of hostile Executive–ruling party relations is to aggravate the credibility gap of the state. Gaining the trust of reform skeptics was a constant uphill battle for the Pérez administration (Rodríguez, interview).

7. Middle-level officers resented higher-level officers for more than economic reasons. They disliked having been used against their own people [the Caracazo], arbitrary promotion standards, generational differences, and skill differences (see Norden 1996).

8. The lodge was called the Movimiento Bolivariano Revolucionario 200, in commemoration of the two-hundredth anniversary of Bolívar's birth. It was formed in the wake of the economic crisis of 1982 (*Globo*, October 14, 1997, 10). The founding members were Jesús Urdaneta, Felipe Acosta, and Hugo Chávez.

9. Francisco Arias Cárdenas, a commander involved in the coup attempt, acknowledged that they considered inviting several AD politicians, such as Luis Raúl Matos Azócar, into the new transition government (*El Nacional*, March 25, 1994, D2; see also Zago 1998, 100).

Nevertheless, the government managed to make some progress, as evidenced by the cooperation of industrialists with Pérez's trade liberalization program. Many industrialists suffered substantial costs as a result of tariff reduction (see Naím and Francés 1995). And yet the sector learned to accept the reform, in part because the government was able to signal credibility and transparency in its liberalization program (Corrales and Cisneros 1999).[10]

However, as Executive–ruling party relations deteriorated, the government found it increasingly harder to uphold the trust of reform skeptics. In a September 1991 speech, in the middle of AD's internal elections, Pérez acknowledged the decline in state-business cooperation: "The Venezuelan private sector has had less trust than foreign investors when it comes to investment decisions. . . . Many believe that the delay in implementing some measures is the result of demagogic temptations or partisan/union pressures, that it is the result of the traditional tendency to try to please everyone and in the end pleasing no one at all." Pérez was thus recognizing the connection between the inability of the state to rein in the populist sectors and the decline in business confidence.

The real breakdown in business confidence occurred in 1992. Following the February 1992 coup attempt, Pérez switched to a policy of yielding to every anti-reform demand of the party. Although the February coup was defeated militarily, the coup received widespread societal support. The government realized the magnitude of its isolation and sought help from AD.[11]

AD leaders accepted Pérez's call for help, but at a very high price. AD demanded, first, major cabinet changes: almost all *técnicos* were sacrificed in favor of AD-friendly ministers. Second, AD demanded an end to all reforms: privatizations, price hikes, and economic measures were halted. Third, AD demanded "leaving politics to the politicians": that is to say, allow AD leaders such as Luis Alfaro Ucero and Humberto Celli to make the most important policy decisions and conduct negotiations with opposition groups. In short, AD demanded—and obtained—both inclusion in policymaking and reform abdication.

Unable to afford its isolation, the government accepted AD's admonition and most of its conditions (Virtuoso 1992).[12] Pérez faced a no-win situation

10. An example of government capacity to negotiate with business occurred in July 1991. In its annual meeting, Fedecámaras issued a statement criticizing many government policies. A few days later, after some discussions with government officials, Fedecámaras retracted its statement and reiterated its support for the reforms.

11. Several polls revealed that close to 65 percent of those surveyed sympathized with the coup plotters. One TV station began to use images of Chávez in its publicity campaigns.

12. Pérez made these cabinet appointments: Carmelo Lauría (AD, Interior), Celestino Armas (AD, Presidency), Alirio Parra (AD, Energy and Mines), Ricardo Hausmann (Cordiplan),

in 1992. Had he attempted to resist AD demands, he not only would have alienated the only political force that was capable of keeping him in office,[13] but also would have reaffirmed the image of inflexibility that so many people believed was his main political vice. He had no option but to yield to the party, now under the control of vindictive leaders.

Pérez was thus forced to shift from a policy of party neglect to a policy of party yielding. This shift had devastating consequences for state-society relations because it exacerbated the state's credibility gap. The state could no longer offer guarantees of continuity because it could not rein in the populist forces that surrounded the Executive. This had damaging effects on each type of reform opponent.

For the anti-establishment opposition, the switch to party yielding corroborated its suspicions that partyarchy was alive and well in Venezuela. Once again, this group could read Venezuelan politics as one more instance in which an unelected party oligarchy was running the show. For cost-bearing sectors, the weakness of the Executive and the admonitions of AD represented opportunities to free themselves from the cost of adjustment.

This explains why anti-reform and anti-establishment forms of political behavior rose throughout 1992, as evidenced by the rise in street protests, labor strikes, the growth of Causa-R, and a second coup attempt in November 1992. In addition, a loose coalition of small left- and right-wing anti-establishment parties, baptized as Convergencia, emerged in 1993. Arguing that COPEI had not opposed the reforms with sufficient vigor, Rafael Caldera quit COPEI to assemble this coalition. Convergencia won the presidential elections of December 1993, and one of Caldera's first acts as president was to release Hugo Chávez (on March 27, 1994), the leader of the February 1992 coup attempt, and to impose price and exchange rate controls. That Caldera would decide to run for office was clearly motivated by his intense anti-reform preferences. That he would break with a party that was not only his own child but a signatory of the Punto Fijo Pact was also the ultimate anti-establishment statement. That the Christian Democrat Caldera would form an alliance with leftists and right-wing groups was the ultimate

---

Miguel Rodríguez (Central Bank), Pedro Mogna Lares (Information), and Armida Quintana Matos (Justice). Lauría was quickly replaced by Luis Piñerúa Ordaz (AD). Pérez also agreed to form an "Advisory Council" to recommend possible reform modifications. It consisted of Ramón J. Velázquez, Julio Sosa Rodríguez, Domingo Maza Zavala, Pedro Pablo Aguilar, Pedro Palma, Ruth de Krivoy, Pedro Rincón Gutiérrez, and José Melich Orsini.

13. Pérez also sought a rapprochement with COPEI (March 10), for which COPEI demanded two cabinet posts. However, COPEI leader Fernández was so criticized for this that he terminated the alliance in June 1992.

example of the marriage of strange bedfellows described at the beginning of this chapter.

Party Yielding and Mistrusting Sectors: The Prisoner, the Prison Guard, and the Judge

The effects of party yielding were even more serious on mistrusting sectors. Party yielding destroyed any possibility of obtaining the cooperation of this sector. Hostile Executive–ruling party relations converted the relationship between the state and business groups into a classic prisoner's dilemma: mistrusting sectors refused to cooperate with potentially beneficial reforms because they stopped believing in the capacity of the government to deliver them.

The decline of trust is evident from public opinion polls. By August 1992 the government's approval ratings had dropped below 20 percent in the highest and lowest income groups and below 10 percent among white- and blue-collar workers (Templeton 1995, 85). The dramatic decline in trust on the part of the rich precisely followed the switch to party yielding. Shortly after the February 1992 coup and prior to the switch to party yielding (March 1991), 24 percent of those in the upper-income category thought highly of the government. It is the only group that experienced a dramatic increase in trust in the government following the coup, suggesting higher-than-average desire to see Pérez conclude his stay in office. However, by August, when Pérez's party-yielding policy was in full swing, the percentage of rich sectors with a favorable attitude toward the government dropped to 16 percent. In less than five months, the government lost the trust it had among the wealthy.

More significant evidence of the decline of trust on the part of mistrusting sectors is the actual political behavior of business groups. In 1992, Venezuela's leading business groups went from a position of negotiated acquiescence to a complete refusal to cooperate with two central areas of reform—privatizations and tax reform. Prior to 1992, business had cooperated with privatizations. In addition, business leaders were beginning to understand the need for fiscal reform in order to defeat inflation. In fact, deficit reduction became the central demand of business groups in 1991.

But in 1992, business lost interest in cooperating with these policies. Private sector interest in purchasing SOE shares virtually disappeared. As the then-president of Fedecámaras, Freddy Rojas Parra, said, "During the economic boom of 1989–92, the private sector hesitated" (in *Primicia*, August 3, 1999, 18). The reason for this was that business groups expected the government to be unable to sell SOEs in relative "labor peace" and sufficiently streamlined, thus handing over "social bombs" to the private sector.

Business groups also refused to cooperate with a fiscal reform proposed by the government in July 1992, the Paquete Solidario Fiscal. The politics of this resistance are worth detailing because they illustrate well the effects of party yielding on business groups.

The Paquete Solidario Fiscal included a series of tax increases, which the government urgently needed to address the fiscal deficit. The government's proposal went through several stages, each vetoed by either the ruling party or mistrusting sectors, or both. First, the government simply proposed large tax increases. At this stage, mistrusting sectors acted as the leading veto players. Business leaders concluded that the government, now captured by party populists, would simply misspend any new revenues, leaving the fiscal deficit unattended.

In response, the authorities modified their plans, proposing a modest increase in taxes accompanied with spending cutbacks. Although more palatable to mistrusting sectors, this proposal was vetoed by AD, now adamantly opposed to any form of austerity.

Then the government offered yet a third proposal: a package of modest tax increases, modest spending cutbacks, and an increase in borrowing. The problem with this proposal was that borrowing would fuel inflation, plunging the government into the classic populist trap of covering deficits through inflation-generating debt. The government was going to increase taxes a bit (still hurting capital holders), cut spending a lot (still upsetting AD), and borrow heavily (generating inflation, in the end defeating the whole purpose of the package). The mistrusting sectors, naturally, were horrified by this tax-your-way-to-greater-inflation arrangement and simply rejected this initiative.

In sum, once the government had abdicated its autonomy in favor of the anti-reform ruling party, business cooperation with the Executive became too risky. Government efforts to persuade business sectors that their fears were ungrounded were interpreted—to borrow from Rodrik (1989)—as mere "promises, promises." Beholden to AD, the government could not offer assurances that it would be able to uphold fiscal austerity or "clean up" SOEs prior to their sale. This explains why in June 1992 Fedecámaras began to demand that any type of agreement with the government be made "without party participation or at least at the margin of the party" (Rojas, interview; Sonntag and Maingón 1992, 60). Business groups wanted the government to be freed from the conditions imposed by the anti-reform party. The Executive could not meet this condition. Consequently, business opted for "defection."

Hostile Executive–ruling party relations also led business groups to expect an easy victory in challenging the reforms that they disliked—the Executive was isolated, and AD was ready to support reform challengers. Consciously or not, AD legislators began to take sides with Fedecámaras. For instance, in justifying its opposition to tax reforms, AD leaders replicated Fedecámaras's position: "This Executive has shown no responsibility in managing public revenues" (Ramos Allup, interview). AD thus not only opposed increasing state revenues (uncharacteristic of populists), but justified its position with neoliberal arguments (the state cannot be trusted to be fiscally responsible). The availability of AD as a de facto business ally encouraged business groups to turn against the state far more aggressively.

A no-win game emerged. Business groups, assuming the role of "judge" of the Executive's performance, demanded greater independence and more signs of "good behavior" on the part of the Executive. But because the Executive was a "prisoner" of the populist AD, it was unable to meet business demands. Business reacted in turn by using the prison guard as an ally in its effort to punish the prisoner.

AD thus engaged in an act of seeming irrationality in 1992. On the one hand, it was defending the right of Pérez to stay in office; on the other hand, it was as critical of Pérez as the opposition. This sent bizarre signals. AD appeared to be supporting a political cause that even the party deemed unworthy of defense. For AD enemies, this provided further evidence that the ills of partyarchy were growing; for cost-bearing sectors, it provided justification for their plight; for the mistrusting sectors, it provided evidence that the Executive was utterly unreliable.

The unavoidable outcome of this dynamic was not only the deterioration of the economy (the unattended fiscal deficit began to put brakes on the economy by late 1992), but more important, the complete collapse of reform sustainability. An Executive that had become beholden to the anti-reform forces of AD gave reasons and incentives for all opposition groups to become active and disruptive. And by signaling its willingness to "understand" them, AD made almost every opposition group estimate that the chance of success in challenging the state was high. Ironically, the Executive pursued party yielding as a way to reduce societal unrest and achieved exactly the opposite.

Reflecting on his party-yielding policies between 1992 and 1993, Pérez declared: "Although the events of February 4 [1992] required a profound rethinking, I should have never allowed the main government initiatives—the modernization of the economy and political decentralization—to come to a halt" (in Prieto 1998). In many ways, Pérez had no option but to yield to the party, but his remarks nonetheless reveal that by yielding, Pérez had essentially dug his own grave.

Pérez's Premature Resignation

Hostile Executive–ruling party relations played a role in Pérez's resignation in May 1993. Throughout 1992 some AD leaders were more eager to remove Pérez from office than even some opposition leaders.[14] In November 1992, these leaders made the Senate consider submitting the issue to a national referendum, in essence, a type of civilian coup attempt against the president. This effort did not prosper. But when more concrete charges of corruption were levied against Pérez in December 1992, the more recalcitrant sectors of AD obtained the support of most party leaders.[15]

This final attack against Pérez was decisive in forcing him to resign. Just as AD's reservations about the reforms had a spillover effect throughout the 1989–92 period, AD's desire to force Pérez's resignation also spilled over across the rest of the political elites, including some of Pérez's earlier collaborators. The person who gathered most of the evidence against Pérez and took the case to the Supreme Court was Pérez's own attorney general, Ramón Escovar Salom. In the words of the CTV's secretary-general, César Olarte: "There are government officials that instead of helping the chief executive, are only making matters worse" (*El Universal*, May 13, 1993). AD provided the "institutional green light" for other anti-Pérez politicians to actively pursue his early removal.[16]

14. The AD leaders in favor of removing Pérez were Humberto Celli, Carlos Canache Mata, Arístides Hospedales, Octavio Lepage, and Henry Ramos Allup. However, not every Adeco supported these efforts. AD's president, Luis Alfaro Ucero, actually preferred to keep Pérez in office (for the sake of regime stability) while simultaneously relaxing the reform program (for the sake of peace, both inside AD and nationwide). COPEI leader, Eduardo Fernández, also opposed Pérez's early departure: "The Armed Forces owe obedience to President Pérez. The majority of Venezuelans gave him their trust as well as a mandate that can only be revoked through voting and not by means of a military or civilian coup attempt" (statement made on November 12, 1992; in Agüero 1993, 194).

15. A few days before Pérez's decision to resign, and before the ruling by the Supreme Court declaring that there were sufficient grounds for bringing him to trial, Celli publicly called for Pérez's resignation (*El Universal*, May 14, 1993, 1–12). This was necessary, Celli explained, because "there is no reason for AD to be burdened with the sanction related to the Bs 250 million. . . . That is Pérez and his ministers' problem." Celli's declaration was the ultimate act of AD rebellion. Although the CEN of AD censured Celli (*El Universal*, May 16, 1993, 1–12), it could not conceal the popularity of Celli's position inside and outside AD. Only three AD leaders truly supported Pérez: David Morales Bello, Lewis Pérez, and half-heartedly, Luis Alfaro Ucero. The censure came too late. By then, everyone in Venezuela had heard AD's secretary-general calling for Pérez's resignation.

16. In May 1994 the CEN of AD decided to expel Pérez from the party, after he was sent to jail. Seventy percent of delegates to the Comité Directivo Nacional ratified this decision (*Revista SIC*, July 1994).

It should also be clear that AD's opposition to the reforms under Pérez was not the result of opposition to the economics of the reforms or inability to understand the need for reforms. Instead, AD's opposition stemmed from a political dispute with an administration that it did not trust. For most AD leaders, it was not the reforms themselves, but rather their implementation by a party-unfriendly government that was objectionable. Evidence of this comes not just from my interviews (see Chapter 5), but also from these acts:

- AD agreed to grant Pérez's successor, Ramón J. Velásquez, sweeping powers to reform the economy, including measures that they had always denied to Pérez, such as the capacity to tax by decree.[17]
- AD selected a pro-reform presidential candidate for the December 1993 elections, the ex-mayor of Caracas, Claudio Fermín.[18]
- When Rafael Caldera became president in 1994 and announced sweeping anti-market measures, AD criticized him. (Eventually, AD began to cooperate with the Caldera administration, but that is discussed in another chapter.)

The key point is that following the demise of the Pérez administration, AD embraced pro-reform positions, proving that AD's trouble with Pérez had more to do with politics than economics.

What Executive–Ruling Party Relations Cannot Explain (Fully)

This chapter has attributed most of Pérez's reform blunders to one single variable: the nature of Executive–ruling party relations. However, this variable cannot explain every political headache or policy blunder of the Pérez years. For instance, it cannot explain the virulent attack against the reforms launched by certain media groups starting in 1990.[19] It cannot explain why

17. One might argue that the political sector was generous to Velásquez out of concern for the future of democracy. If this had been the true motivation, however, one should have expected the political sector to be generous to Pérez when the democratic regime was threatened.

18. Claudio Fermín ran on a pro-reform platform. Although the nomination of Fermín was far from unanimous, it received the support of even anti-*Perecista* AD leaders (*Veneconomía*, July 1993, 8-9).

19. In the 1980s, Venezuelan newspapers seldom attacked government policies. Newspaper owners were highly dependent on paper imports. Because the state had discretion on the tariff level of paper imports and the price level at which they would sell dollars to paper importers, newspaper owners were at the mercy of the government. By eliminating exchange rate controls

Pérez chose to align himself with sinister cronies who made it impossible for the government to ever offer a convincing image of probity.

It cannot explain either an even more serious policy blunder: the government's lack of interest in liberalizing the financial sector. At the start of the reforms, the banking sector, like the rest of the private sector, suffered from all kinds of ailments stemming from the excessive penetration of a state that was both highly interventionist as well as highly porous (see Chapter 4). The banking sector remained an unchecked oligopoly, controlled by a few financial groups (García-Herrero 1997). In cabinet meetings, several ministers argued strongly on behalf of liberalizing the banking sector together with strengthening the state's supervisory capacity (Pedro Rosas, interview).[20] But these reforms were repeatedly delayed by the president of the Central Bank, Pedro Tinoco, himself the president of one of Venezuela's largest and most inefficient banks.[21] In mid-1991, the reforms were finally submitted to Congress,[22] but Congress blocked progress and Tinoco remained unmoved.

The non-reform of the banking sector damaged reform sustainability because it led to resentment within the banking community and across business

---

and liberalizing trade, the Pérez administration "liberated" newspapers from the possibility of being punished by the state. One media group in particular took advantage of this newly gained freedom to launch virulent and recurrent attacks against Pérez's reforms. Like AD, this media group essentially embraced every anti-reform/anti-government grievance (e.g., excessive corruption, lack of transparency, disregard of social issues, favoritism). Many of these accusations were unfounded, but in some ways, predictable. The "liberation" of newspapers, in a context in which the state was imposing costs across society, provided the right opportunity for critical headlines.

20. Several ministers even drafted two major reform bills: the General Law of Banks (which opened the bank to foreign competition, increased reserve requirements, and fortified state supervisory capacities) and the Law of the Venezuelan Central Bank, which granted greater autonomy to the Central Bank.

21. The appointment of Tinoco as president of the Central Bank is perhaps one of Pérez's most serious mistakes (or acts of corruption). Although Tinoco was a reputable businessman, in 1988, his Banco Latino owed the largest debt to the Central Bank of all Venezuelan banks. As president of the Central Bank, Tinoco was responsible for measures that directly benefited Banco Latino: e.g., liberalizing interest rates (which permitted Banco Latino to charge more for loans and to enter into new businesses), blocking the efficient supervision of banking practices (which insulated Banco Latino from the scrutiny of regulators), and opposing the opening of the banking sector to foreign investment (which protected Banco Latino from foreign competition) (*El Nacional*, January 28, 1994, 9). Between 1989 and 1993, Banco Latino went from the fifth- to the second-largest bank in Venezuela.

22. The reforms were submitted at a time when the minister of finance was traveling. The acting-minister of finance, Imelda Cisneros (also minister of industry), took advantage of this opportunity to submit the bills to Congress that had been sitting on the desk of the Ministry of Finance for several months.

groups. Efficient banks saw this non-reform as evidence of state favoritism toward inefficient banks. In addition, business sectors that were liberalized felt cheated as well. Industrialists could not understand why they had to bear the cost of adjustment while banks were exempted. This asymmetry in the distribution of costs led to enormous intra-business and state-business tensions.

As the political and economic system became more precarious toward the end of 1992, the inefficiency-ridden and unsupervised banking sector began to experience heavy losses. Deposits fell by 11 percent in real terms in 1993 with respect to 1991 (García-Herrero 1997). Banks responded by raising lending interest rates (which depressed the demand for loans), keeping deposit interest rates low in order to reduce liabilities (but which lowered the supply of deposits), and increasing the level of self-lending. By 1993, 70 percent of banks' assets were self-loans. When the country entered into a recession in 1993, these banking practices proved unsustainable. Not surprisingly, the first casualty was Banco Latino, the very bank owned by Tinoco. A massive run on the other banks ensued, which, together with the new administration's mishandling of the crisis, brought down Venezuela's entire banking system. By the time the crisis was stabilized in late 1995, losses amounted to 20 percent of Venezuela's GDP (García et al. 1998).

Although these irregularities cannot be attributed directly to Executive–ruling party relations, their independent impact on the politics of reform implementation should not be overstated. Most administrations that conduct deep market reforms are equally subject to virulent attacks from media groups. Many accomplished reformers have also associated themselves with cronies and failed to implement reforms uniformly across all sectors. In both Mexico and Argentina, for instance, numerous sectors, including the banking sector, were left unreformed for quite some time, also leading to political troubles and, later, to economic crises. And yet these governments survived these strains.

The key question is, therefore, why did these "problems" prove so devastating in Venezuela? Here, it becomes necessary to invoke again the role of Executive–ruling party relations. If the government had had a more cooperative relation with its ruling party, it would have been better prepared to neutralize, maybe even defeat, the information campaign launched by media groups. But this was not the case. Media groups attacked the government simply by quoting directly from anti-reform statements by AD leaders. The ruling party actually provided the media with ammunition. Likewise, in delaying financial reforms, the president of the Central Bank was not acting alone. He was able to count on the support of an informal alliance between anti-reform banking lobbies, the first two ministers of finance, and legislators from AD and COPEI The banking lobby pressured against approving the reforms. The first two ministers of finance, both Adecos, defended the president of the Central Bank every time other ministers questioned the lack of progress in financial reforms. And legislators bowed to these banking pressures by delaying approval of reforms once they were submitted to Congress. In sum, although these political obstacles were not the direct result of hostile Executive–ruling party relations, the latter made possible, and in some way exacerbated, the devastating impact that these obstacles produced.

Conclusion

Numerous analysts (e.g., Romero 1997, Templeton 1995, Naím 1993b, Sonntag and Maingón; and Fajardo Cortez 1992) explain Venezuela's political troubles between 1989 and 1993 with sociological explanations, arguing that reforms were rejected, first, by society at large, and then, by representative institutions. This view supposes that parties were smart enough to detect societal sentiments, compelling them to seek distance from the reformers. It is based on the assumption that political institutions act simply as "representatives" of societal sentiments. Parties reflect, rather than shape, societal actions. Another set of explanations attributes the troubles to changes in civil-military relations. As some argue, the coup of 1992 was itself the culmination of accumulated erosion in civil-military relations. And this coup killed an otherwise well-running reform effort.

This chapter, however, makes a different argument. Rather than "reflect" societal sentiment, political institutions actually shape these preferences and responses. Specifically, the growing estrangement in Executive–ruling party relations galvanized and even encouraged crucial political actors at the society level to rise against the state. Societal resistance could have been better managed if AD had not abandoned Pérez in 1991, and the coup itself was more a symptom of this abandonment than an independent cause of Pérez's demise.

There are theoretical and empirical reasons for believing that the line of causality goes from the nature of Executive–ruling party relations to state-society relations. It is clear that AD's reaction to the reforms did not follow societal sentiment. Shortly after the Caracazo (February 1989), AD gave the government its strongest support ever. In contrast, when public opinion toward the government was recovering in 1990, AD began to distance itself from the government. Once AD formalized its break from the government, there was a noticeable deterioration of state-society relations.

This chapter also offers an explanation for this finding. Reformers face a double predicament. First, there is the Huntingtonian predicament: unlike the revolutionary, the reformer must manage multipolar attacks, a constantly changing opposition, and the complexities of enacting gradual change while simultaneously avoiding chaos. But there is yet another predicament: market reforms generate a mostly "counterrevolutionary" type of opposition encompassing three groups: cost-bearing, reform skeptics, and anti-establishment. Whether this resentment against the reforms actually takes the form of societal upheaval or not, this chapter argues, depends on a "third variable"—the stand of the ruling party vis-à-vis the Executive.

Hostile Executive–ruling party relations shape societal reaction through various mechanisms. First, hostile Executive–ruling party relations aggravate the information gap with which any reform government starts. The ruling party not only refused to defend the program, but actually provided reasons for societal actors to mistrust and disparage the government's results, thus legitimizing opponents and delegitimizing reformers. Second, Executive–ruling party estrangement produces a "black hole" in the political system. The isolation of the Executive acts as the hole that attracts power-seekers to take center stage; the willingness of the ruling party to side with these claimants acts as the "gravitational pull" that spurs disaffected groups to take action. Cost-bearing sectors took to the streets (the escalation of protests beginning in October 1991); mistrusting sectors ended their cooperation (Fedecámaras' New Years Eve speech); and anti-establishment sectors launched attempts to seize the political vacuum (e.g., the Notables, the February 1992 coup attempt, the rise of Causa R, the cacerolazos of 1992, the November 1992 coup attempt, the rise of Convergencia). Hostile Executive–ruling party relations also signal a weak Executive, which increases the expectations of success of potential saboteurs and spreads the perception that the ruling party is available as an institutional avenue to challenge the state. In short, hostile Executive–ruling party relations increase the transaction costs of the reforms, delegitimize the government's public relation efforts, and solve collective action problems for anti-reform pressure groups.

Following the February 1992 coup, Pérez switched from a party-neglecting to a party-yielding approach. The state became a prisoner. In exchange for AD's support, the Executive began to yield cabinet positions and policies. Most reform enemies saw in this evidence of the very same factors that precluded their cooperation. Anti-establishment sectors saw evidence of the entrenchment of partyarchy; cost-bearing sectors found allies willing to embrace their plight; and mistrusting sectors saw evidence of the state's inability to rein in the populist forces. Consequently, state-society relations broke down completely in 1992–93.

No government in Venezuela since 1959 had experienced such a dramatic upheaval in intra-society and state-society relations. The nature of Executive–ruling party relations explains this. Several arguments could be levied to challenge the power of the Executive–ruling party variable. One counterargument would stress, for instance, that AD simply no longer possessed the capacity to "shield" the government" and "shape" societal preferences. Thus siding with the Executive could not have prevented societal repudiation of the reforms. The problem is that Venezuela was not a case of AD trying and in the end failing to mobilize public support. It was a case instead of a ruling party engaged in slandering its own government and rescuing the opposition. Second, the mere act of forsaking the government constituted a sufficient incentive for societal unrest. Third, the 1994 electoral results contradict the notion that the capacity of the party to shape societal preferences was inconsequential. That AD finished second in the race, despite the total discrediting of one decade of AD administrations, suggests that AD retained some capacity to mobilize the electorate.

8

the
ruling party
as a
partner

argentina,
1991–1997

Between 1991 and 1997, Executive–ruling party relations in Argentina became the mirror-image of those in
Venezuela. Menem abandoned his party-neglecting
approach in favor of party accommodation. This entailed
addressing some of the most important "points of repulsion" in Executive–ruling party relations discussed in
Chapter 5. In exchange, the ruling party granted the
Executive an extraordinary permit to deepen the reforms.
The result was a dramatic change in Executive–ruling
party relations—from dislocation to greater harmony.
This chapter explains how party accommodation allowed

Menem to escape the spiral of rejection that had besieged his government until 1991, transforming the PJ into a reliable partner of the state.

The Switch to Party Accommodation

Chapter 5 identifies the "points of repulsion" that set off a dislocation in Executive–ruling party relations: the party's desire to preserve some degree of participation in decision making, ideological consistency, custodianship over economic institutions, and the capacity to compete favorably in elections and to broker between the state and interest groups. Party accommodation consists of any policies and attitudes designed to address these concerns. The point of accommodation is to make the party, including dissenters, feel part of the act of governance. Party accommodation does not involve, in fact ought not involve, surrendering economic policymaking to the party. Instead, it involves doing everything else possible to persuade party leaders that their political interests are not being entirely slighted. The goal is to make the party as an organization feel that it matters. In 1991, Menem switched to a policy of party accommodation. These were the main components of this new approach.

Cabinet Changes

Menem took advantage of the Swiftgate scandal of January 1991 to carry out a massive reordering of his cabinet. This was done in a way that accommodated key political concerns of the PJ. For instance, with the resignation of Álvaro Alsogaray in January 1991, the "alliance with the enemy" was deemphasized in favor of an alliance with Peronist-friendly independents (e.g., Domingo Cavallo, Ramón "Palito" Ortega, and Carlos Reutemann).[1] Menem did make more alliances with the Ucedé later on for some local elections, but he never showcased these alliances as the hallmark of his political project. In addition, Menem removed from the cabinet the most conflictive representatives of each of the rivaling bandwagoners (the Celestes lost Roberto Dromi, and the Rojo Punzó lost Alberto Kohan, Luis Barrionuevo, and César Arias). He also incorporated those "creditors" who were willing to cooperate, such

1. Ramón "Palito" Ortega was an actor in Argentine musical films in the 1960s. He joined the PJ in 1991 to run for governor of Tucumán. Carlos Reutemann joined the PJ in 1991 to run for governor of Santa Fe. Unlike the Ucedé leaders in the government, these non-Peronists were more acceptable to the PJ because they were not historical enemies of Peronism.

as the *Cafierista* Guido di Tella. From this moment on, cabinets in charge of social services (e.g., education, health, social assistance), were reserved for party leaders.

With this change in cabinet, Menem accomplished two tasks. First, he put to rest the image of a government captured by enemies of the ruling party. Second, he signaled that willingness to collaborate with the government, more so than historical loyalty to him, would be rewarded. This gave Menem's detractors one more opportunity to make amends. For the most part, Menem adhered to this standard of cabinet appointments throughout his two administrations.

Ideological Consistency

Menem also launched a vigorous campaign to *aggiornar*, update, the PJ. Menemists had always talked about the importance of updating the PJ's ideology. On March 16, 1991, Menem finally took this idea seriously. A massive party congress was organized, titled Justicialist Mobilization for Political and Doctrinal Updating *(Movilización del justicialismo para la actualización política y doctrinaria)*. This congress was an exercise in Peronist adulation and party care-taking. Stating that he came to the congress "feeling more Peronist than ever before," Menem delivered perhaps one of the most crucial speeches of his administration. He addressed head-on every controversial issue in Executive–ruling party relations, such as the issue of doctrinal betrayal: "Betrayal would be to remain petrified in the world of 1946.... Today, more than ever, we need to be anti-system. . . . In Argentina, we have demolished many 'Berlin Walls' in the last two years. . . . To liberate our country from its backwardness, what is required is not to be less of a Peronist, but more of a Peronist" (Menem 1991). Essentially, Menem argued that, rather than betrayal, the reforms restored the vanguard foundationalism of the party. Menem then alerted the party to the disarray of state-society relations in 1991: "Twenty months into my administration, we must recognize that the reconstruction of a new authority capable of taking Argentina out of prostration, is pending. . . . This government is confronting very powerful enemies, and no Peronist can remain indifferent to these enemies" (ibid.). Menem also addressed the disarray of Executive–ruling party relations: "Various sectors of Peronism have questioned the correspondence between the administration's current plan and the ideals of Perón. . . . Various aspects that are dear to Peronist sentiments are in crisis today, and they need to be updated. . . . We have had too much infighting . . . too much cannibalism" (ibid.). By linking the disarray in state-society relations with the "cannibalism" inside Peronism, Menem reminded Peronists of their tragic past, in which enemies frequently took advantage of the party's internal turmoil to undermine Peronist governments.

Menem then announced what would become the Executive's new policy toward the PJ:

> Our goal is to assign to Peronism the paternity of an unprecedented process of change in our history. . . . The point is not to destroy the political parties, but to insert them in a model of social democracy. . . . The point is for the movement and the party to educate leaders capable of governing, not simply capable of conquering the vote. . . . And at the same time, [PJ leaders] must serve as receptors and containers of the new social demands. . . . The crisis is not going to defeat the responsibility of the party to govern the destinies of the fatherland. (Ibid.)

Menem thus announced a new policy toward the party. From a position of neglect, the party was called to be the protagonist of the reform process. This meant not only more involvement in policymaking, but more important, in demand-containing, that is to say, in placating anti-reform elements and deflecting societal grievances against the reforms. And to rally the party on behalf of this enterprise, Menem employed a clever oratorical device: he argued throughout his speech that Perón would have done everything that he was doing, including privatizing all SOEs. The word "Perón" (in reference either to Juan Domingo or Evita) was mentioned thirty-one times.

This speech constitutes one of the most explicit rhetorical attempts in Latin America to make neoliberalism compatible with populism. It contrasts sharply with Pérez's discourse of highlighting the dichotomy between AD's populism and the *Gran Viraje*. The importance of addressing the ideological question for dealing with the party cannot be exaggerated enough. As Panebianco (1988) argues, ideology plays a doubly crucial role in parties: (1) it is the primary source of collective incentives (that is to say, the benefits or promise of benefits that all organizations must distribute equally among participants); and (2) it conceals the selective incentives (benefits distributed to only a few members of the organization). By Peronizing neoliberalism, Menem gave party leaders a tool for covering up the asymmetry in the distribution of costs and benefits that the reforms imposed among the rank-and-file. This was an effort to inflate the ego of the party.

Menem's speech did not succeed in "converting" skeptical Peronists. Levitsky (1999a) even finds that the speech had little lasting power: few rank-and-file

Peronists in 1997 remembered it. But its effect in 1991 was decisive. It disarmed those who were making the very same criticism that overwhelmed Pérez—that this was not a party-friendly government. The speech deactivated the "who in the government is a real Peronist" debate (Díaz, interview) at a time when this debate was drowning the government.

The Marriage of Technocrats and Politicians

Menem did not surrender the management of the economy to the party. Economic affairs remained firmly under the control of technocrats strongly committed to market reforms, namely Domingo F. Cavallo. But Menem encouraged his economic technocrats to work closely with, rather than ignore, the ruling party.

The PJ, especially its unions, had a historical aversion to technocracy; neoliberal technocrats had an equally strong aversion to things partisan (see Chapter 4). To bridge this divide between the PJ and technocrats, Argentina's reform czar Domingo Cavallo took a number of party-accommodating actions as well. He allowed the Ministry of the Economy to virtually become the PJ's electoral headquarters for the late 1991 midterm elections. In August 1991, Cavallo met with a number of Peronists who were running for office to "train" them to defend the program in public or, more important, to deflect any criticisms that they might encounter as they campaigned (*Review of the River Plate*, August 30, 1991). By reaffirming his "friendly" intentions vis-à-vis the PJ's electoral ambitions, Cavallo succeeded in turning the PJ into the state's principal public relations instrument, or at least, a shield against societal criticism.[2] He also created an office within his ministry—the Subsecretariat of Institutional Relations, headed by Guillermo Seita and the very Peronist José Luis Tagliaferi—in charge of conducting negotiations with the PJ. Cavallo realized that he himself lacked the personality and patience to negotiate thoroughly with Peronists (Cavallo, interview). Rather than forgo this task, as many economists would have done, Cavallo decided to entrust it to an office within his ministry (Corrales 1997).

An example of the Subsecretariat's political work was a business-labor meeting organized in October 1992. That month, Congress was taking a while to approve certain reforms. The Subsecretariat decided to jump-start congressional action by deploying "Peronist instruments." It organized a business-

---

2. Cavallo's subsequent involvement in the electoral affairs of the PJ generated more friction than it resolved because, unlike in 1991, he would choose sides.

labor meeting (the "National Economic Council for Productivity, Investment and Growth"), whose goal was to obtain a strong endorsement of the participants in order to compel congressional action. The main inspiration for this meeting was Perón's historic 1944 "Postwar National Council" and his subsequent consultations with corporate groups. The Subsecretariat circulated among PJ leaders a document that demonstrated this Peronist inspiration (Ministerio de Economía 1992). The Council's response was overwhelmingly favorable. Even the first vice president of the UIA, Héctor Massuh, declared that this was the minister's best speech since taking office (*Clarín*, October 8, 1994, 4). Following the Council's endorsement of Cavallo, Congress yielded as well. In short, this was a replication of Menem's 1991 correctives: the use of Peronist symbols and tactics to round up ruling-party support.

Although few party leaders ever believed that Cavallo was truly committed to safeguarding the party's interests and dogma, they nonetheless came to appreciate his overtures. Most of the PJ leaders I interviewed recognized that Cavallo made a great effort to talk with them (see Table 5.2, question 3). This marriage of technocrats and politicians was always a rocky union, but it was a union nonetheless, especially in the 1991–95 period. It was responsible for much of the cooperation between the Ministry and the Congress.

This was far more than Venezuela ever attained. Many Adeco sectors shared a similar historical disdain of technocrats. A leading Adeco labor leader stated it clearly: "The 1981 thesis indicates that the national destinies cannot be left in the hands of technocrats" (Arrieta A. 1991, 354). Venezuela's reform-czar Miguel Rodríguez also tried to talk to party officials, hoping to alleviate the anti-technocratic sentiment. Yet he failed. He never convinced Adecos that he harbored "friendly" intentions toward the party. Adecos always complained that Rodríguez spoke to them in a condescending and patronizing style. Rodríguez himself never concealed his disdain of politicians, often interpreting AD's opposition as a sign of a lack of intelligence and education. But the truth is that there was no systematic effort to institutionalize channels of communication between the Ministry and the party, as in Argentina. Consequently, Rodríguez never felt that he had the support, let alone the trust, of AD leaders (Rodríguez, interview), and AD leaders never felt that Pérez's economic team was committed to the party.

Redefining Property Rights to Convert Unions into Market Participants

The Executive also made it easy for PJ unions to participate in newly created profit-making activities. For instance, the oilworkers union obtained facilities to set up its own private firms to participate in the privatization of the oil sector. Some unions and *Obras sociales* were also allowed to buy shares in newly privatized firms and to form investment alliances with the newly privatized pension funds. The government also accepted a congressional modification to the privatization of the pension system stipulating that any organization, regardless of legal status, could serve as a pension fund manager. This would allow labor unions to be part of the new pension management business. This redefinition of property rights on behalf of party interests contributed to the party's assimilation of the reforms (Azcurra, interview; Cassia, interview). In Venezuela, although privatization officials considered adopting measures that ensured business opportunities for AD sectors, the overall policy was to "leave the party alone" and, to some extent, exclude it from the market.

Respecting the Autonomy of Governors

It is frequently argued that one reason for Menem's success in obtaining party support was his colonization of the party hierarchy (Palermo and Novaro 1996; Novaro 1994; Acuña 1994). This explanation is half valid. No doubt, Menem tried to colonize the party hierarchy in mid-1990 by imposing his own candidates and economic views on party posts. Yet not all party posts were taken over by Menemists. Moreover, colonization cannot explain why even Menem's detractors within the PJ became bandwagoners, including Antonio Cafiero. Menem also channeled significant side payments to the PJ (discussed in Chapter 9). But these side payments, like Menem's colonizing efforts, were insufficient, in part because "money" itself was not the preeminent concern of the PJ. Instead, the PJ was concerned about its "place in the sun," and this is what Menem delivered after 1991.

The real reason that the party cooperated was not colonization, but the granting of autonomy. For the most part, the Executive learned to respect what Levitsky (1999a) aptly describes as "mutual autonomy" in Executive–provincial relations: provincial leaders refrained from attempting to exert influence over national policy, in return for substantial autonomy and power resources within their own provinces. Several violations of this mutual autonomy occurred under Menem, but never to an excessive degree. For the most part, Menem decided (or was forced) to accept non-Menemist PJ leaders at the provincial level, and Cavallo was often forced to accept non-neoliberal economic practices at the provincial level (e.g., the failure to streamline deficits, to privatize local-level SOEs; see Gibson and Calvo 2000). PJ governors who consolidated solid political machines in their provinces were able to preserve their autonomy vis-à-vis the Executive.[3] The result is that by 1997, only four of the PJ's twenty-four provinces were controlled by Menemists, and these contained only 14.8 percent of the overall electorate (Levitsky 1999a, 340). Provincial governors paid in kind: except on a few occasions, Peronist governors never went too far in challenging Menem. They expressed criticisms, but they never organized challenges against Menem, at least until 1997. And with the sole exception of José Octavio Bordón (PJ governor of Mendoza), no governor left the party.

Renegotiating the Rules of Engagement with Congress

Much has been written about Menem's use of decrees (Ferreira Rubio and Goretti 1998; O'Donnell 1994). Less attention is given to the fact that the PJ rarely complained. This is because starting in 1991 the Executive negotiated a new rule of engagement with the ruling party. The PJ had a strong presence in Congress (see Chapter 3), and as such, it developed a stake in preserving the prerogatives of the legislature. The PJ would have been distraught had Menem forgone congressional involvement, in part because that would have involved bypassing the PJ.

Menem's response was to reformulate the rules of engagement with the legislative branch as follows:

- Ministers and reforms would go to Congress more frequently;[4]
- legislators would be allowed to introduce modifications to the proposed bills and even halt progress on labor-market reforms; but
- the Executive reserved the right to veto all or parts of congressional output.

Rather than demand complete acquiescence, the Executive opened the possibility for policy negotiations with Congress. One of Cavallo's first acts as minister of the economy, for instance, was to grant Congress the right to approve subsequent privatizations. In addition, in 1991 Cavallo became the minister of the economy who most frequently visited Congress in recent

3. Examples include Eduardo Duhalde in Buenos Aires, Rodolfo Gabrielli in Mendoza, Rubén Marín in La Pampa, Néstor Kirschner in Santa Cruz, Adolfo Rodríguez Saá in San Luis, Vicente Joga in Formosa, Julio César Humada in Misiones, and Jorge Busti in Entre Ríos (Levitsky 1999a, 312–22).

4. Some top PJ leaders (e.g., Alasino, interview) expressed that this was a personal promise made by Menem to PJ legislators.

Argentine history. As he often argued: "We need to stop managing the economy with memos, resolutions, and decrees . . . these are easy to reverse. Their lack of legislative status signals lack of necessary consensus" (Cavallo 1991). After 1993, Cavallo visited Congress less frequently, but his secretaries continued the practice.

This new rule of legislative engagement was specifically applied to privatizations. Almost every privatization project between 1991 and 1995 went to Congress (see Llanos 1998, 750). Legally, there was no need to do this; the Law of State Reform of 1989 authorized the Executive to privatize on its own. Politically, however, this practice was smart, since it satisfied the PJ's interest in having reforms go through Congress.

In return, the Congress (essentially, the PJ) approved almost every privatization bill, albeit with modifications. Most modifications sought to preserve some degree of state presence (e.g., privatization of pension system), some degree of congressional oversight over the implementation (e.g., privatization of YPF), and some concessions to specific interest groups (Llanos 1998, 756). For instance, the Executive branch wanted to sell most of YPF's shares. Congress changed this, requiring the state to keep 20 percent of its shares and to hold two seats in the executive board of the privatized YPF (ibid.). Congress introduced similar provisions in almost every other privatization. PJ legislators were thus asserting, and the Executive accepting, the party's desire for participation in decision making.

The rise in Executive-legislative exchanges is also evident from the volume of congressional "requests for reports" to the Executive, especially the Ministry of the Economy. These are requests for more information on specific bills under study or already enacted. A study by the Ministry (Ministerio de Economía 1994) revealed that, by October 1994, Congress had requested almost three times more reports from the Menem administration than from the Alfonsín administration (Table 8.1), most of which took place between 1991 and 1993 (more than 450 per year).[5] The "volume" and "speed" of response to these requests also increased after 1991. The Ministry of the Economy, for instance, responded to 85 percent of its requests after 1991 (up from 79 percent between 1989 and 1991, and 71 percent under Alfonsín). Furthermore, the "speed" of response increased from an average of three hundred days in 1991 to approximately one hundred in 1993 and eighty in 1994.

5. During the first two years of the Menem administration and during the entire Alfonsín administration, the volume of requests per year never exceeded 250.

Table 8.1 Argentina: Requests for Reports by the Legislature to the Executive

Entity	Menem Administration*	Alfonsín Administration
Economy	1059	348
Defense	103	31
Justice/Education/Culture	177	46
Health	196	94
Labor	58	55
Interior	101	50
Foreign Relations	98	33
Other	398	55
Total	2190	712
Requests per week	7.99	2.60

* Until October 1994.

Source: Ministerio de Economía (1994).

These numbers reveal the extent of Executive–legislative engagement. At the very least, the legislature was very busy with reform-related work. That the Ministry responded overwhelmingly (both in volume and speed) after 1991 suggests a ministry that took better care of relations with Congress.

This new rule of engagement, often overlooked by analysts of the Menem administration, was an important departure in Executive-legislative relations in Argentina. It transformed relations with the ruling party because it addressed some of the grievances accumulated by the PJ since 1989. Allowing PJ legislators to present modifications to laws gave the PJ a say in the reform process. It also gave the party the opportunity to save face vis-à-vis its clients. The "you modify, I might veto" formula is more functional to the clientelistic interests of the party than the "you watch, I decree" scheme that prevailed prior to 1991. The latter highlighted the irrelevance of legislators; the former allowed the party to present itself as a relevant actor in the battle. Even if the modifications were subsequently vetoed by the Executive, legislators could still return to their clients with a "decorous defeat," which is far more preferable than the "spectator role" to which they had been relegated until then. Moreover, the party could justify these defeats by blaming the intransigent minister of the economy, rather than the irrelevance of the party.

The Executive was rewarded handsomely. Together with the support of minor parties, the PJ overrode the opposition of the UCR to the reforms (Table 8.2). This does not mean that all Peronists endorsed all laws or that all Radicals rejected all laws, but it shows the extent to which the PJ came around.

Table 8.2   Argentina: Reform-Crucial Laws* Approved by Congress, 1989–1993

Law (Date)	Voting by Party**	
	PJ	UCR
A. Disharmonious Executive–Ruling Party Relations, 1989–91		
1. Reform of the State (8/17/89)	Yes	No
2. Administrative Emergency (9/1/89)	Yes	No
3. Tax and Provisional Penal Code (2/7/90)	Yes	Yes
4. Fund for the Financing of Private Productive Activities (9/28/90)	Yes	Yes
B. Harmonious Executive–Ruling Party Relations, 1991–93		
5. Convertibility Law (3/27/91)	Yes	No
6. Negotiable Obligations (7/4/91)	Yes	Yes
7. Financing for the National Social Pension Regime (7/18/91)	Yes	Yes
8. Debt Consolidation Bond (7/31/91)	Yes	No
9. 1991 Budget (8/14/91)	Yes	No
10. National Employment Law (10/2/91)	Yes	No
11. On-the-Job Accidents (10/2/91)	Yes	No
12. Patrimonial Restructuring of Labor Union Associations (10/2/91)	Yes	No
13. 1992 Budget (12/19/91)	Yes	No
14. Privatization of Electric Power Areas (12/18/91)	Yes	No
15. Tax Code Reform (8/18/92)	Yes	No
16. Privatization of Gas del Estado (5/20/92)	Yes	N/Q
17. Restructuring of the Banco Hipotecario Nacional (5/20/92)	Yes	Yes
18. National Law of Ports (6/3/92)	Yes	No
19. Agreement between the Federal Government and the Provinces (8/19/92)	Yes	No
20. Privatization of YPF (9/24/92)	Yes	N/Q
21. Privatization of Caja de Ahorro and Banade (9/30/92)	Yes	No
22. Control of the Administration (9/30/92)	Yes	No
23. 1993 Budget (12/23/92)	Yes	Yes
24. Federal Law of Education (4/14/93)	Yes	No
25. Reform of the National Social Pension System (9/23/93)	Yes	N/Q
26. 1994 Budget (12/23/93)	Yes	N/A

Notes:
* As per the criteria of the Minister of the Economy (Cavallo).
** Decision in favor or against made by the party's faction in Congress. It does not necessarily mean that all party members adhered to the decision.
N/Q: No Quorum—the UCR decided to be absent the day of the voting.

Source: Based on data from the Ministry of the Economy, Subsecretariat of Institutional Relations.

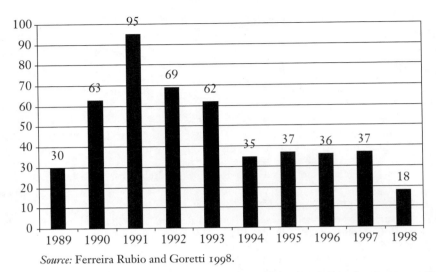

Source: Ferreira Rubio and Goretti 1998.

Fig. 6   Argentina: total number of "need and urgency" decrees, July 1989–August 1998

Endorsement did not mean submission. Executive-legislative relations became livelier after 1991, sometimes even stormy. At times, the PJ rejected bills (e.g., the 1991 Aguinaldo bill).[6] In other cases, the Executive vetoed provisions introduced by the legislature. All of these violations of the tacit Executive–ruling party agreement led to friction between the two. This, however, ought not be construed as evidence of disharmonious Executive–ruling party relations. Quite the contrary, it was the result of the space created by the normalization of these relations. Menem's new rule of engagement with the ruling party called precisely for this type of exchange. By allowing Congress to participate in the reforms, even argue with the Executive openly, the interests of legislators of having greater participation in policymaking was addressed. This explains the paradox that just as congressional challenges increased after 1991, so did the number of reforms approved by Congress.

6. The Aguinaldo bill was an attempt by Cavallo to reform a law that required the state to pay public employees a semiannual bonus (*aguinaldo*). Many Peronists considered this law to be a pillar of Peronism because it was instrumental in allowing Perón to mobilize labor unions in the 1940s. The problem was that in 1991 this bonus accounted for more than two-thirds of the projected fiscal deficit. Arguing that paying this bonus in full would be inflationary, Cavallo proposed in May 1991 to move toward monthly, rather than semiannual, installments. The IMF was keen on this reform, declaring it essential for signing the latest "Letter of Intent" drafted by the government (*Review of the River Plate*, June 28, 1991). The PJ rejected Cavallo's idea, proposing instead a reform that ensured that 90 percent of pensioners and 70 percent of workers would continue to receive their bonus semiannually. The UCR decided to deny quorum, thus killing even the Peronist-amended proposal.

The rise in congressional engagement did not mean an end to *decretismo*, which some of Cavallo's closest advisors lamented (Llach 1997, 123). However, after peaking in 1991, the incidence of decrees declined (see Fig. 6). And more important, the response of the PJ to these decrees changed as well. Prior to 1991, the PJ reacted to *decretismo* by virtually refusing to consider bills. After 1991, the PJ tended to react by seeking negotiations with the Executive and, often, endorsing the decrees.

Any attempt by the Executive to undo this rule of engagement provoked instant ire within the PJ. An example was Cavallo's failed efforts to get special powers from Congress at the end of 1994. Worried about rising deficits, Cavallo wanted Congress to allow him to privatize every remaining SOE and lay off as many public sector employees as necessary for the next four years without the need to go to Congress (Article 14 of the 1995 Budget Bill). Cavallo argued that this would generate the U.S.$1 billion needed to end Argentina's increasing deficit (*Clarín*, November 8, 1994, 3). But this amounted to a break in the rule of Executive-legislative engagement. Unsurprisingly, the PJ rejected Cavallo's request for special powers. Despite two subsequent economic crises (1995 and 1998–99), the Congress under Menem never granted the Executive branch any special powers to bypass the legislature.

This also raises questions about some common views of the Argentine Congress. The normalization of Executive–ruling party relations in Argentina had an overlooked institutional side effect: the engagement of the legislature in economic policymaking. In some ways, this was a step forward in the development of Argentina's democratic institutions. Congressional involvement in economic policymaking was unusual compared to Venezuela from 1989 to 1993, and Argentina prior to 1991. It emerged under Menem, mostly as a result of his party-accommodating policies. The Congress did not just act as a representative of parochial, particularistic interests (see Mustapic 2000), nor did it entirely neglect its task of "controlling the administration" (Jones et al. 2000). Instead, Congress began to exercise some accountability functions toward the Executive.

This was not perfect accountability by any means. One key problem was that this accountability was somewhat biased and incomplete, mostly because it consisted of "control within the family," that is to say, among Peronists. Excluding the opposition from these arrangements was an important democratic drawback that is discussed in subsequent chapters. Nevertheless, there is no question that the PJ in Congress did not act as a mere rubber stamp on the Executive, and this constituted a step forward in enhancing the accountability functions of the legislature.

To summarize, the Executive in 1991 inaugurated a policy of party accommodation that, with few interruptions, lasted until mid-1997. Menem's

efforts at placing more Peronists and fewer PJ-enemies in the cabinet, blend-
ing Peronist and neoliberal rhetoric, encouraging technocrats to negotiate
rather than bypass the party, helping unions participate in privatizations,
respecting the autonomy of elected Peronist leaders throughout the
provinces, providing some space for detractors, allowing the Congress to
modify laws, and addressing many of the political grievances of the PJ
allowed the Executive to improve relations with the ruling party. As long as
PJ leaders were willing to accept the economic reforms and defend the Executive, the state was willing to accommodate many of their interests.

The PJ as a State Partner

Menem's party-accommodating measures transformed Executive–ruling
party relations almost instantly. In August 1991, Cafiero and Menem publicly
exchanged compliments for the first time since Menem had become president
(*Clarín*, August 27, 1991, 21). Evidence of a turnaround in Executive–ruling
party relations was the PJ's response to Menem's massive deregulation decree
of late 1991.[7] Despite discontent among Peronist labor bosses and the UCR,
the PJ leadership, including Cafiero, refused to criticize it. Another piece of
evidence was the PJ's more generous interpretation of the 1991 elections. As
discussed in Chapter 3, the PJ made some inroads in these elections (e.g., it
came out ahead of the opposition), but also experienced setbacks (e.g., the
loss of three governorships and a lower share of the vote than in 1989 and
1987). PJ leaders reacted by minimizing the importance of the losses and
instead celebrating the electoral victories. This contrasts sharply with AD's
reaction to the first midterm elections of December 1989, in which the party
ignored the electoral achievements (e.g., winning elections in the most
adverse and unlikely-to-be-repeated economic and political circumstances),
and focused instead on the decline of the votes.

Remarkably, this rapprochement in Executive–ruling party relations
occurred at a time when the economic scenario was improving, but was
not yet altogether stable or even promising. In August 1991, inflation was
significantly lower, but as always, there were enormous doubts about the

---

7. Decree No. 2284 contained 122 articles and two annexes repealing regulatory legislation in industry, farming, commerce, social security, labor matters, and services. A mass of
bureaucratic regulatory agencies were abolished. Menem announced it to the nation in an eight-
een-minute speech.

sustainability of the new stability. Inflation had not disappeared completely. If anything, inflation levels in late 1991 looked remarkably similar to inflation levels a few months after the 1985 Austral Plan, which collapsed soon after (Guerchunoff and Llach 1998). Moreover, although indicators of country risk in 1991 were the best in Menem's period, they were still alarmingly high and almost identical to the country-risk level in February 1989, when the first Argentine hyperinflation broke out.[8] Doubts also existed about the rest of the reform package. In short, 1991 was a year of economic uncertainty, and yet the PJ endorsed the government—a true act of faith. The PJ was rewarding the government for making political concessions, rather than for its economic achievements.

The rapprochement extended beyond the party leadership. A 1992 survey of five hundred Peronists revealed that the PJ rank-and-file supported the Executive and the reforms.[9] And compared to other government policies, the "reform of the state" had the highest approval rating among Peronists. For a reform process that only a year before had been labeled a "betrayal of Peronism," these survey results illustrate a significant change in Executive–ruling party relations.

That the PJ remained solidly aligned behind the Executive branch between 1991 and early 1997 challenges two commonly held views about the PJ during this period—that it was obsequious to the Executive and that it was resentful of the Executive. Neither was true. More accurately, Torre describes the PJ as "a political system in and of itself, simultaneously acting as a ruling and opposition party" (Torre 1999, 44–45). An even more precise way to describe the PJ is as a partner. The party reacted to the Executive branch cooperatively rather than submissively—it accepted the overall direction of policy preferred by the Executive, as long as it retained the right to introduce modifications. The party did not become monolithically enthusiastic about the reforms and the reformers either. Opinions about the reforms and the president varied significantly. Often, for instance, PJ leaders went out of their way in support of the state. Other times, PJ leaders were quite critical. But even critics refused to cross certain lines. Two examples show these parameters.

An example of the PJ's overwhelming support for the Executive occurred during the congressional discussions about the privatization of YPF in 1993,

8. This indicator of country-risk is the difference between the returns of Argentine bonds and those of thirty-year bonds issued by the U.S. Treasury (Llach 1997, 189).

9. The approval rating of the president among Peronist affiliates was 60 percent. The approval ratings for the "reform of the state" and "privatizations" were 69 percent and 46 percent (*Clarín*, May 17, 1992, 10).

one of the most significant privatizations of the Menem era.[10] Opposition to this privatization emerged from predictable groups: firms that conducted a lot of business with YPF (Cámaras de Empresas Petroleras Argentinas), labor groups in the oil sector (SUPE, the oilworkers union), moderate politicians (including pro-government Peronists), and the opposition party (UCR). The UCR in particular did everything possible to stop this privatization.[11] Yet after several meetings with Cavallo, the PJ came out in favor of the Executive in April 1993, issuing an official statement lashing out at the UCR for "devoting itself to destroy rather than fix" the privatization process (*La Nación*, April 28, 1993). The PJ support went beyond mere words. In July 1993, when Cavallo was invited to the Chamber of Deputies to talk about the privatization of YPF, he worked out a "secret" agreement with PJ leaders Eduardo Bauzá, Jorge Matzkin (president of the PJ block), Carlos Ruckauf, Miguel Ángel Toma (deputy), and Oscar Lamberto (budget commission) that the PJ would stand behind the minister. Cavallo could not imagine the extent of the PJ support. During the meeting, as tensions rose between Cavallo and the UCR, the UCR legislator Noel Breard threw a glass of water in Cavallo's face. Immediately, a PJ deputy, Antonio Guerrero, jumped on Breard. A fight broke out between the two that ended only after six other legislators intervened (*Clarín*, July 9, 1993, 18). Guerrero's response personified one side of the PJ's pro-government new role: fully supportive and relentless against opponents.

Yet that was only one dimension of party behavior. Another dimension was cooperation, but less unconditional. Not all PJ leaders, for instance, were enthusiastic about Menem. Some PJ leaders actually remained quite critical. But these criticisms remained within bounds. A good example of this was a meeting of discontented Peronists that took place in 1994 during the PJ's deliberations about its agenda for the forthcoming constituent assembly. A thorny issue was the amount of money to be transferred by the federal government to the provinces. Strong critics of the government within the PJ demanded far more. Cristina

10. YPF was one of the largest SOEs in Argentina, controlling more than half of the domestic oil market, with annual revenues of U.S.$5 billion and exports of U.S.$600 million in 1993. This was the first profit-making firm to be targeted for privatization. Prior to its sale, the government carried out one of the most profound restructuring projects in the history of state-owned enterprises. From a loss of U.S.$579 million in 1991, YPF achieved a U.S.$256 million profit in 1992 and U.S.$703 million profit in 1993. Staff was reduced from 52,000 to approximately 6,000 (*Clarín*, July 14, 1994, Economía 2–3).

11. For instance, days before the placement of YPF shares in international markets, the head of the UCR national committee sent telegrams to the U.S. Security and Exchange Commission asking for cancellation of the sale on grounds of government corruption (*Review of the River Plate*, April 16, 1993, 18). One of the government's main critics was UCR senator, Fernando de la Rúa, who complained that Menem was "rushing" the privatization of YPF and avoiding "dialogue" with societal sectors (*Clarín*, March 17, 1993, 20–21).

Fernández de Kirchner, wife of Néstor Kirchner, PJ governor of Santa Cruz and one of Menem's harshest critics inside the PJ, addressed a crowd of angry Peronist delegates. Fernández de Kirchner took sides with all the claimants, lambasting the government's policy toward the provinces.

Yet at the end of her speech Fernández de Kirchner said: "We cannot blame Menem or Cavallo . . . if we ourselves are unable to raise the issues that we deem to be just" (*Clarín*, August 5, 1994, 6). Fernández de Kirchner simply refused to blame the Executive. If anything, the blame belonged to the rank-and-file for failing to make alternative proposals. The audience gave Fernández de Kirchner a standing ovation.

In the 1991–97 period, therefore, the PJ was never free of government critics, and these critics were never quiet. Yet not even the staunchest critics wavered from the party's commitment to defend the presidency. There were a few attempts by PJ leaders to challenge Menem from within, but all failed. For the most part, as the next chapter will show, party leaders became major defenders of the administration, shielding it from attacks coming from both outside and within the party. PJ leaders seldom crossed the line of publicly bashing the Executive branch, let alone, siding with Menem's opponents—a line that was so frequently violated by the Adecos in Venezuela.

Conclusion

Menem's party accommodation addressed the erosion in the consultative, custodial, and brokerage roles of the party caused by a process of economic reform. It is one of the reasons for the "production of party discipline," or at least cooperation, exhibited by the PJ under Menem and which surprised many scholars (see Mustapic 2000).[12] The most important consequence of this rapprochement was that the Executive obtained a negotiated permit from the ruling party to go ahead with the reforms. At a time when most economic agents were predicting an impending economic collapse (late 1991), the ruling party was extending to the president its willingness to cooperate. This was not a blank check by any means, but it was the largest vote of confidence ever received by Menem.

12. Mustapic (2000) argues that party discipline in Argentina is not the automatic result of institutional variables such as the degree of party control over nominations. Nominations in Argentine parties are not monopolized by centralized party committees. Party cooperation, therefore, must "be produced" through the allocation of incentives on the part of the Executive and each party.

9

harmonious

executive–ruling party

relations and

reform sustainability

The formidable partnership between the Executive and the ruling party in Argentina after 1991 transformed state-society relations. It conferred upon the state the political resources to solve the political obstacles that in the past had hindered reform sustainability. Specifically, it gave the state an unprecedented jolt of credibility. For the first time in decades, the state was able to convey the conviction that nothing would stand in the way of the reforms.

According to many political economists, a rise in credibility ought to generate greater cooperation between interest groups and the state (see Chapter 4). This occurred in

Argentina, but only among reform skeptics. Having fewer justifications for their skepticism about the prospects of reforms, reform skeptics significantly relaxed their opposition to Menem. The credibility jolt, however, did not have such a benevolent impact among cost-bearing groups and opposition parties. Rather than abate, the opposition from these groups intensified. Now that these groups could be confident that the reforms would proceed, they had more reason to worry about suffering the costs of reform. They thus redoubled their efforts to stop the reforms. The rise of credibility, counterintuitively, gave rise to intense opposition from cost-bearing groups and opposition political parties.

In the past, this reactivation of societal opposition would have killed any reform program. This time it did not. The reason was the alliance between Menem and the PJ. By siding with the Executive, rather than with cost-bearing groups, the ruling party disarmed the latter. Left isolated, cost-bearers and political opponents had no option but to come to terms with the reform. Recalcitrant postures began to give way to more pragmatic negotiating strategies.

Closing the Credibility Gap

The principal consequence of improved Executive–ruling party relations, and the concomitant increase in congressional sanctioning of reforms, was the closure of the state's credibility gap. Prior to 1991, the Executive tried every possible means to achieve credibility, mostly through extra-partisan avenues: by seeking alliances with conservative sectors (e.g., the Ucedé), by incorporating business representatives (e.g., appointing Roig and Rapanelli as ministers of the economy), by packing the Supreme Court with loyalists, by rushing privatizations and bypassing PJ legislators and labor leaders, by realigning with the West and sending ships to the Gulf War, by concentrating powers, issuing decrees, and imposing harsh monetarism (e.g., Plan Bónex). None of this worked. In April 1991, economic agents remained as skeptical as ever.

Only when Menem made the ruling party the centerpiece of his administration did the reform process experience a credibility boom. The Executive could signal that it controlled the populist forces that surrounded him. And because this support translated into congressional endorsement of reform bills, the reforms acquired a degree of institutional grounding (*seguridad jurídica*) that further enhanced credibility (Corrales 1997). The alliance between the Executive and the ruling party allowed the state to emerge as a

Table 9.1   Argentina: Country Risk Premium (percentages)

Year	Bonex YTM* (1)	6-month LIBOR (2)	Country Risk Premium (1–2)
1981	16.2	16.7	−0.5
1982	16.6	13.6	3.0
1983	18.1	9.9	8.2
1984	22.2	11.3	10.9
1985	18.9	8.6	10.3
1986	15.8	6.9	8.9
1987	18.3	7.3	11.0
1988	23.4	8.1	15.3
1989	28.7	9.3	19.4
1990	29.4	8.4	21.0
Mar 1991	19.4	6.3	13.1
Jun	17.9	6.6	11.3
Sep	11.9	5.6	6.3
Dec	11.0	4.3	6.7
Mar 1992	10.8	4.6	6.2
Jun	9.9	4.1	5.8
Sep	10.5	3.4	7.1
Dec	12.6	3.6	9.0
Mar 1993	9.6	3.6	6.0
Jun	7.2	3.5	3.7
Sep	7.0	3.4	3.6
Dec	7.0	3.4	3.6

Notes: For the 1980–90 period, the YTM (year-to-maturity) for Bonex includes averages for each statistical series; for 1991–93 the 1989 Bonex YTM was used. LIBOR (London inter-bank offered rate) is the interest rate at which funds on loan are offered to first-class banks in London.

Source: de la Balze (1995).

formidable, invincible, unstoppable contender in the reform process. A reversal of expectations followed: actors could expect with certainty, for the first time in decades, that the state would deepen, rather than abandon, the reforms.

One indicator of rising credibility is the "country risk premium": the difference between the international and the domestic cost of money. Governments facing a high credibility problem cannot easily raise money through bonds (since lenders do not trust them), which forces them to sell bonds at rates far above those of the international market. Thus, the higher the difference between what a government pays to attract lenders and international interest rates, the higher the credibility problem. Table 9.1 shows this difference for the Argentine case. Argentina's country risk premium declined from 21.0 in 1990 to 3.6 by December 1993.

Experts tend to attribute this change to the technical merits of the remarkable Convertibility Law (1991), the hallmark of Argentina's stabilization.[1] This law banned the Central Bank from printing money and tinkering with the exchange rate. It mandated the Bank to defend a fixed exchange rate. And it required the government to hold dollars, foreign currency, and gold in the same amount as there were pesos in circulation or deposited in the Central Bank.

What many economists often ignore is that what sustained the Convertibility Law was a political anchor: the rise in harmony in Executive–ruling party relations. The law worked not so much because of its technical correctness, but because of its political grounding. Technically, the law was quite risky.[2] But politically, it was quite sound. This was the first time in Argentina that a stabilization package had been attempted by means of a law (the 1985 Plan Austral and the 1990 Plan Bónex were decrees), which in turn was only possible because the PJ was willing to endorse it.

Why did the PJ endorse this harsh stabilization measure? First, the PJ liked the law's nationalist flavor. The Executive promoted it as a law inspired, not by the IMF, but by Argentina's late-nineteenth-century experience with the gold standard. The PJ also liked its statist orientation. The law imposed state controls over exchange rate markets. As Cafiero explained his support: "With these decisions, Domingo Cavallo has restored the prestige and power of the state over markets" (*Ámbito Financiero*, April 10, 1991, 40). But more important, the PJ liked the law because it addressed the party's "foundational" and "custodianship" concerns. By placing the PJ-dominated Congress in charge of the exchange rate, the law implicitly made the PJ the "founding father" of a new economic regime.

The Convertibility Law, therefore, was one of the first products of the Executive's new party-accommodating approach. It was approved a week after the party congress of March 16, 1991. It occurred after Cavallo spent several weeks trying to normalize relations with Congress, including agreeing to grant Congress the right to approve each subsequent privatization.

---

1. For more on the political economy of the Convertibility Law, see Pastor and Wise 1999b, Guerchunoff and Llach 1998, Llach 1997, Corrales 1997, Starr 1997, and Acuña 1994.

2. In assessing which economies are better candidates for a currency board, Corden (2000) offers the following criteria: (1) the economy must be small by world standards; (2) fiscal policy and monetary policy must be conservative; (3) the central bank must be independent; (4) the levels of liberalization must be low; (5) labor market flexibility must be high; and (6) most trade must occur with the United States. At the time of the Law, Argentina violated all criteria except the third, which the Law itself established. For these reasons, the adoption of the Currency Board in Argentina was technically risky.

The measure was a law rather than a decree, hence addressing the political concerns of the PJ.

It is this firm political grounding—rising harmony in Executive–ruling party relations—that explains the sustainability of the law. The PJ unremittingly defended the foreign exchange regime mandated by the law, even when so many other experts and actors lobbied against it between 1991 and 1993. No economic guru at the time, including the IMF, approved of the law (Cavallo and Cottani 1997, 19). In fact, virtually every sector of public opinion expressed doubts about the state's capacity to sustain the new exchange rate regime. After all, no one could believe that a country with such a history of instability and international volatility would be able to maintain the dollar-peso parity. The only political actor that wholeheartedly defended the law, other than the Executive, was the PJ. The PJ consistently refused to participate in any debate about its merits or to listen to any actor pressuring for a devaluation. Without this backing, the Convertibility regime would have succumbed to devaluationist pressures. This political backing compensated for the law's technical frailty.

The Rise of Credibility and the Rise in State-Society Tensions

The immediate impact for state-society relations of this credibility boost varied according to the type of opponent. Reform skeptics reacted to the credibility boost by relaxing their mistrust. The main evidence of this was the relative tranquillity in both exchange rate and price markets between 1991 and the external shock of early 1995 (see Chapter 10). Except for a few occasions, the demand for dollars (in Argentina, an inverse indicator of the state's credibility) remained historically low and stable until 1999. Even the IMF, which was quite skeptical of the Convertibility Law, came around: in March 1992 the IMF and Argentina finally signed an extended facility agreement, providing the financial base for Argentina's entry into a debt-relief program (the Brady Plan). Private foreign capital also responded favorably, as evidenced by the spectacular return of capital from abroad. Dollar deposits as a percent of GDP increased from 3.6 in March 1991 to 23.4 at the end of 1994, whereas interest rates on deposits declined from 193.3 in March 1991 to 9.6 percent in 1994 (Llach 1997, 220).

This is not to say that skepticism disappeared completely. For many actors, the economic stability of this period seemed "too good to be true," or at least, to be everlasting. In the past every episode of stability had eventually collapsed. And by mid-1992, numerous economic actors still expected the same to happen to the Convertibility regime; however, the Convertibility regime attacked some of the historical sources of inflation that previous stabilization attempts never had (e.g., fiscal and quasi-fiscal deficits, Central Bank indiscipline), but not all of them (e.g., trade deficit, overvaluation). Furthermore, reform skeptics remained disappointed at the Executive's failure to secure certain reforms such as labor market flexibility (more on this later). Doubts about the sustainability of the regime never quite disappeared. Reform skeptics remained vigilant, but far less skeptical than ever before.

The anti-establishment opposition reacted by ceasing its efforts to topple the regime. Argentina's leading anti-establishment sector, the military, had been quite unruly since the founding of the democratic regime in 1983: Alfonsín suffered three military uprisings; Menem suffered one in December 1990. Yet there were no more military uprisings thereafter. This was all the more surprising given that the Executive had reduced the size of the military by a third, abolished the draft, and privatized military-linked SOEs. Public repudiation of the 1987 coup attempt, the military's internal divisions, and Menem's strong punishment of the 1990 coup participants no doubt contributed to this change in the military behavior (Norden 1996; Acuña and Smulovitz 1995). But an equally important factor was the image of invincibility gained by the Executive as a result of its alliance with the PJ. Menem's was the first civilian administration since Perón in 1946 that did not exhibit the internal vulnerabilities that in the past proved so inviting to anti-establishment groups.

Once the coup route was foreclosed, anti-establishment sectors became less and less anti-establishment, preferring instead to influence the political system through other means. One way was to "negotiate" directly with the president, rather than to demand concessions and domains of autonomy (see Diamant 2000). Another was the electoral route. A political party emerged that sought to capture this sector: the ultranationalist Movement for National Dignity and Independence (MODIN). Founded by the leader of the 1987 coup, Lieutenant Colonel Aldo Rico, MODIN attracted those who had supported the December 1990 insurrection. The rise of credibility altered the expectations of MODIN. Rico was convinced that the implementation of the reforms would benefit MODIN—the reforms would increase the number of cost-bearers and these would join MODIN (Aldo Rico, interview). This is one reason Rico placed his bet on the electoral route. Yet his expectations never materialized. MODIN experienced a modest and short-lived rise (see Chapter 3). Part of the reason for MODIN's stagnation was that the PJ leaders ensured that at least cost-bearing Peronists (urban and suburban non-white collar workers with low income and low levels of education) would not defect (see Gervasoni 1998 and Gibson 1997), as the next section shows.

Whereas the rise of credibility neutralized the opposition of reform skeptics and anti-establishment groups, it had the opposite effect among cost-bearing groups: it alarmed them. Many cost-bearing sectors actually panicked.

The economic expansion of 1991–94 did nothing to allay their fears. First, while the end of inflation is enthusiastically welcomed by the population at large, in countries with long-standing histories of high inflation, stability also generates the perception of economic loss in the medium term (Corrales 1997). With price stability, citizens gain purchasing power, but simultaneously lose the illusion of rapid social improvement. During high inflation, when prices are constantly renegotiated, actors know that there will always be a future opportunity for correcting their lot. For instance, wage earners might accept a "bad" salary today in the expectation that they will renegotiate a raise on the next round. The possibility of social progress through price negotiation (illusory in some cases, real in others) comes to an end with macroeconomic stability (see also Acuña 1994). Moreover, inflation does not disappear automatically (e.g., Argentina's annualized inflation rate in mid-1992 was around 20 percent), and becomes even higher in some nontradable sectors. Within a few years, Buenos Aires became one of the most expensive cities in the world (comparable to Frankfurt), while its wage levels lagged far behind (a third of Frankfurt levels) (see Table 9.2).

Second, economic prosperity brings a resurgence of populist appetites. Once the country is perceived to be "normal again," actors feel that it is appropriate to revive populist claims on the state. Rent-seekers estimate that the state can once again afford such claims, and cost-bearing sectors feel entitled to compensation for their sacrifice. Still another group of actors interprets the economic recovery as evidence that there is no more need to persevere with austerity and structural reforms.

Finally, Argentina's economic prosperity was uneven. The introduction of market forces led to Schumpeter's "creative destruction"—the inevitable (and for Schumpeter, desirable) demise of noncompetitive sectors. While some industrial sectors experienced unprecedented booms,[3] others experienced significant contractions.[4] And while labor groups in some industries (automotive,

---

3. In 1994, the Secretariat of Industry of the Ministry of the Economy revealed that most of the post-1991 industrial expansion was focused on five sectors of the economy, of which the automobile industry was the biggest beneficiary (in *Clarín*, September 2, 1994, Suplemento económico 2). Indeed, the Association of Automobile Manufacturers confirmed that between 1991 and 1993 the sector's production increased by 150 percent; in 1993, the production was 16 percent higher than the historical record set in 1973 (*Clarín*, October 22, 1994, 25).

4. The most affected sectors were capital goods, petrochemicals (fifteen plants were shut down), textiles (exports declined 56 percent), and paper and cellulose (15 percent of plants shut down) (*Clarín*, September 24, 1994, 18).

Table 9.2   Prices and Earnings, Cities of the World (U.S.$)

City	Prices of Goods and Services*		City	Net Income per Hour**	
	1991	1994		1991	1994
Tokyo	2008	2569	Zurich	16.0	17.3
Oslo	2016	1974	Tokyo	10.9	15.3
Zurich	1746	1946	New York	10.5	12.8
Copenhagen	1594	1842	Copenhagen	10.1	11.7
Paris	1425	1650	Frankfurt	9.7	11.3
New York	1454	1620	Oslo	10.2	10.3
Seoul	1018	1604	Montreal	9.0	10.1
Buenos Aires	**980**	**1564**	Amsterdam	7.8	9.2
Frankfurt	1300	1529	Paris	7.3	8.5
London	1470	1354	Taipei	5.5	8.2
Amsterdam	1145	1339	Madrid	8.0	7.5
Hong Kong	1114	1330	Milan	8.5	7.3
Taipei	1471	1324	Sydney	8.3	7.2
Tel Aviv	1175	1312	London	7.4	7.1
Milan	1431	1253	Tel Aviv	4.3	5.1
Sydney	1236	1203	Seoul	5.2	5.0
Montreal	1269	1186	Athens	4.9	4.9
Madrid	1638	1180	**Buenos Aires**	**2.0**	**4.7**
Athens	940	1059	Hong Kong	4.5	4.4
São Paulo	854	1054	Lisbon	3.0	4.0
Bogota	661	1028	Johannesburg	3.8	3.8
Lisbon	980	1001	Bogota	1.8	2.8
Mexico City	869	976	São Paulo	1.8	2.7
Johannesburg	892	930	Mexico City	0.9	2.6
Manila	698	926	Manila	0.6	1.1
Caracas	**1064**	**795**	**Caracas**	**1.7**	**1.0**
Nairobi	785	610	Nairobi	0.9	0.4

Notes:
* Total costs of a basket of 109 (for 1991) and 108 (for 1994) goods and services, excluding rent, that is weighed by consumer habits. Basket includes 39 foodstuffs.
** Actual hour earnings of 12 occupations after taking into account working time, holidays and vacations, weighed by occupation.

Source: UBS (1994, 1991).

communications, retail) experienced wage and size expansions, in other industries (e.g., textiles and steel) they experienced severe losses. Many privatized firms experienced substantial labor reductions (e.g., more than 90 percent in railroads and maritime transportation, more than 50 percent in SOMISA, more than 80 percent in YPF). Provinces that relied heavily on federal monies also experienced hard times (e.g., Santiago del Estero). To compound the problem, the economic boom encouraged previously inactive sectors to rejoin the labor force, increasing the labor force from 200,000 in the 1980s to 320,000 in the mid-1990s (Llach 1997, 252). This combination of industrial reduction and reentry of previously inactive jobseekers led to a rise in unemployment. And despite the spectacular economic growth between 1991 and 1994, the decline in levels of poverty was quite modest (see Fig. 7).[5]

Although the net economic effect of this process was positive in the aggregate (in terms of overall economic and industrial expansion), the existence of losers was undeniable. At the very least, this was a society divided by winners, lesser winners, and losers.

Thus there were many reasons why good economic times did not bring political rejoicing throughout Argentina between 1991 and 1994. Cost-bearers had ample reason to complain, and this translated into political trouble for the administration. Cost-bearing industrialists elected the most protectionist leadership in the UIA in years. Privatizations continued to generate opposition. Strikes by agrarian federations occurred repeatedly.[6] After peaking in June 1992 at 900 points, the Buenos Aires stock market declined to 300 points by October. There was a strong run on the dollar in November 1992. The provinces, which negotiated a favorable resource-sharing agreement with the federal government in 1992, began in 1993 to demand more (a 10 percent increase in their share of resources) in exchange for extremely minor reforms at home (*Review of the River Plate*, April 16, 1993, 10–11). UCR legislators became more anti-reform, voting against reforms or denying quorums in Congress. There was a major uprising in Santiago del Estero in December 1993. So why were these opponents unable to derail the reforms, as happened in Venezuela in 1991–93 and in Argentina in previous stabilization attempts?

5. The question of what impact the reforms had on poverty levels is controversial. Even using data from the same source—e.g., the Ministry of the Economy, published under the Menem's successor, Fernando de la Rúa—justifies different stories depending on the period examined (Fig. 7). If one looks at the percentage of households below the poverty line from circa the beginning of the Menem administration (October 1989) to circa the end of his first term (October 1995), the story is that the reforms reduced poverty (from 38.2 percent to 18.2 percent). If one looks at the period circa the start of the Convertibility Law (October 1991), the story is that the reforms increased poverty (from 16.2 percent to 18.2 percent). If one looks at the period between the end of the Alfonsín administration (May 1989) and the end of the second Menem administration (October 1999), the reforms had an insignificant impact on poverty (from 19.7 percent to 18.9 percent) (Ministry of the Economy 2000).

6. These were (1) a work stoppage by the Argentine Agrarian Federation (FAA) and Coninagro (March 19–22, 1992); (2) a work stoppage by the Argentine Rural Confederations (CRA), FAA and Coninagro (November 2 and 3, 1992); and (3) a march along Plaza de Mayo by FAA, CRA, and Coninagro (July 27, 1993).

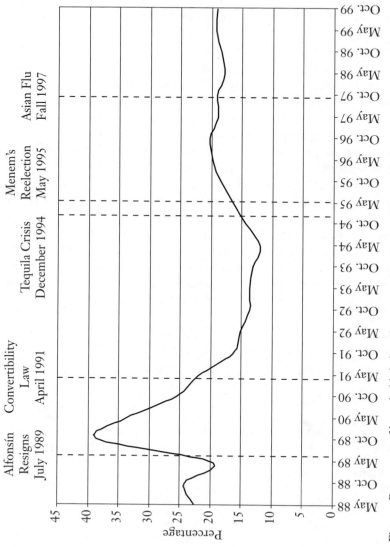

Fig. 7 Percentage of households below the poverty line, greater Buenos Aires

Note: Includes Federal Capital and 19 counties of Buenos Aires.
Source: Ministry of the Economy (2000).

Harmonious Executive–Ruling Party Relations and Cost-Bearing Groups

The explanation for the survival of the reform effort is the strong Executive–ruling party alliance. The normalization of Executive–ruling party relations reversed the traditional role played by the PJ vis-à-vis cost-bearing groups. The PJ changed from being a legitimizer of social protest to a promoter of trust in the state, and from being a vehicle for anti-reform interest groups to a shield against them.

Filling the Information Gap, Shielding the Government,
and Delegitimizing Societal Protests

In his March 1991 speech to the party, Menem called the PJ to become "receptors and containers" of social grievances. Because of the normalization of Executive–ruling party relations, the PJ went along. Prior to 1991, the PJ stood ready to embrace many of the prevailing societal and group-based claims (e.g., the right to strike, the critique of the military amnesty, the slowdown of ENTEL's privatization). After 1991, it reversed roles. The PJ began to disregard or pay only lip service to most societal claims against the reforms, such as demands to alter the dollar-peso parity, fire Cavallo, stop privatizations, reintroduce protective tariffs, and increase the level of social spending). It continuously placed ads in newspapers in support of the government (see Appendixes 5–7). Many Peronist leaders even campaigned on behalf of the government (see Table 5.2, question 6). In the 1991 midterm elections and throughout 1992, party members designed campaign strategies explaining to the rank-and-file the need for defending the government following the crisis, or at least, for postponing action on their grievances (*Clarín*, January 22, 1992, 4–5; January 23, 1992, 2–3). Party leaders even recruited Peronist unions for these campaigns (Cassia, interview).

Two unexpected examples of PJ defending the government against cost-bearing groups were the conflict with the CGT in November 1992 and the conflict with the pensioners throughout the 1990s. Until late 1991, the CGT was split between a more reform-accepting (CGT-San Martín) and a more reform-challenging faction (CGT-Azopardo). The return of credibility alarmed both factions.[7] Even the CGT-San Martín feared that the government would violate

7. Specifically, Menem's decision in January 1992 to tackle the *obras sociales* prompted this unification. The *obras sociales* are union-controlled health insurance funds that expanded into all kinds of businesses (tourism, recreation, legal services, school services, etc.) serving almost 17.6 million beneficiaries, more than half the population. Being tightly controlled by Peronist unions,

its promise not to liberalize labor markets.[8] Consequently, the two factions reunited and called for a general strike for early November 1992. After an initial wavering, the highest leadership of the PJ (including former labor bosses such as Jorge Triaca) unequivocally repudiated this strike. It drafted a document rejecting the CGT's actions for being "eminently political" and published newspaper ads criticizing the strike. The banner of one such ad was "Justicialism always stands by the people," implying that the CGT was not with the people (see Appendix 5). Individually, numerous top PJ leaders expressed very harsh criticism of the "error" of the *compañeros peronistas* in the CGT.

The efforts of the party to stop the strike failed. On November 9, approximately 70 percent of workers along Argentina's industrial strip stopped working (according to UIA estimates; other nongovernmental estimates [see, for example, McGuire 1997] suggest lower adherence rates). However, for the strikers, the strike was a disappointing lesson in the new political reality of the nation: the PJ would not stand behind them. This is one reason that allowed Menem to feel that the strike was inconsequential: "The strike was an absolute failure. . . . Not even 1,000 strikes like this one will make the government change course" (*La Nación*, November 10, 1992). Although the strike returned welfare collection to unions and delayed the government's plan to reform collective bargaining, it did not produce wage hikes or increases in state pensions, exactly what the CGT was demanding (Murillo 1994). The CGT discovered its isolation.

Had the party lent its support to the strikers, the government would have been pressured to yield to the CGT, which most likely would have prompted the CGT to intensify its resistance to the reforms. In fact, the most important concession that the government ever granted to the CGT, the promise not to pursue labor flexibilization, was negotiated in 1991, by petition of PJ leaders in Congress. But because the PJ sided with the Executive in the 1992 labor dispute, the capacity of the CGT to intimidate the Executive declined. Judged against the intention of the strikers, the 1992 strike was a colossal political failure despite its success on the streets. Consequently, the CGT had little choice but to change strategies after 1992: rather than seek to sabotage or block the reforms, the CGT began to seek ways to "participate" in their implementation.

---

allegations abound that they are the primary source of labor corruption. In January 1992, Menem sent a bill to Congress empowering the state (not the unions) to collect monthly contributions and permitting beneficiaries to belong to any *obra social* (see McGuire 1997).

8. In addition, the Peronist labor leaders were concerned with the reduction in the number of labor-based members of Congress.

The other example was the conflict with the pensioners. The pensioners represented one of the most seriously affected victims of Argentina's economic crisis in the 1980s and the austerity of the 1990s. In early 1991, this so-called new poor began to organize. Unlike the plight of organized labor, the plight of the pensioners enjoyed substantial support from public opinion. Instead of accepting the pensioners' demand for a U.S.$450 monthly check, Menem offered the pensioners some modest help and pegged it to an eventual reform of the social security system and the privatization of YPF. In short, the Executive gained more than it yielded. And again the PJ sided with the Executive and not the pensioners, endorsing Menem's controversial solution. The PJ even published full-page ads addressed "To the Argentine Retirees," telling them to accept the settlement (see Powers 1995).

The repudiation of the CGT and the pensioners represented audacious acts for the PJ to take. The CGT was the historical backbone of the party; the pensioners were a symbol of the "inhumane" nature of austerity. They were the groups that the PJ would have eagerly embraced in the past. That it did not support them this time is crucial evidence of the reversed role of the PJ.

Foreclosing Institutional Avenues for Sabotaging Reforms

Another consequence of the greater harmony in Executive–ruling party relations was that the PJ became unavailable as an institutional avenue for interest groups to sabotage the government. This too contrasts sharply with the situation in Venezuela. As a party that was in the opposition for thirty-one of its forty-five years, the PJ by 1991 had become quite comfortable as the refuge of almost every disaffected sector of Argentine society. The party not only survived the beatings it received from every military regime prior to 1983, but it actually contributed to undermining each of these regimes by serving as an institutional avenue through which societal actors could challenge the state.

A common tactic was for the PJ and industrialists to exchange political favors.[9] In exchange for labor protection, the PJ would provide industrialists

9. This insight comes from O'Donnell's (1978b) argument about the "defensive alliance" between Argentina's labor sectors and the weaker urban bourgeoisie (the non-oligopolistic and domestic-oriented industrial sectors). For O'Donnell, Peronism was the preeminent expression of this alliance. Always strong enough to frustrate the political programs of the more powerful bourgeoisie (agro-exporters and internationalized industrialists), the alliance was still not powerful enough to impose its own. Thus, this alliance stopped stabilization and economic opening efforts, but never succeeded in carrying out its own "socially just capitalist development" project. For O'Donnell, this explains Argentina's cycle of political and economic instability between

with a commitment to protect domestic markets. Other times, the PJ simply allowed itself to be used by industrialists. For instance, in order to oppose liberalization, industrialists typically threatened the government with massive layoffs, hence labor unrest. Clearly, the key to labor unrest was in the hands of the PJ, not the industrialists. Thus, for their threats to be credible, the industrialists needed the PJ to "play the game." Often, the PJ went along. The PJ and the urban-based, inward-oriented industrialist sectors not only shared many interests but also *de facto* exchanged political services. All of this changed with the normalization of Executive–ruling party relations in 1991. The PJ refused to act as an avenue for cost-bearing groups. The following sections show some examples.

The Privatization of Somisa   One of the largest steel plants in Argentina, Somisa was targeted to be the first major privatization under Cavallo. The government promised to avoid all the mistakes of the past and deliver an exemplary privatization—transparent, consensual, and profitable. In addition, Somisa, unlike ENTel and Aerolíneas, would be reconverted prior to the sale, which meant laying off approximately 60 percent of its personnel.

These plans provoked virulent opposition. In the past Somisa was used as a "dumping ground for paying off political favors" (*Review of the River Plate*, October 17, 1991). Opposition to its privatization was thus predictable. Led by Naldo Brunelli, the opposition was based primarily in Somisa's small home town, San Nicolás, where Somisa distributed handsome benefits: salaries alone amounted to U.S.$10 million every month. Opposition was not confined to Somisa's workers; the national branch of the Steel Workers Union (UOM), led by Lorenzo Miguel, and numerous private firms (mostly suppliers and contractors of Somisa) supported the anti-privatization campaign.[10] The Peronist mayor of San Nicolás also supported this coalition. The administration confronted a large anti-privatization alliance of labor, business, and local politicians.

1956 and 1976. What O'Donnell misses is that on repeated occasions, even the large industrialists (i.e., the UIA) joined this alliance. In February 1985, for instance, amid rumors of an upcoming stabilization plan (the Austral Plan), CGT leader Jorge Triaca and UIA president Roberto Favelevic jointly presented the Alfonsín administration with an alternative plan (the "20 Points Plan" by the Group of Eleven), calling for rapid economic growth, an exchange rate that would promote both export promotion and further import substitution, and a return to union welfare funds (Epstein 1992b).

10. According to Somisa's privatizer at the time (and former Peronist labor boss), Jorge Triaca: "The most virulent opposition . . . stemmed, undoubtedly, from the sectors with vested interests in Somisa. . . . Those who sell Somisa 70 percent of its inputs and those who purchase 70 percent of its production. . . . These are firms that do not face any competition. Somisa works exclusively to feed them" (*La Nación*, October 28, 1991).

Tensions escalated throughout 1991, culminating with a major strike in San Nicolás on October 3, followed by more hard posturing and threats of a nationwide strike. However, a dramatic turnaround occurred on October 26: Somisa's assembly of workers overwhelmingly approved the management's reconversion scheme; in essence, this was a sudden acceptance of the privatization plan. In a matter of forty-eight hours, therefore, the anti-privatization coalition changed its preferences completely.

The unavailability of the PJ as an ally for the Somisa protesters explains this turnaround. The protesters were aware that their only chance of defeating the government lay in making the conflict nationwide, that is to say, obtaining the support of a political ally of national stature and access to the government. The support of the UOM was not enough. Only the endorsement of the PJ (and its labor federations) would provide the necessary clout. Expecting this support was not unrealistic: a year earlier the PJ would have embraced their cause.

Consequently, Brunelli and Miguel paid a visit to the PJ faction in Congress. The only result was an equivocal offer by its head, Jorge Matzkin, to "mediate" the conflict (*Ámbito Financiero*, October 16, 1991, 1, 12). In reality, Matzkin did little to help. To prevent Congress from considering the Somisa case, he even decided to "freeze" congressional activities until November. This was a crucial door-closing act. Frustrated, Brunelli then went directly to the CGT-San Martín and the CGT-Azopardo, but both refused to endorse a general strike as well (*Página/12*, October 24, 1991). It is historically remarkable that even the CGT-Azopardo refused to cooperate. The CGT-Azopardo was the most contestant of the two federations and a known enemy of Somisa's privatization. In 1986, when Alfonsín announced the possibility of privatizing Somisa, Ubaldini took his union to the streets to block the action (de Pablo 1994, 142). Ubaldini's refusal to do the same in 1991 was decisive.

Once the PJ option was foreclosed, the Somisa protesters lost all hope of victory. Unrest abated, and statist labor negotiations with the government for Somisa's privatization began.[11] Somisa was privatized in 1992, after laying off approximately 6,200 employees and provoking the shutdown of 2,500 private contractors (*Clarín*, August 14, 1994, 22–23).

The PJ and the Cost-Bearing Private Sector   The unavailability of the PJ as an institutional avenue to sabotage the reforms had a significant impact on state-

11. By January 1992, Brunelli declared: "Today, we are no longer discussing whether Somisa ought to belong to the state" (*Clarín*, January 8, 1992, 3); "What we want is 10 percent of the shares to go to the UOM" (*Ámbito Financiero*, January 8, 1992).

business relations as well. Two of Argentina's most powerful private sectors—protected industrialists and agricultural exporters—were cost-bearers. Industrialists faced unprecedented foreign competition; agricultural exporters faced an overvalued currency that hurt export profits. The former wanted more protection; the latter complained about the fixed exchange rate regime.

Under other circumstances, the PJ would have embraced both claims, but not this time. Disaffected agricultural exporters and industrialists had lost their most significant political avenue to press the state. The leading federation of agricultural exporters, the Argentine Rural Society (SRA), reacted to its isolation by simply withdrawing from the battle. The SRA did not even support the various rural-based strikes that took place. The reason was: "We simply estimated that the chances of success in prompting a change in policy course were minimal. . . . Once the Peronists changed, the possibility of allies changed as well" (De Zavalía, interview). Lacking institutional support, the SRA concluded that the chance of winning a war against the government was minuscule. Instead of wasting political energy in futile skirmishes, the SRA's strategy became "to side with the Executive in the hope of negotiating better concessions rather than to challenge the Convertibility" (ibid.). By 1992, the SRA had fully acquiesced to the new overvalued monetary regime—another historical rarity. Because the SRA refused to endorse the three agricultural strikes of the 1991–94 period, the smaller federations had no chance of having any political impact on overall economic policy.

The UIA, however, did not give up so easily. Its reaction to the government's renewed vigor was to attempt to challenge the government openly and unilaterally. In May 1991, for the first time in years, the UIA elected an openly protectionist leadership (Israel Mahler and Manuel Herrera). The UIA discontinued its ties with the moderately pro-market think tank FIEL in June 1991 and began to openly criticize each of the pillars of the new regime, such as the fixed exchange rate, the overvaluation of the currency, trade opening, especially vis-à-vis Brazil, and the lack of industrial subsidies.

Amazed at the intensification of the UIA's anti-reform posture, a leading news magazine remarked: "The UIA . . . is an unlikely place to look for strong open opposition to the government. Subtle hints at formal lunches and private talks to ministers are the usual methods of making suggestions and expressing disapproval. It was, therefore, a surprise when Manuel Herrera, secretary of the organization, came out with a forceful attack on present economic policy" (*Review of the River Plate*, January 29, 1993, 45). This statement underestimates the enormous disruptive capacity of the UIA in the past, but the *Review*'s surprise is justified. In the past, the UIA had always maintained a pro-market facade in its public statements belying a protectionist preference in its private dealings with the government. Because the PJ was often available to "play the game" and "provide services" on behalf of the UIA, the latter had no need to openly show its true colors, hence its duplicitous personality.

However, after 1991, the UIA could no longer count on the PJ to defend it. The novelty is that for the first time the UIA became protectionist in both its public and its private dealings. Unlike the SRA, the UIA overestimated its capacity to conduct the battle alone. The UIA leadership hoped that, by declaring its position openly, it would attract support from any cost-bearing sector now forsaken by the PJ. This was the Peronization of the UIA—an effort to play the role of "refuge of the disaffected" left vacant by the PJ.

The UIA's confrontational efforts failed. Devoid of an entry door into the government, the UIA's claims against the regime had little impact on policymaking. Few groups endorsed the UIA's ineffectual position. Sure enough, the government negotiated certain concessions with industrial firms, but these negotiations were conducted mostly outside UIA channels. And compared to the magnitude of the UIA claims, these concessions were far from meaningful victories.

By mid-1993, the UIA finally desisted. A more conciliatory leadership was elected. One of its first public statements was to accept the dollar-peso parity. Despite huge complaints by industrialists regarding the government's lack of "industrial policy" (that is to say, a plan of targeted subsidies) (see *Clarín*, July 27, 1994: Suplemento Económico 6), the UIA remained unwilling to seek a change in the new economic regime. Instead, it sought to negotiate with the government policy specificities on a case-by-case basis (Casullo, interview). In 1994, the president of the UIA, Jorge Blanco Villegas, declared: "Trade opening has been truly hard, very hard, and has led to painful changes; but in my opinion they were necessary" (*Clarín*, September 9, 1994: Suplemento Especial, 7). This was a complete change in Executive-UIA relations in Argentina. For the first time since the mid-1970s, the UIA desired to work with, not sabotage, a liberalized economic regime.

The change in Executive–ruling party relations thus changed the nature of state-society relations. Reform skeptics felt less justified in mistrusting the Executive; cost-bearers felt politically isolated and unable to challenge the reform. As a result, both groups switched political strategies, from noncooperation to cooperation, and in some cases, from recalcitrance to willingness to negotiate. All of this was the result of the PJ's change from being an enemy of the state to its closest partner.

The Gaps in the Reforms

Party accommodation policy, despite its payoff in terms of improved state-society relations, came at a price nonetheless—gaps in the reform process. In return for cooperation, the ruling party placed certain demands on the government. The most important in Argentina was to go easy on labor market reforms. Etchmendy and Palermo (1998) show that reforms in the labor sector between 1989 and 1995, compared to privatizations, were indeed far more timid, proceeded at a much slower pace, and were frequently blocked by Congress. During this period, Congress approved nine out of the ten privatization bills it received, but only eight of the twenty labor reform bills. Slow labor market reform constituted a crucial gap in the reform agenda. It was a hard pill for the technocrats to swallow.

This gap was especially costly for the government, not so much for its presumed economic impact (the government claimed that low market flexibility explained the rise of unemployment), but for its political impact. It led to tensions with the business sector, and it eroded somewhat the hard-earned credibility of the state.

Nevertheless, the government found ways to manage this tension with business groups, mostly by playing a curious game. Until 1994 this game took this form:

1. The government submits a labor reform bill to Congress;
2. Congress rejects the bill;
3. Menem accepts defeat (that is to say, he does not enact the law by decree);
4. Menem encourages *técnicos* to draft a new, watered-down bill;
5. Repeat steps 1 through 4.

This game differed from the "You modify, I might veto" rule that characterized the politics of other economic reforms. First, Congress (led by the PJ) repeatedly rejected the reforms. Second, Menem repeatedly acquiesced.

Nevertheless, this game helped the government to counteract the credibility problem that arose vis-à-vis the business sector by not delivering labor reforms. By accepting Congress's rejection, the Executive was conforming to the agreement with the PJ of leaving labor rights untouched, thus keeping the PJ satisfied. Had Menem decreed the reforms, he would have pleased business, technocrats, and international advisers, but at the cost of alienating the party and violating his own party accommodation policies. And yet, by taking steps 4 and 5, Menem still managed to signal to business, technocrats, and international groups that he had not given up on them. By forcing the *técnicos* to resubmit a modified bill that was closer to PJ demands, the government even courted the PJ's desire to feel it had an impact on policymaking

After 1994, this game changed somewhat, taking shape as follows:

1. The Ministry of Labor (not Economy) drafts a new reform bill.
2. The bill is submitted to discussion in meetings between labor unions (CGT) and business unions (UIA).
3. These negotiations produce a "compromised" bill in which neither of the three actors obtain what they desired the most, but their interests are not entirely slighted either.
4. The modified bill is sent to Congress.
5. Congress approves it without difficulty.

This new regime restored elements of the old Peronist corporativist setting: tripartite negotiations between the leading labor federation, the leading business federation, and the state (always a bit more biased toward labor groups), which pleased the PJ enormously. For this reason, the game was far more productive in terms of legislative output. Between July 1994 and December 1995, the government was able to obtain a new law for small and medium-sized firms, flexibility in hiring contracts, reform of work accident laws, a new law of bankruptcy, a law for mediation to reduce labor conflicts, and a few reforms of the *obras sociales* (Etchmendy and Palermo 1998).

Another important gap in the reform was the rise of neopopulism. An important component of Menem's party accommodation policy was to place Peronists in charge of ministries that managed social spending, precisely the areas with the largest budgets and the largest budget increases in the 1990s (the notable increase in social services in 1993 was due to the inclusion of retirement and pension systems) (see Table 9.3).[12] Social service expenditures did not decline even during the 1995–96 recession. They did decline in 1997, but mostly because of the need to devote more resources to the public debt.

The resilience of public sector spending in Argentina's budget was not accidental. Social spending was directed by Peronist ministries. In fact, the Ministry of Labor and Social Security in 1996 controlled almost half of the

---

12. Social services consist of health promotion and social assistance, social security (largest component), education and culture, science and technology, work, housing and urban affairs, and drinking water.

Table 9.3   Argentina: National Budget, 1991–1997 (percent of total for the year; peso amount in parentheses in billions)

	1991	1992	1993	1994	1995	1996	1997
Administration	13.41	15.27	9.75	9.75	10.16	9.54	9.36
	(2.0)	(2.7)	(3.9)	(3.9)	(4.2)	(3.9)	(4.1)
Defense	15.05	16.25	8.60	8.96	8.43	8.34	7.46
	(2.3)	(2.9)	(3.4)	(3.6)	(3.5)	(3.4)	(3.3)
Social Services	34.72	29.59	61.11	64.19	64.97	65.19	63.40
	(5.3)	(5.3)	(24.2)	(25.7)	(26.7)	(26.8)	(27.9)
Economic Services	28.09	2.46	11.50	9.30	6.94	6.64	6.43
	(4.2)	(4.4)	(4.6)	(3.7)	(2.9)	(2.7)	(2.8)
Public Debt Service	8.73	14.19	9.04	7.80	9.51	10.30	13.3
	(1.3)	(2.6)	(3.6)	(3.1)	(3.9)	(4.2)	(5.9)
Total	100.00	100.00	100.00	100.00	100.00	100.00	100.0
	(15.1)	(18.0)	(39.7)	(40.0)	(41.2)	(41.2)	(44.0)

Source: Cicioni (1997, 28).

national budget (Cicioni 1996, 43). The minister of the economy lobbied for less spending; the PJ ministers lobbied for more. The result was less spending than was needed from the point of view of "socioeconomic needs" (Cortés and Marshall 1999), but more than would have happened from an exclusively "fiscally conservative" perspective. Most of the changes in the 1997 budget were increases imposed by Congress in the area of social services. The government originally budgeted 27.0 billion pesos for social services; the Congress approved 27.9 million pesos, reducing spending in most other areas (Cicioni 1997, 28–29). This suggests a deliberate strategy by the PJ to fund social spending over other programs and a deliberate strategy by the government to accommodate the PJ.

The party was thus responsible for adding a more "human face" to Menem's neoliberalism. A purely technocratic government probably would not have accepted this. But this human face came with blemishes: many of these funds went to promote neopopulist and party-promotion activities. In the province of Buenos Aires, controlled by Eduardo Duhalde, public social spending skyrocketed. Duhalde's wife, Mrs. Hilda Duhalde, chaired the Consejo de la Familia y Desarrollo Humano, the province's welfare agency with an annual funding of some U.S.$280 million, which ran a multitude of social assistance programs. As the head of the army of 17,000 women volunteers, Mrs. Duhalde was seen as responsible for the daily hand-outs of food and milk to 600,000 poor, drawing comparisons even with Eva Perón (Economist Intelligence Unit 1997, 13). There is reason to believe that these funds gave the local branch of the PJ ample opportunities for patronage.[13]

There is no question that Menem's technocrats were aware of the use of these funds for neopopulist/party-promoting activities. Yet most of them were careful not to criticize this. In 1994 Cavallo even defended Duhalde's use of public monies (*Clarín*, October 16, 1994, 1–3). This "don't ask, don't tell" stance exemplified the pros and cons of party accommodation. Granting autonomy to the party generated party endorsement of market reforms, but at the cost of policy gaps and some erosion in transparency.

Conclusion

Political parties, especially statist ruling parties in the context of market reforms, have a comparative advantage, not just as aggregators of collective

---

13. Levitsky finds that more than two-thirds of the base units he surveyed were run by activists with government jobs, and in more than a third of these base units, at least two other activists also held government jobs (1999a, 288).

Table 9.4 Argentina: How Harmonious Executive–Ruling Party Relations Mediate the Effects of Credibility Booms, 1991–1994

Economic Effects of Credibility Boom		Political Effects of Credibility Boom on:			
Positive	Negative	Cost-Bearing Sectors	Opinion-Makers	Mistrusting Sectors and Winners	Anti-Establishment
• Inflation ends • Economy grows • Credit returns • Capital returns • Consumption booms • Investment booms • Jobs expand • Productivity rises	• Trade deficit increases • Inflation in non-tradeables increases • Currency overvalues • Wage differentials between labor in competitive and noncompetitive sectors expand • Rent-dependent sectors lose income • Unemployment rises	• Intensify their opposition	• Highlight the negative sides of the reforms	• Increase their cooperation with the state	• Dissatisfied
Impact of Harmonious Executive–Ruling Party Relations on Each of These Dimensions					
PJ helped disseminate these results	PJ downplayed these results	PJ provided little political support	PJ relied on state technocrats to counteract these challenges	PJ's alliance with the Executive signaled continuity	PJ precluded the rise of a political vacuum at the top

interests, but also as instruments of governance. Attempting to carry out economic change without the support of a ruling party deprives the Executive of crucial links with its natural constituencies and further undermines relations with nontraditional constituents. On the other hand, a strong alliance with the ruling party serves the Executive well, not just because of what the party is willing to do (shield the state), but also because of the less intentional signal that it transmits: the capacity to forge ahead. It also forecloses the institutional avenues through which reform opponents can undermine the government.

Table 9.4 summarizes the influence of the ruling party in containing resistance to reforms. Harmonious Executive–ruling party relations generate a credibility boost, which in Argentina generated an economic boom. This softened the opposition of some groups (mistrusting sectors), but not of others (cost-bearing sectors). The capacity of the state to survive and even overturn the sabotaging activities of cost-bearing groups is directly related to its alliance with the ruling party. With respect to society as a whole, and the Peronist rank and file in particular, the party served to delegitimize protests, contain grievances, and disseminate information on behalf of the government and the reforms. With respect to leading interest groups, the PJ simply refused to serve as an ally. This posture allowed the Executive, for the first time since the 1950s, to survive the simultaneous pressures of the CGT and the UIA.

In 1990, Menem declared: "There will not be national unity if there is no unity within the party" (*La Nación*, March 31, 1990). Events proved him right. The new rules of the game brought about by the harmony in Executive–ruling party relations compelled interest groups to change tactics from opposition to acceptance of reforms, or at least a willingness to negotiate. In many ways, the new relationship unhinged the formidable "defensive alliance" (O'Donnell 1978b) of labor and the bourgeoisie that, in the past in Argentina, had been every government's headache.

10

more

crises in

executive–ruling party

relations

If the argument that harmonious Executive–ruling party relations generate societal cooperation with reforms is true, then one should be able to verify the effects of the opposite condition. That is, a crisis in Executive–ruling party relations should lead to some sort of crisis in reform sustainability. The evidence exists, not just in Venezuela under Pérez, but also in Venezuela under Caldera and in Argentina under Menem and Alfonsín.

The 1992 Mini-Crisis in Argentina

On November 12, 1992, a major run on the dollar began in Argentina in what became the first financial panic of the Convertibility era. The run was surprising because it occurred at the most economically robust time of the Menem years. Part of the cause was external: starting in the summer of 1992, European currency markets became unstable, leading to devaluations in Italy, the United Kingdom, and other countries. But this is not the whole explanation. Those devaluations occurred in September and did not affect Argentina's currency throughout much of the third quarter of 1992.

A more important trigger was the sudden deterioration of Executive–ruling party relations after October 1992. Signs of deterioration were everywhere. The CGT held its general strike on November 9. Cabinet infighting intensified: Cavallo had public disputes with key PJ cabinet members such as Julio César Aráoz (Health and Social Action) and Rodolfo A. Díaz (Labor) (*Clarín*, November 12, 1992). There were rumors circulated that the head of the Subsecretariat of Institutional Relations, Guillermo Seita, would resign (ibid.). The 1993 budget and the pension system reform were stalled in Congress. Finally, rumors circulated that a group of PJ governors led by Eduardo Duhalde (governor of the province of Buenos Aires and Menem's former vice president) were drafting a memo to the president proposing a "split" (*desdoblamiento*) of the Ministry of the Economy to create a "Ministry of Production" to be led by a politician. It is not coincidental that the run occurred in the midst of these events. The run reflected the return of the fears of the mistrusting sectors.

Just as a sudden change in Executive–ruling party relations triggered the speculative run, a subsequent rapprochement contributed to its resolution. By Monday, the PJ decided to endorse the Executive unequivocally. Some of the governors alleged to be conspiring against Cavallo, including Duhalde, strongly denied such allegations and issued instead a vigorous endorsement of the reforms and the reformers. By the next day, the run on the dollar stopped (the dollar actually declined in price), and the value of trading in the stock exchange surged. The return of confidence was so sweeping, as evidenced by the decline in demand for dollars, that the Central Bank was forced to buy U.S.$22.2 million in order to keep the dollar-peso parity.

The following day, in a speech during an act of concessions of federal lands to families, Menem once again delivered an ultra-Peronist speech, mentioning the names "Perón" and "Evita" repeatedly. He argued that "privilege-laden sectors are attempting to destabilize my performance, much as they tried to do under Perón" (*Clarín*, November 20, 1992, 4–5). Perhaps this

"Peronization of the presidential discourse" was Menem's way of thanking the PJ for its support. It was the party, rather than the economic authorities, that received the president's praise.

The Crisis of the Second Half of 1995 in Argentina

A second and more serious crisis in Executive–ruling party relations occurred in the third quarter of 1995, right after the May presidential elections. In the first half of 1995, Argentina suffered its most serious external shock since the Convertibility Law—the ripple effects of the December 1994 devaluation of the Mexican peso (the Tequila Crisis). Given Argentina's overvalued currency and trade deficits, international investors believed that Argentina, like Mexico, would soon devalue. This expectation led to a huge outflow of portfolio investments from Argentina, generating enormous devaluation pressures in the first quarter of 1995. The government held steady, meeting the demand for dollars in full. It lost 30 percent of reserves between the end of 1994 and the first quarter of 1995 and provoked a severe recession and a rise in unemployment by mid-1995 (see Table 10.1).

Until the middle of 1995, the government enjoyed harmonious Executive–ruling party relations. Except for Cavallo's request for emergency powers (which would have been a violation of the rule of Executive–ruling party engagement negotiated in 1991), the PJ fully supported the government's orthodox postures, including the *Ley de Solidaridad Previsional*, a few labor-flexibilization laws, and several financial reform laws. Many PJ leaders had reservations, but they decided that the presidential race was not the time to

Table 10.1   Argentina: Aftershocks of the Tequila Crisis

	1994		1995				1996			
	III	IV	I	II	III	IV	I	II	III	IV
GDP (% annualized)	7.1	6.6	2.7	−5.2	−8.1	−7.0	−3.2	4.8	6.7	8.8
Unemployment		12.2		18.4		16.6		17.1		17.3
Wholesale inflation (% yearly)	3.7	3.6	4.8	4.2	2.7	1.8	0.4	−0.2	0.1	0.3
External reserves (U.S.$ billions)	16.6	17.9	12.5	15.0	15.3	18.5	18.8	20.0	18.4	20.5
Deposits (U.S.$ billions)	37.5	37.0	31.2	31.2	32.9	34.3	38.6	39.9	40.6	42.8
Merval (stock market) index	605	460	382	406	432	519	509	607	558	650

Source: Llach (1997, 232).

Table 10.2   Argentina: Assessment of the Economic Program According to
PJ Voters in Prior Elections (percentage)

	Nov 94[a]	Dec 94[b]	Feb 95[c]	Aug 95[d]	Aug 96[e]	Jan 97[f]	May 97[g]	Feb 98[h]
Very good	7.2	16.8	18.1	15.3	4.4	2.6	0.0	0.8
Good	17.2	39.3	46.2	13.8	34.4	32.6	9.9	12.6
Regular	40.3	19.0	25.9	38.4	33.7	13.8	83.0	41.1
Bad	23.3	6.5	5.9	24.0	21.3	25.1	7.2	21.9
Very bad	12.0	10.4	1.1	7.1	4.8	25.3	0.0	13.1
Doesn't know/ Doesn't answer	0.0	8.0	2.7	1.4	1.3	0.5	0.0	10.5

Notes:
[a] Poll in the Federal Capital, 600 cases, PJ voters for the Constitutional Assembly.
[b] Poll at the national level, 1,200 cases, PJ voters for the Constitutional Assembly.
[c] Poll in Greater Buenos Aires, 1,000 cases, PJ voters in 1993 elections.
[d] Poll in the Federal Capital, 400 cases, PJ voters in the 1995 presidential elections.
[e] Poll in the Federal Capital, 500 cases, PJ voters in the 1995 presidential elections.
[f] Poll in the province of Buenos Aires, 1,600 cases, PJ voters in the 1995 presidential elections.
[g] Poll in the Federal Capital, 300 cases, PJ voters for national deputy elections.
[h] Poll at the national level, 1,000 cases, PJ voters in the 1995 presidential election.

Source: SOFRES (Buenos Aires).

bicker with the government. And as before, the support for the Executive extended beyond party leaders. One public opinion poll, for instance, revealed that the popularity of the reforms among PJ voters, always high, increased further after the new round of reforms were announced in early 1995 (Table 10.2).

This cooperation, together with the backing of the multilaterals and the banking reforms of early 1995, paid off. The PJ faced the elections with a fair degree of unity, contributing to Menem's overwhelming victory. By mid-1995, signs of an economic recovery were already visible. It seemed that the impact of the Tequila Crisis would be contained.

However, Executive–ruling party relations deteriorated immediately after the May elections. The key issue was the government's response to the unemployment problem, a theme that had obsessed the PJ since 1994. Several PJ leaders had revived the idea of forcing Cavallo to create a new ministry that would be in charge of employment promotion. After the elections, the PJ felt that it was safe to vent criticisms against Cavallo's adamant refusal. In retaliation, Cavallo gave a speech in Congress accusing an Argentine businessman (Alfredo Yabrán) as being the head of "a mafia inlaid in the power structure" and hinting complicity on the part of government and legislative figures (Cavallo 1997, 275–76). This speech embarrassed—and angered—the PJ. For the first time ever, PJ leaders called openly for Cavallo's resignation. And as Table 10.2 shows, discontent with the reforms soon spread to the rank-and-file.

This third quarter of 1995 constitutes the most serious crisis in Executive–ruling party relations since 1991. Predictably, the effects on credibility and, hence, state-society relations were adverse. Economic actors panicked after the election, largely in response to this bickering. Industrial production, which had begun to recover in July, dropped to a new low in November. Peso deposits declined again in July and did not recover until November. After rebounding in July–August, the stock market declined continually during September–November, reaching the same low levels as in the height of the Tequila Crisis (April 1995). The GDP experienced its most severe decline in the third and fourth quarters of 1995.

Normally, economic agents are more uncertain during, rather than after, a presidential race. But in the words of Llach: "The post-electoral uncertainty was, undoubtedly, more harmful" (Llach 1997, 240 and n. 9). Post-electoral Executive–ruling party animosity produced "more recession" than economic conditions warranted. The December 1994 external shock dealt a serious blow to the Argentine economy in the first half of 1995, but the deterioration of Executive–ruling party relations in the second half of 1995 significantly magnified and prolonged its effect.

The 1997–1999 "Re-Reelection" Crisis in Argentina

The most serious crisis in Executive–ruling party relations began in mid-1997, and continued until the end of the Menem administration. Its effects on reform sustainability were as serious as those of the 1989–91 crisis. Despite the continuity of variables pushing in the direction of more reform (external pressures from the IMF and an "economic change team," led by Minister Roque Fernández, that shared the same commitment to market reform as the Cavallo team), the reform process slowed down between 1997 and 1999. Several macroeconomic accomplishments of the 1991–97 period were allowed to deteriorate, pushing Argentina very close to bankruptcy.

The most important cause of this crisis in Executive–ruling party relations was Menem's decision in mid-1997 to seek a third term in 1999—what various newspapers baptized as the "re-reelection" drive. This constituted a clear violation of the 1994 Constitution, which explicitly banned the reelection of an incumbent president after a second term. More important, it was a violation of Menem's party accommodation policy. Until 1997, the PJ leaders had agreed to cooperate with Menem, provided that he would, at the end of his term, allow new leaders to rise to the top. The party consented to Menem's stewardship over the economy, not to Menem's self-perpetuation in power.

The party always expected that other Peronists would have a fair shot at rising to the top. By seeking a third term, Menem threatened to block upward mobility opportunities for other Peronist leaders. For this reason, his decision to run again infuriated many party leaders, not to mention most Argentines (approximately 80 percent expressed disapproval).

Resistance within the PJ was so strong that even the defeated Eduardo Duhalde was able to stage a political revival by capitalizing on this resentment.[1] By late 1997, Duhalde reemerged as the leading force inside the PJ, mobilizing a huge coalition of Peronists intent on blocking Menem. Duhalde called Menem's attempt to seek a favorable court ruling on behalf of reelection "a juridical coup d'etat" (*Microsemanario 305*, February 13–17, 1998). For the first time since 1991, the Executive was at odds with a large portion of the party leadership. By February 1998, polls suggested that less than 13 percent of prior PJ voters had a positive view of the economic program, a significant drop from 1997 (see Table 10.2).

Menem's detractors in the PJ gained ground quickly. A poll in early 1998 revealed that in a hypothetical primary inside the PJ, Duhalde would win 60 percent of the votes, whereas Menem would obtain 17 percent (*Carta Económica*, March 1998). To protest Menem's re-reelection drive, crucial party leaders refused to attend a party congress convened in mid-1998 (*Carta Económica*, August 1998). Previously neutral PJ leaders, such as Alberto Pierri, began to join the anti-Menem camp (*Carta Económica*, February 1999). As in Venezuela in the early 1990s, Executive–ruling party relations turned hostile.

The Return of Menem the Populist

This hostility in Executive–ruling party relations undermined reform sustainability in the 1997–99 period. Feeling isolated and devoid of sufficient political support, Menem became uninterested in further economic adjustments. Then vice-minister of the economy, Carlos Rodríguez, explained Menem's posture toward his team as follows: "Menem told us: 'I will not reject your proposals, but I will not promote them'" (Rodríguez, interview). This contrasts sharply with the 1991–97 period, in which Menem actively campaigned on behalf of the measures proposed by the Ministry of the Economy. Concerned about the lack of support for his re-reelection drive, especially inside his party, Menem simply could not afford policies that would alienate the very allies he needed for his campaign.

---

1. Duhalde invested huge resources in the failed campaign to elect his wife, Hilda "Chiche" Duhalde, to Congress from the province of Buenos Aires in the October 1997 elections.

Table 10.3   Argentina: Selected Macroeconomic Indicators, 1995–2000

	1995	1996	1997	1998	1999	2000[c]
GDP at constant prices (percentage change)	–2.8	5.5	8.1	3.8	–3.4	–0.5
Average deseasonalized industrial production (percentage change)	–4.8	4.8	8.6	1.6	–6.4	–0.1
Unemployment (October)	17.4	18.8	14.3	13.3	14.4	14.7
Fiscal revenue[a]	23.2	22.1	23.2	23.7	24.3	24.5
Noninterest expenditure[a]	23.6	23.2	22.9	23.2	25.1	24.1
Primary balance[a]	–0.4	–1.1	0.3	0.5	–0.8	0.5
Interest[a]	1.9	2.1	2.3	2.6	3.4	4.0
Overall balance[a]	–2.3	–3.2	–2.1	–2.1	–4.2	–3.6
Outstanding government external debt[b]	67.2	73.5	74.8	82.4	85.4	85.7

Notes:
[a] Consolidated public-sector operations (includes federal and provincial operations). Figures are percent of GDP.
[b] Billions of U.S.$, end of period.
[c] Preliminary.

Source: IMF (2000a, 2001).

The most immediate consequence of Menem's lack of interest in reforms was the failure to contain the rising debt. Economic officials recommended increasing taxes, decreasing expenditures, and using privatization proceeds to pay the ever-rising debt—to no avail. No one at the top—neither the president nor his detractors within the PJ—cared. Rather than decrease spending, Menem actually proposed increases in his 1998 budget. In early 1998, an IMF mission sounded the alarm, warning about rising deficits and indebtedness. Sounding more like the populist president of Peru in the 1980s, Alan García, than the neoliberal Menem of 1991, Menem responded: "Nobody tells Argentina what to do." That same year, Congress rejected Minister Roque Fernández's watered-down proposal to increase taxes and expand VAT coverage to exempted sectors. In January 1999, the Argentine government promised the IMF a primary surplus of 1.2 percent of GDP by year's end (IMF 1999, 3). Instead it delivered a deficit of 4.1 percent. Like Pérez's economic ministers in the 1991–92 period, Menem's economic officials were desperate for presidential backing. Without such backing, economic officials had no option but to "stay on automatic pilot," as Fernández was fond of saying. They were unable to contain the debt (Table 10.3), and the state began to delay payments to public sector suppliers (Economist Intelligence Unit 1998).

The New Spending Race

The other side of Peronism responded in kind. PJ governors began to increase provincial spending. Duhalde became the most preeminent populist of Argentina's leading politicians. The province of Buenos Aires, where Duhalde was governor, underwent a gigantic expansion of public expenditures, transforming a low and below-average fiscal deficit in 1996 (7 percent of current revenues) into a huge and significantly above average deficit in 1999 (25 percent of current revenues) (World Bank 2001). Most of these expenditures were related to increases in personnel—a proxy of clientelism. The pronounced expansion of personnel spending in the province of Buenos Aires contrasts sharply with that of other provinces. Between 1995 and 2000, personnel spending in the province of Buenos Aires increased by 61 percent; the overall increase of the other provinces was 10.2 percent. Personnel spending in most major jurisdictions (e.g., Córdoba, Santa Fe, City of Buenos Aires) actually declined or remained stable in this category. The expansion of spending and deficits in the most economically weighty province of Argentina significantly undermined the country's macroeconomic performance.

With an Executive in desperate need of allies and a group of party leaders in an all-out-effort campaign to contain his ambitions, the political grounding for austerity simply evaporated. That the opposition parties, the UCR and FREPASO, formed a coalition in 1997, the so-called Alianza, heightened the feeling of threat of each of these forces within the PJ. Each side of the civil war in the PJ realized that more austerity would imperil its own political objective.

Another consequence of the 1997–99 crisis in Executive–ruling party relations was the return of Menem's penchant for power concentration. One clue is the dramatic increase in the amount of social spending funds that the Office of the Presidency came to control. Between 1993 and 1999, the Office of the Presidency more than doubled the percentage of social spending under its control (from 6.3 to 13.5 percent of total), a formidable increase in a very short period of time, greater than the overall increase in social spending (Table 10.4). The presidency obtained control of types of social spending that it did not control in 1993 (culture, water utilities, housing, and social welfare). The proportion of social spending controlled by the Ministry of the Economy shrank considerably, a proxy of the declining leverage of this ministry in Menem's cabinet toward 1999.

It is unclear why the Office of the Presidency, rather than the relevant ministries, needed control over these monies. It is hard to justify this on technical grounds. Yet this is consistent with a president obsessed with maximizing his spending capacity in the hope of expanding his own bargaining leverage vis-à-vis the PJ.

Table 10.4   Argentina: Who Controls the "Gasto Público Social"?, 1993–99 (Millions of Pesos)

| | Total | | Controlled by | | | | | |
| | | | Presidencia[a] | | Ministry of the Economy | | Relevant Ministry | |
	1993	1999	1993	1999	1993	1999	1993	1999
Education: basic	130.15	735.20	0	0	0	0	130.15	735.20
Education: secondary and higher	1,421.83	2,133.92	14.8	11.46	0	2.1	1,305.03	1,854.14
Education: culture	78.88	156.61	0	124.65	0	0	52.08	2.11
Education: general	273.93	66.86	0	15.25	0	0	48.63	47.43
Science and Technology	498.72	648.80	292.18	72.45	139.02	167.06	43.13	368.89
Health[b]	792.49	3,026.01	22.97	201.69	0	0	578.74	2,563.63
Water and Sewers	67.17	131.77	0	131.77	67.17	0	0	0
Housing and Urban Affairs	935.85	768.28	0	761.78	0	0	904.96	6.5
Social Welfare[c]	812.77	1,786.44	42.52	262.28	28.38	50.1	152.2	0
Sports	42.52	23.38	0	23.38	0	0	0	0
Employment	837.54	2,381.31	0	0	0	0	796.67	2,381.31
Total	5,891.85	11,858.58	372.41	1,604.70	234.57	219.26	4,011.59	7,959.21
Percent of total			6.3	13.5	4.0	1.8	68.1	67.1

Notes:
[a] Includes Office of Chief of Ministers (Jefatura de Gabinete).
[b] Includes Prestaciones de salud de Pensiones No Contributivas after 1997.
[c] In Spanish: "promoción y asistencia social." Funding transferred to Obligaciones del Tesoro" by 1999.

Source: Based on data from Ministerio de Economía (1999).

Menem thus concluded his years in office with more concentration of power resources than at any other point since 1991. He had come full circle. He finished his second term exactly as he had begun his first: trying to mobilize the party's rank-and-file against the party's leadership and triggering a huge conflict within his own party. Only this time, it was the party's leadership that prevailed.

The Decline of State-Business Cooperation

The cost of this unnecessary "political shock" was high. Menem's re-reelection drive constituted not only a serious affront to the Constitution, but also to the economy. In two years, Menem undid the coalition of business leaders, regional PJ bosses, and rank-and-file that he skillfully built after 1991 (see Palermo 1999, Gibson 1997, Starr 1997, and Palermo and Novaro 1996). The tension between Menem and his party restored the credibility deficit that plagued the state prior to the 1990s. Argentina began to relive the same ills in state-society relations that prevailed prior to 1991. For instance, the Executive branch began to emit contradictory policy signals. At the same time that economic officials were trying to obtain congressional approval of tax increases, Menem was promoting a gigantic infrastructure project (*Clarín*, March 17, 1998, 20). Once again, the Argentine state was in the business of cheating private agents, repeating its predatory behavior of the 1980s, and undermining its own credibility.

The dispute between Menem and the party "officially" ended in mid-1999 with the nomination of Duhalde as the PJ's candidate. Yet this did not allay business skepticism. In his effort to block Menem, Duhalde had gone out of his way to disparage the reforms, tarnishing his reputation forever among business skeptics. This was a major turnaround from 1992, when Duhalde acted as one of most ardent defenders of the reforms among labor and business groups (*Clarín*, July 28, 1992, 8). As early as November 1997, business leaders began to express "deep concern" over the rise in anti-reform discourse in the PJ triggered by the re-reelection dispute (*Clarín*, November 5, 1997, 2–3).[2] Six months later, when the aftershocks of the Russian crisis hit Argentina, the "concern" of business skeptics turned into panic. Bank deposits declined. Argentina entered into a recession.

2. In July 1998, Carlos Rodríguez expressed the negative effects of Executive-ruling party discord as follows: "It is very difficult to manage the economy of a country undergoing not only political turmoil regarding whom and what will come next, but also uncertainty about which labor and tax codes we will have. . . . The investor who is looking at Argentina cannot tell which Constitution there will be, which candidate each party will nominate, and which tax and labor codes will emerge. Even inside the same party there are candidates who support the economic

In short, Menem's re-reelection drive led to a crisis in Executive–ruling party relations that destroyed the economy. The predictable effects of such crises reappeared: policy incoherence, economic officials devoid of political power, rescue measures to cover reform holes, and a pervasive credibility deficit. The crisis thus exacerbated the economy's vulnerability to the external shock of 1998. Not unlike the situation of 1988, in which reform skeptics did not know whether any of the two presidential candidates were truly committed to end statism, investors in 1999 felt uncertain about the future. In this context of a credibility deficit, it is not surprising that the Argentine state had such a difficult time recharging the economy—investors were refusing to invest. While the South American nations most affected by the Asian Crisis began to recover in 1999 (Chile and Brazil), the recession in Argentina proved to be one of its most intractable of the last two decades of the twentieth century. The main reason for this stagnation was not the defection of foreign investors (as was the case during the Tequila Crisis), but the credibility deficit brought about by disharmonious Executive–ruling party relations in 1997–99. Only an Executive with a strong relationship with its ruling party would have been capable of solving this economic disaster. Menem's successor did not enjoy such a privilege, and Argentina plunged into its worst crisis in decades (see Chapter 13).

The 1987–1988 Collapse of the Austral Plan

Another important test case that highlights the causal power of Executive–ruling party relations is the Alfonsín administration (1983–89). Alfonsín's failure to restructure the economy made stabilizing it impossible (Machinea 1993; FIEL 1990),[3] which led to perhaps one of the darkest periods of economic governance in Argentina's history.

Alfonsín's failure to consolidate his reforms is often attributed to technical incorrectness (some see the Austral Plan as too heterodox), to lack of political

---

model while others call for changing the model. We are making too much noise, and these mistakes will prove to be costly. . . . It is obvious that Duhalde does not support our economic model. . . . Menem is the one who supports the model the most because he was the one who created it. But I feel it is necessary to give stronger signals" (*Clarín*, July 14, 1998).

3. Alfonsín not only failed to privatize his pet projects (ENTel and Aerolíneas), but also to control SOE outlays (which increased from 19.7 percent of GNP in 1984 to 23.9 percent in 1988) (FIEL and CEA 1990, 22). Provincial spending also increased (by 13 percent from 1984 to 1988). This failure was not the result of lack of trying. Alfonsín implemented one of the most far-reaching stabilization programs (the 1985 Austral Plan) and recruited one of the most technically competent staffs ever.

commitment,[4] or to the virulent opposition from interest groups (industrialists and labor) and the opposition party (the PJ) (see Torre 1993 and Machinea 1993). An overlooked factor is the estrangement in Executive–ruling party relations produced by the reforms. UCR leaders had come to power on the assumption that they could return to the old models of politicians controlling and regulating the economy, practicing patronage (Machinea 1993, 134; Cavarozzi and Landi 1992, 209, 211), and advocating economic policies that were identical to those of their Peronist rivals (Kaufman 1990, 74). Alfonsín responded by trying to bypass his party: relying on decrees, reducing party involvement in the cabinet, avoiding consultations with the party, resisting sending ministers to Congress, etc. Thus Cavarozzi and Grossi (1992) describe the 1985–87 period as "the President's Government." There was some initial success in economic governance—marked reductions in inflation and the fiscal deficit—but these proved short-lived. Although the reforms were popular across the electorate (the government won the 1985 elections), they were resented by the UCR itself. Moreover, after the initial success of the Austral Plan, the commitment for austerity among the UCR, never strong to begin with, waned even further (Torre 1993, 80–81). Many UCR legislators, "dubious" about Alfonsín's stabilization policies, joined the Peronists in demanding the discontinuation of the reforms (Canitrot 1994). By 1987, the UCR had "distanced itself from the economic team and, to some extent, from the president" (Cavarozzi and Grossi 1992, 183).

The government's political response focused more on winning allies among business groups and placating Peronist labor groups than in regaining the trust of the UCR (Smith 1992, 34; Damill and Frenkel 1993, 56–59). The frustration of the UCR increased.[5] At some point, Alfonsín tried to make amends (appointing a party leader as secretary of agriculture), but this was too little too late. Executive–ruling party relations had become too contentious for these overtures to make any difference. Not surprisingly, the Austral Plan collapsed. And after this collapse, the UCR did little to rescue the reform efforts. A major confrontation between the party and the minister

4. Those who take this position (e.g., Casas 1991, 119–20) point to statements by Alfonsín himself. In his last annual speech in Congress, for instance, two weeks prior to the presidential elections of 1989, Alfonsín declared: "There were [adjustments] that we did not want to do, at times postponed, or simply decided not to do . . . because they entailed social costs and sacrifices for important sectors of our society in the short-term" (in Novaro 1994, 60 n. 16).

5. An important battleground was control over the Central Bank. In 1986, Alfonsín wanted to replace the head of the Central Bank, the Radical economist Alfredo Concepción, with a more fiscally austere leader, José Luis Machinea. The UCR fiercely resisted, attempting to fill the board of directors with faces friendlier to the UCR. In mid-1986, Alfonsín vetoed these efforts and went ahead with the appointment of José Luis Machinea. The UCR continued to press for further concessions (Kaufman 1990, 89–90).

of the economy took place in the party's November 1987 congress in Córdoba (Gaudio and Thompson 1990, 197). In 1987, Alfonsín's relations with the PJ (controlled by the Renovators) were better than with his own party.[6]

An Imperfect Solution: Accommodating the Opposition in Venezuela, 1996–1998

Venezuela under Rafael Caldera (1994–99) exemplifies a case in which an Executive decides to compensate the dislocations within his ruling coalition by seeking to "buy" support from opposition parties. In 1996, Caldera launched a program of structural adjustment ("Agenda Venezuela") comparable to that of Pérez. But unlike the case under Pérez, Caldera's ruling party was quite weak from the start—a last-minute alliance formed in 1993 between an ad-hoc coalition of minute parties (Convergencia) and a historically small socialist party (Movimiento al Socialismo, MAS). Although this Convergencia-MAS alliance won the 1993 presidential elections, it came in third in every congressional, gubernatorial, and mayoral election. This alliance became even more atomized following the unveiling of Agenda Venezuela in 1996; sectors of Convergencia began to defect, and MAS began to break apart. Executive–ruling party dislocation climaxed in 1998 when MAS endorsed none other than Hugo Chávez for the December 1998 presidential elections. Chávez was the most anti-reform of all candidates. In protest against this choice, the government's economics czar and founding father of MAS, Teodoro Petkoff, resigned from MAS in July 1998.

Caldera's response to the growing disarray in his ruling coalition was to attempt to buy the support from the strongest opposition force, AD—ironically, the very same party that Caldera had vilified during the 1993 elections. He gave AD a few ministries, supported AD's nominations and several laws, and preserved AD's presence in the bureaucracy. In return, AD supported some of Caldera's initiatives, such as the suspension of economic guarantees, provisions for a debt-rescue fund, funds for the bail-out of the banking system, and a watered-down privatization law. After the 1995 midterm elections, in which AD rebounded, the ruling party MAS sought to counterbalance AD by forming alliances with the other opposition forces—COPEI and Causa R. In short, the government spent most of its time forming and undoing alliances with opposition parties.

Compared to a party-neglecting strategy, a policy of accommodating the opposition as practiced in Venezuela in 1995–98 offered the advantage of

---

6. While the PJ began to cooperate with the Executive on some economic reforms (e.g, tax reform), the UCR heightened its criticisms of Alfonsín's economic policy, which they blamed for their 1987 electoral setback.

compensating the administration for its fragile ruling coalition with borrowed supporters. This allowed for a certain degree of reform sustainability. However, compared to party accommodation vis-à-vis the ruling party, party accommodation vis-à-vis the opposition does not produce impressive levels of reform implementation. Unlike a ruling party, the opposition has no interest in seeing the incumbent succeed, since its ultimate goal is to weaken the incumbent in order to regain the presidency. Hence, the opposition sells its support at a much higher price and with greater reservation. This explains AD's haphazard support of the Caldera administration despite Caldera's overtures: it supported certain reforms (usually the most modest), but it never shied away from opposing the government whenever it perceived an opportunity to score electoral points (e.g., supporting striking workers, or supporting the protectionist demands emerging from Fedecámaras).

Consequently, reform implementation under Caldera did not go far, even after Caldera decided to push them full force. Caldera privatized a few firms (e.g., Sidor), opened up the oil sector, and liberalized the banking sector, but he failed to bring inflation below the best year of the Pérez administration (31 percent in 1991). Some of Venezuela's most needed structural reforms—e.g., the creation of a stabilization fund to manage windfalls in oil revenues, the flexibilization of labor markets, and the revamping of the tax system—were continually postponed. This proved devastating at the end of 1997, when oil prices declined precipitously to levels not seen since 1986, plunging Venezuela into the fourth fiscal and foreign exchange crisis since Caldera took office (see Corrales 2000b).

Conclusion

The five cases discussed in this chapter show that reform sustainability varies in relation to the nature of Executive–ruling party relations. The more conflictive the relationship (Venezuela, 1991–93; Argentina, 1987–89 and 1997–99), the harder it is to sustain a major effort to overhaul the economy. The case of Argentina under Menem in 1997–99 also shows that presidents have enormous discretion in altering the relationship. With his re-reelection drive, Menem succeeded in single-handedly destroying the very same pillar that sustained him during the 1991–97 period. The case of Venezuela under Caldera shows that one possible solution to such problems is to seek accommodation with the opposition party. This accommodation, however, is suboptimal because opposition parties never respond as cooperatively as a ruling party would. In short, conflictive Executive–ruling party relations are a major obstacle to state governance.

party systems,

external shocks,

and internal

party structures

institutional

determinants

of executive–ruling party

relations

Up to this point I have presented the nature of Executive–ruling party relations as a crucial independent variable of reform sustainability. In this chapter I treat
Executive–ruling party relations as the dependent variable. Here I seek to provide a deeper understanding of
why Executive–ruling party relations became so harmonious in Argentina and so hostile in Venezuela.

The Executive's policy toward the party—whether
party-accommodating or party-neglecting—is not the
sole determinant of party response. Also important are a
series of institutional variables. The first is a historical-

institutional variable: degrees of interparty cooperation. It is common to think, along with Haggard and Kaufman (1995), that cooperative, nonpolarized party systems enhance governability. However, this chapter will show that, under certain conditions, cooperative party systems (such as existed in Venezuela) can actually undermine governability because they can fuel Executive–ruling party dislocations. For dissenters in the ruling party to openly challenge the Executive, they must feel comfortable standing on the same side of an issue as opposition parties. In less cooperative party systems such as in Argentina—characterized by high mistrust among parties—ruling party dissenters, averse to siding with the opposition, will think twice about challenging the president. Excessive party system collusion, in some way, exacerbates Executive–ruling party dislocations.

Features of the party system, however, cannot fully explain the dynamics of Executive–ruling party relations, as I will argue in this chapter. A second and more powerful explanation can be found in the features of the parties themselves, specifically, the level of internal party fluidity. Recent literature on political parties has focused on the factors that compel political parties, especially Western European social-democratic parties, to adapt to new circumstances. A prominent debate focuses on which factors are more important in explaining party transformation—external shocks (e.g., economic crises, electoral setbacks, changes in values of voters) or internal party features (e.g., extent to which leadership, factions, and structures are entrenched). Kitschelt (1999, 1994), for instance, takes the latter position. He argues that internal characteristics of parties—institutional structures, ideological traditions, and leadership—better account for party adaptation ("strategic flexibility"). For Kitschelt, the more organizationally "entrenched" parties (that is to say, parties with mass membership, formal ties with ancillary organizations, and large bureaucracies) have more trouble adapting.

However, as Berman (1997) points out, some very entrenched European parties managed to successfully transform themselves in the 1990s, suggesting that entrenchment is not an absolute barrier to party adaptation. By the same token, the PJ, like AD, was highly entrenched, and yet it adapted to the new circumstances of the 1990s.[1] Thus, as Berman suggests, the key to party adaptation must involve both external and internal variables. Specifically, external variables such as a "particularly stinging" electoral defeat, contribute

---

1. For Levitsky (1999a), the PJ's adaptation occurred along two axes: (1) coalitional adaptation—i.e., recrafting its original coalition to include more than the industrial working-class base; and (2) programmatic adaptation—i.e., recrafting its program to conform with the requirement of a post-statist economy. See also Gibson 1997.

to party adaptation because they soften internal party rigidities (Berman 1997, 113; see also Coppedge 1998, Harmel et al. 1995, and Wilson 1980).

In essence, Berman revives Downs's (1957) argument about the transformative impact of electoral defeats. According to Downs, parties are preeminently vote-getting machines, specializing in the business of getting like-minded individuals into office. Parties will do anything, even self-transform, if they fail to maximize their vote-getting potential. Electoral crises— that is to say, electoral performances that fall dramatically short of the leaders' expectations or historical averages—induce parties to self-transform. As party elites strive to find a new winning formula, everything from leadership to ideologies becomes subject to revision. While the direction of change is unpredictable, change is virtually inevitable after exposure to electoral setbacks.

Downs (1957) has been criticized for providing a reductionist view of parties and exaggerating their mutability.[2] With respect to Argentina and Venezuela in the 1980s, Berman's adaptation of Downs's parsimonious hypothesis is sufficient. Between 1983 and 1985 the PJ suffered a series of external shocks, that is to say, electoral losses, that unleashed a crisis of hegemony with the party. For the first time, PJ leaders feared that their electoral dominance was in peril. This realization led to a process of internal change that ultimately made the PJ "readier" to assimilate the post-1989 reforms. This process of change did not make the party neoliberal, but it did make the party more amenable to accepting the risks associated with the new direction proposed by Menem.

In short, this chapter argues that a combination of internal party variables (levels of entrenchment) and external shocks (electoral reversals) explain party transformation. This, in turn, helps explain the nature of Executive–ruling party relations during the implementation of the reforms.

Variations in Degree of Centrifugality in Executive–Ruling Party Relations

When Menem and Pérez took office in 1989, they faced the same practical problem: the need to find leaders within their parties, preferably highly

---

2. Sartori (1976), for instance, argues that not all parties are vote-maximizers. Parties can be (a) witness parties uninterested in maximizing votes; (b) ideological parties, interested primarily in indoctrination; (c) responsible parties, which do not alter their policies to maximize votes; (d) responsive parties, for which winning elections is a priority; and (e) purely demagogic parties, which are only vote-maximizers. Sartori thus proposes an alternative definition of party: "Any political group capable of placing through elections candidates for public office" (327). He also challenges Downs's view that parties are primarily vote-getting machines. Parties compete for "staying in the market," i.e., being relevant for influencing policy. Votes are just the means.

trained, who would be willing to implement market-oriented reforms. Of the two, Pérez was harder pressed to find any potential recruits. According to Pérez, he sought but could not find leading Adecos who understood, let alone believed in, the reforms. This compelled him to do more recruiting outside AD (Pérez, interview). To some degree, therefore, Pérez's policy of party neglect was itself a function of this initial constraint—the party had to be excluded because there were few Adecos that could be included.

This difference in the "supply" of pro-reform party leaders was a symptom of a deeper phenomenon: AD as a whole was less prepared than the PJ to assimilate the reforms. The number of bandwagoners in the PJ was always greater than in AD. Even Pérez's enthusiasts within AD were less committed to the new government than the average Peronist leader. Menem's detractors eventually yielded more gracefully to the reforms than most analysts expected. Cafiero could have prolonged and intensified his challenge of Menem, but he refused to do so. Even the ultra-cafierista "25" unionists soon became eager bandwagoners (McGuire 1997, 226–34). The PJ also tolerated a degree of Executive imperiousness even after 1991 (e.g., partial vetoes of PJ-sponsored bill modifications), which in Venezuela would have provoked instant outrage from AD.

In many ways, the PJ was readier to embrace the risks of reform. In the early 1990s, AD had fewer members prepared to support experimental policies and exhibited less enthusiasm for the reforms and greater willingness to express dissent than the PJ. This is not to say that a resolution of Executive–ruling party relations in Argentina was easy or assured, but it suggests that centrifugal forces were more intense in AD than in the PJ.

How Levels of Interparty Cooperation Affect the Risks of Voice

One explanation for greater centrifugality in Venezuela's Executive–ruling party relations is the degree of interparty cooperation. Variations in interparty cooperation can either mitigate or exacerbate the risks associated with ruling party dissent. Ruling party dissent is risky for at least two reasons. The first risk is that by protesting, dissenting ruling party members might provoke the failure of the administration, thus giving voters more reasons to vote for an alternative party in subsequent elections. The second risk is provoking the ire of Executives, who, especially in Latin America, command significant power resources to punish detractors. Therefore, AD's decision to challenge Pérez took some courage.

Ruling party dissent is more likely to flourish to the extent that there are factors attenuating the risks of voice. High levels of interparty cooperation can have this effect.[3] Ruling party leaders are more likely to take the risk of opposing the president when they know that they are not alone. The availability of possible political allies or collaborators defrays the risks of voice. The opposition thus plays a key role in this calculus: it can act as an ally that mitigates the risk of dissent, but only if ruling party members feel comfortable siding with the opposition. Where there is a history of interparty cooperation, the conditions are ripe for greater ruling party dissent.

At the start of the reforms, the two leading parties in Argentina were less comfortable cooperating with each other than in Venezuela. It was unthinkable for disaffected Peronists to side with the UCR, despite some initial convergence of interests in stopping the reforms. This was not just because the UCR left the government in total disrepute. Rather, it was the result of a history of animosity between the UCR and the PJ that dated back to the very founding of the PJ. The idea of Peronists accepting UCR leadership was out of the question in Argentine politics. For twenty-six years (1946–72), the animosity between Peronists and Radicals was almost as intense as the animosity between Peronists and conservative military sectors. The Radicals always resented the bursting onto the scene of Peronism in the 1940s. Prior to that, the UCR was Argentina's preeminent anti-oligarchic, antimilitary party. Peronism stole these banners from the UCR, and in Perón's first administration, deployed informal repressive tactics against the UCR. In addition, Peronists ridiculed and often violated many of the Republican "institutions" installed by the UCR. Radicals always saw Peronists as political bullies who were disrespectful of democratic procedures.

Peronists, in turn, always saw Radicals as accomplices, or at least as too tolerant, of the efforts by the military to proscribe the PJ. The fact that President Arturo Frondizi (UCR, 1958–62), who owed his victory to the secret backing of Perón, reneged on his promise to relegalize the PJ further fueled this historical mutual mistrust.

Not until 1972, with the much celebrated "embrace" between UCR leader Ricardo Balbín and Juan Perón, did a rapprochement between the parties

3. In both Argentina and Venezuela, the constitutional clause preventing the reelection of presidents, in effect in 1989, was another factor that diminished the probability of the first risk. Because presidents were banned from running for reelection, party officials knew that they could offer a totally new candidate in the next elections. This made certain leaders of the ruling parties feel that the party could survive the experience of a failed administration. They hoped that voters would interpret the choice of a different candidate as a healthy attempt by the party to distance itself from an unpopular administration.

begin (Cavarozzi 1986, 166).[4] And yet this entente was neither too popular (many Peronists and Radicals, including Raúl Alfonsín, objected to it) nor too lasting (Perón's successor, Isabel Perón, made few overtures to the UCR). When the UCR returned to office in 1983, relations improved (e.g., Executive-congressional relations on noneconomic matters were fruitful), but not on economic matters.

This history of minimal interparty cooperation put a lid on a potential Peronist revolt against Menem. Peronists did not want to be on the same side as the UCR. When Alfonsín attempted in August 1992 to group into one movement all the dissenters against the new economic model, including disaffected Peronists, by founding the "Movement for Social Democracy" (Movimiento para la Democracia Social, MODESO), he was in for a major disappointment (*Noticias*, August 1992).[5] Even the staunchest PJ dissenters (e.g., the Group of Eight) repudiated Alfonsín.[6] The initiative died quickly.

The issues of "refuge" possibilities discussed here and "party accommodation" discussed in Chapter 8 help to explain the "Bordón crisis." After the defeat of Cafiero in 1990, José Octavio Bordón became Menem's main challenger inside the PJ. Bordón was a Renovator in the 1980s and a supporter of privatizations in 1989–90. However, Bordón had always criticized the government's neglect of science and technology, its lack of transparency in regulating post-privatized sectors, its laxity about private sector oligopolies, and Menem's efforts to expand his power within the party. And yet Bordón decided to stay within the party throughout most of the adjustment period, refusing to quit in 1990 with the Group of Eight and ignoring Alfonsín's call to join MODESO in 1992. He finally left the PJ in September 1994 to join the FREPASO as its main presidential candidate for the May 1995 elections. Why did Bordón stay until 1994? Part of the answer was the unavailability of refuge opportunity: siding with the UCR was inconceivable,[7] and joining the

4. Balbín and Perón signed "The Hour of the People," an accord in which both parties recognized each other's political demands and agreed to moderate their rhetoric.

5. This was not the first time that Alfonsín attempted to steal Peronist masses from the PJ. When President Isabel Perón began to move to the right and defy Peronist labor unions in 1975, Alfonsín urged the UCR to move to the left in order to capture disaffected sectors within Peronism. As president, Alfonsín also tried to de-Peronize the labor unions by having them adopt more democratic internal elections and trying to establish the "Third Historical Movement" (Gaudio and Thompson 1990). On both occasions, Alfonsín repelled, rather than attracted, the very Peronists he was trying to court.

6. The leaders of the Group of Eight (later baptized Frente Grande, and later on, FREPASO) did not form an alliance with the UCR until mid-1997.

7. When Alfonsín was discussing the MODESO, Bordón reiterated his intentions to stay with the PJ legislative fraction (*Clarín*, August 25, 1992).

Group of Eight was "unreasonable because back then these leaders had very little political weight" (Bordón, interview). Why leave in September 1994? Part of the answer was the emergence of a new refuge opportunity: the rise of FREPASO, which gained political vigor following the 1994 elections to the Constituent Assembly. Another part of the answer was a major violation of party accommodation: Menem's vacillation in scheduling the party's internal primaries in the PJ.[8]

In contrast, the history of interparty cooperation was richer in Venezuela. The hallmark of Venezuelan politics since 1958 was joint-rulership of political institutions among political parties, what Rey (1989) calls the "populist system of concertation among elites." While AD remained electorally dominant, COPEI's presence in labor unions, professional associations, government agencies, and civic associations in general was always significant and tolerated by AD. Joint-rulership was a stipulation of the Punto Fijo pact of 1958 that both parties respected. Adecos even learned to live peacefully under two COPEI administrations.

Interparty cooperation encouraged many AD leaders to take the risk of challenging Pérez. AD dissenters felt more comfortable defying Pérez because they did not feel uncomfortable standing on the same side as COPEI. They even accepted operating under the leadership of COPEI in one of their major acts of defiance against Pérez (e.g., the Caldera Law). This granted a risk cushion to disenchanted Adecos. Ironically, therefore, an ingredient for governability under normal times (interparty collaboration) acted as an ingredient of ungovernability under market reforms.

External Shocks, Internal Party Fluidity, and Party Transformation

Degree of interparty collaboration, however, is not a complete explanation for variations in centrifugality. The most remarkable aspect about the Venezuelan case is that, despite some defections, the ruling party eschewed a division such as the one it experienced in the 1960s. Most of the dissenters

---

8. Bordón was confident that he would perform decently in such elections. Refusing to set a date for the primaries, Menem then tried to persuade Bordón to stay by deploying an alternative party-accommodating strategy—offering him the vice presidency. But at this point, it was too little, too late (Bordón, interview). Bordón claims that he left in order not to weaken the PJ, but rather to force the party to think about certain issues. He knew he could not win the elections, but he still wanted to show to the PJ that his postures had a not-insignificant electoral weight and thus were worthy of incorporating into the administration's agenda.

stayed and prospered within the party. And in Argentina, cooperation between disaffected Peronists and Radical legislators did occur (e.g., eleven Peronist legislators collaborated with the UCR in 1993 to slow the passage of the Pension Reform bill).[9] More important, the rise of Frente Grande in 1993, later FREPASO, provided a non-UCR partnership and "refuge" opportunity for disaffected Peronists. And yet no major PJ leader other than Bordón joined the Frente Grande. Frente Grande stole voters mostly from the UCR rather than the PJ (Gervasoni 1998; Levitsky 1998). Thus, even when a viable exit and alliance opportunity did arise, it hardly affected Executive–ruling party harmony.

A more powerful explanation for the different degrees of centrifugality in Executive–ruling party relations is variations in party transformation during the 1980s—high for the PJ, low for AD. Two crucial variables played a key role in determining this transformation: internal party fluidity and external shocks.

Internal fluidity refers to the ease with which internal party leadership changes. There existed in AD a series of practices that ensured party leaders a long tenure at the helm of the party. Tenure was insulated from the effects of electoral outcomes: even if the party lost an election, or a new AD administration moved in, old party leaders retained their posts. Once a member of the CEN, an AD leader was almost never required to retire. The number of retirements always lagged far behind the number of new entrants (Martz 1998, 69). The fact that Venezuelan presidents were guaranteed a seat for life in the Senate assured the continuity of old party leaders at the national scene, and by extension, within their own parties.

Low levels of leadership exit had two main consequences. One was the rise of cartel-like thinking among party leaders. Because the top party posts hardly ever became vacant, opportunities for new blood to move in were scarce. Existing leaders were not eager to admit new members. To move in, new members had to either persuade the party to expand the number of seats in the leadership structure (which happened, but with great difficulty) or achieve superhuman political feats. Barriers to leadership renewal were, in a word, extraordinary. The other consequence of low leadership retirement was intense internal bickering. The permanence of old leaders gave rise to

9. However, most episodes of PJ-UCR collaboration were qualitatively different from episodes of AD-Copei collaboration in Venezuela. PJ legislators after 1991 did not seek to sabotage the reform or even to embarrass the government, but to force the government to accept more PJ-based conditions. Collaboration with the UCR was mostly a tactical bargaining strategy, rather than an attempt to torpedo the Executive.

intense resistance both from newcomers, who often resented the reduced space for them, and from rivals of old leaders, who resented the permanence of their nemeses.

The return of Pérez in the 1980s exemplifies this situation. Pérez finished his first term in office in disrepute, especially within AD. Not only was he unable to secure a victory for AD in the 1978 elections, but his administration ended amid accusations of corruption. In 1981, COPEI legislators tried to pass a resolution declaring Pérez guilty in an overpricing-kickback deal (the *Sierra Nevada* affair). AD legislators abstained (Coppedge 1994b, 24), revealing (1) the extent to which Pérez's popularity had declined among AD, but also (2) the staying power of old leaders. AD leaders, despite their resentment toward Pérez, could not bring themselves to sanction such a party veteran.[10] Pérez then proceeded to use his continued presence in the party to mount his historic comeback of 1987–88. And this comeback, like previous efforts of "outs" to take the party back, generated enormous tensions.

Second, AD developed restrictions in internal contestation, which also decreased internal fluidity. There was no direct election for membership in the CEN. In the 1980s, the party's leadership devised a series of informal controls to limit eligibility for participation in internal primaries, thus assuring the victory of their preferred candidates (Martz 1999–2000, 645). Given that the CEN had complete control over promotions and nominations within the party and Congress, there was a built-in incentive for party delegates to cater to the interests and preferences of existing CEN members (Crisp 2000). In addition, the electoral system for congressional representatives and municipal assemblies—a closed list determined by CEN members—also allowed the CEN to maintain tight control over legislators. The desire to secure a top position in the slates made AD politicians obsequious vis-à-vis the CEN (see ibid. and Martz 1998). In Congress, party discipline was so high that roll calls were rarely made (Coppedge 1994b).

Third, there were restrictions in AD's exposure to external contestation. Until the late 1980s, governors were appointed by the president. Thus, winning only 55 percent of the vote in a presidential election granted the ruling

10. Many analysts attribute AD's conflict with Pérez in the 1990s to this troubled history within the party. However, petty factionalism was not the root cause of Executive–ruling party estrangement. The Pérez-Lepage dispute, though intense, was not the first episode of factionalism in AD. It was not even the first time that an "out" had challenged the "ins" (see Coppedge 1994b). In the past, these factors had never led to hostile Executive–ruling party relations. There is no question that Pérez was a conflictive person in AD in the 1980s, but much of this animosity subsided once Pérez became AD's candidate in 1987 and the "ni ni" leaders endorsed Pérez. In addition, the party's response to Pérez in 1989 was still generally supportive, despite reservations.

party 100 percent control of the provinces and the capital city. The party thus gained total state presence for less-than-total electoral achievements.

These institutional features—restrictions in retirements, in internal contestation, and in external contestation—insulated the CEN from the pressures that in other democratic societies encourage parties to renew themselves. The result was one of the least internally fluid parties in Latin America. Not surprisingly, the "openness" of party leadership diminished, bureaucratization of the leadership increased, decision making concentrated further in a smaller number of leaders, ideological conflicts subsided, and the degree of internal democracy declined over time (Martz 1992).

The PJ, however, had a fair degree of internal fluidity. The PJ did exhibit some of the features of entrenchment suggested by Kitschelt (1994, 1999). For instance, the PJ, like AD, had mass membership, as well as ancillary institutions—links with social groups, regional organizations, and labor unions. In some areas, the PJ was decidedly more entrenched than AD. It held a monopoly of representation in unions, for instance (see Levitsky 1999a). However, in many other respects, the PJ was less entrenched than AD. First, this was a party that had spent most of its existence in the opposition, often underground and suffering the repression of military governments.[11] Second, and as a consequence, the PJ had a less developed bureaucracy. A sign of the PJ's underbureaucratization is the fact that the PJ did not have a physical headquarters in Buenos Aires before the 1990s, whereas AD had at least two major installations in Caracas (a high-rise tower and a massive compound, appropriately called the bunker). This bureaucratic deficit meant the absence of an organization that could impose vertical control (from top-tier to bottom-tier entities) or horizontal links (linking territory-specific units with each other) (Levitsky 1999a). In addition, although the PJ is "organizationally strong" (it is well organized and enjoys ample geographic coverage, strong linkages to trade unions, and strong loyalties), the party's rules and procedures were underinstitutionalized, or "under-routinized," to use Levitsky's (1999a, 1998) label (see also McGuire 1997). Leadership structures were porous. There were no established career paths for leaders, and the written party rules differed considerably from informal practices. In short, the PJ was weak in terms of adherence to consistent internal rules for upward mobility.[12]

---

11. It is important not to exaggerate this point. Living under military regimes did not completely destroy the party. The party learned to adapt to these restrictive circumstances, often negotiating secret agreements with the military regimes. Military repression was hard on the party, but in some ways, it allowed certain leaders of the party to solidify their positions.

12. Levitsky (1999a) categorizes the PJ as scoring very high on the fluidity variable. I, however, would give the party a medium-high score. In 1983, the leaders of the party (at the national

The PJ's institutional fluidity, always significant, increased further, the more the party became exposed to internal and external contestation in the 1980s. Compounded by the effects of several stinging defeats in the 1980s, the result was party transformation. The first such defeat was the 1983 presidential elections—a particularly traumatic election for the PJ. This was the first time ever that Argentina's iron law—that given fair and open elections, Peronism wins—was broken. The PJ not only lost the elections, but lost them in a big way—a 20 percent decline in votes since the previous elections of September 1973. The PJ lost in most of the suburban counties surrounding the capital, which were traditional bastions of Peronism. Although the PJ was able to maintain its core constituency, the party failed to attract new voters. Party leaders could not explain this decline, especially coming at the heels of a military regime, which the party took credit for undermining. For a party that saw itself as the true soul of the nation and the symbol of resistance to militarism, the 1983 defeat was a catastrophe.

To make matters worse, the PJ's electoral misfortune continued beyond 1983. In the 1985 congressional elections, the PJ's electoral performance (34.9 percent) was even lower than in 1983 (39.9 percent). The party was shrinking. It could no longer claim to be "the party of the Argentine people."

These defeats unleashed a serious internal crisis. Debates and cleavages began to multiply regarding the question of how to reconstruct the party (Snow and Manzetti 1993). Always internally chaotic, the PJ went into complete disarray after 1983, to the point of beginning to look like a "Persian Bazaar" (Cavarozzi and Grossi 1992, 190–91).

The contrast with AD could not be starker. AD was both less exposed to contestation and completely exempted from electoral shocks in the 1980s. After its 1983 triumph (with almost 58 percent of the votes, its highest share since 1963), AD began to enjoy an unprecedented "power feast." AD not only obtained solid control of the Executive, both houses of Congress, and after May 1984, the municipalities, but virtually colonized the entire state apparatus. In exchange for total control of party affairs, Lusinchi agreed to place party leaders in high positions throughout the state bureaucracy. He even appointed all the provincial secretaries-general of AD as governors of their respective provinces in sheer disregard of a long-established norm prohibiting party leaders from simultaneously holding Executive public offices (Magallanes 1993). In the words of one observer: "Lusinchi placed the party above the government" (Sweeney 1990, 17).

---

level and lower-tier levels) tended to be the same as in the 1970s. The survivability of this leadership despite the passage of time and the presence of a military regime suggests a degree of "stickiness" of existing leadership structures.

To summarize, differences in three crucial internal party variables explain differences in party adaptation in the 1990s: levels of internal fluidity (high in the PJ, low in AD), degree of internal contestation (high in the PJ, low in AD), and exposure to external contestation (high in the PJ, low in AD). Combining these internal characteristics with the stinging electoral defeats of 1983 and 1985 triggered a huge crisis inside the PJ, characterized by enormous internal changes. Party leaders panicked and began to think about ways to regain competitiveness. AD, in contrast, was exposed to none of these change-inducing factors. Thus while the PJ was undergoing a dramatic transformation, AD was comfortably ensconced in power, facing no incentive to change, and becoming even more cartelized.

Differences in Party Transformation

The PJ's transformation was all-encompassing, covering almost every aspect of the party. AD, however, remained impervious to change. Comparing the evolution of both parties in the 1980s makes this clear.

The Emergence of Real Renovators in the PJ

The first effect of the 1983–85 crisis of hegemony was the emergence of a group of Peronists deeply committed to transforming the party. In March 1984, the Peronist Renovation Front (Frente de Renovación Peronista) was founded by Antonio Cafiero with Carlos Grosso and Carlos Menem, an act that was entirely consistent with Downs's (1957) proposition about the consequences of electoral setbacks. The Renovators' goal was to find a new winning formula for recovering the PJ's lost dominance. Their strategy was to challenge the leadership of the party, the so-called Orthodoxy. They advocated (1) giving the party a more modern and moderate "face";[13] (2) adopting greater internal democracy;[14] (3) assuming a more cooperative attitude toward

13. They wanted to rid the party of the image of radical and violent intransigence symbolized by the then PJ leaders, Ítalo Lúder and Herminio Iglesias. As acting president while President Isabel Perón was ill and, as her lawyer after the 1976 coup, Lúder was seen as too close to an administration that many Argentines saw as chaotic and violent. Labor leader Iglesias himself was accused of labor racketeering and having links with death squads. At the end of the 1983 campaign, Iglesias burned a coffin draped in Radical colors in a televised rally with two million participants (Snow and Manzetti 1993, 65), fueling the image of intransigence that Renovators actually wanted to jettison.

14. The first act of the Renovators was to call for direct elections per single district. Although there was a hidden agenda in the proposal—to use elections to challenge the Orthodox

the Executive office, even if controlled by the UCR;[15] and (4) reducing the predominance of militant labor unions[16] (see Levitsky 1999a, McGuire 1997, Palermo 1992, Cavarozzi and Grossi 1992, and de Ípola 1987). These proposals were so radical that some sectors of the party even considered expelling Renovator leaders.

AD Renovators, despite their label, never made such far-reaching proposals. Rather than an ideological or programmatic challenge, AD Renovators in the 1980s were simply a party faction. They sought greater internal power, not a "different" party. Coppedge (1994b) more accurately labels them "Outs," since they were chiefly individuals who lacked access to the party's top positions. Policy issues played little role in AD's cleavages in the 1980s and before.[17] For Coppedge, insofar as any issue divided the "Ins" from the "Outs," they were attitudes toward party discipline, candidacies, nomination procedures, government-party relations, and interparty competition. Indeed, prior to Pérez's 1988 embrace of some of COPRE's recommendations, very few AD Renovators seriously advocated liberalization (economically or politically, internally or nationwide).

Increasing Ideological Elasticity

Another key by-product of the crisis of hegemony (and the subsequent search for a new winning formula) in the PJ was the onset of ideological revisionism within Peronism. Peronists in the 1980s began a fierce debate about Peronist doctrine. Renovators were at the forefront of this effort. They began to discuss the various ways in which the Perón project had gone "awry" since Perón's death (de Ípola 1987). Carlos Grosso argued that "one of the major causes of our electoral losses was the fact that we kept considering societal options that no longer corresponded to reality" (in Snow and Manzetti 1993,

---

leadership—the end result was to install the first democratic primaries for the selection of national presidential candidates, thus expanding the party's exposure to internal contestation.

15. Of all Peronist governors in the 1980s, Menem had the closest relationship with Alfonsín (Cerruti 1993). When Cafiero obtained control of the PJ in 1987, relations between the PJ and Alfonsín improved dramatically. At some point, Alfonsín obtained Cafiero's support for a bill to increase taxes.

16. The Renovators came to feel that labor unions had become too autonomous, obstructionist, and uncontrollable.

17. Despite the lack of a general correlation between policy preference and faction, Coppedge did find that the "Outs" were more likely to prefer Keynesian policies (e.g., "stimulate demand" rather than stimulate production) and to oppose Lusinchi's austerity policies (1994b, 143–44), suggesting that insofar as AD Renovators had an economic orientation, it was statist.

65). Self-criticism, ideological revisionism, and the creative use of Peronist writings to justify new positions became commonplace. Not even the Orthodox leaders could escape these debates, because at the very least, they had to provide ideological rebuttals to the Renovators.

Although some demythologization of statism occurred, and some Peronists embraced more market-oriented positions, the main result of this ideological revisionism was neither a shedding of populism nor the full acceptance of neoliberalism.[18] The effect was instead an increase in ideological elasticity. Ideological elasticity had always been a feature of Peronism. Communists, fascists, nationalists, corporativists, and democrats could always find ideological justifications based on Peronist writings. PJ members were accustomed to "tinkering" with ideology and questioning party dogmas. But in the 1980s, this elasticity was stretched further to encompass, for the first time, an issue that had always unified Peronism—the sanctity of heavy state involvement. For the first time, Peronist leaders questioned the desirability of too much statism.

AD, however, underwent no ideological review, let alone revision, in the 1980s. Since party leaders were uninterested in searching for a new winning formula, the need to revisit ideology was minimal (see Coppedge 1994b and Martz 1992). Despite the debates regarding the new role of states and markets taking place internationally and domestically (e.g., the "Roraima Project," COPRE's recommendations),[19] AD remained impervious to and dismissive of these debates. The party's "Political Thesis," which was last changed in 1964, remained unexamined.

Perhaps the most serious proposal for party change occurred in 1980 with the "Documento de los 70," a letter to party bosses Rómulo Betancourt and Gonzalo Barrios signed by more than seventy Adecos. The letter called on AD to address internal problems such as divisions, corruption, lack of debate, decline in militancy, and nonrenewal of leadership (see Magallanes 1993). The "Thesis of the Labor Bureau" underwent a revision in 1981. That a call for party change (the "Documento") and an actual change (the Labor Thesis) would occur while AD was in the opposition is compatible with the argument in this chapter that party change is more likely in the context of electoral

18. Although more democratically oriented, rule-respecting, and fiscally conscious, few PJ Renovators in the mid-1980s were advocates of market reforms. Renovators criticized Alfonsín's Austral Plan as a continuation of the economic policies of the military dictatorship and the IMF (Cavarozzi and Grossi 1992).

19. The "Roraima Project" was a highly visible group of thirty to forty Venezuelan elites who in the early 1980s began to call for a "unanimous commitment to austerity," "less government intervention," and "more room for private initiatives" (Grupo Roraima 1985).

setbacks. However, for all their worth, these impulses were very modest and not necessarily in the direction of greater liberalization. The "Documento" was virtually ignored by the CEN. In addition, it said nothing about adopting political and economic liberalization. If anything, the "Documento" called for tightening internal party discipline (e.g., prohibiting electoral competition for the posts of local secretaries-general, banning reelection after two terms for all secretaries-general, and restoring the "mystique of struggle"). Likewise, the most significant innovation in the Labor Thesis (co-management by workers and executives at the firm level) was far less dramatic and revolutionary than the new positions being discussed inside the PJ in the 1980s (partial privatizations). Another opportunity for ideological adaptation occurred in 1985 with the Ninth Congress of the CTV, in which AD politicians, intellectuals, and labor leaders convened to discuss the "CTV's strategy vis-à-vis the crisis" (Godio 1986). The title of this congress reveals that the unions were aware of Venezuela's chronic economic problems. But once again, the proposed changes were modest in scope and effect.

Therefore, when Pérez launched his reforms, he unleashed the first process of ideological revisionism in decades. A joke among Adecos when this process began in 1989 was that no one in the party knew where AD's founding documents were. Whereas Menem's challenge was to resolve in his favor an inherited process of ideological elasticity, Pérez's challenge was to instigate it and then survive it. This placed the Venezuelan Executive at a disadvantage. AD's ideology had not been rendered elastic, and party leaders were "untrained" for (and uninterested in) ideological revisionism. The state was forcing a process of ideological revisionism that in the PJ occurred as a result of the external shock of the early 1980s, rather than by presidential command.

Leadership Replacement

The 1983–85 electoral results also propelled a major leadership shift in the PJ: the replacement of Orthodox leadership by Renovators. As the faction in control of the PJ, the Orthodox bore the brunt of the party's 1983 and 1985 electoral setbacks (McGuire 1997, 189–90). In addition, in their effort to oppose the UCR, they picked the "wrong side" on two crucial electoral issues. They opposed the government's proposal (1) to create a National Commission for Disappeared People (CONADEP), which was to investigate human rights abuses under the dictatorship, and (2) to settle border disputes with Chile over the Beagle Islands. They described the former as a mere witch hunt; the latter, as an act of treason. Because both initiatives turned out to be popular among the electorate, the Renovators, who supported these initiatives, were able to argue that the Orthodoxy was "out of touch."

With each electoral setback, the Orthodox leadership yielded positions,[20] and the Renovators gained them. Although the PJ's performance in the 1985 congressional elections was dismal, Renovators tended to outperform the Orthodox.[21] This allowed the Renovators to gain control of the PJ gradually, first in the province of Buenos Aires and, by 1987, throughout the nation. In the 1987 gubernatorial elections, with the slogan "Yes, change is possible," the Renovators won in nineteen of the twenty-four provinces. By winning the governorship of the province of Buenos Aires, Cafiero automatically became the party's strongman. By 1987, the Renovators had conquered the party's hierarchy.[22]

Crises of hegemony produce an urgency to find new vote-attracting leaders. Consequently, the PJ's never-too-stringent "admissions requirements" became even more relaxed, and its "underinstitutionalization" became even more pronounced. New leaders (and affiliates) began to be welcomed less on the basis of demonstrated Peronist credentials (e.g., student militancy, labor collaboration, or a history of struggle against dictatorship) than on the basis of their capacity to attract new votes. This amounted to a fair degree of indiscriminate party permeability: it became easier than ever for anyone to join the party, including the leadership ranks, increasing the eclectic nature of the party's leadership.

The case of Domingo F. Cavallo illustrates this. Cavallo was the antithesis of Peronism in terms of background and ideas. He was neither a party affiliate nor a populist.[23] Nevertheless, Renovators in Cavallo's province of Córdoba

20. One of the first to yield was former president Isabel Perón. Although not an explicit member of the Orthodoxy, she was the foremost representative of "Peronism gone awry." In 1983 she refused to be involved in an increasingly divided party, deciding instead to return to Spain, continue her "sepulchral silence," and officially resign as a PJ leader in 1985. After the 1985 defeat, Herminio Iglesias (secretary-general) and Senator Vicente Saadi (first vice president) stepped down. Saadi was later reinstated as "honorary and effective president," but resigned again after the poor showing of the Orthodox candidates in 1987.

21. For instance, in the province of Buenos Aires, the Renovators' slate of candidates overwhelmed the Orthodox slate by almost three to one.

22. Cafiero became president; Menem, vice president; José María Vernet, first vice president; Roberto García, second vice president; Grosso, secretary-general; and José Manuel de la Sota, political secretary.

23. For instance, rather than an urban industrial worker from Buenos Aires, Cavallo was the son of middle-class immigrants in the not-so-Peronist province of Córdoba. Rather than resist the military dictatorship, Cavallo served as a government official under the military government (1981 and 1982). Rather than a statist-populist, Cavallo was a market-oriented economist and president of one of Argentina's most market-oriented think-tanks (IEERAL) (see Corrales 1997).

invited Cavallo to run for the National Congress as a Peronist-associate in 1987. The crisis within the PJ and the search for a winning formula explains this surprising invitation. The PJ's electoral performance in Córdoba in the 1980s was ghastly. The PJ's image in the province was so negative that no one in the party, not even the Renovators, could easily recruit prominent local figures to run for office under the PJ banner. In addition, the PJ in Córdoba, as in the rest of the country, needed figures to appeal to the middle class and to the "new Center" (see Levitsky 1999a). To address these deficiencies, a Renovator from Córdoba, José Manuel de la Sota, persuaded Cavallo to join the PJ and run for office (Santoro 1994).

In Venezuela, bringing a Cavallo into AD would have been unthinkable. AD's Orthodox remained in control of the party structure throughout the 1980s, because of the disconnection between power holding and contestation. The need to fill party positions, so acute in the PJ, was a moot point for AD. Actually, because AD was enjoying a "power feast," party leaders had incentives to raise, rather than lower, barriers to entry. It was hard enough for militant Adecos to obtain leadership positions, let alone for individuals with non-Adeco backgrounds. Stricter admission standards and opportunities for upward mobility in AD further precluded leadership renovation. Thus the old leaders of the 1960s were still in the CEN in the 1980s (e.g., Gonzalo Barrios, Luis Alfaro Ucero, Octavio Lepage, and Manuel Peñalver). The only challenge occurred late in the Lusinchi administration and only from within—Pérez's victory in the 1987 primaries. And yet this victory did not displace the Orthodoxy because of the restrictions in elite rotation already discussed.[24] Stricter admission standards also encouraged "brain drain." Many young, highly trained professionals quit the party, or did not even try to join it, since they knew that the prospects for upward mobility within it were bleak.

Again, party permeability within the PJ did not mean the predominance of neoliberal thinking, but it did mean the availability of individuals with softer commitments to "old Peronism." The opposite was the case in AD, in which increasing cartelization in the 1980s reduced the availability of ideological and programmatic "experimenters."

24. AD's secretary-general and leading anti-*Perecista*, Manuel Peñalver, resigned shortly after Pérez's triumph in the primaries. Elections for secretary-general were held, and Orthodox leader Humberto Celli beat the more conciliatory Pedro París Montesino, although by a very small margin (Lauría, interview). Thus the party remained in the hands of Orthodox leaders, although their grip on power was also unstable and weak.

The Heterogeneity (and Hence Fragility) of the Renovators

Although the crisis of hegemony in the PJ had led to leadership change, the new leadership never had a chance to develop a firm grip on power. Their grip on power was neither unified nor secured. This fragility was compounded by the fact that most Renovators had very few real constituents. For the bulk of the Peronist rank-and-file, especially union members, the Renovators were too white-collar. Indeed, the Renovators saw themselves as modernized social democrats, à la Felipe González in Spain. This had little appeal among the PJ core rank-and-file. For them, the moderate and sophisticated discourse made the Renovators "look too much like the Radicals" (Kohan, interview). Moreover, the fact that Renovators had displaced the preferred leaders (the Orthodoxy) of the unions and embraced an anti-union discourse further alienated a crucial sector of the party's base.

In short, the PJ in general, and its Renovator leadership, remained in flux. It was a leadership that lacked cohesiveness and organized constituents. This was fertile ground for yet another political takeover—which Menem carried out in 1988. Menem challenged Cafiero's nomination for the presidency, which had the support of most PJ leaders and governors.[25] He did this by mobilizing the forsaken and resentful Orthodox constituency with promises to reconquer a place for them in the party.[26] Few Renovators sided with Menem in the July 1988 primaries, but many endorsed him during the campaign. This was also the result of Cafiero's loose grip and the Renovators' less entrenched loyalties.

Different Opponents

The internal party detractors of Menem and Pérez at the start of the reforms differed not just in their initial enthusiasm for the Executive, but more fundamentally, in their political values. Menem's detractors were the Renovators; Pérez's detractors were the Orthodox. This too contributed to the variation in centrifugality in Executive–ruling party relations in the 1990s.

By mobilizing the party's orthodox rank-and-file against the Renovator leadership, Menem incurred a political debt that, at one level, tied his hands. Menem's supporters were precisely the sectors of the party that contained the most cost-bearers. But at another level, this gave Menem a "more responsible"

---

25. Sixteen of twenty-two provinces had Peronist governors; thirteen of them supported Cafiero.

26. Menem's platform "picked up" everything that the Renovators abandoned (Cerruti 1993). "*Menemism* became a mix of leftists and right-wingers, of nationalists without votes and local caudillos without scruples" (Morales Solá 1990, 90).

internal opposition. Having the most democratic, rule-respecting, change-experimenting wing of the party as the core of his internal opposition served Menem well during the reform process. It meant that his party detractors would react less disruptively. As a Renovator, Cafiero had always advocated a more cooperative attitude toward the Executive office. An Orthodox opposition would have given Menem much more trouble. This is clear from the Venezuelan case, where Pérez's detractors were the traditionalists. The hallmark of the Orthodoxy (in both Venezuela and Argentina) was hard posturing against challengers and questionable esteem for electoral processes.[27] Pérez's detractors (unlike Menem's) were thus less "awed" by Pérez's electoral comeback.

Returning to Power versus Losing Power: Dependence on the State and the 1989 Disjuncture

One final variable that mattered was differences in levels of dependence on state sinecures. Since the mid-1940s, the PJ had been in the opposition for thirty-four years; AD had been a ruling party for more than twenty-three. This amounted to a significant difference in each party's level of dependence on state resources—high for AD, low for the PJ. Thus 1989 marked a crucial turning point in the political trajectories of the PJ and AD. For the PJ, it marked a return to power after thirteen years in the opposition. For AD, it marked the end to five years of intense state-party fusion. This explains why the reforms of the 1990s hurt AD more.

AD won the presidency in 1989 with a remarkably high 55.6 percent of the vote, but it lost its majority in Congress. As Pérez remarked, "In 1989 I won, but the party lost" (interview). In reality, AD lost much more than Congress: it lost control of the state. Pérez launched not only a process of state shrinking, but also a policy of party neglect. Just as AD was asked to engage in more political competition (e.g., the December 1989 elections for the governorships), it was being denied the resources to compete that it had always enjoyed—state sinecures.

Menem's 1989 triumph, however, represented the return of Peronist glory. Menem brought back not only the masses to the PJ, but most important, the state. A party that had long been deprived of these two trophies was

27. In fact, the Orthodox attempted to stop Pérez's candidacy by proposing further restrictions in contestation. For instance, Secretary-General Manuel Peñalver distributed a leaflet among AD leaders claiming that AD's founding father, Rómulo Betancourt, never pursued reelection. Peñalver wrote: "But I guess that not all politicians have the vision" that Betancourt had (in Carvallo and López Maya 1987).

bound to feel more grateful to the leader who reclaimed them. In addition, a party with lower dependence on state resources was bound to see the reforms as less costly. The new administration, even with its call for a smaller state, was still far preferable to the status quo ante, which was political oblivion for the party as a whole.

Menem's recovery of the masses and the state was not sufficient to counter the centrifugal forces in Executive–ruling party relations. At one level, the PJ's return to power introduced new tensions. The PJ returned to office with a "splurge" mentality, desperate to indulge in the privileges of governing, hence its initial distaste for the reforms. Menem's challenge was to contain the state-exploiting proclivities of a power-hungry party that had long been waiting for the opportunity to take control. His initial response to the party's splurge mentality was to deny it opportunities for splurging (party neglecting), which intensified the animosity in Executive–ruling party relations that the reforms triggered. Once he allowed some room for party indulgences (the switch to party accommodating), tensions with the ruling party eased.

Conclusion: Mitigating and Exacerbating Institutional Factors

It is now possible to return to the initial questions: why did Pérez and Menem adopt a similar policy of party neglect at the start of the reforms? Why did Menem (but not Pérez) later change toward a party-accommodating policy? The answer to the first question is a combination of hubris, technocratic advice, and demagoguery. Hubris mattered in that both Menem and Pérez seriously believed that they could carry out the reforms alone. Both leaders had taken power without the support of the party leadership, and they estimated that they could similarly conquer the economy. Technocratic advice mattered in that many high-level technocrats, disdainful of all things political, at first recommended avoiding close alliances with populist/clientelistic parties to avoid sending inconsistent signals. Demagoguery mattered in that these presidents thought that bashing parties, or at least appearing to act independent of parties, would score popularity points among an electorate that exhibited anti-party sentiments. Finally, the policy was an understandable response to a party that had strong reservations about market reforms.

The answer to the second question, however, is different. Halfway into the reforms, Menem discovered that the party was somewhat responsive to Executive overtures. This is explained by the variables discussed in this chapter. The tension in Executive–ruling party relations in both cases shared mitigating and

Table 11.1   Mitigating and Exacerbating Factors in Executive–Ruling Party Dislocation, circa 1989

A. Mitigating Factors		
Common to both	Stronger in or unique to:	
	Argentina	Venezuela
Party is weak vis-à-vis the Executive	• Party leadership controlled by Renovators • Party leadership, structure, and ideology in flux • Availability of policy experimenters among leadership ranks • Outside alliances were unappealing (due to history of low inter-party cooperation)	• Long tradition of democratic centralism in the party (granting the Executive autonomy and curtailing the autonomy of mid-level leadership)
B. Exacerbating Factors		
Executive pursues party-neglecting policies	• Party comes to office with a splurge mentality • Rivalries among bandwagoners (Celestes vs. Rojo Punzó)	• Party returns to office with poor electoral showing (low majority status in Congress) • Leadership controlled by the Orthodox wing • Historical discontinuity (from "power feast" under Lusinchi to "party neglect" under Pérez) • No prior crisis of hegemony • Issue of corruption intensified party fears • Availability of outside partners (history of cooperation with COPEI)

exacerbating factors, as Table 11.1 details. However, the net balance of mitigating factors was greater in Argentina, whereas the net balance of exacerbating factors was greater in Venezuela. Some of these mitigating circumstances were the result of peculiarities in the cases (e.g., AD was historically a more institutionalized party than the PJ). Others, however, were the result of predictable forces. This is the case of the process of transformation that the PJ underwent along "Downsian" lines: electoral setbacks triggered a search for new winning formulas, which in turn softened internal rigidities.

Given these mitigating circumstances, Menem found possibilities for reconstructing Executive—ruling party relations. The party's response to Menem's initial overtures (e.g., the March 1991 party congress) was positive, which in turn reaffirmed Menem's decision to persevere in his new party-accommodating approach. In contrast, when Pérez made comparable overtures in 1991 (e.g., allowing the party to scrutinize the privatization process), the party's response was more circumspect: it agreed to the privatization of CANTV but not much else. Pérez's overtures were too little (given the gravity of Executive—ruling party relations) and too late (given how long Pérez waited to address party grievances).

This is not to say, however, that the task of realigning the party with the Executive in Argentina was easy or inevitable. Not every sector of the party responded gracefully to Menem's overtures. Curtailing the "splurge mentality" of a power-hungry PJ was challenging. Menem could have prolonged his policy of neglect and forever alienated the party. The Executive and the party were indeed heading toward a showdown in 1991. Menem seriously considered disbanding Congress. Menem and Pérez, therefore, had to address similar problems in dealing with their parties. Pérez's obstacles might have been more onerous, but they were not insurmountable, and Menem's possibilities might have been more numerous, but he could have easily missed them, as in fact he did during the first part of his administration.

To recapitulate, market-oriented economic reforms impose common costs and risks among ruling parties. The PJ, however, was better prepared than AD to assimilate those costs and risks. Centrifugal forces in Executive—ruling party relations were simply more intense in Venezuela. Two sets of institutional factors explain this.

One is a historical-institutional difference: variation in interparty collaboration. Political scientists tend to agree that polarization undermines governability. However, in situations of Executive—ruling party dislocation, such as the ones generated by market reforms, high levels of interparty collaboration (as in Venezuela) might actually undermine governability. This is counterintuitive, but nonetheless real. Low levels of interparty collaboration encourage dissent within the ruling party. Easier prospects of collaborating with the opposition gives dissenting ruling party members external partners as well as an external refuge that cushion the risk of challenging the Executive.

However, interparty collaboration is not a complete explanation. It cannot account for the fact that AD avoided an internal split as happened in the 1960s and as this argument would predict. In addition, it cannot account for the fact that few Peronists actually engaged in open dissent and defection once a more "politically viable" external ally and refuge became available (the Frente Grande in 1993). It cannot explain either why in the past party polarization did not prevent Executive–ruling party tensions under previous Peronist administrations.

A more powerful explanation for the variation in centrifugality in Executive–ruling party relations is the transformation of the PJ and the stagnation of AD prior to the reforms. This was the result of three variables: (1) internal fluidity (medium-high in the PJ, low in AD), (2) exposure to both internal and external contestation (high in the PJ, low in AD), and (3) external shocks in the form of electoral defeats (high in the PJ, low in AD). The result was transformation in the PJ, what this chapter described as a crisis of hegemony that weakened internal structures further. Electoral shocks triggered a process of change; internal fluidity made it possible.

Elements of this transformation were predictable for any party experiencing a crisis of hegemony. Old structures were dismantled, ideologies became more elastic, policy experimenters gained more space in the party, and loyalties became less entrenched. In addition, the PJ became more accustomed to internal heterogeneity—in its program and in its membership. When Menem increased this heterogeneity by welcoming non-Peronists after 1989, the PJ exhibited less revulsion, unlike the Adecos, who never forgave Pérez for his "non-Adeco" cabinet. In short, a more internally fluid party that was less bound to the past was more likely to adjust to the circumstances.

Other aspects of the PJ's transformation in the 1980s were less predictable, but nonetheless fortuitous for Menem, such as the rise of a more moderate and democratic leadership. The rise of a new leadership was to be expected, but there was nothing that guaranteed that this leadership would be more moderate and rule-conforming. This accidental change in values conferred on Menem a more responsible and adaptive internal opposition.

Furthermore, the PJ's lesser dependence on the state, by virtue of its many years in the opposition, made the PJ more likely to accept the post-1989 situation. Even Menem's smaller state and not-so-indulgent attitude toward the party were far more acceptable to party leaders than the status quo ante—no control of the state and no electoral dominance.

In contrast, AD spent the 1980s enjoying a "power feast," with solid control of the state, protected from political threats, and spared the ordeal of a crisis of hegemony. After the fat years of the 1980s, the party was bound to feel more intensely the lean years of the 1990s. Because AD faced no need to change (that is to say, to find a winning formula), it underwent no change. Leadership structures remained entrenched; ideologies, fixed; and admission standards, strict. If anything, the party moved further away from internal liberalization. The leadership further cartelized under the sectors of the party that were most attached to old ideas of statism and democratic centralism. AD remained closed to new ideas at a time when Venezuela was declining and other nations were experimenting with market-oriented solutions. Already a highly ossified party, AD ended the 1980s even more ossified and thus less adaptable.

Party transformation in the PJ and nontransformation in AD also contributed to the different Executive policies toward the ruling party in the 1990s. Menem was able to find a supply of policy experimenters within the party, who in turn could be recruited to carry out the reforms and, simultaneously, establish links with the rest of the party, a luxury not that available to Pérez in 1989. This made Pérez more inclined to pursue party neglect. Pérez did not need to ignore the party to the extent that he did, but he could not incorporate the party into his administration to the extent that party leaders wanted either.

These propositions have implications for our understanding of how democratic institutions contribute to the rise of market institutions and, more specifically, to economic change. One common argument stresses that democracy contributes to market reforms because it encourages stable and transparent rules, which markets need in order to thrive (e.g., Domínguez and Purcell 1999; Chapter 1). Another common argument is that democracy facilitates market reforms because it allows for nonreformers to be voted out of office, making room for new officials (e.g., Remmer 1991b). This chapter suggests an alternative route through which democracy helps economic change—namely, political parties. High degrees of democracy within and around parties facilitate economic transformations. The higher incidence of electoral contestation in the PJ relative to AD in the 1980s exposed the party to change pressures that precluded entrenchment of old practices. These pressures were painful for the PJ. They could have produced a number of different outcomes. But without them, party adaptation in the 1990s would have been less likely. This is clear from Venezuela, where AD experienced almost no electoral contests from mid-1984, remaining insulated from potential pressures to self-transform.

Democracy matters for economic change, perhaps more at the level of parties than at the level of the regime at large. Both Argentina and Venezuela were fairly democratic at the national regime level, but unequally democratic at the party level. This latter difference contributed to party adaptation in Argentina, and hence governability because it softened the internal rigidities that often prevent parties from adapting to new external circumstances.

PART FOUR

the
state-without-party
condition
in latin america

12

the

"state-without-party /

party-without-state"

condition

latin

america

in the

1990s

The argument of this book can now be integrated into a unified theoretical proposition: whenever a state lacks the support of a strong ruling party or, alternatively, whenever a dominant party fails to gain access to the state, political turmoil is likely. In the case of a state without a party, the turmoil will consist of severe conflicts between the state and society during reform implementation. In the case of a dominant party without a state, the turmoil will be located mostly within the party in the form of a crisis of hegemony. Table 12.1 summarizes this "state-without-party / party-without-state" proposition.

Table 12.1   The "Party-Without-State / State-Without-Party" Argument

Case	Independent Variable	Dependent Variable
Argentina 1983–87	**Party without state**: The PJ suffers unprecedented and unexpected electoral defeats (1983 and 1985).	**Crisis of hegemony**: Party leaders wrestle over a new winning formula, giving rise to changes in ideology, structure, and leadership.
Venezuela 1983–89	**Party with state**: AD wins the 1983 elections and is incorporated fully into the state apparatus.	**No crisis**: Party remains exempt from pressure to change.
Early Stages of Reform		
Argentina June 1989– mid-1991	**Party and state begin to unite**: Electoral success of 1989 helps to placate the crisis within the PJ, but prevailing party-neglecting policies slow down the resolution of crisis.	**Crisis of hegemony subsides but not completely**: The result is tense Executive–ruling party relations, hurting reform sustainability. However, opportunities exist for an Executive–ruling party rapprochement.
Venezuela Jan 1989– Aug 1991	**Party and state begin to separate**: AD wins presidential elections but feels detached from the state as a result of reforms and party-neglecting policies.	**Crisis of hegemony erupts**: The result is tense Executive–ruling party relations, hurting reform implementation.
Culmination of Reforms		
Argentina late 1991–95	**State with party**: The Executive adopts a party-accommodating strategy. The PJ feels integrated in reform governance.	**Harmonious Executive–ruling party relations**: The crisis within the party ends. The party endorses the reforms. Political instability in state-society relations declines or is managed by the state
Venezuela late 1991– mid-1993	**State without a party**: AD breaks completely with Pérez and his reforms.	**Hostile Executive–ruling party relations**: The ensuing power vacuum exacerbates state-society conflicts.

Peronism between 1983 and 1989 epitomized the party-without-state condition. Its historic 1983 and 1985 electoral defeats, which effectively blocked its access to state office, led to a crisis of hegemony that culminated in party transformation. In contrast, AD experienced a level of state-party fusion in the 1980s that was unprecedented in its history, blocking all impetus for internal transformation.

Between 1989 and 1991, the PJ began to experience a relaxation—but not a full resolution—of the party-without-state condition. The party and the state began to unite as a result of the party's return to office. However, the launch of market reforms (which reduced the party's control over the economy and the state), coupled with Menem's party-neglecting policies, ensured that the party remained detached from the state. Consequently, the crisis inside the party subsided relative to the 1980s, but not completely: the party developed internal divisions, suffered an identity crisis, and vacillated in supporting the Executive. The crisis within the party made the party unsuitable as a governing ally, thereby impairing reform sustainability. To survive, the Executive resorted to "reform rescue" measures (e.g., decretism, rushed privatizations, and threats to use the military against protesters and to close down Congress).

In Venezuela (1989–91), the state and the party began to grow apart, coming close to the same state-without-party condition prevalent in Argentina. At first, the separation was not absolute: AD was still the ruling party. But the launch of the reforms, together with the president's party-neglecting policies, led AD to think that it was losing access to the state. This precipitated an internal crisis in AD, which only served to corroborate the Executive's initial hunch that AD was unsuitable as a governing ally. A vicious circle emerged: party-neglecting policies fueled a party crisis, which in turn, justified the Executive's continuation of party-neglecting policies.

By mid-1991, Argentina had moved toward the party-with-state condition. By addressing crucial political grievances of the party, Menem succeeded in obtaining a "negotiated consent" from the PJ to deepen the reforms. The emergent harmony in Executive–ruling party relations transformed state-society relations. Skeptics had fewer reasons to doubt the state; cost-bearers were deprived of viable political allies; and anti-establishment sectors faced slim chances of overthrowing the state. Governability thus received a major boost. In Venezuela, however, where the Executive never adopted a policy of accommodating the ruling party, the crisis within the party deepened, culminating in the revolt of the orthodox. Governability suffered a major blow. Hostility in Executive–ruling party relations gave skeptics more reason than ever to mistrust the government's capacity to sustain the reforms, gave cost-bearers more reason to feel that their plight was justified, and anti-establishment groups, more opportunities to take center stage. Following the February 1992 coup attempt, an isolated Executive had little option but to yield to a vigorously anti-reform and vindictive party.

The state-without-party condition was thus a crucial impediment to reform implementation in Argentina and Venezuela—but not just there. It has been equally damaging to other Latin American countries. The state-without-party condition could very well be one of the most serious obstacles to governance in Latin America. Numerous administrations in Latin America have attempted to introduce reforms in a state-without-party context. Inevitably, the result has been setbacks in reform sustainability.

Market Reforms and Democracy in Latin America in the 1990s

In the late 1990s, scholars both sympathetic to and critical of market reforms reached the conclusion that Latin America had undergone a "silent" neoliberal revolution (Stallings and Peres 2000; Oxhorn and Ducatenzeiler 1999; Yergin and Stanislaw 1998; Glade 1998; IDB 1996; Edwards 1995). The assumption is that while Latin American countries at the end of the 1990s differ in the extent to which they advanced certain economic reforms, there was a fair degree of "convergence" in the overall picture, namely, that there was an overall shift to market economies (Morley et al. 1999; Varas 1995). A consensus emerged that Latin America essentially completed the "first generation reforms" (economic stabilization and restructuring) and was ready to embark on the so-called second-generation reforms intended to address areas such as income inequality and inefficient delivery of social services (Stallings and Peres 2000; Korzeniewicz and Smith 2000; Pastor and Wise 1999a).

However, there is a risk of overstating these assumptions. In many countries, the transition to market economies has been neither silent nor particularly far-reaching. At times, the transition has come with a rise in political instability, political paralysis, reform reversal, and democratic erosion. Figure 8 ranks most major Latin American administrations that initiated market reforms in the 1990s according to two dimensions: (1) political freedom and (2) degree of market opening near the end of their terms in office.

The ranking on political freedom comes from the Freedom House World Survey, which ranks countries according to the extent of political and civil

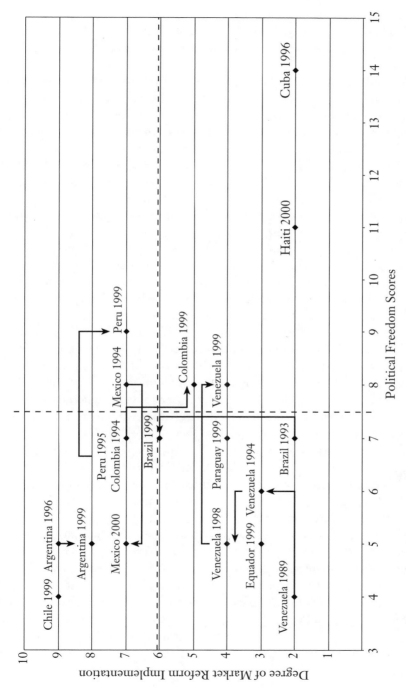

Fig. 8   Latin America: political freedoms and market reforms in the 1990s

rights enjoyed by citizens. Although the methodology of the Freedom House ranking has been criticized for being too "overspecific" (Munck and Verkuilen 2000), it is useful for this purpose because, unlike other rankings, it covers the entire 1990s.

The ranking on degree of market opening is my own assessment based on overall levels of economic freedom according to the Heritage Foundation ranking, openness of deregulation (a subset of the former), inflation rates for the country and in relation to the region, fiscal deficits, private investment as a share of the GDP, and accumulated value of privatizations. Looking at all these indicators together provides a more complete panorama of the extent of market opening. Based on those indicators, I have ranked administrations in terms of degree of market opening (see Appendix 4).

Figure 8 reveals two important trends in the 1990s. First, there is significant variation in the extent to which Latin American countries achieved democracy and market opening. Countries can be classified according to four categories: (1) high democracy and high market opening (upper left quadrant); (2) low democracy and high market opening (upper right quadrant); (3) low democracy and low market opening (lower right quadrant); and (4) high democracy and low market opening (lower left quadrant).

The second observation is that some countries experienced moves along these dimensions. Some countries changed positions regarding their levels of democracy. For instance, a deep economic reformer such as Mexico improved its democratic standing, whereas a deep economic reformer such as Peru underwent a democratic decline. In addition, a poor economic reformer such as Venezuela experienced democratic decline (from 1989 to 1994), followed by a democratic renewal (1994–98), and then another decline (1998–2000). Other countries changed position regarding their degree of market opening. For instance, Colombia became less market-oriented in the 1990s, whereas Brazil became much more market-oriented. All this corroborates the idea, discussed in Chapter 2, that there is no obligatory relationship between democracy and market reforms.

What Figure 8 does not convey, but is nonetheless an important part of the politics of market reforms in the 1990s, is the degree of political instability during the implementation period. Some democratic countries experienced high political instability such as coup attempts, impeachments, recurrent street protests, and political violence (Venezuela from 1992 through 1994, Ecuador since 1994, Paraguay since 1995, Colombia since 1994). And some less democratic countries are more stable than others (compare Cuba, for example, with Haiti).

How can this variation in levels of democracy, market opening, and political stability be explained? I contend that the state-without-party condition is the key to this puzzle.

The State-Without-Party Condition in Latin America

The state-without-party condition emerges whenever either of the following two situations is present. One is a rebellion from within a ruling party that has been historically strong, as happened in Venezuela under Pérez. The second occurs when the Executive wins office by means of a loose, ad hoc coalition of minor political forces and movements or last-minute coalition building. Either condition—a rebellion of the ruling party or a last-minute fabrication of a ruling party—bodes trouble.

The state-without-party condition confronts Executives with a difficult governability problem—the lack of suitable political allies capable of shielding and connecting the state. Presidents simply find it impossible to reform the economy in such isolation. Executives will respond to the state-without-party condition in multiple ways, each with significant economic as well as political consequences, shaping both the degree of market opening and the health of democratic institutions. The list of cases discussed is not exhaustive, but it is representative of the variety of responses.

The State-Without-Party Condition, Version 1

The first type of state-without-party condition occurs whenever a dislocation in Executive–ruling party relations surfaces. Any reform-minded Executive that comes to office with the support of a dominant party is susceptible to this. A sector of the ruling party will resent the reforms and will try to curtail the autonomy of the Executive. The outcome of this dislocation will have significant political repercussions. These are some possible outcomes:

1. Reform-minded Executives alleviate this dislocation through party-accommodating strategies—the Menem (1991–97) response. This boosts reform sustainability, but it also leaves illiberal gaps in the reform process.
2. Reform-minded Executives fail to solve the dislocation in Executive–ruling party relations and consequently confront a showdown with the party. Two scenarios are possible:

a. either the orthodox sectors of the party strike, forcing the Executive to yield completely; or

b. the Executive strikes against the party and the party system. Either scenario may imperil reform sustainability.

3. Executives can avoid a showdown with the orthodox sector by yielding to them preemptively. This response produces the most watered-down economic reform possible and vindicates anti-reform political sectors. The effect on political stability is hard to predict. On the one hand, the reduction of Executive–ruling party tensions tends to contain state-society tensions. On the other hand, the failure to control the economic crisis can fuel state-society tensions.

The following sections contain examples of each of these outcomes.

Harmonizing Executive–Ruling Party Relations: Mexico (1988–1994)

Perhaps the case that resembles Argentina (1991–97) the most is Mexico (1988–94). Much has been written about Mexico's market-oriented reforms, among the most far-reaching in the world. It is often said that the Mexican state achieved reform sustainability by seeking the support of extra-partisan allies: technocrats and new societal groups that were either reform "winners" or simply marginalized sectors of society, at the expense of traditionalist sectors of the PRI (see Golob 1997, Gibson 1997, Grindle 1996, Centeno 1994, Teichman 1995, and Heredia 1994). However, I propose a different interpretation: Mexico's market reforms were made possible—and shaped by—the Executive's efforts to accommodate, rather than suppress, the internal dissent within the PRI.

Salinas had a more difficult time achieving harmony in Executive–ruling party relations than Menem, in part because the divisions in the party and the impacts of the reforms were more complicated than is the case on parties operating in more democratic settings. Mexico was one of the least democratic regimes in Latin America in the 1980s (see Chapter 4). The PRI had enjoyed a stranglehold over the political system for more than sixty years. Market reforms split the PRI not just along the issue of the desirability of economic liberalization and inclusion into decision making but also on the desirability of overall political liberalization.

In the 1980s, two factions emerged in the PRI holding different views on each of these options (Table 12.2). One faction was unenthusiastic about both economic and political liberalization—Quadrant IV, pejoratively called the dinosaurs. Another faction was enthusiastic about economic liberalization but

Table 12.2   Mexico: Economic and Political Preferences of Political Parties, 1980s

		Economic Liberalization	
		Enthusiastic	Hesitant
Political Liberalization	Enthusiastic	Quadrant I PAN	Quadrant II
	Hesitant	Quadrant III PRI (*técnicos*)	Quadrant IV PRI (dinosaurs)

less so about political liberalization—Quadrant III, the *técnicos*. This group occupied positions in the most autonomous government agencies (the Central Bank and the Finance Ministry) (see Heredia 1994). In the 1980s, this group gained ground, conquering the presidency with the rise of the Miguel de la Madrid administration (1982–88). To complicate matters, de la Madrid also confronted a rising opposition party, the PAN, which advocated both economic and political liberalization—Quadrant I (see Chand 2001).

De la Madrid responded to this dual challenge—an internal split in the PRI and the rise of the PAN—by pushing ahead with economic liberalization, but also by acceding to one crucial demand of the dinosaurs: slowing down political liberalization. De la Madrid adopted a hard-line position vis-à-vis the PAN and electoral fraud (Morris 1995, 141). But this proved insufficient to placate the PRI dinosaurs because it did not necessarily make room for them—there was no accommodation of the dinosaur's desire to have greater political power (see Baer 1993, 53–54). In some ways, de la Madrid had the same effect that Pérez had in Venezuela: he inaugurated the party-without-state crisis in Mexico. Consequently, Executive–ruling party relations deteriorated.

By 1986, Quadrant IV experienced an internal split of its own. A faction emerged clamoring for more internal democratization of the PRI and accountability for the Executive, the so-called Democratic Current, led by Cuauhtémoc Cárdenas. De la Madrid's selection of another member of Quadrant III as his successor in the presidency, the *técnico* Carlos Salinas de Gortari, further infuriated everyone in Quadrant IV. Accusing the government of "betraying the Revolution" (Centeno 1994, 49), the *Cardenistas* left the PRI and formed a new party, the PRD. This meant the entry of a new political force in Mexican politics—occupying Quadrant II. The PRD advocated political liberalization (in order to defeat the PRI) and little economic liberalization.

Those "dinosaurs" who stayed in the PRI now faced a double threat: the rising *técnicos* in the PRI and the defecting PRD. Turmoil inside the PRI escalated as the party approached the 1988 elections. In the last months of his

Table 12.3   Mexico: Economic and Political Preferences of Political Parties, post-1988

		Economic Liberalization	
		Enthusiastic	Hesitant
Political Liberalization	Enthusiastic	Quadrant I PAN, PRI ("*modernos*")	Quadrant II PRD
	Hesitant	Quadrant III PRI (Salinas in 1988)	Quadrant IV PRI (dinosaurs)

administration, de la Madrid faced the most uncooperative Congress in decades. Labor leaders were openly calling for a complete abandonment of economic models (Burgess 2000; Centeno 1994, 15; Adler Lomnitz, Lomnitz-Adler, and Adler 1990, 20).

By 1988, yet another faction began to emerge within the PRI—supporters of both economic and political liberalization (see Table 12.3). This new group (the *modernos*) argued that the party's best chance to regain legitimacy and recover votes was to portray an image of a newly revamped political party, willing to embrace competitive politics (see Colosio 1993). A new faction of the PRI thus made its way into Quadrant I.

Carlos Salinas de Gortari (1988–94), originally committed to Quadrant III, faced attacks from every quadrant of the political system (the PAN and the PRI *modernos* in Quadrant I, the PRD in II, and the PRI dinosaurs in IV). He recognized that it would be difficult to continue with de la Madrid's hard-line position toward the opposition, but he also recognized the need to reunite the party (PRI operators were refusing to mobilize voters to attend Salinas's campaign rallies) (Coppedge 1993, 132).

His response to these challenges was to accommodate each of the two major factions inside the PRI. More so than de la Madrid, Salinas took "excruciating pains to keep the ruling party united" (Castañeda 2000, 90). He deployed a sophisticated policy of party accommodation. He catered to the *modernos* by deepening economic reforms started by de la Madrid and by overturning de la Madrid's more blatant hard-line policies toward the political opposition. But he also catered to the dinosaurs, a point often overlooked by many analysts. Although Salinas took away some of the old privileges of the PRI's old guard, he also preserved many of their organizational and political privileges.

Salinas went beyond simply giving the traditionalists space within his administration (that is to say, positions in the cabinet, local/gubernatorial offices, and party congresses). He also compromised some economic objectives to please them. For instance, the government abandoned its intention to reduce annual inflation below 10 percent, allowing it to hover between 18 and 20 percent, in order to satisfy the party's demand for fiscally stimulated economic growth (see Baer 1993, 57, and Buendia 1996, 559). Other concessions included the non-liberalization of the financial sector, which contradicted the logic of trade liberalization with the United States, but which protected some of the PRI's major financiers (Kessler 1998); the nonflexibilization of labor markets, which protected many PRI-friendly unions;[1] the nonliberalization of petrochemicals and energy, which protected a source of state income for the PRI; and the mishandling of interest rates in 1994, which satisfied the traditionalists' desire for a loose monetary policy during an election year, but which also provoked the 1994–95 Tequila Crisis (Kessler 2000).[2]

More important, the Executive devoted significant resources to enhancing the party's capacity to compete electorally (in contrast to de la Madrid's strategy of simply denying victories to the opposition) (Colosio 1993). Salinas injected massive resources into the PRI's electoral campaigns (ibid., 93–104). The 1993–94 electoral code reforms established very high ceilings for private contributions (approximately U.S.$65,000 for an individual contribution, as compared to a maximum of U.S.$20,000 in the United States), allowing the PRI to outspend its rivals (Cornelius 1996, 58). Another electoral booster was PRONASOL (Programa Nacional de Solidaridad), a huge state program with a U.S.$3 billion budget nominally intended to fight poverty through public works, but de facto, a populist machine to enhance the PRI's electoral chances. Essentially, the government used proceeds from Mexico's vast privatization to fund PRONASOL (Kessler 1998, 52). PRONASOL's first leader was a PRI traditionalist, Manuel Tello. Its budget was targeted to areas where the PRI had experienced electoral defeats (e.g., Michoacán, Juchitán, Oaxaca) (Dresser 1991). Although monies went from the president's office directly to local offices, thereby bypassing some traditional "corporatist" party chiefs, PRONASOL monies constituted nonetheless a huge overture to the party because it provided "investments" in the geographic areas where the PRI was electorally needy (Centeno 1994, 65; Cornelius 1996, 59), or where the PRD was strong (Horcasitas and Weldon 1994). Although PRONASOL was

1. There were other concessions to unions. The telephone workers' union, for instance, accepted the privatization of Telmex in return for a lucrative share deal for its members (*The Economist*, October 23, 1999, 35). Salinas refused to reform the closed shop, whereby only one union is recognized in each company. He allowed the leading labor union, the Confederation of Mexican Workers (CTM), to become the dominant union in export-oriented industries, an area where the CTM had had little representation in the past. And toward the end of his administration, Salinas restored "sectoral" (i.e., labor union) representation in party lists (see Burgess 2000).

not the panacea that Salinas had anticipated (many PRI corporatist chiefs resented it because it appeared to be a "parallel political party," see Baer 1993, 57–60, and Dresser 1994, 157), it is nonetheless a classic example of Salinas placing the goal of party building above the interest of neoliberalism.

Another dimension of Salinas's party-accommodating strategy was his policy of selective opening: "concerting and negotiating with the PAN, while isolating and undermining the support accruing to Cárdenas and the PRD" (Morris 1995, 98; see Camp 1999, 198). By siding with the PAN, Salinas accommodated the PRI *modernos*, who demanded more signs of a commitment to democratization. And by disfavoring the PRD, he catered to those PRI dinosaurs who disliked the PRD while simultaneously changing the expectations of those dinosaurs who still felt attracted to the PRD. As argued in Chapter 11, the extent of ruling party dissent can depend on the viability of external partners. If the PRD had been allowed to grow, its attractiveness to this group of PRI dinosaurs might have increased, further exacerbating the "leak" in the party.

The result was a negotiated settlement with the rebellious, disgruntled elements of the ruling party. In return for political concessions, the PRI dinosaurs agreed to economic reforms. The PRI dinosaurs began to look like the mirror image of the PRD—they accepted economic liberalization while still supporting slow progress on political liberalization. By mid-1991, the PRI was fully behind the slogan "Uno, dos, tres, Salinas otra vez" (Centeno 1994, 3). Perhaps in gratitude, Salinas's initial choice to succeed him as president was party-operative Luis Donaldo Colosio, preferred over the less PRI-friendly finance minister, Pedro Aspe, and the more antagonistic mayor of Mexico City, Manuel Camacho.[3]

2. In 1994, Mexico made the policy mistake of trying to defend the currency against devaluation pressure without ensuring fiscal restraint. The government increased spending, lowered interest rates, sterilized capital outflows, increased development bank lending, and replaced peso-denominated bonds with dollar-denominated securities (Starr 1999, 222). These fiscally loose policies were incompatible with the stated goal of defending the currency, but they were compatible with the goal of placating the PRI's old guard. The old guard disliked Salinas's initial choice to succeed him, Luis Donaldo Colosio, because he was seen as a direct continuation of Salinas. On the very day Colosio was assassinated, about twenty party veterans sent a letter to Salinas insisting on participating in the selection of Colosio's replacement, followed by pronouncements of support for a rival of Salinas's candidate (Starr 1999, 220). To preserve party unity, Salinas granted the old guard these policy concessions, together with influence over the coming campaign, often at the expense of some Salinas loyalists.

3. In an interview, Salinas was clear about what each of these candidates contributed politically to his administration. He praised Aspe for his international accomplishments, especially for reviewing "Mexico's stance with regard to our foreign debt." He praised Camacho for "govern-

Thus Salinas's legacy to his successor, President Ernesto Zedillo (1994–2000), was a fairly consolidated economic model that was mostly neoliberal, but still contained illiberal gaps (policy inconsistencies). He also left a more modernized party, but one that still provided a comfortable home for traditionalists. Much of Zedillo's task was precisely to deal with these inconsistencies both at the level of the economy and the party.

The Party Strikes Back: Paraguay (1993–1998)

Some of the most dramatic cases of reform sustainability problems in Latin America have occurred as a result of virulent rebellions from reform-resistant sectors of statist ruling parties. The pattern is similar to that of Venezuela (1989–93). The crisis within the party creates problems within the cabinet, within the legislature, and throughout society at large. The dissenting faction of the ruling party helps to galvanize—often even lead—opposition to the reforms. Facing gridlock, the Executive tends to respond by yielding to traditionalists, thereby compromising the reforms.

A clear example was Paraguay. President Juan Carlos Wasmosy (1993–98), of the populist-statist Asociación Nacional Republicana, better known as the Partido Colorado, unveiled a program of market reforms shortly after coming to office. This package included the typical structural economic changes of the Washington Consensus, with one added component—the demilitarization of state and party structures.[4] This gave rise to opposition from both sectors of the ruling Partido Colorado—the traditionalist civilians (led by Luis María Argaña) rejected the efforts to roll back the state, and the military sectors of the party (led by General Lino César Oviedo), who opposed the

---

ing Mexico City the way I asked him to." But only Colosio was praised for his party-accommodating skills. "As party president, Colosio immediately undertook a process of approaching the PRI constituency in each state of the republic and mending relations that had been strained by the conditions in which many legislators had lost in the 1988 elections. He worked intensely to support the candidates who had lost their respective elections and attended to those who, even having won, lacked the overwhelming majorities they had enjoyed in the past. It was necessary to bring them together and begin the internal restructuring of the party for the upcoming National Assembly. . . . He showed great ability to unify the party and knew how to use the work of the government in the party's favor, thereby facilitating the important election results [of 1991] that we achieved" (in Castañeda 2001, 215–17). Given a choice between an international economist, a controversial mayor, and a party operative, Salinas picked the last, which was consistent with his party-accommodating strategy.

4. In 1995, Wasmosy signed a pact with Congress banning the military affiliation with and involvement in the affairs of the party and reducing the size of the military budget. The military, however, got a hefty salary increase in return.

efforts to subordinate the military.[5] For a while, Wasmosy pursued a party-neglecting strategy (e.g., he hired Hernán Büchi, the architect of Pinochet's neoliberal reforms in the 1980s as his private economic adviser), which predictably aggravated the resentment of Colorado traditionalists.

Hostile Executive–ruling party relations in Paraguay hindered reform implementation. Wasmosy's supporters among Colorado legislators were a minority. Argaña began to encourage Colorado labor sectors to strike and protest against privatizations. He even pushed for a national referendum on privatizations as a way to stop them. In 1996, the party as a whole issued an official declaration against neoliberalism, privatizations, and Mercosur. At this point, the state began to suffer from the credibility gap typical of the state-without-party condition. Business support for the government, initially high, waned by 1996, as business groups complained about the failure of the government to carry out promised reforms. As the orthodox sectors of the Partido Colorado gained the upper hand, Wasmosy had no option but to begin to yield. Few privatizations were completed, wage increases were granted, and the number of state employees increased. Progress also slowed down in military reform. Although Wasmosy refused to impede Congress from pursuing military reform,[6] he agreed to many of Oviedo's demands, such as the construction of the lavish stadium for military parades, the so-called Linódromo (see Britez et al. 1996). Some generals were actually removed for criticizing Oviedo.

And yet party yielding failed to placate the orthodox sectors. In April 1996, Oviedo staged an unsuccessful coup d'etat, widely supported by most orthodox Colorados. Although the government defeated the coup, it lost in the September 1997 primaries to the very same forces. Oviedo came in first, followed by the anti-reform faction of Argaña, leaving the government's candidate, Carlos Facetti, in a humiliating third place. As in Venezuela, the turn from party neglecting to party yielding led to reform slowdown, with no real decline in political instability.

The Executive Strikes Back: Haiti (1994–1999)

An alternative resolution to hostility in Executive–ruling party relations is for the Executive to strike back. Frustrated by the internal bickering within the ruling party, and its effects on the cabinet, the legislature, and society at large,

---

5. On the authoritarian and populist history of the Colorado, see Rivarola 1991.
6. Interview with Carlos Mesán Galli, chief economic adviser to Wasmosy, July 10, 1995.

the Executive decides to strike against the party, usually by disrupting the electoral process. Pérez and Menem considered this option, but decided against it. The prime minister of Haiti, René Préval (1995–2001), went ahead. In January 1999, Préval dissolved Congress, postponed elections, and began to govern by decree. This was the culmination of a four-year struggle with his ruling party, the Lavalas Political Organization (LPO). Préval was elected in 1995 with an overwhelming 87 percent of the vote in Haiti's first election since a U.S. military force of 22,200 returned Jean Bertrand Aristide to power in 1994. Aristide himself hand-picked Préval. Problems for Préval began when, shortly after taking office, he announced sweeping market reforms. Previously, Aristide flirted briefly with market reforms (the so-called Emergency Economic Recovery), but quickly gave them up in the face of opposition from the LPO.[7] Préval, however, decided to try reforms. In 1996, he appointed a relatively pro-market prime minister, Rosny Smarth. The split within the LPO escalated. Aristide, who commanded the anti-reform faction of the LPO—the La Fanmi Lavalas (Bevan 1999, 225)—began to stir state-society conflicts, organizing "popular" groups and mounting general strikes. Soon, Aristide succeeded in getting Préval to yield (Morrell et al. 1999). In 1997, the La Fanmi Lavalas faction rigged the legislative/municipal elections, without much protest from Préval. Unwilling to tolerate Préval's acquiescence to Aristide, Prime Minister Smarth resigned (*The Economist*, June 14, 1997).

From this point on, the anti-Aristide faction of the party (the Organization of People in Struggle), which controlled the Senate, counterattacked by blocking almost any initiative coming from Préval. Essentially, Préval became caught between the anti-reform sector of the party led by Aristide and the anti-Aristide sector sitting in the Senate. The pro-Aristide faction created trouble in the streets; the senators created trouble in Executive-legislative business. Consequently, starting in 1997, Haiti began to operate without a prime minister, without a complete cabinet, without a budget, without any form of economic program, and with rising societal tensions. The internal factions of the Lavalas in parliament rejected every one of Préval's nominees for prime minister, which in one case consisted of a pro-reform, former Inter-American Development Bank officer (Eric Pierre). This "politics of no compromising" led to a serious deterioration of the economy (Morrell et al.

---

7. Toward the end of his administration, Aristide turned once again into a staunch critic of market reforms (*The Economist*, September 30, 1995). He did this in part to ingratiate himself with the majority in his party in order to get party support for a second term in office. Aristide's bid for a second term failed, but he nonetheless managed to emerge as the leader of the anti-reform wing of the party.

1999). Corruption, contraband, and pockets of famine proliferated. In January 1999, Lafanmi supporters even set up barricades in Port-au-Prince.

It was at this point that Préval responded by striking against the political system. Between 1997 and 2000, Préval postponed elections four times. The strike against elections and against Congress, and hence against his own party, was Préval's response to a state-without-party crisis. Party yielding to the anti-reform sectors had not worked. Neither the economy nor state-society relations had improved. Préval then proceeded to strike against the political system, producing one of the bluntest interruptions of democratic rule in the Americas in the 1990s.

The Executive Yields Preemptively: Cuba (1993–1999) and Colombia (1994–1998)

Yet another resolution to the Executive–ruling party dislocation is to surrender preemptively. The Executive simply yields to the orthodox sectors of the ruling party early on, before the dislocation in Executive–ruling party relations gets out of control. Cuba and Colombia are good examples of this response.

Facing one of the most dramatic economic collapses in the Western Hemisphere since the Depression (more than a 35 percent economic contraction in 1989–94), the communist government of Cuba was compelled in 1993 to introduce some market reforms: the decriminalization of dollar-holding, self-employment in a few trades, cooperativization of state farms, and full liberalization of foreign investment. Most of Cuba's international allies, trading partners, and even top economic officials, such as Carlos Lage, insisted on far deeper economic reforms (e.g., expanding self-employment and profit-making possibilities of Cuban citizens; privatizing or liquidating SOEs; and allowing the emergence of medium-sized, domestically owned private firms, capable of forming joint ventures with foreign investors). However, the reforms never went this far and, in fact, slowed down after 1996 (see Pastor 2000, 34–36).

Part of the explanation for this reform timidity is the Executive's decision to yield to the orthodox sectors of the ruling party almost from the start of the reforms. Since the 1991 Fourth Party Congress, the Cuban Communist Party had split into the typical two camps: the reformers and the orthodox. A more far-reaching economic reform, leading to fewer SOEs and fewer state employees, threatened the leadership of the communist party, which ran these SOEs (Pérez-Stable 1999, 71; Centeno and Font 1997; Inter-American Dialogue Task Force on Cuba 1995). Thus, orthodox sectors—essentially the bulk of the party leadership—wanted to set brakes on the reforms.

Castro responded by yielding to the orthodox.[8] Between 1991 and 1993, Castro simply refused to introduce any major economic reforms. When reforms were no longer postponable, Castro introduced very modest reforms in 1993–95, avoiding the most daring proposals advocated by some of his advisers. Furthermore, for every reform enacted, Castro also enacted an accompanying restriction that reinforced statism and circumscribed the liberalizing measure. For instance, the government allowed Cuban citizens to hold dollars, but also established a state-owned monopoly over retail, ensuring that only the state could capture such dollars. The government allowed citizens to become self-employed, but it also enacted heavy restrictions, ensuring that this market would remain quite small.[9] The government liberalized foreign investment, even permitting 100 percent foreign ownership of firms. Yet only one of Cuba's 370 foreign-owned companies is 100 percent foreign-owned,[10] assuring state involvement in the lucrative external sector. In addition, the state retained the monopoly over the staffing of these foreign companies. Foreign firms must hire their staff from a list drafted by state officials and communist party leaders. This allows the party to continue to reward loyalists with access to the best jobs in the country. Finally, the foreign-owned firms pay salaries to the Cuban government in dollars, and the government then pays the employees in pesos. This allows the state to pocket a significant profit derived from this fixed, overvalued, monopolistic foreign exchange rate regime (Werlau 1997). When foreigners were demanding further reforms, Castro instead yielded further to the orthodox side of the party: he mocked his own economic advisers, reiterated communist clichés, and rejected further reforms.[11] By 1996, the state began to dampen market activities and harass "profiteers" among the self-employed.

The few liberalizing measures enacted have thus come with palliatives for the orthodox sectors of the ruling party. Mesa Lago (1994, 60) described this

---

8. At the 1991 Fourth Party Congress, Castro purged the party of major reformers. Thus, the few reformers that remained were rather timid and disinclined to go too far in economic liberalization (Inter-American Dialogue Task Force on Cuba 1995). Although reformers had made it into important cabinet positions by 1993, the bulk of the party remained orthodox (*The Miami Herald*, January 1, 1994, 11A).

9. The restrictions covered (1) number of trades (only artisans, taxi drivers, food stands, shoemakers/sellers, art restoration, babysitting, plumbers, and electricians were allowed); (2) type of citizen (citizens with college degrees or holding leadership positions were banned); (3) labor conditions (self-employed citizens were not allowed to hire employees); and (4) taxation. See Jatar-Hausmann 1999.

10. Remarks by Sergio Placencia, president of the Central Bank of Cuba, at the Inter-American Dialogue, Washington, D.C., October 25, 2000.

11. For instance, in a speech to the National Assembly, Castro said: "I despise capitalism, it is excrement, it is unjust, it is alienating" (in Mesa Lago 1994, 65). The five hundred deputies applauded vigorously.

pattern of reform as follows: "Occasionally, [Castro] goes further in the implementation of a measure than the initiator originally intended (e.g., in dollarization), but most often Castro goes only halfway, or backs the orthodox side in the introduction of restrictions, or protracts the enactment of regulations for months or even years" (e.g., the authorization of self-employment).

The difference between Castro's party-yielding approach and those of Préval and Wasmosy is that it was preemptive. It occurred before the dislocation in Executive–ruling party relations spiraled out of control. The president was not forced to yield, but rather, chose to yield early on to avoid a major showdown with the party. Avoiding this dislocation helped to contain state-society conflict, at the cost of circumscribed economic reforms. These restrictions on economic liberalization served the purpose of granting the state, and hence the party hardliners, new powers in Cuba's new economy.

A similar case of preemptive party yielding was Colombia under Ernesto Samper (1994–98). Here, the rebellion of the orthodox sectors of the ruling party had less to do with economic liberalization than with allegations of a drug-money scandal, but the consequences for reform sustainability were similar. Samper's predecessor, César Gaviria (1990–94), implemented one of the most far-reaching economic reforms in the region.[12] Samper was elected on the promise of deepening such reforms. However, soon after taking office, Samper was accused of receiving drug money to finance his electoral campaign. Samper had no option but to allow the attorney general to conduct an investigation, which naturally targeted fellow members of his Liberal party. This infuriated Liberal leaders, who blamed Samper for unleashing this process and doing little to stop it. Facing the possibility of impeachment, Samper was placed in a very weak bargaining position vis-à-vis his own party. He desperately needed his party's support in order to survive impeachment. Conditions simply would not permit him to seek its support for deeper market reforms as well.

---

12. Gaviria had to deal with a split in his party between the populist faction led by Ernesto Samper and the faction that supported the slain leader Luis Carlos Galán. The reason for this split was the unorthodox way in which Gaviria had obtained the nomination for his party. The leading candidates were Samper and Galán. But Galán was assassinated in 1989. At the funeral, Galán's son unilaterally declared Gaviria, who had served as Galán's campaign manager, to be his family's choice (Martz 1999, 655). The outpouring of sympathy for the slain leader led to an overwhelming show of support for Gaviria. Both the Samper faction and many Galanistas were furious (Minister Jaime Niño, interview). Gaviria deployed extensive party-accommodating strategies, especially vis-à-vis the Samperistas. He incorporated powerful, dissenting members of the Liberal party into his cabinet and insisted that his administration would be committed to widespread consultation. Samper was nicely rewarded with the Ministry of Development, a position that allowed him to establish links with the business sector, which proved enormously beneficial when he decided to launch his own campaign in 1993.

Samper responded to this crisis by yielding to every anti-reform and anti-austerity demand stemming from his own party. As in Cuba, party yielding took a heavy toll on reform sustainability. Few new reforms were implemented, and many previous accomplishments (e.g., fiscal discipline, trade opening) were compromised. Consequently, Colombia switched from being one of Latin America's most impressive reformers in the early 1990s to one of the weakest. When the Asian Crisis hit in 1997–98, Colombia's fiscal condition was so deteriorated that the exchange rate regime collapsed and the country plunged into one of the most severe recessions in Latin America. Two decades of sound fiscal management came to an end with Samper's party-yielding administration.

The State-Without-Party Condition, Version 2

The state-without-party condition can also occur when presidents win office by avoiding links with existing parties and forming their own last-minute electoral movements. This electoral strategy is inevitable in countries with fragmented party systems, but it has also occurred in countries with stable party systems, when presidents, hoping to capitalize on the antiparty sentiment of the electorate, run as independents. Even when these ad hoc parties obtain a majority of seats in the legislature, the result can still be a state-without-party. These ad hoc electoral movements and coalitions are typically too fragile to provide the kind of political grounding that reforms require and that more solidly grounded parties can provide. The Executive will soon find him or herself isolated at the top, in need of stronger political allies. The following are possible outcomes of this state-without-party condition:

1. Executives negotiate directly with opposition parties. Executives always need to negotiate with opposition parties, but when they operate under weak or ad hoc ruling coalitions, they depend on the opposition even more. Negotiating with the opposition confers some degree of reform sustainability, albeit less than would be the case in a state-with-party context. This is because opposition parties will sell their support at a high cost. Venezuela under Caldera (see Chapter 10) is a perfect example. The extent to which the Executive concedes to the opposition depends in turn on the strength of the ruling coalition. The weaker the ruling coalition vis-à-vis the parties of the opposition, the lower the bargaining leverage of the Executive, and hence, the more reform sustainability is compromised.

2. Executives find it impossible to reach agreements with the opposition. This is most likely to occur when both the ruling party and the opposition parties are weak, ad hoc, or fragmented. The Executive cannot find a single political entity with which to ally himself: even the opposition is fragmented and unable to provide sufficient grounding. In turn, the opposition parties have little incentive to make a pact with an Executive whose own forces lack political weight. The result is an exacerbation of all the ailments associated with a state-without-party condition: a credibility crisis, uncontainable opposition from cost-bearers, and a black hole in the political system.
3. Executives strike against the party system as a whole. Presidents might decide to undermine both the opposition party and the ruling party. This may boost reform sustainability, but at the expense of democracy.

The following sections show examples of each of these responses.

Buying Support from the Opposition: Brazil (1985–1999)

In the 1990s, Brazil underwent a gradual switch from scenario 2 (weak ruling and opposition parties) to scenario 1 (strengthening of the ruling coalition). This resulted in improved reform sustainability, allowing Brazil to escape its status as Latin America's preeminent reform-laggard. Yet market reforms in Brazil have not been free of setbacks, mostly because Brazil has not fully escaped the state-without-party condition.

Between 1984 and 1994, Brazil operated under scenario 2. All three presidents during this period—José Sarney, Fernando Collor de Mello, and Itamar Franco—owed their electoral victories to weak electoral coalitions.[13] Brazil is a paradigmatic case of weak, undisciplined parties and inchoate party systems, a "unique case of party underdevelopment" (Mainwaring and Scully 1995; Mainwaring 1992). In inchoate party systems, the Executive has difficulty marshaling support for administration policies through party channels (Mainwaring 1995). Despite their significant presence in Congress, these ruling coalitions become insufficient providers of governability. The fragility of these coalitions locks the Executive in a state-without-party condition.[14]

13. Sarney owed his victory to an electoral coalition between the populist Brazilian Democratic Movement Party (PMDB) and the Liberal Front Party (PFL), which, according to a Brazilian joke, was a party of great leaders and a tiny following (Siqueira Wiarda 1990).
14. Under Sarney, the ruling party was intensely opposed to market reforms. One of Sarney's finance ministers, the prolific Luiz Carlos Bresser Pereira (April–December 1987), wrote:

Not surprisingly, between 1985 and 1994, Brazilian Executives made more than seven attempts to stabilize the economy and all failed.

Under Collor, the state-without-party condition reached explosive dimensions. Collor campaigned without a party and on an antiparty platform, reaching office with an ad hoc coalition of small parties. Collor was consequently deprived of resources to handle the opposition to his reforms. At first, he tried to bully Congress by flaunting his large electoral victory and high public opinion ratings. When this strategy failed, he began to rely on decrees—issuing 250 of them during his first year in office. The state-without-party condition, together with Collor's party-neglecting approach, led to unprecedented tension between the state and opposition parties. State-society conflicts soon followed. Collor became the quintessential noncredible Executive, prompting the always skeptical business community to turn completely against him by 1991 (Kingstone 1999b).

Collor switched to a party-yielding policy toward the end of his administration. Yet, unlike Caldera in Venezuela, Collor was unable to negotiate with the opposition. By then, the decline of the ruling coalition wiped out any bargaining power he might have had. Collor had no option but to yield to the opposition, showering already angry opposition parties with favors in a desperate attempt to calm them (e.g., he tentatively offered to make it easier for states to roll over their vast accumulated debts, to open the coffers again for states, and bring the PFL into the government). This was too little, too late. The legislature continued to attack Collor and his reforms. In late 1993, having completely killed his reform efforts, Congress proceeded to kill his administration. Congress impeached him on charges of corruption.

Under President Fernando Henrique Cardoso (1994–99, 1999–present), Brazil switched from scenario 2 to 1. The first Cardoso administration constituted the coming to office of a stronger party than Collor's—the Social Democratic Party (PSDB). Although young (founded in 1988), the PSDB quickly became a more autonomous and disciplined party, with a more coherent program of government and technocratic foundation than the average party in Brazil (Resende-Santos 1997). However, the PSDB was neither strong enough nor dominant enough in Congress to exempt Cardoso from the need to build an electoral coalition by accommodating other parties.

"Lack of support for my economic program was clearly the central problem. I did not get support from my president, nor from my party, nor from the broader society for the fiscal adjustment that was necessary" (Bresser Pereira 1995, 351). Party president Ulysses Guimaraes and party leader Fernando Henrique Cardoso "had to mediate between me and the party, which did not accept my views" (ibid., 352 n. 25).

Through a number of concessions, Cardoso put together a governing coalition comprised of a relatively stronger party (PSDB) and other parties of varying electoral strength (the Brazilian Labor Party, or PFL; the Progressive Reform Party, or PPB; the Progressive Party, or PTB; and the Partido do Movimento Democrático Brasileiro, or PMDB).

Brazil's state-without-party condition thus began to relax somewhat relative to Cardoso's predecessors. This helps to explain Cardoso's greater success in implementing economic reforms. However, Cardoso did not escape fully the effects of the state-without-party condition. The tendency for the ruling party to dissent and bicker, and for the opposition parties to sell their support at a high price, continued. Internal tensions within Cardoso's coalitions surfaced with almost every major reform initiative, especially those intended to correct the fiscal deficit, which explains Cardoso's most important policy failure in the 1990s—his inability to erase Brazil's crippling fiscal deficit (see Cardoso 2000). In 1995, Cardoso attempted a reform of the social security and pension system (the Previdencia), designed to restore fiscal health. The upshot of reform was to get Brazilians to work longer for smaller pensions (Kingstone 1999a). Eight pro-government deputies in the fifty-one–member committee defected, including representatives from the PFL, the PPB, and the PMDB (see Kingstone 1999a and Faucher 1999). This internal split not only spoiled aspects of the reform (the fiscal deficit ballooned), but also agitated state-society relations. After the defection of ruling party members, the leading union went on strike against the privatization of the state-owned oil company. Cardoso had no option but to shelve this reform.

Cardoso responded to this quasi state-without-party condition on a case-by-case basis. In some instances, he resorted to explicitly party-neglecting approaches (e.g., condemning the dissidents and threatening to punish them). Other times, he resorted to explicit party-yielding approaches (granting concessions that imperiled reforms); and other times, he pursued a party-accommodating strategy (granting some concessions to those party dissenters who were willing to compromise, including devoting significant effort to ensuring the support of Antonio Carlos Magalhaes, leader of his main coalition partner, the PFL).

Thus, Cardoso faced a situation similar to that of Venezuela under Caldera—the need for "political help" from opposition parties. The state has not been as susceptible to societal attacks as was the case under Collor or Pérez, in part because Cardoso escaped the extreme state-without-party condition. Cardoso has also been more successful in sustaining reforms than Caldera was because he has kept the ruling coalition strong in relation to the opposition. This has conferred on the state a bargaining leverage vis-à-vis the opposition, and hence, greater capacity to sustain reforms. But this has not exempted him from having to buy support—both from opposition and coalition partners. The result is a watered-down reform program—more far-reaching than those of previous Brazilian presidents, but pale in comparison to those of Menem and Salinas.

Negotiation with Opposition Parties Proves Impossible: Ecuador (1992–2000)

When both the ruling and the opposition parties are weak, it is impossible for the Executive to negotiate political support from the opposition. This is what happened in Ecuador in the 1990s. Whereas Brazil underwent a relaxation of scenario 2, Ecuador underwent a deepening of it: both the ruling and opposition parties became increasingly prone to fragmentation.[15] Consequently, Ecuador remained Latin America's most notorious reform-laggard in the 1990s. Between 1992 and 2000, six presidents tried to stabilize the economy. All failed. Two were removed from office—one by Congress, the other by a military coup. At the root of this instability was an acute state-without-party condition.

President Sixto Durán Ballén's party, the Partido Unión Republicana (PUR), split off from the Partido Social Cristiano in 1991, when the latter refused to endorse Durán's bid for the presidency. To win the elections, Durán had to put together a last-minute coalition of small and disaggregated political forces. This left him with a fragmentation-prone ruling coalition that was unable to marshal societal support for reforms and neutralize societal opposition. Although initially pro-reform, his ruling coalition ended up opposing him. The coalition weakened further after the mid-term congressional elections (it lost nine of its eighteen seats in the seventy-seven–member Congress). Durán was never able to implement his much-needed fiscal reform. In October 1995, besieged by a dramatic corruption scandal, Durán Ballén acknowledged that the country "is living through the worst political crisis in its democratic history" (*The Economist*, October 28, 1995). The opposition parties took advantage of the political vacuum at the top and aligned themselves

---

15. Rather than weak, parties in Ecuador are deeply compartmentalized. They have strong links to either a geographic region (coastal-highland divide) or socioethnic group (Native Americans versus migrants versus elites). These regional and ethnic divisions magnify the rivalries among parties, so that interparty cooperation is difficult even when ideologies overlap (McConnell 2001).

against the reforms, including the privatization of the hydro-energy sector, and threatened to impeach ministers. Labor strikes against the privatization of the telecom company and the opening of the oil sector proliferated between 1995 and 1996.

The next president, Abdalá Bucaram (*El loco*, the loony), faced an even more severe state-without-party condition. Shortly after winning office with 54 percent of the vote with the most populist, anti-IMF campaign in Latin America,[16] Bucaram underwent the typical Latin American post-election conversion: he announced a sweeping neoliberal reform program, including a convertibility plan similar to Argentina's. In the context of state-without-party, this was bound to fail. Although the second-largest party in the then seventy-eight–member Congress (with seventeen seats), Bucaram's party was mostly a collection of personal friends. Few political parties were willing to make an alliance with a man who had been so critical of parties during the election and whose own party was so insignificant. His only allies (two small parties) soon defected. The opposition parties were quick to exploit Bucaram's isolation, blocking every reform effort and encouraging labor unrest. Soon, the streets were filled with angry protesters. In February, the Congress voted 44 to 34 to remove Bucaram with the unproven charge of "mental incapacity."

After Bucaram, Ecuador went from being a case of a state without a major party to a state without any ruling party at all. Bucaram's successor, Fabián Alarcón, was a party-less leader. Alarcón's Frente Radical Alfarista held three seats in Congress, including Alarcón's. The thirteen or so other parties in the now eighty-two–member Congress essentially refused to support any of Alarcón's reforms. Alarcón's response was to yield to the parties in opposition: he gave up on economic reforms altogether (one of his first economic measures was to revoke some of the subsidy cuts Bucaram had ordered) and focused instead on an alternative, more politically viable project: organizing a constitutional assembly. Though political tensions were contained, abandoning the reforms took a heavy toll on the economy. By mid-1998, the country entered a recession, with a fiscal deficit hovering around 7 percent of GDP and an escalating inflation rate.

In 1998, Ecuadorans elected Jamil Mahuad, the first president whose party (Popular Democracy) held a significant presence in Congress (28 percent of

---

16. Bucaram's angry campaign included denunciations of the "oligarchies," end of privatizations, calls for increasing public spending, and promises to "make the rich vomit." (He even gave a hero's welcome to Lorena Bobbit, the Ecuadorian-American who made headlines worldwide by cutting off her husband's penis.)

seats), albeit still short of an absolute majority. Although party fragmentation abated somewhat (four parties obtained more than 80 percent of the vote) and the economic crisis worsened, Mahuad still failed to find political support for his program. He tried an alliance with a center-right party (the Social-Christian Party, or PSC), but this forced him to give up most reform measures (changes to income and value-added taxes, and increases in prices of oil products) and still failed to stop Congress from approving a deficit budget. By early 1999, there were strikes by teachers, electricity workers, taxi drivers, and bus drivers against the reforms. In March, the PSC broke completely from the government and launched a debate in Congress to revoke Mahuad's emergency powers. Mahuad began to yield further, even agreeing to reduce fuel prices, and making concessions to small left-leaning parties.

Ecuador's economy went into a tailspin by the end of 1999, verging on hyperinflation in the context of a hyperrecession and an imminent run on the banks. In desperation, the government announced a radical stabilization policy based on dollarization. One week before the plan was to go into effect, Mahuad was overthrown by the military, who took advantage of an indigenous protest that was brewing.

Ecuador is thus a classic case of the state-without-party condition. All presidents since 1992 came from small, personalistic, or even nonexistent parties. All four needed allies in Congress, but unlike Venezuela under Caldera, these ruling parties were too weak to command respect from opposition parties, and the opposition parties in turn were too weak to offer any real help. Reform sustainability suffered, political turmoil escalated, one president gave up on reform, and two pro-reform presidents were forced to leave office prematurely.

Attacking All Parties: Peru (1990–1992)

A final escape of the state-without-party condition is to strike against the system completely. Peru under Alberto Fujimori (1990–95, 1995–2000, 2000) is an example of this situation. Fujimori went out of his way to weaken both opposition parties and, even more unusually, his own ruling party. The only way to survive this extreme state-without-party condition—and implement deep economic reform—is for the Executive to find an extra-partisan ally and to undermine the future growth of opposition parties. In Peru, the extra-partisan ally was the military, and the strategy to undermine the opposition included informal erosion of political freedoms. Peru showed that militarism and authoritarianism are very likely outcomes of states seeking to reform the economy under an acute state-without-party condition.

In the late 1980s, Alberto Fujimori ran for president deliberately avoiding links with any party, relying instead on allies from technical sectors, international groups, and the military (see Mauceri 1995 and Kay 1996) and cultivating the image of the "untainted leader who was above the fray of partisan politics" (Roberts 1995, 94). His electoral machine, Cambio 90, was cobbled together shortly before the elections and was nothing more than a loose coalition of personal acquaintances in business and academic circles. Once in office, Fujimori continually criticized the established political parties and did little to institutionalize his own electoral machine (Levitsky 1999b; Degregori forthcoming).

Despite the severe economic crisis he had inherited (e.g., an annual inflation rate of approximately 7,500 percent in 1990) and the ample powers that he obtained from Congress at the beginning of his term, opposition to reforms escalated between 1990 and 1992, especially among labor. Lacking a strong ruling party, Fujimori was unarmed against these society-based challenges. He resorted to reform rescue measures—by late 1991, he had enacted 120 new laws by decree power. In April 1992, he faced an impasse in Congress, which was trying to prevent him from governing by decree and granting privileges to the military (see Degregori forthcoming; Weyland 1996b, 195). Fujimori responded by staging his famous *auto-golpe* of 1992—a coup against the Congress and the existing parties.

Scholars tend to explain Fujimori's self-coup as the result of military pressures, the strong resistance of opposition forces, the authoritarian values of the president, or a combination of these. Some critics also argue that Fujimori actually provoked a confrontation with the legislature by demanding approval of a set of prerogatives that no reasonable Congress would ever agree to. Fujimori wanted absolute power, not just powers to reform the economy, and this, critics argued, produced the Executive-legislative gridlock of late 1991.

Nevertheless, it makes sense to think of the 1992 self-coup as the result of the state-without-party condition. Deprived of a strong ruling party and unwilling to form an alliance with the second-largest party, Fujimori felt deprived of political capital to balance his adversaries or to push ahead with his programs. In 1991, former president Alan García was elected secretary-general of the main opposition party, APRA, signaling a rebirth of the leading opposition party. The Senate declared the presidency "vacant" on the grounds of lack of moral authority. As one government official put it, the point had come "where either the government would kill the president, or the president would kill the Congress" (quoted in Cameron 1997, 56). Fujimori knew that his capacity to contain the opposition was in jeopardy. He was facing all the symptoms of the state-without-party condition, including a deep credibility deficit. All of this prompted him to rely more and more on the military, which infuriated his adversaries further. As the crisis in Executive-legislative relations deteriorated, Fujimori calculated that a self-coup was the only way to restore credibility (that is to say, to demonstrate that he was unencumbered) (Cameron 1997, 61–62).

After the self-coup, Fujimori formally restored political liberties, but informally did everything possible to undermine opposition parties. He censored the press, used thugs against the opposition, and outspent his rivals in elections. Opposition parties remained weak, fragmented, and chaotic, a point that the literature on Peru makes abundantly clear. What is less well known is that Fujimori went out of his way to keep his own ruling coalition equally weak. He continually intervened in the staffing of his party to ensure that only loyalists held important posts, and even they, for not too long. Fujimori impeded the emergence of rules for determining party ascendance. No party headquarters was ever established. Rather than a party, Fujimori's ruling movement remained a "state of mood" (Degregori forthcoming): an agglomeration of yes-men and obscure technocrats. The former handled electoral mobilization; the latter handled the reforms.

With a fragmented opposition, an obsequious cadre of yes-men politicians and technocrats, and the full support of the military, Fujimori emerged virtually unencumbered in Peruvian politics after 1992. He was thus able to implement one of the most far-reaching reform efforts in the Americas, matching if not surpassing Menem's record. Yet the lesson is clear: pushing for reform under a state-without-party condition is only possible through significant erosion of democratic institutions.

Conclusion

Theorists of comparative politics have long stressed that political outcomes are the result of (1) historical-institutional factors, which limit the choices available to actors, and (2) the ingenuity of actors themselves, which allows them to manipulate, even rise above, institutional constraints. This chapter illustrated this proposition. The state-without-party condition has been a historical-institutional obstacle to reform sustainability in Latin America in the 1990s. It seriously constrained the extent to which Executives could achieve economic reform. Yet presidents have displayed significant ingenuity in responding to this constraint, in some cases even discovering innovative escapes.

The state-without-party crisis is the result of either of two conditions: (1) a severe conflict between the Executive and a strong ruling party, or (2) a president who comes to office independent of existing parties, or supported by a last-minute, ad-hoc coalition of small parties. Even highly technocratic governments facing economic crises find it impossible to sustain reforms in a state-without-party context.

The state-without-party condition is not a situation of equilibrium. At some point, actors in the political system must give in. The president might seek to accommodate the ruling party (including overtures to dissenting sectors), succumb to the pressure from orthodox sectors, find alternative sources of support, or strike against the party and the party system. Each of these responses has different effects on reform sustainability.

Neglecting the ruling party is the most explosive option. Attempting to implement economic reforms by bypassing a strong ruling party and dismissing it as an obstacle intensifies the aggravation of the party. Revisiting Figure 5 in Chapter 5, this party-neglecting response is represented by point Y_1 in Figure 9. At first, party neglect allows the Executive to register some progress in reform implementation, but nowhere near the level of implementation desired by the Executive—the distance between the dotted line and point Y_1. The Executive will feel compelled to implement reforms through decretism, shock measures, little political consultation, and high-profile alliances with nonpartisan forces such as international actors, the military, or business conglomerates, coupled with an antiparty or anti-Congress discourse. Confrontation between the Executive and both the ruling and the opposition parties is likely.

If the ruling party is strong, the confrontation will center on the president and the ruling party. If the ruling party is weak or coalition-based, the ruling party will tend to weaken and produce defectors. The Executive will be left devoid of political allies. Opposition parties will take advantage of the isolation of the Executive and intensify their attacks against the reforms. The information and credibility gaps will deteriorate. A political black hole will set in, with repercussions across the rest of society. Opposition parties, interest groups, opinion-makers, and skeptics will adopt increasingly recalcitrant positions. Reforms proceed with difficulty, if at all.

Because party-neglecting strategies exacerbate conflicts in Executive–ruling party relations, which in turn disrupt state-society relations, they are inherently unstable: the tension that they generate is unsustainable over time. At some point, one of the entities will have to strike: either the ruling party, often in conjunction with opposition parties, blocks the power of the president to govern

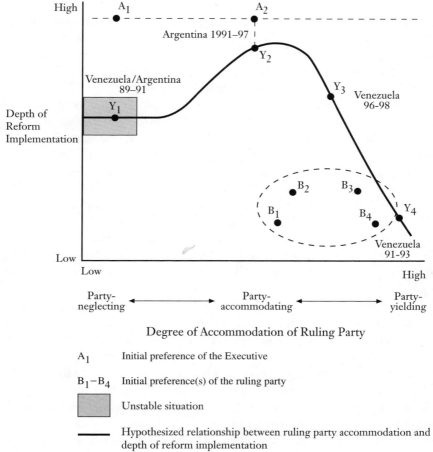

Fig. 9   Reform implementation and Executive–ruling party relations

the economy, or the president strikes against the political system, that is to say, attempts to supersede or reorder the political system.

Presidents might be able to avoid this showdown by switching to a party-yielding response (point Y_4). This means capitulating completely to the anti-reform sectors both within and outside the ruling party. Often, party yielding is the inevitable outcome of party neglecting. As they become increasingly frustrated with the Executive's party-neglecting policies, anti-reform sectors in the ruling party gain the upper hand. The Executive becomes isolated, and thus prone to yield. The economic consequence of this approach is lack of improvement of economic variables.

The political impact, however, is harder to predict. There might be less tension between the president and the parties, which should translate into a decline in state-society tensions. Equally plausible, however, is that parties might seek to exploit the president's weakness and incite societal actors to rebel. The combination of declining economic conditions and rising political gridlock could lead to higher societal discontent.

A third escape from the state-without-party condition is to try to form ad hoc coalitions with the main opposition parties (point Y_3). This approach is a second-best compromise. It avoids the economic paralysis of party yielding and the political tensions of party neglect. However, it is not without costs. Opposition parties will sell their support at a very high price, demanding tough concessions. After all, opposition parties seek to minimize the victories of the incumbents. Economic reforms will be considerably watered-down. Moreover, granting concessions to the opposition party might further aggravate the ruling party. The outcome is thus some reform sustainability, but never as far-reaching as would be the case under the content of a strong Executive–ruling party alliance. The weaker the ruling coalition vis-à-vis the opposition, the more watered-down the reforms.

Finally, there is the possibility of reconciling the ruling party and the state (point Y_2). Of all the options available to Executives, this state-with-party condition brings the highest payoff. The Executive rallies the party on behalf of the reforms by offering political concessions to both liberalizers and traditionalists, such as participation in the cabinet, consultations, addressing ideological questions, expanding party access to the market, subsidizing the party's electoral activities, and ensuring pockets of autonomy within the ruling party. The result is an expansion of the Executive's capacity to deepen the reforms. If the ruling party is historically dominant, the realignment in Executive–ruling party relations acts as a disincentive for societal actors to sabotage or mistrust the reforms. The ruling party will act as a shield for the state and neutralizer of societal opposition. Reversing the reforms becomes difficult, even if the opposition takes a recalcitrant stand.

However, the government will still fail to achieve the levels of reform implementation initially intended (the gap between points A_2 and Y_2). Party accommodation, by definition, entails granting the party certain concessions that translate into gaps in the reform process. The state-without-party argument is related but different from Haggard and Kaufman's argument that party system fragmentation is an impediment to governability. It is related because in highly fragmented party systems, the possibility of ad-hoc ruling coalitions is more likely. However, the state-without-party condition can come about even in nonfragmented party systems. Ultimately, Haggard and Kaufman's thesis places the locus of the conflict between the president and opposition forces. My argument, by contrast, places the locus at the level of the Executive and its ruling party.

Table 12.4 summarizes the argument and evidence presented in this chapter. It shows the two different historical-institutional variables that presidents inherit ("starting condition") and the various ways in which Latin American Executives have reacted to them ("responses"). Each of these responses affects both the degree of reform sustainability and the health of democracy of the regime. The variation in terms of economic freedom and political freedom presented in Figure 8 is now easier to understand.

In addition to affecting reform sustainability and the health of democracy, the response of presidents to the state-without-party condition also affects another variable: the general political stability of the regime. Four combinations are possible:

Possibility 1. Both stability and democracy improve. This is more likely under party accommodation. A strong Executive–ruling party relation discourages anti-establishment behavior on the part of political actors. It also encourages opposition parties to find more efficient ways to negotiate with the Executive (e.g., by trying to display greater technical competence rather than merely ideological attacks against reforms, and by stressing the need to correct the illiberal gaps rather than reverse the reforms). These strategies can restore the competitiveness of opposition parties. The result could very well be that both the ruling and opposition parties can emerge stronger, offering the electorate more interesting platforms of governance. All this favors democratization.

Possibility 2. Both stability and democracy decline. This occurs whenever the president and the ruling party engage in severe conflicts. Either the president ends up striking against the political system (Haiti 1999) or the ruling party challenges the Executive, often through unconstitutional or highly disruptive means (Paraguay 1997–98).

Possibility 3. Stability improves but democracy declines. This can occur if either the president resorts to extra-partisan actors such as the military (Peru in the 1990s) or yields to the orthodox sectors of the ruling party (Cuba). The former entails the rise of blunt authoritarian practices. The latter means a decline in conflicts between the president and the party, which, as argued in previous chapters, translates into more stable state-society relations. But this fortifies the hardline sectors of the party, which might make it harder for democratization measures to proceed.

Table 12.4 Responses to the State-Without-Party Condition and Their Economic and Political Outcomes

Starting condition	Response	Outcomes			Examples
		Reform sustainability	Health of democracy	Political stability	
Dislocation between Executive and strong ruling party	Party accommodation	High	Improves	Improves or changes little	Mexico (1989–94) Argentina (1991–97) Colombia (1990–94) Chile (1990s) Bolivia (1980s)
	Hostility: Party strikes back	Low	Fragile	Declines	Paraguay (mid-1990s) Venezuela (1992–93) Haiti (1997–98)
	Hostility: Executive strikes back	Low	Declines	Declines	Haiti (1999)
	Party yielding	Modest reforms	Declines	May or may not improve	Cuba (mid-1990s) Colombia (1994–98)

Table 12.4 *(cont'd)*

Starting condition	Response	Outcomes			Examples
		Reform sustainability	Health of democracy	Political stability	
Weak, ad-hoc ruling coalitions	Negotiations with opposition parties	Mixed	Improves	Improves	Venezuela (1996–98) Brazil (1994–99)
	No agreements with opposition parties	Low	Fragile	Declines	Ecuador (1990s) Brazil (1980s–1993)
	Extrapartisan allies (e.g., military)	High	Declines	Improves	Peru (1990s)

Possibility 4. Stability deteriorates but democracy improves. Situations in which the political parties strike against the president are politically complicated. On the one hand, the parties could be accused of acting undemocratically by trying to depose presidents through technicalities of dubious constitutional merit. If this is the case, then democracy is jeopardized. On the other hand, if the outcome of this process is to establish a more balanced distribution of power between the Executive and the legislative branches, then one could conclude that the party strike against the president helped democracy.

Finally, the state-without-party / party-without-state argument has implications for the literature on state governance. Essentially, the relationship between state autonomy (vis-à-vis the ruling party) and state capacity to implement reforms is not linear, but rather curved. Too much autonomy from the ruling party (party-neglecting policies) and too little autonomy from the ruling party (party yielding) are detrimental for reform sustainability. The former is inherently unstable; the latter is a recipe for reform paralysis.

13

conclusion

between autonomy
and inclusion—
a theory of
governance

Why did Argentina manage in 1991 to escape from years
of economic decline and implement far-reaching market
reforms and Venezuela did not? This was the central question of this book. It is a question that goes to the core of a
central issue in comparative politics: under what conditions do states manage to carry out policies that are economically necessary but nonetheless incompatible with the
preferences of vested interests? It is a question about how
states govern their economies in the face of political resistance. It is a question about the conditions for self-reform
and the sources of stateness in contemporary democracies.

The key to reform sustainability in Argentina was the rise, halfway into the reforms, of a harmonious relationship between the Executive and the ruling party. Once the Argentine state obtained the ruling party's consent for the reforms, a powerful political alliance was born—the "state-with-party" condition. For the first time since the 1950s, the PJ, the most powerful party in Argentina, became a partner of a reformist state, rather than a champion of particularistic grievances. This had dramatic repercussions for state-society relations. The state's credibility and information gaps were reduced. Disaffected societal sectors were deprived of an institutional ally. Mistrusting sectors had fewer reasons to doubt the state's commitment to change.

In Venezuela, however, Executive–ruling party relations became intensely acrimonious, producing the equivalent of a black hole in the political system. For the first time since the 1960s, the strongest party in Venezuela, AD, became an enemy of the Executive—not just of the Executive's choice of successor, but of its very authority. Forsaken by its natural ally, the Executive was left in limbo, devoid of political grounding. The decision of many AD leaders to "defend the people before defending the government" served as the gravitational pull that spurred disaffected actors to take center stage. From anti-establishment sectors to skeptical business leaders, societal groups were able to find reasons and inducements for challenging the Executive. The result was the collapse not just of the reform program but of the state's capacity to govern.

In seeking answers to the question of what determines reform sustainability, scholars have tended to ignore the Executive–ruling party relation variable, contending instead that the key lies in economic factors, the internal features of states, the ideologies of parties, or the interplay between the Executive and opposition interest groups and opposition political parties. This book does not deny the importance of these variables, but it suggests that in many ways, these factors are significantly shaped by the nature of Executive–ruling party relations. The specific orientation of the ruling party— whether statist or pro-reform—is less important. What matters is that the Executive manages to form a cooperative relationship with a strong ruling party.

A second question was: why was the Executive in Argentina, and not in Venezuela, able to forge such an alliance with the ruling party? The answer combines agency, choice, and preexisting institutions. First and foremost, the Executive's policy vis-à-vis the ruling party mattered. Party-neglecting policies alienated the party. Party accommodation, however, permitted a rapprochement.

These policy choices, in turn, were facilitated or encumbered by the receptivity of the party, that is to say, its propensity to cooperate with the state. This receptivity was in turn contingent on various institutional factors. One is variation in interparty cooperation. Where interparty cooperation was historically low (Argentina), detractors within the ruling party felt discouraged from rebelling out of fear of siding too closely with the opposition. Where interparty collaboration was more customary (Venezuela), dissent within the ruling party was more likely because dissenters did not mind siding with the opposition. In contexts of Executive–ruling party dislocation, collusive party systems can, paradoxically, imperil economic governance because they can fuel this dislocation.

Furthermore, the internal and external institutional contexts of the party mattered. The PJ, but not AD, came to office with a more fluid institutional makeup, which was the result of a process of significant transformation in the 1980s. A combination of internal factors (less-entrenched leadership) and external factors (more exposure to contestation, less dependence on state resources) contributed to softening the party's internal structures, ideologies, and loyalties. When confronted with a severe electoral shock in 1983–85, the party's internal rigidities weakened further. The party actually plunged into a crisis. Every element of the party—from the leadership to the ideology—was subject to questioning as various factions began to search for a new winning formula. A never-too-entrenched party became even more malleable.

None of this happened to AD. Facing no perceivable threats to its hegemony and grip on power (few electoral contests, little internal democracy, high dependence on state sinecures), AD faced no incentive to change prior to 1989. Despite the domestic economic and social crisis taking place in the country, and the increasing international debates about the new role of states and markets, AD remained unmoved. Pérez inherited an ossified party that if anything, was more cartelized, unbendable, and fearful of openness than ever before. That is why the reforms of the 1990s had such a pounding, cracking impact on it. Unlike the PJ, which proved too flexible to break, AD was too rigid to bend.

Democracy does contribute to market reforms, but my argument is not identical to others who have reached similar conclusions. Domínguez and Purcell (1999), following Przeworski (1991), for instance, stress that democracy contributes to market reforms because it maximizes stable and transparent rules, which are necessary for markets to thrive. North and Weingast (1989) argue that democratic institutions permit credible precommitments, which are also necessary for markets to thrive. Remmer (1991b) suggests that democracy facilitates market reforms because it allows for nonreforming incumbents to be voted out of office, making room for reform-minded officials. I argue, differently, that democracy, *both inside and outside dominant parties*, contributes to market-oriented reforms because it can soften the internal rigidities that often prevent political parties from taking the risk of embracing change.

Conciliating the Autonomy versus Inclusion Dilemma

The conclusion that economic governance is predicated on the state-with-party condition has theoretical implications. Specifically, it helps to reconcile two seemingly incompatible prescriptions in the literature on governability.

In the 1980s, some political scientists argued that a condition for "revolutions from above" is the autonomy of the state, specifically, the degree to which reformers are detached, or not recruited, from the sector whose privileges are being revoked (e.g., Waterbury 1992, Haggard and Cheng 1987, Evans et al. 1985, Trimberger 1978). If Krueger (1974), Olson (1982), and Tullock (1990), among others, are correct in positing the predatory nature of interest groups, the need for some degree of independence from these groups seems unquestionable. In the words of Schmitter and Karl (1991, 81), effective democratic governance necessitates that popularly elected officials "exercise their constitutional powers without being subjected to overriding (albeit informal) opposition from unelected officials." State-autonomy scholars thus focus on the internal structural characteristics of the states, such as technocratic competence, internal cohesiveness, and bureaucratic insulation from vested interest groups, what Poggi (1990, 97–105) describes as the "state-centered understanding of the state."

By contrast, theorists of corporatism (see Held 1987) and democratization (e.g., O'Donnell et al. 1986) argue that while the capacity to act independently from interest groups is valuable, democratic governance requires incorporating societal groups into decision making. Governance is about eliciting trust from all sectors of society, including opponents, and inclusiveness is a necessary starting point. In the words of a key exponent of the corporatist school: "The key to differing degrees of governability lies less in the 'objective' magnitudes of macroeconomic performance, social cleavages, and class relations than in the way differentiated interests are 'intermediated' between civil society and the state" (Schmitter 1981, 292). For corporatism and democratization theorists, the antidote to ungovernability is to integrate politically those actors who are affected by economic change.

These positions are not only incompatible, but individually untenable. Stressing one prescription over the other can actually be detrimental to governance. The reform experiences of Argentina and Venezuela make this clear. For instance, the Executives' pursuit of power concentration and decretism (the statist prescription) led to societal discontent.[1] Granting vast powers to technocratic actors (under Miguel Rodríguez, Ricardo Hausmann, and Teodoro Petkoff in Venezuela, or Juan Sourrouille, Néstor Rapanelli, and Erman González in Argentina) was insufficient for generating the intended economic results and societal acceptance. But at the same time, incorporating the direct representatives of interest groups into the cabinet (the corporatist prescription) also exacerbated state-society conflicts. For example, Pedro Tinoco, the president of Venezuela's Central Bank and owner of one of the country's largest banks, not only blocked the full liberalization of the banking sector, but also made the state susceptible to accusations of favoritism, pitting industrialists against the financial sectors represented by Tinoco. Incorporation of targeted sectors thus led to reform paralysis as well as intersectoral conflicts.

In many ways, therefore, the challenge of governing the economy under hard times—the ultimate test of stateness—consists of finding a way to combine the prescriptions of these two seemingly contradictory logics. Reformers must act with independence from predatory groups (the autonomist point), but simultaneously command the loyalty and participation of societal actors (the corporatist/democratization point).

In the early 1990s, some scholars began to try to solve this dilemma. Huber (1995), Evans (1995, 1992), and the authors in Migdal et al. (1994), for instance, argue that neither pure autonomy nor pure inclusion is the route to state capacity. Instead, it is "embedded autonomy": a combination of internal coherence and external connectedness with societal actors. Scholars of Asia have belabored this point, arguing that the key to the success of East Asian states is their ability to provide administrative guidance to (Johnson 1982), even to coordinate (Stiglitz 1996), the business decisions of business groups. The problem is that while these "state-in-society" arguments highlight the need to find networks of connection with society, they do not clearly specify how to prevent these networks from becoming bridges through which interest groups can capture the state.[2]

How can reform-minded states achieve the appropriate connection with society—that is to say, linking state and society without entrapping the state? The answer offered by this book is that states need to avoid the state-without-party

---

1. See also Grindle 1996, 10, and Conaghan 1996, 43–44, for similar points.
2. For a comparative review of Evans 1995, see Schneider 1998.

condition. In essence, states must govern in close alliance with a political party. The following sections show why.

Shielding (versus Sabotaging) the Reformers

A harmonious Executive–ruling party relation can shield the Executive from the actions of potential saboteurs at the society level. The PJ established a range of societal grievances that it would not embrace, e.g., criticizing the overall direction of the reforms, questioning the authority of government officials (especially economic authorities), and refusing to implement approved policies. Although the PJ often debated with the Executive over the details— and sometimes the wisdom—of some reforms, these debates seldom sought to undermine the authority of the Executive or the direction of the reforms. The ruling party sided with the Executive in repudiating obstructionist sectoral pressures.

In contrast, AD became the champion of these pressures. At the very least, it took seriously the criticisms stemming from disaffected sectors of society. More often, it actually sought to curtail the autonomy of the state, criticized the government publicly, and even questioned its judgments. The ruling party mobilized public discontent. Rather than shield the state, AD led the firing squad.

Closing (versus Widening) the Information Gap

The state-with-party condition also ameliorates the information gap, which is a recurrent curse of most market reform programs. This information gap occurs for many reasons. Many sectors of society are misinformed about the mechanisms and objectives of the reforms. Technocrats fail to communicate their policies in a way that makes sense to nonexperts. Organized opponents of reforms tend to do a better job at launching public information campaigns than reform beneficiaries.

An Executive–ruling party rapprochement helps to offset this asymmetry of information. The PJ in 1991 began to campaign on behalf of the reforms, even forcing state technocrats to reveal more information about their policies than they would have without this pressure. A political system does not need a ruling party to do this; the opposition can do it just as well, if not better. Where the ruling party makes a difference is in disseminating the information that is extracted from technocrats. This is what the PJ accomplished. Although at times party leaders simply called on citizens to postpone their grievances and show patience, very often, especially during the crucial

1991–94 period, they actually conducted mass public campaigns on behalf of a given policy. In a way, the PJ became a conveyer belt of information between technocrats and society at large.

No doubt, some PJ leaders decided to stay silent. But even this silence was better than the alternative—open attacks against the government, like AD in Venezuela. In their battle against the government, AD leaders distorted information, emphasized the inconsistencies in the design and results of the program, failed to rebut myths about the reforms, and were the first to express doubts about government-generated information. The public normally expects the opposition party to question government-provided information, but when the ruling party is at the forefront of this questioning, the damage to the image of the government is more severe because it alienates the administration's natural supporters.

Political parties, then, continue to have a comparative advantage as socializing agents. Although secular trends (e.g., the rise of the mass media, the proliferation of newer sources of information, the discrediting of politicians) have reduced the advantage that parties have in this domain, they nonetheless perform a crucial information-affecting role in modern democracies. Citizens do not maximize the time that they spend gathering information, especially about complex public policy issues. They tend to resort to "information shortcuts" in order to fill in their information gaps, that is to say, they follow cues from technical experts, peers, opinion-makers, public relation campaigns, or favorite politicians. Parties are not alone in this market of information shortcuts, but they have not been displaced from it either.

Political Grounding (versus Political Black Hole)

An Executive who governs in harmony with a strong ruling party also obtains a strong *piso político* (political grounding). Having the support of a large, organized political machine that is strongly rooted across societal sectors is an enormous power resource. This partnership is likely to bring congressional endorsement of the reforms (if the ruling party is predominant), which bestows a degree of institutionalization and irreversibility on the reforms. If the ruling party happens to be a statist party, the payoff is even higher. Statist-populist parties traditionally enjoy close links with organized societal groups, e.g., labor unions, industrialists, professional associations, university students, intellectuals, local and regional groups, and clubs. Harmonious relations between the Executive and these types of parties help align some of these societal groups with the state. In contrast, hostile relations translate into state detachment from societal groups—a type of a black hole in the political system. The isolation of the Executive, in and of itself, is a hard-to-resist opportunity for state challengers to take center stage.

Credibility Boost

Perhaps the most important consequence of harmonious Executive–ruling party relations is to boost the credibility of the state. It allows the Executive to persuasively convey that nothing, especially the populist forces that surround the Executive, will stand in the way of the reforms. This has a decisive impact on state-society relations. It does not necessarily turn all sectors of society more cooperative with the reforms. But it better equips the state to address the new state-society conflicts that the credibility boost gives rise to.

Eliciting the Support (versus Reaffirming the Fears) of Mistrusting Groups   The one sector of society that will respond cooperatively to the credibility boost, that is to say, increase its willingness to support the reforms, are the reform skeptics. The ability to convey that the populist forces will not block the reformers leads skeptical sectors to relax their mistrust. Ruling party endorsement of the reforms can offer guarantees that other economic actors are less likely to cheat. This allays business fears of being left with the "sucker's payoff." Also, party endorsement signals policy continuity. Insofar as governing with the party entails legislative cooperation, it reduces the possibility of reversibility. This also allays business fears that the rules of the game will change unexpectedly.

Thus, for instance, the PJ-approved Convertibility Law inaugurated a period of remarkable stability in the foreign exchange and financial markets, two of the most trust-sensitive markets. If PJ legislators had ever discussed changing the value of the currency after April 1991—a move that by law was within their power—this stability would have been jeopardized. But the PJ, honoring the tacit agreement that was part of its partnership with the Executive, rarely discussed this possibility in public, despite the fact that the "appropriateness" of the exchange rate has been the most hotly debated topic in Argentina (and abroad) since 1991.

The Venezuelan Executive, however, unable to convey his ability to rein in the populist forces, became the ultimate noncredible reformer. Mistrusting groups came to expect that the Executive would falter in its commitments, changing their reaction to the reforms from acquiescence to noncooperation by 1992.

Thus statist ruling parties have a role to play in shaping the behavior of not just affiliates and ancillary organizations, but also extra-partisan actors such as business groups.[3] By serving as the network of connection with labor and Congress, the ruling party addresses some of the most important reasons business often refuses to cooperate with costly change: (1) the expectation that labor will defect; and (2) the expectation that the reforms will not endure. This way, harmonious Executive–ruling party relations help to influence state-business relations.

Neutralizing (versus Encouraging) the Cost-Bearing Sectors   Unlike mistrusting sectors, cost-bearing sectors react apprehensively to the credibility boost. The expectation that the state will deepen the reform frightens and galvanizes them to protest. Moreover, the return of normalcy (economic recovery) increases societal appetite for more fiscal spending or, at least, for relaxing austerity.

However, the very same factor that made possible this credibility boom, and hence this new type of societal pressure—harmonious Executive–ruling party relations—serves as an antidote against these pressures. By siding with the Executive, the ruling party ceases to act as the institutional vehicle through which cost-bearers challenge the reforms. This alters the expectations of societal actors. Cost-bearing sectors estimate that they have a smaller chance of defeating the Executive. Some will give up automatically (e.g., the SRA); others might decide to put up a fight by themselves (e.g., the UIA). But sooner or later, most realize the futility of their efforts and will gradually relinquish sabotaging tactics in favor of attempts to negotiate participation in the reforms.

In sum, political parties in modern democracies, even statist ruling parties, enjoy a comparative advantage, not just as vote-getters and preference-aggregators, but also as instruments of governance. They contribute to governance, not because they help shape the design of policy (Boix 1998), but rather because they help shape its implementation. They contribute to sustainability, not just because of what they are willing to do (shield the state, close the information gap), but also because of the signals that they transmit (nothing will stand in the way of the reforms) and the institutional avenue that they foreclose. Attempting to carry out the reforms without the support of ruling parties deprives the Executive of instruments to deal effectively with noncooperative, disloyal, or mistrusting attitudes.

3. Political scientists generally do not regard parties as suitable for the task of mobilizing business support because business sectors demand political goods that parties cannot easily offer, namely, investment returns. This contrasts with labor groups, many of whose demands parties can more easily provide (e.g., exemption from the cost of adjustment, inclusion in the decision-making, labor security, etc.).

This argument represents a move beyond the state/societal structuralism that Skocpol popularized, in which scholars focus on both the internal features of states (their "organization and interests"), and those of society—the "organization and interests of socioeconomic groups" and their relationship with the state (Skocpol 1985, 20). These structuralist perspectives have a difficult time explaining political transformations that are not accompanied by major transformations of structures. The 1991 turnaround of Argentina is one such transformation. Back then, state structures were as weak as ever, and the organization and interest of society were as reform-averse as ever. The state-with-party condition was an institutional change that explains Argentina's escape from this structure-imposed constraint.

Testing Causality

The "nature of Executive–ruling party relations" is analytically separate from, and causally related to, societal reactions to the reforms, a key component of reform sustainability. This variable cannot explain every aspect of the reform process in Argentina and Venezuela, but it nonetheless passes at least three major tests of causality.

Timing

The first test of causality is the question of timing. If the connection between Executive–ruling party relations and state-society relations is posited to be causal, the question of timing is crucial: Executive–ruling party relations need to improve before state-society relations improve or, alternatively, deteriorate before state-society relations deteriorate. This was shown to hold true in Argentina and Venezuela. One of the benefits of the research methodology employed in this study (interviews, event tracing, detailed case study) is that it permitted analyzing the chronological sequence of important incidents and their effects on actors. In Venezuela, AD launched its war against the Executive by mid-1990, long before the marked deterioration of public opinion, societal unrest, and military instability that brought down the government (October 1991). In Argentina, the PJ normalized its relations with the Executive at a time when public discontent and skepticism toward the reforms were at an all-time high (early 1991). In addition, the PJ stood by the Executive even when state-society tensions rose, rejecting even popularly supported causes (e.g., the pensioners, devaluation). And when relations turned hostile again (1997), reform sustainability receded thereafter (1998–99).

Controlling for Policy Measures

Another crucial test of the causal effect of Executive–ruling party relations is to control for policy initiatives. Several policies that were attempted—to no avail—in the context of disharmonious Executive–ruling party relations in Argentina actually prospered in the context of harmonious Executive–ruling party relations: fixed exchange rates, fiscal reforms, investment incentives, privatization. This change in policy success was due in part to changes in levels of societal resistance, which, in turn, were linked to the nature of Executive–ruling party relations. For instance, under Lusinchi (harmonious Executive–ruling party relations), societal challenges against the state did not prosper (e.g., the Caldera bill stayed dormant in Congress, the CGT did not strike against the 1983–85 austerity measures, and disaffected sectors of the military did not stage coups despite their discontent). Under Pérez (negative Executive–ruling party relations), all these societal challenges—and more—prospered.

Variations in Executive–Ruling Party Relations

A final test of causality is that variations in the independent variable must correlate with changes in reform sustainability. This book shows different ways in which the state-without-party condition varied, both within the same country and across countries. In Argentina, for instance, the most significant episode of harmonious Executive–ruling party relations (1991–97) was preceded and followed by episodes of Executive–ruling party discord (the Alfonsín administration, the first year and a half of the Menem administration, and to a lesser degree, the last two years of the Menem administration). In Venezuela, the discord of the Pérez administration (1989–93) was preceded by harmony (the Lusinchi administration, 1994–89). And throughout Latin America, sharp differences in the state-without-party condition were documented. In each of these episodes, the finding was the same. The deeper the state-without-party condition, the harder it was for Executives to sustain economic reforms.

Party Accommodation as Institution Building: Argentina versus Peru in the Late 1990s

In his discussion of the Peruvian reforms in the 1990s, Roberts (1995) argued that "Fujimori has crafted a mixed political strategy that combines technocratic neoliberalism with microlevel populism." Indeed, most successful reformers that come from statist political parties also used similar neopopulist tactics to seduce incumbent forces and gain new allies. What makes these tactics "neo" is that the new populism comes with a new economics—that is to say, a high regard for fiscal discipline and restraints on state intervention in productive activities. It is "populist" in that these parties continue to use state resources (derived from the new fiscal health) to mobilize previously unmobilized societal groups (see Gibson 1997) and to reward loyalists.

Despite this commonality, Argentina's path toward the market in the 1990s differed from that of Peru. Argentina relied on party accommodation and, hence, boosting of the ruling party; Peru relied instead on party deflation. Party accommodation is intrinsically a type of institution building, which, despite its dark side, served Argentina's democracy. The best evidence of this is to contrast the different fates of the reckless reelection bids of Menem and Fujimori.

Both Menem and Fujimori ended the decade with a disproportionate sense of triumphalism and indispensability. Both sought to extend their stays in office despite constitutional prohibitions. Both tried all kinds of tricks, legal and illegal, to overcome widespread opposition to their plan. Fujimori succeeded, but Menem was forced to give up. The reason for this was variation in the state-without-party condition. In Argentina, after six years of party accommodation, the ruling party itself was able to emerge as the most forceful obstacle to Menem's efforts to overstay his welcome. Efforts on the part of the Executive to escape the parameters of what was permissible in Executive–ruling party relations were bound to give rise to resistance within the party. The party had the incentive to avoid Menem's blockage of the mobility for future leaders, as well as the resources to stop him. Party accommodation in the 1991–97 period permitted party resistance in the 1997–99 period.

In Peru, however, where there was never any party accommodation, no political force existed close to the president that could have played such a balancing role against Executive imperiousness. The opposition protested against Fujimori, but this went nowhere. Fujimori felt uninhibited to proceed with his reelection drive. As long as the military consented—which it did—there was no other force capable of stopping him.

The fundamental paradox of the state-with-party condition lies precisely in the complexity of the resulting partnership with the Executive. Party accommodation gave rise to a ruling party that, to paraphrase Argentine sociologist Juan Carlos Torre, played simultaneously the role of loyal opposition as well as partner. The partnership aspect of this relationship served to undermine mechanisms of presidential accountability and set the stage for illiberal lacunae. But at the same time, party accommodation allowed the ruling party to develop the autonomy and resources necessary to act as a check on presidential abuse.

The Costs of Party Accommodation: Neoliberal Reforms and Illiberal Gaps

The way to normalize Executive–ruling party relations is for Executives to deploy party-accommodating policies. Yet party accommodation involves important trade-offs. It permits reform sustainability, but at the cost of "illiberal" gaps in both the reform process and within the ruling parties.

The illiberal gaps stem from the compromises that the Executive needs to reach with the traditionalists in the ruling party. Placating the sense of threat that market reforms provoke on traditionalists might require introducing policies that contradict the spirit of the reforms. For instance, PJ leaders were offered privileged access to revenues from privatizations, control of social spending, autonomy to conduct patronage, debt relief, and so forth. More important, the Executive inflated the party's sense of self-importance. The PJ wanted its place in the sun as a condition for reform endorsement—and Menem complied. As a result, the PJ left office with a bigger sense of "indispensability" than ever before. Once again, a Peronist Executive had nurtured the party's self-perception as the "founding father" of the nation, the custodian of its institutions, and the political force whose say should matter the most. In short, the Executive reinforced the messianic proclivities of the PJ.

Many cases of successful Executive–ruling party rapprochement on behalf of market reform have occurred on the basis of similar overtures to the party. For instance, in Mexico and Colombia in the early 1990s, and in Bolivia in the 1980s, the ruling parties were given access to privatization and tax revenues, supposedly to be used for social policy, but *de facto* to be used for party-mediated patronage. Even in Venezuela between 1983 and 1985, Lusinchi obtained party consent for austerity by reinforcing party penetration of the state apparatus and agreeing not to liberalize the political system. In Mexico in the 1980s, party accommodation even included decelerating the liberalization of political competition among parties. Party-tolerated corruption has been reported ad nauseam in all of these cases. Furthermore, party accommodation reduced somewhat the accountability of both the Executive and the ruling party, since each tolerated and protected from scrutiny the political abuses of the other. In short, to persuade the party to embrace economic liberalization, the Executive has had to condone party practices that contradict the spirit of liberalization. And in return, the Executive has obtained some protection from societal scrutiny.

In short, this research adds to the explanation for the emergence of "illiberal" lacunae in countries that, paradoxically, went a long way in introducing neoliberal economic reforms. Both at the political and economic levels, Executives found it necessary to create these lacunae. Some aspects of the economy remained exempt from reform; some aspects of the political system remained exempt from accountability.

The Costs of the State-Without-Party Condition

However serious the costs of party accommodation, the costs of the alternative—a state-without-party—are certainly worse. Once again, Venezuela (post-Caldera) and Argentina (post-Menem) illustrate why trying to govern in the absence of supportive, competitive ruling party impairs economic governance.

Venezuela Post-Caldera

Venezuela in the 1990s became neither a case of reform avoidance nor of neoliberal transition, but rather of reform nonconsolidation—the prototype of a "reform-lagging" country, one of the few Latin American countries to have had not one, but two "lost decades." Venezuela suffered some sort of economic emergency in eight of the twelve years from 1988 to 1999—a critical fiscal deficit, a banking crisis, a currency crisis, an economic recession or a combination of these. More than two-thirds of the population now live below poverty levels. A recent report estimates that for an average Venezuelan with twelve years of schooling the probability of ending up poor is 18.5 percent, up from 2.4 percent only a decade ago (Congreso de la República). Education—a common antidote against poverty—has simply ceased to work.

This economic plunge is deeply connected to the collapse of the party system. Toward the end of the Caldera administration, the party system fragmented further. The leading parties—AD, Convergencia, and COPEI—were summarily defeated in a series of elections in 1998–99. Old parties were completely repudiated, both in the presidential elections (December 1998) and the elections for the delegates to the constitutional assembly (July 1999). Unwilling to align themselves with existing political parties, opposition candidates ran as independents in the July elections. Opposition voters thus faced a plethora of opposition candidates from which to choose. Their votes were dispersed among many candidates, making it difficult for opposition candidates to amass enough votes to win seats.

These two outcomes—economic collapse and party system collapse—are intimately related. Venezuela's repeated failure to reform its economy made existing politicians increasingly unpopular, who in turn responded by privileging populist policies over real reforms. The result was a vicious circle of economic and political party decay. During the Caldera administration, the erosion of the state-without-party condition forced the Executive to court the very same parties that he had campaigned against—AD and COPEI, which in turn sold their support at a very high price (Chapter 10). Once again, a reform-minded administration gave the image of being trapped by political parties, fueling citizen's disgust with party politics. But in reality, Venezuela was trapped by the exact opposite, the state-without-party condition.

When Hugo Chávez assumed office in early 1999, Venezuela's party deficit reached an all-time high. Opposition parties essentially fragmented or disintegrated. AD even declared itself to be financially bankrupt. The president assumed office with another quickly assembled coalition of small ruling parties, the Polo Patriótico. If Chávez ever converts to market economics, just as most Latin American populist-militaristic leaders did in the 1990s, he will clearly enjoy favorable political assets—a devoted following and a demoralized opposition. However, he could still be encumbered by the same political constraints imposed by the state-without-party condition: the propensity of his ad hoc ruling coalition to fragment upon launching market reforms. Chávez's ruling coalition, the Polo Patriótico, is almost identical to Caldera's—an ad hoc, last-minute mélange of small, marginal parties of the left and the military sector, with support from defecting factions of some traditional parties. This coalition is also susceptible to the same structural instability as the preceding one. None of the parties in the Polo Patriótico has developed a strong political machine, which might compel Polo's leaders to use state resources to build political machineries. This is tantamount to pressures for populism from within.[4]

Chávez thus confronts the options available to statesmen without parties. He could attempt to build his own party (the MVR), negotiate with the oppo-

---

4. The other problem is the nonrenewal of the old left-Chávez's closest allies. Like the traditional politicians of AD and COPEI, the leaders of the old left have been historically exempted from the need to compete for votes to justify their leadership positions within their respective parties. Until the 1980s, the old left held a permanent minority status—a status that its leaders resigned themselves to. This resignation meant exempting themselves from pressures for self-renewal and elite rotation.

sition, succumb to policy paralysis, strike against the party system, or rely on the military. So far, he has shown a preference for the latter two options. His first year in office was devoted to undermining the opposition by way of plebiscite-style elections in which the opposition fared poorly. He used his popularity to approve a new constitution that weakens opposition parties. The new constitution even bans state financing of political parties. This gives his own party an enormous advantage—Chávez can easily divert state resources for the MVR and deny such funds to opposition parties.

The overture to the military is even more dramatic. In two years in office, Chávez appointed high-ranking military officers to head the ministries of Infrastructure, Interior, Justice, and Defense and to the presidencies of PDVSA, Citgo, and CVG. Most social assistance programs are being carried out by the military. For the first time since the 1950s, the military in Venezuela is displacing civilians from the control of civilian institutions. Many civilians, including members of the Polo Patriótico, resent this, which has given rise to yet another cleavage within the ruling coalition.

Bullying the opposition and catering to the military are inauspicious for democracy. Yet they are natural consequences of the state-without-party condition.

Argentina Post-Menem

In mid-1998, Argentina's fast-growing economy entered into a recession. Despite a new administration, several adjustment packages, a U.S.$39.1 billion credit line from the IMF, and a U.S.$29.5 billion bond swap later, the recession simply got worse in 2001. This is Argentina's longest recession in recent memory. In less than three years, Argentina went from being a country with a promising economic future to a country posing a huge danger to global finance. What went wrong in Argentina?

Alas, the state-without-party condition is part of the problem. Argentina's ruling party between 1999 and 2001, the Alianza, was an alliance of two center-left parties, the old UCR and the FREPASO. It was formed in 1997 with the explicit purpose of taking Argentina through "post-adjustment" politics (that is to say, increase transparency, channel resources to social sectors), not through "pre-adjustment" politics. The problem is that Menem's last two years in office were so disastrous that he brought back Argentina to a pre-adjustment stage (see Chapter 10). Menem left a cocktail of rising deficits, debt, and recession, the latter exacerbated mostly by state-induced mistrust on the part of economic agents. Prior to coming to office, Alianza leaders spent most of their time debating—and agreeing on—how to invest state resources, but not enough time debating what to do in the event of revenue shortfalls. They prepared to govern Argentina in good times, but not in bad times. When the Alianza took office, it confronted a political problem—recession, high debts, and high deficits for which it had neither contingency plans nor consensus.

In dealing with the politics of adjustment, de la Rúa was much more constrained than Menem ever was. De la Rúa could not devalue (as Cavallo did prior to launching the 1991 Convertibility Plan) nor privatize, since there was nothing left to privatize. The only options left were spending cutbacks, tax increases, and tax creation designed to yield almost U.S.$2 billion (the December 1999 package, otherwise known as the "impuestazo"). These are unpopular measures, and for many economists, suboptimal because they are intensely recessionary and, thus, inadvisable in the context of a deep recession such as that of the fourth quarter of 1999. The administration thus made its debut by displeasing two important groups: the center-left sectors who elected the president and the private sector that longed for a supply-side economic stimulus.

Once again, the politics of adjustment generated a huge dislocation in Executive–ruling party relations. Protests on the part of Alianza leaders, both inside the cabinet and in the legislature, were publicly voiced by the first month of the administration (*Clarín*, January 14, 2000; January 17, 2000) and grew louder thereafter. Even Alfonsín, supposedly the "mentor" of de la Rúa's first minister of the economy, José Luis Machinea, turned against the government. In October 2000, he declared on national TV: "The Convertibility Law of 1991 is the gravest episode in economic affairs of this century," a clear attack against Machinea's policy of continuing to uphold the exchange rate regime (Microsemanario 420, October 20, 2000). The following day, the government felt compelled to offer a harsh rebuttal: "The Convertibility Law is the fulcrum [*piedra angular*] of our monetary, credit, and financial markets" (Chrystian Colombo, ibid.).

The Alianza thus maintained a mixed stand toward Machinea. The small wing of the UCR supported the minister, although not whole-heartedly, whereas the non-*Alfonsinista* radicals and the *Frepasistas* never came around. Thus the ruling coalition proved unable to digest de la Rúa's adjustment package. It should not be surprising at this point why the de la Rúa administration had such a difficult time gaining the trust and cooperation of economic agents to reignite economic growth. The state-without-party condition was the crucial ingredient in Argentina's failure to restart its economy between 1998 and 2001.

The state-without-party condition had the same political effects in Argentina in 2001 that it had had in Venezuela in 1993. Economic agents increased their mistrust of the state (evidenced by continued decline in industrial investments). The administration resorted to desperate rescue measures, including the reappointment of none other than Domingo Cavallo, who attempted in vain to get "special powers" from Congress. Perceiving the weakness of the Executive, the opposition turned increasingly uncooperative. Even the external allies lost confidence in the state and abandoned de la Rúa (in November 2001, the IMF decided not to provide further relief). In utter isolation, the government announced a bank holiday to contain the run on the banks, unleashing widespread looting, not unlike what happened in Argentina in 1989. The following day, President de la Rúa resigned, yet another casualty of the state-without-party condition.

Conclusion

Parties remain indispensable for economic governance in democratic nations. Economic transformation occurs more smoothly in the context of a cooperative relationship between an Executive and a strong ruling party, which, in turn, is only possible where competitive political parties exist to begin with. Parties contribute to economic governance, not because they shape policy, but because they shape policy sustainability. Countries with weakened political parties face a governance handicap.

Since the 1970s, scholars have been reporting and debating the consequences of the "decline" of political parties, in both Western democracies and Latin America. Many scholars argue that old parties lost touch with the new post-materialist realities of citizens, became impermeable to new leaders and ideas, responded slowly to new issues, suffocated rather than stimulated civil society, and became semi-cartels interested mostly in protecting the "in" groups. Parties came to be seen as either impediments or pollutants of democratic governance. Hopes for democratic renewal were placed instead on the plethora of new social movements that began to proliferate in the 1970s.

In the late 1990s, however, several scholars have begun to lament, rather than celebrate, the disrepute of political parties in Latin America. Although parties in the region have been the culprit of enormous political vices, the demise of party life, where it has occurred, has come at a huge cost. For many scholars, the cost has occurred at the level of societal representation—what some label a "crisis of representation" (Hagopian 1998; Domínguez and

Giraldo 1996)—which has deprived citizens of "talk-back mechanisms" vis-à-vis the state (Conaghan 1996).

This study adds its voice to these alarm signals, but it highlights a different cost associated with party deficits—economic governance. States that attempt to escape from economic crises without the benefit of competitive, reformed, and cooperative political parties, both in office as well as in the opposition, are handicapped. Countries that manage to renew, rather than displace, their old parties stand a better chance of escaping deep economic crises, even when those very same parties were responsible for bringing on the crisis to begin with.

appendixes

Appendix 1: Argentina and Venezuela: Examples of SOEs (late 1980s)

Category	Argentina	Venezuela
Ports	Administración General de Puertos	Instituto Autónomo Aeropuerto Internacional de Maiquetía
		Instituto Nacional de Puertos
Transport (air and sea)	Aerolíneas Argentinas	Línea Aeropostal Venezolana
		Venezolana Internacional de Aviación (VIASA)
	Líneas Aéreas del Estado	Inversiones de Transporte
	Empresa Líneas Marítimas Argentina (ELMA)	Venezolana de Motores Aeronáuticos e Industriales
		C.A. Venezolana de Navegación (CAVN)
		Transportadora Marítima
Utilities	Agua y Energía Eléctrica	C.A. Administración y Fomento Eléctrico
	Com. Mixta Argentino-Paraguaya del Río Paraná	Electricidad del Caroní
	Entidad Binacional Yacyretá	Energía Eléctrica de Barquisimeto
	Hidroeléctrica Norpatagónica	Energía Eléctrica de Venezuela
	Obras Sanitarias de la Nación	Instituto Municipal del Aseo Urbano
	Servicios Eléctricos del Gran Buenos Aires (SEGBA)	Instituto Nacional de Canalización
	Gas del Estado	Instituto Nacional de Obras Sanitarias
Shipyards	Astilleros y Fábricas Navales del Estado	Astilleros Navales Venezolanos
	Talleres Navales Dársena Norte	Diques y Astilleros Nacionales
Forestry	Centro Forestal Pirane	C.A. Venezolana de Reforestación
Railways	Ferrocarriles Argentinos	Instituto Autónomo Ferrocarriles del Estado
	Comisión Mixta Ferroviaria Argentino-Boliviana	
Housing	Construcción de Viviendas para la Armada	Instituto Nacional de la Vivienda
Foodstuffs and agricultural warehouses	Corporación Argentina de Productores de Carne	Almacenes y Depósitos Agropecuarios
	Compañía Azucarera las Palmas	Centrales Azucareros
		Fondo de Desarrollo Frutícola

Category	Argentina	Venezuela
Communications	Emp. Nacional de Telecomunicaciones (ENTel)	Fondo Nacional de Cacao Mercados, Silos y Frigoríficos Palmavén C.A. Teléfonos de Venezuela (CANTV)
Nuclear power	Emp. Nuclear Argentina de Centrales Eléctricas	
Tourism, media, entertainment	Emp. Operadora Mayorista de Servicios Turísticos Hoteles Nacionales del Min. de Bienestar Social Various horse-racing tracks 71 radio stations; Telam; 9 TV stations	C.A. Zona Turística Oriental Corporación de Turismo de Venezuela Inst. Autónomo Círculo de las FF.AA. Instituto Nacional de Hipódromo (Caracas, Valencia, Maracaibo) C.A. Venezolana de Televisión; several radio and TV stations
Basic industry	Forja Argentina SOMISA Altos Hornos Zapla	14 basic industry and infrastructure enterprises under the Corporación Venezolana de Guayana (CVG), including: Siderúrgica del Orinico (SIDOR) and Venezolana de Aluminio.
Mining	Hierro Patagónico de Sierra Grande Yacimientos Carboníferos Fiscales	C.A. Minas de Naricual; Carbones del Zulia; Compañía Nacional de Cal; Empresa Nacional de Salinas; Ferrominera Orinoco
Military	14 military factories	Almacenes Militares C.A. Venezolana de Industrias Militares
Petroleum and petrochemicals	Yacimientos Petrolíferos Fiscales (YPF) 5 petrochemical companies	Petróleos de Venezuela (PDVSA) Seven subsidiaries in associated downstream activities (e.g., natural gas, petroleum distribution, fertilizers, petrochemicals)

Appendix 1 *(cont'd)*

Category	Argentina	Venezuela
Financial	40 banks, including credit agencies Instituto Nacional de Reaseguros; 11 provincial insurance and 1 air insurance companies	27 banks and financial institutes
Misc.	143 wholly owned provincial enterprises 19 wholly owned municipal enterprises, including the Buenos Aires subway system 28 mixed ownership firms 10 intergovernmental enterprises	70 smaller SOEs operating in tourism, agricultural export industry, manufacturing; Centro Simón Bolívar (office complex); Empresa Venezolana de Artesanías; C.A Metro de Caracas

Sources: IMF 1988; World Bank 1993; and Minsburg 1991.

Appendix 2: Research Strategy, Interviews, and Translations

To obtain information about the preferences and actions of the ruling party as well as other information relevant to this book, three research strategies were employed. The first consisted of a conventional examination of primary and secondary materials (e.g., journalistic pieces, party literature, speeches, and scholarly works). Second, open-ended interviews were conducted with more than 150 political actors or observers. These interviews took place during various trips to Argentina (July–August 1991, June–July 1992, and June–December 1994), various trips to Venezuela (December 1993–April 1994, Summer 1997) and various trips to Washington, D.C. Some interviews took place in Cambridge, Massachusetts. An effort was made to include not just party leaders but also other types of elite, such as state officials, business representatives, civic leaders, opposition figures, labor bosses, and local analysts. The research on Venezuela profited enormously from the opportunity to interview presidents Carlos Andrés Pérez and Rafael Caldera, and on Argentina, Minister Domingo Cavallo.

In general, interviews tended to last between an hour and an hour and fifteen minutes. Appendix 3 provides the names of interviewees and their most politically relevant posts during the Pérez and Menem administrations.

As an information-verifying device, the interviews generally adhered to two tactics: third-party questioning (that is to say, asking the subjects about not just their own activities but also about those of others) and double-checking (that is to say, corroborating the information conveyed by interviews with different subjects). Requests for anonymity were strictly respected. Although an effort was made to cover similar ground in each interview, no set pattern was followed.

A third and crucial research strategy for assessing ruling-party positions consisted of asking the top party leadership to respond to a fixed questionnaire at the end of each interview (see Table 5.2). This questionnaire was conducted in the first half of 1994 in Venezuela and the second half of 1994 in Argentina. Thus, this strategy controlled for the timing of the questions, approximately five years after the launch of the reforms in each country. Each interviewee was read the same list of statements and asked to respond by indicating the extent to which he or she agreed or disagreed with it. Three answer choices were available: (1) I agree strongly or mildly, (2) I am neutral (e.g., ambivalent or unwilling to answer), or (3) I disagree strongly or mildly.

Interviewees for this questionnaire were selected on the basis of two criteria. First, interviewees must have been members of the party's central committee at any moment during the reform process. In AD, this meant membership in the National Executive Committee (*Comité Ejecutivo Nacional*, CEN), a body of party officials, which had thirty-five members in 1989. In the PJ, it meant membership in the Executive Board (*Mesa Ejecutiva*), which had twenty-six members in 1989 (increased to thirty-three after 1991). The CEN and the Executive Board are the decision-making organs of each party. They typically meet at least once a week, often with the Executive when the party is in office. Membership in either the

CEN or the Executive Board is irrespective of career background (elected officials, intellectuals, technical experts, business leaders, etc.) or current professional position (legislator, provincial governor, cabinet member, fund raiser, adviser, etc.).

The second selection criterion was that interviewees could not be members of the government at the time of the interview. This criterion was irrelevant in the case of Venezuela (since the government was out of office at the time of the survey), but it served to exclude four potential interviewees in the case of Argentina (who held joint appointments in the government and in the Executive Board): Carlos Menem, Guillermo Seita, Eduardo Bauzá, and Carlos Corach. The purpose of this criterion was to avoid the bias toward a pro-government opinion that state officials were likely to have. The remaining CEN and Executive Board members were not interviewed because they were either unavailable (due to travel, death, or illness) or unwilling to meet.

As a result of these criteria, the questionnaire was presented to twelve CEN members and ten Executive Board members. The interviewed CEN members are Carlos Canache Mata, Humberto Celli, Paulina Gamús, Liliana Hernández, Alberto Herrera, Arístides Hospedales, Carmelo Lauría, David Morales Bello, Ángel Reinaldo Ortega, Pedro París Montesino, Luis Piñerúa Ordaz, and Henry Ramos Allup. The interviewed Executive Board members are César Arias, José Azcurra, Oraldo Britos, Antonio Cafiero, Antonio Cassia, Alberto Conca, Remo Costanzo, Alberto Kohan, Ricardo Romano, and Luis Rubeo. The main advantage of the questionnaire is that it provides quantifiable, and thus, comparison-friendly answers. The main disadvantage is that, at best, the answers apply mostly to the situation at the moment of the interview.

All sources in Spanish, including interviews, were translated into English by the author, unless otherwise specified in the text.

Appendix 3: List of Interviewees (Name / Highest Post, 1989–94 /
Date and Place of Interview)

Venezuela

1. Alfonzo H., Rafael
President of Conindustria
February 7, 1994, Caracas

2. Álvarez Paz, Oswaldo
COPEI governor of Zulia State and
1993 presidential candidate
March 23, 1994, Caracas

3. Álvarez, Víctor
Adviser in the Ministry of Development and Corpoindustria
March 18, 1994, Caracas

4. Beltrán Petrosini, Luis
Attorney General
March 17, 1994, Caracas

5. Blanco, Carlos
Minister of COPRE
March 16, 1994, Caracas

6. Bottome, Robert
Director of *Veneconomía*
Several occasions, Caracas

7. Caldera, Rafael
Two-time president of Venezuela
1993, Cambridge, Mass.

8. Canache Mata, Carlos
CEN member, chief of AD's legislative bloc
April 11, 1994, Caracas

9. Carmona, Jesús
Minister of the Presidency, Minister of Congressional Relations
April 7, 1994, Caracas

10. Celli, Humberto
CEN member, AD secretary-general
April 6, 1994, Caracas

11. Chacón, Carlos
Privatization Officer (after Pérez)
January 14, 1994, Caracas

12. Cisneros, Imelda
Minister of Development
Several occasions, Caracas

13. Coles, Jonathan
Minister of Agriculture
Several occasions, Caracas

14. Díaz, Rolando
Labor Analyst
March 29, 1994, Caracas

15. Febres, Carlos Eduardo
CTV representative
February 7, 1994, Caracas

16. Fernández, Eduardo
COPEI president and 1988
presidential candidate
Several occasions, Caracas

17. Freites, Luis Alfredo
Presidential Trustee for National
Concertation
March 27, 1994, Caracas

18. Gamús, Paulina
CEN member, AD legislator
April 14, 1994, Caracas

19. García, Gustavo
Economist and adviser to finance
minister
Several occasions, Caracas

20. García, Haydée
Adviser to the Ministry of Labor and
Family
January 13, 1994, Caracas

21. García Mendoza, Oscar
President of Banco Venezolano de
Crédito
April 6, 1994, Caracas

22. Gil Yepes, José Antonio
Director, VeneConsultores; director,
Veneconomía
February 28, 1994, Caracas

23. Gómez, José Rafael
AD deputy
February 2, 1995, Cambridge, Mass.

24. Hausmann, Ricardo
Minister of Cordiplan
Several occasions, Caracas and
Washington, D.C.

25. Hernández, Liliana
CEN member, AD deputy
April 13, 1994, Caracas

26. Herrera, Alberto
CEN member and president of
Federación Campesina
March 17, 1994, Caracas

27. Hospedales, Arístides
CEN member
March 22, 1994, Caracas

28. Jatar, Ana Julia
Superintendent, Pro-Competencia
Several occasions, Washington, D.C.

29. Juan, Ellis
Adviser to FIV and World Bank
Consultant
December 1, 1993, Washington, D.C.

30. Kastner, George Th.
Managing Director of Arthur D. Little
Venezuela
March 30, 1994, Caracas

31. Keller, Alfredo
Pollster, president of Consultores 21
March 30, 1994, Caracas

32. Kelly, Janet
Dean (and political scientist), IESA
Several occasions, Caracas

33. Lauría, Carmelo
CEN member and president of
Chamber of Deputies
April 18, 1994, Caracas

34. Márquez, Trino
Vice-minister, COPRE
February 8, 1994, Caracas

35. Márquez, Walter
MAS deputy
April 19, 1994, Caracas

36. Morales Bello, David
CEN member, Pérez's campaign officer
April 12, 1994, Caracas

37. Naím, Moisés
Minister of Development
Several occasions, Washington, D.C.

38. Nebreda, Julián
Technical Assistant for Venezuela,
Inter-American Development Bank
December 1, 1993, Washington, D.C.

39. Parel, Chris
Venezuela Country Officer, World
Bank
October 29, 1993, Washington, D.C.

40. París Montesino, Pedro
CEN member, President of the Senate
April 4, 1994, Caracas

41. Pérez, Carlos A.
Two-time president of Venezuela
April 22, 1994, Caracas

42. Piñerúa Ordaz, Luis
CEN member, Minister of the Interior
April 5, 1994, Caracas

43. Otero, Miguel H.
Director, *El Nacional*
March 24, 1994, Caracas

44. Quintero Núñez, Eduardo
President, FIV
Various occasions, Caracas and Cambridge, Mass.

45. Ramos Allup, Henry
CEN member, AD deputy
April 14, 1994, Caracas

46. Rangel Mantilla, Beatriz
Minister of the Presidency
March 16, 1994, Caracas

47. Rivas, Orángel
Adviser, Cordiplan
February 24, 1994, Caracas

48. Rodríguez, Miguel
Minister of Cordiplan
July 6, 1994, Washington, D.C.

49. Roig, Jorge
Causa R deputy
April 21, 1994, Caracas

50. Rosas, Pedro
Minister of Finance
February 22, 1994, Caracas

51. Stambouli, Andrés
Political scientist
February 8, 1994, Caracas

52. Suzzarini, Abdón
Adviser to the Ministry of Development, and Central Bank
February 11, 1994, Caracas

53. Torres, Gerver
President of FIV
September 27, 1995, Washington, D.C.

54. Vélez, Francisco
Adviser, FIV
December 2, 1993, Washington, D.C.

55. Villalba, Julián
President, FIV
February 25, 1994, Caracas

56. Vollmer Jr., Gustavo
Business leader
March 28, 1994, Caracas

57. Zermeño, Mayra
Venezuela section, World Bank
October 29, 1993, Washington, D.C.

Argentina
1. Alasino, Augusto
PJ senator
September 28, 1994, Buenos Aires

2. Alemann, Roberto
Economist
June 1992, Buenos Aires

3. Alexander, Myrna
World Bank representative
Various occasions, Buenos Aires

4. Arias, César
EB member, PJ deputy
October 6, 1994, October 28, 1994,
Buenos Aires

5. Azcurra, José
EB member, PJ labor secretary,
November 3, 1994, Buenos Aires

6. Bárbaro, Julio
PJ leader,
August 18, 1994, Buenos Aires

7. Bordón, José Octavio
Governor of Mendoza (PJ), presiden-
tial candidate (FREPASO)
November 3, 2000, Washington, D.C.

8. Britos, Oraldo
EB member, senator, and labor leader
October 5, 1994, Buenos Aires

9. Bullrich, Patricia
PJ deputy
October 7, 1994, Buenos Aires

10. Cafiero, Antonio
PJ president, governor of Buenos
Aires Province, and senator
November 8, 1994, Buenos Aires

11. Cafiero, Juan Pablo
Group of Eight
November 1, 1994, Buenos Aires

12. Cahn, Francis
Vice President, Techint
August 5, 1991, Buenos Aires

13. Carballo, Carlos
Adviser, Minister of the Economy
(under Erman González)
August 26, 1994, Buenos Aires

14. Cardoso, Oscar Raúl
Journalist, *Clarín*
September 22, 1994, Buenos Aires

15. Casas, Juan Carlos
Business journalist
November 2, 1994, Buenos Aires

16. Caselas, Víctor
Adviser, Argentine Union of Suppli-
ers to the State
July 30, 1991, Buenos Aires

17. Cassia, Antonio
CGT and SUPE president
October 18, 1994, Buenos Aires

18. Cassullo, Eduardo
Executive Director, UIA
October 5, 1994, Buenos Aires

19. Cavallo, Domingo F.
Minister of the Economy and Public
Works and Services
Several occasions, Buenos Aires

20. Conca, Alberto
PJ leader
September 30, 1994, Buenos Aires

21. Costanzo, Remo
EB member, PJ senator
September 28, 1994, Buenos Aires

22. Cottani, Joaquín
Adviser, Ministry of the Economy
June 1992, Buenos Aires

23. de Barrios, Félix
Director, Argentine Businessmen
Council
August 7, 1991, Buenos Aires

24. de Zavalía, Eduardo
President, SRA
September 26, 1994, Buenos Aires

25. Dagnino Pastore, José
Economist
June 1992, Buenos Aires

26. Díaz, Rodolfo A.
Minister of Labor
Various occasions, Buenos Aires and
Cambridge, Mass.

27. Fernández Otero, Ricardo
General Coordinator, National
Council of the PJ
November 4, 1994, Buenos Aires

28. Fraga, Rosendo
Director, Centro de Estudios Unión
para la Nueva Mayoría
August 30, 1994, Buenos Aires

29. Giordano, Osvaldo
Adviser, Ministry of the Economy
June 1992, Buenos Aires

30. González Fraga, Javier
President, Central Bank
August 8, 1991, Buenos Aires

31. Grondona, Mariano
Journalist
Various occasions, Buenos Aires

32. Heymann, Daniel
UCR Economic Adviser
June 1992

33. Kusznir, Juan Carlos
Subdirector, IEERAL
June 1992

34. Liendo Jr., Horacio
Adviser, Ministry of the Economy
September 30, 1994, Buenos Aires

35. Kohan, Alberto
Minister of Social Action
October 13, 1994, Buenos Aires

36. Maffei, Marta
Labor union leader
November 7, 1994, Buenos Aires

37. Magariños, Carlos
Secretary of Industry and Commerce
July 1992, Buenos Aires

38. Molina, Pedro
President of PJ Legislative Bloc
October 4, 1994, Buenos Aires

39. Olivera, Enrique
UCR Legislator
June 1992, Buenos Aires

40. Otaño Piñero, Jorge
Secretary, National Electoral Board
November 4, 1994, Buenos Aires

41. Redrado, Martín
Director, Comisión Nacional de
Valores
October 26, 1994, Buenos Aires

42. Ribas, Armando
Director, Banco Extrader
November 3, 1994, Buenos Aires

43. Rodríguez, Carlos Rafael
Vice-Minister of the Economy
(1996–98)
August 17, 2000, Buenos Aires

44. Romano, Ricardo
PJ leader
September 18, 1994, Buenos Aires

45. Rubeo, Luis
PJ senator
September 19, 1994, Buenos Aires

46. Stafforini, Eduardo
Adviser to the PJ
September 22, 1994, Buenos Aires

47. Tagliaferri, José Luis
Jefe de Gabinete del Ministro
Various occasions, Buenos Aires

Appendix 4: Ranking of Depth of Market Reforms

To rank the extent of market reforms in a given administration, it is important to look at various indicators (see Chapter 3). A raw quantitative assessment of the degree of market reforms would consider, at the very least, the extent to which the administration managed to achieve or maintain relatively: (1) high levels of economic freedom and regulatory openness; (2) low levels of inflation; (3) low levels of public-sector deficits; (4) significant levels of private investments relative to GNP; and (5) significant degree of privatization.

The following table provides data on these categories for several reform-minded administrations in Latin America in the 1990s. It also provides data on regional averages for many of these categories in order to situate a country's performance in relation to Latin America as a whole. Based on my own assessment of these figures, I have classified administrations according to different degrees of market openness. Scores range from 0 (low market reformers) to 10 (high market reformers). My rankings appear in column L.

| Country | Year | Economic Freedom | | Consumer Prices | | Public-Sector Deficits | | G | Change in Private Investment/ GDP | | J | Privatizations | Ranking |
		A	B	C	D	E	F		H	I		K	L
Argentina	1996	2.3	2	0.1	18.2	-1.8	-1.2	1989–96	12.2	16.8	4.6	6.1	9
	1999	2.25	2	-1.7	9.6	-2.1	-3.2	1996–98	16.8	18.2	1.4	8.6	8
Brazil	1993	3.3	4	2489.1	876.6	-0.8	-1.2	1989–93	21.1	15.5	-5.6	0.7	2
	1999	3.25	3	8.0	9.6	-9.0	-3.2	1993–98	15.5	16.5	1.0	10.9	7
Chile	1999	2	2	2.6	9.6	-1.5	-3.2	1989–98	18.2	22.1	3.9	3.4	9
Colombia	1994	3.05	3	22.6	333.1	1.0	-1.9	1989–94	9.6	15.2	5.6	0.9	7
	1998	2.9	3	16.7	10.3	-3.4	-2.7	1994–98	15.2	9.7	-5.5	4.5	5
Cuba	1996	4.85	5	N/A	N/A	-2.3	-1.2	1989–96			N/A	N/A	2
Ecuador	1999	3.45	4	53.5	9.6	-4.0	-3.2	1989–97	11.6	13.3	1.7	0.6	3
Haiti	1999	3.9	5	10.1	9.6	-2.6	-3.2	1989–98			N/A	0	2
Mexico	1994	3.1	4	7.1	333.1	-0.3	-1.9	1989–94	13.0	15.6	2.6	5.6	7
	1999	2.95	4	13.9	9.6	-1.3	-3.2	1994–98	15.6	19.8	4.2	5.9	7
Paraguay	1999	3.2	4	4.6	9.6	-1.5	-3.2	1989–98	16.0	14.2	-1.8	0.2	4
Peru	1995	2.9	4	10.2	25.8	-0.6	-1.5	1989–95	13.1	19.6	6.5	7.9	7
	1999	2.5	3	4.8	9.6	-2.6	-3.2	1995–98	19.6	20.7	1.1	13.2	7
Venezuela	1994	3.5	3	70.8	333.1	-13.8	-1.9	1989–94	7.2	8.2	1.0	3.6	3
	1998	3.3	3	29.9	10.3	-4.0	-2.7	1994–98	8.2	9.8	1.6	6.1	4

Notes and Sources:

A. Degree of Economic Freedom, as per Heritage Foundation (various years). To measure economic freedom and rate each country, 50 independent economic variables are studied, which fall into 10 broad categories—trade policy, fiscal burden of government, government intervention in the economy, monetary policy, foreign investment, banking, wages and prices, property rights, regulation, and black-market activity. The grading scale runs from 1 to 5: a score of 1 signifies an institutional or consistent set of policies that are most conducive to economic freedom; 5 signifies a set of policies that are least conducive. These scores are averaged for an overall score. The period of study is generally examined for the period covering the last half of the year through the first half of the next year.

B. Degree of Regulatory Rigidness, as per Heritage Foundation (various years). This measure is a subset of the economic freedom score. Numbers indicate how easy or difficult it is to open and operate a business. A very low score of 1 indicates that corruption is nonexistent and regulations are minimal and applied uniformly. A very high score of 5 indicates that corruption is rampant, regulations are applied randomly, and the general level of regulation is very high.

C. Consumer Prices for the Country, based on ECLAC (various years). Data based on information provided by official sources in the countries. Data for 1993–98 cover December–December variations; data for 1999 cover November 1998–November 1999, except Haiti, October 1998–October 1999.

D. Regional Average of Consumer Prices for the Year, based on ECLAC (various years).

E. Public-Sector Deficits for Country. Data for all countries based on ECLAC (various years), except for Cuba, which is drawn from Jatar-Hausmann (1999:87). Data cover the nonfinancial public sector, except for Argentina, which covers the national nonfinancial public sector (i.e., it excludes provinces and municipalities), and Haiti and Peru, which covers the Central Government.

F. Public-Sector Deficit for the Entire Region (average).

G. Period of Coverage

H. Amount of Private Investment/GDP at the beginning of the period, as per IFC (2000).

I. Amount of Private Investment/GDP at the end of period, as per IFC (2000).

J. Change in points during the period (H–I).

K. Accumulated Privatization Revenues as a Percentage of GDP, based on data from the Inter-American Development Bank. Data tend to underestimate the privatization record of countries that privatized early on, such as Chile, Argentina, Peru, and Mexico.

L. Author's ranking of the administrations based on the degrees of market openness.

Appendix 5: "El Justicialismo siempre junto al pueblo" (Attached)

SOLICITADA

EL JUSTICIALISMO
SIEMPRE JUNTO AL PUEBLO

Ante la decisión cupular de la Confederación General del Trabajo de convocar a una huelga general para el próximo día lunes 9 de noviembre, el Consejo Nacional del Partido Justicialista tiene la obligación de hacer conocer al país las siguientes consideraciones:

1) El Gobierno Nacional, expresión de la voluntad política del Justicialismo, avalado por la inmensa mayoría del pueblo argentino, conduce un proceso transformador de estructuras caducas que nos llevaron al atraso, a la miseria, al desempleo, a la hiperinflación y sumieron a nuestro pueblo en la desesperanza del fracaso reiterado.
Hemos rescatado la esperanza de los argentinos, y avanzamos hacia la construcción de una Argentina estable, con crecimiento y justicia social.

Los trabajadores son los principales destinatarios de este gigantesco esfuerzo.

2) Cuando nos hicimos cargo del Gobierno, el principal reclamo social era la estabilidad que se alcanzó, y no ignoramos que hoy el reclamo es el crecimiento con justicia social.

Este Gobierno tuvo la fortaleza necesaria para satisfacer aquella angustiosa primera demanda de la sociedad, y tendrá la misma fortaleza y decisión para cumplir estos objetivos que son parte irrenunciable de la identidad peronista.

Es mucho lo que se ha hecho, y es mucho lo que falta por hacer.

Para facilitar la participación se han creado ámbitos de diálogo y concertación entre los trabajadores, los empresarios y el gobierno, con dos Consejos que se encuentran funcionando.

La opción aparece clara: o se construye aportando en función de estos objetivos que son los del conjunto de la sociedad, o se confronta irresponsablemente promoviendo un paro sin motivos, sin propuestas, con fines políticos subalternos resuelto sólo para satisfacer las demandas de su propio sistema de intereses y de conducción.

Las estructuras dirigenciales del sindicalismo argentino deberían ser parte necesaria de la conducción de este proceso.

No pueden ni deben desertar de sus responsabilidades.

3) El martes todos los argentinos estaremos en el mismo país, con los mismos problemas.

EL JUSTICIALISMO CONVOCA A
RESOLVERLOS TRABAJANDO

PARTIDO JUSTICIALISTA

Consejo Nacional

Appendix 6: "La Fuerza de la Esperanza" (Attached)

CLARIN ★ Buenos Aires, miércoles 27 de mayo de 1992 ★ Página 45

SOLICITADA

LA FUERZA DE LA ESPERANZA

1. Cumplidos tres años de gestión los resultados electorales, las encuestas, la opinión internacional y el sentido común convalidan ampliamente la acción del gobierno del Presidente Menem. Sin embargo, hoy arrecian presiones y ataques de diversos factores de poder que apuntan, justamente, a la cabeza del proyecto.

Cuanto más se afianza la estabilidad más se la pretende contraponer con el crecimiento y la redistribución. Cuanto más se consolidan las libertades públicas, más se nos acusa de autoritarismo.

Cuanto más se afirma el orden jurídico, más se intensifica la acción psicológica que lo desvirtúa. Cuanto más avanzamos en desmontar las estructuras del privilegio y la corrupción más se nos acusa de corruptos.

De este modo los peronistas nos encontramos ante una situación crucial: o retomamos la capacidad de acción política para avanzar hacia el cambio consolidando la estabilidad, la democracia, el orden jurídico y la posibilidad transformadora o la Nación corre el riesgo de volver al pasado de frustración.

La crisis que vivimos es fruto del reacomodamiento a un nuevo modelo de país, que alcanza a todos los sectores e instituciones. Y también es consecuencia de la acción desmesurada de quienes se oponen al cambio. El desafío del peronismo es, una vez más, encarnar la transformación de la sociedad. No precisa demostrar retóricamente su aspiración a la justicia social: en la Argentina ella es el fruto de nuestras realizaciones. Sin embargo, para garantizar el futuro, debemos hacernos cargo del cambio con más fuerza, mayor convicción, más movilización de nuestra base popular. Porque el pueblo siempre apostó a superar la frustración a la esperanza.

2. A fines de 1988 la sociedad argentina ya percibía que estaba terminada la etapa inicial del proceso de recuperación democrática y el agotamiento del gobierno radical. El derrumbe del "Plan Austral" había dejado al alfonsinismo sin programa; y desde entonces todo su accionar se redujo a intentos de manipulación cortoplacista de las variables económicas. Sin voluntad política de transformación estructural, la "Economía de Guerra", el "Australito", el "Plan Primavera solo", fueron cortinas retóricas para ocultar su impotencia y su ignorancia. No podían gobernar la Argentina por una simple razón: no sabían.

A principios de 1989, la situación les explotó en las manos. Y no solamente perdieron las elecciones sino que dejaron al país en la más profunda recesión de los últimos 30 años, con la tasa de desocupación más alta de la historia, con un salario medio de la economía de menos de 100 dólares, jubilaciones de menos de 30, devorados por una hiperinflación del 200% mensual y con episodios de violencia social que amenazaban con extenderse. Y tuvieron que abandonar el gobierno seis meses antes del plazo constitucional.

3. En esas graves circunstancias, el Dr. Carlos MENEM asumió anticipadamente la Presidencia de la Nación. Con él, el Peronismo llegaba nuevamente al gobierno después de un largo y profundo proceso de cambio y modernización. La prisión, el ostracismo, el exilio y la lucha por la recuperación democrática habían promovido una nueva generación de dirigentes formados en el conocimiento y la acción, en la ciencia y la política, de la cual el mismo Dr. Menem es un destacado ejemplo.

Ya en 1987 se había establecido sólidamente en el discurso peronista un nuevo análisis del mundo y del país. La crisis del orden mundial de la posguerra, emergía clara a la lectura atenta de la realidad. Ello planteaba requerimientos distintos para una reinserción soberana de la Argentina en el mundo. Y el diagnóstico de la decadencia argentina de aquellos años denunciaba otras causas que las consideradas hasta entonces. Ese nuevo diagnóstico nos orientó en la búsqueda de otras soluciones; nuevas, distintas.

Pero fueron los cambios en nuestros propios modos de vida política interna los que posibilitaron la encarnadura política de esa nueva propuesta. La democratización partidaria iniciada en el 85 y que culminó —por la tesonera prédica del mismo Menem— en la elección de nuestra fórmula presidencial por el voto directo y secreto de todos los afiliados, convirtiendo al peronismo en el único gran partido argentino y uno de los pocos en el mundo que no consagra su fórmula a través de Convenciones o Congresos.

Los dos millones y medio de peronistas que participaron en la consagración de su candidatura fueron el anticipo de los casi ocho millones de argentinos que lo votaron para elegirlo Presidente de la Nación. Fue a través de este proceso profundo, popular, democrático y transparente que se institucionalizó su liderazgo sobre una sociedad que había depositado en él su último recurso: la Esperanza.

4. Hoy estamos ejecutando un programa de gobierno que funciona y que la Sociedad apoya porque tiene éxito. Es un programa políticamente conducido y técnicamente ejecutado. Está basado en un diagnóstico correcto y original de la situación que ataca y supera las causas de la crisis de decadencia e injusticia que heredamos.

El Programa de este Gobierno no es un programa "de ajuste", sino un "cambio de modelo de país"; porque la causa de nuestros males no estaba en "desajuste" alguno, sino en el tipo de organización económico-social —el "modelo"— que instalaron en la Argentina los gobiernos autoritarios, y que antes de nosotros nadie había podido cambiar.

El modelo del pasado era el "Capitalismo Prebendario" —que la sabiduría popular ya señalaba como la "Patria Contratista" y la "Patria Financiera"— y que describiéndolo en líneas simples funcionaba así: el Estado, a través de la inflación —que es el impuesto más irresistible, más regresivo y más antipopular— le expropiaba riqueza a la sociedad y particularmente a los sectores de ingresos fijos, esto es, a los trabajadores. El mismo Estado, a través de subsidios, contratos del gobierno y de empresas públicas, sobreprecios, excesiva protección y regulación y otras prebendas, transfería esa riqueza a las minorías privilegiadas articuladas con el poder. Era el modelo de la corrupción institucionalizada y la cultura de la especulación.

5. ¿Y qué hicimos? La primera etapa fue frenar el proceso de transferencia de riqueza a los sectores prebendarios a través de una transformación profunda del sistema económico y del Estado. Las leyes de emergencia económica y de reforma del Estado, la eliminación de subsidios, la reforma del Estado, las privatizaciones, la refinanciación de la deuda interna y externa, etc. La segunda etapa fue crear las condiciones que hicieran posible terminar con el impuesto inflacionario a través de la convertibilidad, la desregulación y sus medidas complementarias. Así, hemos desmontado el mecanismo perverso del capitalismo prebendario y hemos creado las condiciones para el desarrollo del nuevo modelo.

6. Nuestro programa se nutre en las banderas de justicia social, independencia económica y soberanía política. Es nuestra doctrina adaptada a los tiempos. No es de ningún modo una receta liberal y es mucho más que un conjunto de medidas y decisiones técnicas: es nuestra revolución, donde lo político totaliza democráticamente los esfuerzos de toda la sociedad para adaptarse a la evolución. Es la acción política la que hace al programa; porque sin política y sin consenso popular, no hay programa. Con este programa y luego de casi dos décadas de estancamiento y decadencia, la economía argentina creció al 5% en 1991, la desocupación se redujo a la mitad, el salario medio de la economía llegó a 450 dólares, la actividad económica, la producción y el empleo aumentaron en todos los rubros. Y aunque queda muchísimo para hacer hemos abierto un horizonte de futuro para el crecimiento con justicia social.

Los cambios de modelo socioeconómico necesitan tiempo para consolidarse definitivamente. Para asegurar su consolidación, es necesario adecuar los plazos de lo político a los requerimientos temporales del programa. Este es el punto central del debate sobre la reelección, que no debe esconderse entre otros temas —por importantes que sean— y que debemos asumir clara y explícitamente.

Se trata de darle al Programa el tiempo para consolidar su éxito, al sistema político la previsibilidad que las circunstancias exigen y al presidente Menem la oportunidad para completar su obra. Si no lo hacemos, comprometeremos el éxito del enorme esfuerzo realizado por el pueblo argentino.

Quienes promovemos la reelección de Menem no pretendemos imponerla. Solo queremos por vía institucional, devolverle al pueblo argentino la posibilidad de ejercer su soberanía y votarlo o no votarlo. Este solo y trascendente hecho no asegura que Menem sea reelecto; lo que asegura es que la decisión sobre la continuidad del programa quede en manos del pueblo.

7. El sistema político argentino es básicamente bipartidista y en él, la soberanía popular le asignó al justicialismo el rol de partido de gobierno; de oficialismo. Y aunque se lograron resultados positivos en la aprobación de leyes en el Congreso y en las elecciones provinciales, el Partido Justicialista ha tenido dificultades para cumplir algunas de las funciones fundamentales del oficialismo democrático, porque no ha completado el debate sobre la naturaleza de los cambios que vivimos. No articuló un discurso homogéneo de explicación y sustento al programa del presidente Menem; no encontró un procedimiento para organizar disciplinadamente los apoyos parlamentarios que el Gobierno necesita, no ha recuperado la capacidad de devolverle a la militancia la motivación imprescindible para su movilización abriendo el partido a su activa participación.

Por eso el Presidente ha debido asumir toda la tarea política personalmente; o casi. El explica, defiende, moviliza. Y aunque está masivamente acompañado por el pueblo, está partidariamente solo; la organización partidaria lo ha dejado solo. Y esta afirmación no debe verse como una crítica "de afuera", sino como un cuestionamiento reflexivo a nosotros mismos, porque los firmantes de este documento somos casi todos autoridades partidarias.

Tenemos que cambiar. No alcanzan las adhesiones "gregarias" al programa, que podrán ser leales pero no explican ni convencen; tampoco las adhesiones "posibilistas", que argumentando que no hay alternativa explican sin convencer. Solo una adhesión "política", fundada en el conocimiento inteligente de nuestro programa podrá sustentar un discurso partidario que lo explique, y sea capaz de convencer, de sumar adhesiones y de movilizar apoyos.

La organización de ese proceso de adhesión política es la tarea interna prioritaria del Partido Justicialista. Generando un discurso político articulado y coherente, que le posibilite participar en el debate social con seriedad y contundencia; una política parlamentaria eficaz y consistente con el Programa del Presidente; una estructura orgánica viva y sensible, útil como vínculo entre el Gobierno y la sociedad que lo sustenta; y un estilo de acción participativo y abierto, capaz de ser a la vez estímulo y referencia para la insustituible acción de la militancia peronista. Solo así podremos asegurar el apoyo político a nuestro programa de Gobierno y consolidar su éxito. Solo así podremos dar la batalla por la reelección y ganar.

A eso convocamos. Eso estamos haciendo: organizar al Peronismo crear la fuerza propia del Presidente Menem y su programa de gobierno: el Poder de la Esperanza.

Firman:

Abed Alberto, presidente de la SIGEP, Presidencia de la Nación; **Acefiola Florencio**, diputado nacional, Tucumán; **Alterach, Miguel Angel**, vicegobernador de Misiones; **Aromando José**, secretario de Coordinación Técnica, Ministerio de Educación; **Arrechea José**, diputado nacional, Chubut; **Baum Daniel**, diputado nacional, Neuquén; **Bello Claudia**, secretaria de Relaciones con la Comunidad, Ministerio del Interior, consejera nacional PJ; **Bermúdez María del P.**, diputada nacional, Jujuy; **Bonifacio Alberto**, director del INAP, Presidencia de la Nación; **Brenda Carlos**, diputado nacional, Formosa; **Brizuela María**, consejera nacional PJ; **Caballos Roque**, presidente del Tribunal de Cuentas de la Nación; **Cavallo Eduardo**, interventor de Obras Sanitarias, consejero nacional PJ; **Conca Alberto**, asesor presidencial, consejero nacional PJ; **Daud Jorge**, diputado nacional, Entre Ríos; **Díaz Lozano**, vicegobernador de Tucumán, consejero nacional PJ; **Díaz Rebello**, ministro de Trabajo y Seguridad Social de la Nación; **Domenicone Héctor**, secretario de Coordinación Administrativa y Técnica, Ministerio de Economía; **Domínguez Julián**, presidente del Instituto Nacional de la Juventud, Ministerio de Salud y Acción Social, consejero nacional PJ; **Domínguez Roberto**, gobernador de Jujuy; **Echeverría Luis**, diputado nacional Buenos Aires, consejero nacional PJ; **Fellner Eduardo**, diputado nacional Jujuy; **Figueroa Alcorta Gastón**, interventor en Administración Inmuebles Fiscales, Ministerio de Economía; **Frangipane Virginia**, presidente del Consejo de Políticas Públicas para la Mujer, Presidencia de la Nación; **Fuks Gabriel**, consejero nacional PJ; **Fusel Juan Carlos**, jefe de asesores, Secretaría de Hidrocarburos, Ministerio de Economía; **Garre Rosalía**, consejera nacional PJ; **Gioja José Luis**, diputado nacional San Juan; **Godoy Julio César**, consejero nacional PJ; **González Roberto**, consejero nacional PJ; **Grabois Roberto**, subsecretario de Relaciones con la Comunidad, Ministerio del Interior, consejero nacional PJ; **Gurdulich Ana María**, asesora programa Arraigo, Santa Fe; **Herrera Bernardo**, diputado nacional La Rioja; **Herrera Juan Carlos**, presidente del INAC, Ministerio de Economía; **Kessler Ana**, subsecretaria de Reestructuración y Gestión, Ministerio de Defensa; **Lassus Alberto**, subsecretario de Seguridad Social, Ministerio de Trabajo y Seguridad Social; **Lemaire Graciela**, consejera nacional PJ; **Lico Miguel Angel**, secretario ejecutivo programa Arraigo, Presidencia de la Nación; **Machicote Jorge**, diputado nacional La Rioja; **Maggi Juan**, diputado nacional Buenos Aires, consejero nacional PJ; **Manfredotti Carlos**, diputado nacional Tierra del Fuego, consejero nacional PJ; **Mendoza Claudio**, diputado nacional Chaco; **Michilie Salomón**, diputado nacional Misiones; **Mundet Eduardo**, subsecretario de Universidad, Ministerio de Educación; **Ocampo Blanca**, ministro de Desarrollo Humano, San Juan; **Ordóñez Melitón**, presidente Comisión Venta Inmuebles Estatales, Ministerio de Economía; **Osorio Alfredo**, subsecretario de Coordinación, Ministerio de Educación; **Parada Alberto**, diputado nacional Chubut; **Pessoli Pedro**, consejero nacional PJ; **Prol Luis**, secretario de Hidrocarburos y Minería, Ministerio de Economía; **Puerta Ramón**, gobernador de Misiones; **Puricelli Arturo**, diputado nacional Santa Cruz, consejero nacional PJ; **Rodríguez Enrique**, secretario de Trabajo, Ministerio de Trabajo y Seguridad Social; **Sánchez Arnaud Juan**, subsecretario de Privatizaciones, Ministerio de Economía; **Soetzl Carlos**, diputado nacional Entre Ríos, consejero nacional PJ; **Sucarla Neyel**, diputado nacional Córdoba; **Talana Jorge**, consejero nacional PJ; **Toto Francisco**, diputado nacional Santa Cruz; **Troyano Silvia**, diputada nacional Salta; **Varas Guido**, consejero nacional PJ; **Varela Néstor**, diputado nacional Tucumán; **Villanueva Ernesto**, director nacional ANSSAL, Ministerio de Salud y Acción Social.

Appendix 7: "Cruzada Menemista" (Attached)

MOVIMIENTO NACIONAL JUSTICIALISTA

Cruzada Menemista para la Actualización Doctrinaria y la Transformación del Estado

La Argentina está viviendo una transformación sin precedentes. El 8 de julio de 1989 se inició una etapa que ha revolucionado la economía, la sociedad, la política y la mente de los argentinos.

La férrea insistencia de un hombre, el Presidente de la Nación CARLOS MENEM, abrió el camino y la gran mayoría del pueblo argentino ratificó en las urnas las bondades de esta revolución en paz. Amplísimos sectores sociales, desde el más modesto trabajador al empresario, han comprendido que el Estado, tal cual lo habíamos entendido, ya no tenía razón de ser.

"Queremos que el Estado se vuelva a ocupar de las cuestiones esenciales como salud, educación, defensa, seguridad, justicia y acción social. No queremos, por Dios, un Estado bobo, indiferente ante las desigualdades sociales, sin corazón frente a los que sufren y necesitan protección. Queremos complementar el estado de derecho con el estado de justicia", dijo MENEM en el Teatro Cervantes el 18 de marzo de 1991, en el "Encuentro para la Actualización Doctrinaria".

Se ha confundido nacionalismo con estatización y fuimos sorprendidos por un Presidente que se puso al frente de un proceso de cambio que no podía esperar.

La velocidad de los acontecimientos, la profundidad del cambio y las dificultades de un país devastado por la crisis, nos confundió y desorientó y hasta no faltaron quienes comenzaran a plantear que había que volver a las fuentes, al 45. Se olvidan que Juan Domingo PERON, fundador del Movimiento Nacional Justicialista, dijo que es preciso actualizarse con los tiempos.

Las tres grandes banderas de Independencia económica, soberanía política y justicia social, siguen teniendo vigencia. Pero la realidad ha mostrado hasta el hartazgo que la Independencia económica no se ha conseguido con un Estado empresario, convertido en pasto de la corrupción y del privilegio de aquellos que lucraron con su ineficiencia.

En un mundo cada vez más integrado, la Independencia económica se logrará si la Argentina persiste en su política de integración con América Latina, cuyo hito fundamental es el Mercosur.

Pero esta integración con el mundo debe realizarse con dignidad, preservando el contenido nacional, tal como lo pretende Carlos Menem. Por eso es necesario un Estado Chico, pero fuerte, un Estado con Soberanía Política que sepa aprovechar las posibilidades del vertiginoso proceso de integración mundial al que asistimos.

Sabemos, lo que sabe mejor que nadie el Presidente, que en la Argentina flaquea la justicia social: "nadie puede venir a contarnos lo difícil de esta situación que estamos viviendo, que en la Argentina hay muchos pobres y marginados. ¿Alguien puede creer que me olvidé de ellos? ¿Alguien puede creer que

no me acuerdo de sus voces, de cada uno de sus reclamos?" remarcó MENEM en el Cervantes.

Y el pueblo demostró en estos últimos comicios que, pese a los problemas que padece, tiene confianza en el Presidente de la Nación. Es que intuye que la justicia social no se logrará de un día para el otro, aunque sufra en carne propia las consecuencias del ajuste que siempre golpea más a los que menos tienen.

Está cercano en el tiempo el momento del crecimiento, del trabajo para todos y de la vivienda digna. Claro que ya no podrá reclamarse que todo lo arregle el Estado, las responsabilidades deben ser compartidas, aunque el gobierno tenga la responsabilidad mayor de establecer una red de seguridad que contenga y proteja de las desigualdades a los más desprotegidos.

Este no es momento para nostálgicos, tampoco para oportunistas que quieran medrar con el prestigio y la autoridad de nuestro Presidente.

Este es el momento de una cruzada, como aquella que hace más de cuarenta años impulsara EVA PERON, la abanderada de los humildes. Una cruzada menemista que devuelva a los justicialistas la mística perdida y el orgullo de ser peronistas. Una cruzada con miles de peronistas dispuestos a difundir y esclarecer la magnitud del cambio que está llevando adelante CARLOS MENEM.

Una cruzada que también abra las puertas a todos los argentinos que adhieren a la política de gobierno, una cruzada que ayude a generar ideas para adecuar y cambiar lo que haya que cambiar en la Argentina.

Los cambios en la economía, la sociedad y la política habrán de reflejarse, más temprano que tarde, también en lo institucional. Si hay aspectos instrumentales envejecidos en la CONSTITUCION NACIONAL, habrá que modificarlos, preservando su parte dogmática, aquella que contribuyó a hacer una nación de nuestra Patria.

Una cruzada que apoye sin retaceos la obra de gobierno de Carlos Menem. Una cruzada que respalde sin especulación alguna a las autoridades electas que comparten el plan en marcha, como por ejemplo el Gobernador electo de la Provincia de Buenos Aires, Dr. Eduardo Duhalde.

Una cruzada sin dueños. Una cruzada menemista que ayude a construir una Argentina fuerte, dinámica, moderna, justa, con un pueblo educado, sano y feliz. Sólo será posible si persistimos por el camino trazado, si despertamos el entusiasmo escondido en el pueblo peronista, sin sectarismos pero con fe y confianza en la tarea que desempeña el Gobierno Nacional.

Los abajo firmantes convocamos a una cruzada convencidos de que quizás sea ésta la última oportunidad de levantar a la Argentina. Esta es la razón de ser de una cruzada que se hará realidad si el pueblo la hace suya.

COMISION PROMOTORA: Coordinador: Jesús GONZALEZ (Diputado Nacional M.C. - Congresal Nacional), Bs.As.; PACAYUT, Abelardo F. (Vicepresidente 1º H. Cámara de Senadores), Entre Ríos; MARTINEZ LLANO, Rodolfo (Senador Provincial).Corrientes; CRUZAT DE PERONE, Lucía (Consejera Nacional), Bs.As.; AMICONE, Agustín (Sec. Gral. Sindicato del Calzado); ROSSI, Domingo (Vicegobernador saliente), E. Ríos; DIAZ COLODRERO, Agustín (Dip. Pcial.), Ctes.; PALACIO, Oscar (Congr. Nac.), Bs. As.; AISENSTEIN, Enrique (Dir. Gral. de Política Mrio. de Defensa); URRISTE, Lelio (Sdor. Pcial.), E. Ríos; PARDO, Angel F. (Dip. Pcial.), Ctes.; D'ONOFRIO, Jorge (Cong. Pcial.) Bs. As.; GALLEGOS, Juan Carlos (Encarg. Comis. de Defensa H. Cámara de Dip. de la Nación); SAINT PAUL, Bernardo (Sdor. Pcial.), E. Ríos; PERIE, Hugo (Dip. Pcial.), Ctes.; FERRARI, Mónica (Congr. Nac.), Bs. As.; BARGADO, Rodolfo (Pte. Cámara de Ind. y Comercio, Merlo), Bs. As.; FALCON, Ricardo B. (Vdor. Direc. Nac. Contruc. Portuarias y Vías Navegables); FOLLONIER, Sixto (Sdor. Pcial.), E. Ríos; ZALAZAN, Mirta (Cjal.), Ctes.; CERCHIARA, Roald (Cong. Nac.), Bs.As.; PERAZZO, Raúl (Empresario), Bs. As.; CETTOUR, Hugo (Sdor. Pcial.), E. Ríos; ORTELLADO, Mercedes (Cong. Pcial.), Ctes.; DAVICO, Miguel (Congr. Nac.) Bs. As.; YEDRO, Mario (Sdor. Pcial. E.R.), BREN, Julio E. (Cong. Pcial.), Ctes.; IBAÑEZ, Héctor (Cong. Nac.), Bs. As.; MARIN, Eduardo (Dip. Pcial.) E. Ríos; GONZALEZ, Juan (Dir. Pol.), Bs. As.; DEMICHELIS, Juan (Dip. Pcial.), E. Ríos; GOMEZ, Gerardo (Sec. Gral. C.G.T.), Ctes.; SEHIAOVONIS, Faustino (Dip. Pcial.), E. Ríos; TANZI, Antonio (Dirig. Pol.), Bs.As.; ORBEGON, Emilio (Cong. Nac.), Bs. As.; TRAMONTIN, Miguel (Intendente de Ibicuy), E. Ríos; BALBUENA, Rogelio (Dirig. Pol.), Ctes.; DEL REY, Hugo (Dirig. Pol.), Cap. Fed.; NOVOA, Rubén (Cong. Nac.), Bs. As.; ARIAS, Eldo (Dirig. Pol.), Bs. As.; PERONI, Oscar (Cong Pcial.), Ctes.; POGGIONE, Hernando (Dirig. Pol.), Bs. As.; SANDONA, Juan (Cong. Pcial.), Ctes.; DE LA MERCED, Eduardo (Dirig. Pol.), Ctes.; TAFALLA, Daniel (Dirig. Pol.), Bs. As.; OLMEDO, Víctor (Cong. Nac.), Bs. As.; HNATIUR, Orlando (Cong. Nac.), Bs. As.; REPETO, Alejandro (Dirig. Pol.), Ctes.; MARTINEZ, Mario (Cjal. Pilar), Bs. As.; SERPA, Hugo (Dirig. Pol.), Bs. As.; GUIDI, Jorge (Cong. Pcial.), Ctes.; DIAZ, Angélica (Dirig. Pol.), Bs. As.; LAZARTE, Oscar (Cong. Pcial.), Bs.As.; BORGO, Juan (Cjal. Mte. Caseros), Ctes.; ASTUDILLO, Omar (Cjal. Pilar), Bs. As.; HIRIBURU, Roberto (Dirig. Pol.), Bs. As.; ACUÑA, Francisco (Vpte. P. J. Mte. Caseros), Ctes.; DIAZ, Angel (Sec. Gral. P.J. Gral. Sarmiento), Bs. As.; DEL PUEYO, Sergio (Dirig. Pol.), Bs. As.; BENITEZ, Pablo (Dirig. Pol.), Ctes.; IGLESIAS, Julio (Sdor. M. C. Bs. As.); GONZALEZ, Aníbal (Sdor. M. C. Bs. As.); FARJAT, Elena María (Dirig. Pol.), Bs. As.; MARTINEZ, Juan Manuel (Dirig. Pol.), Bs. As.; FACHETTI, Carlos (Dirig. Pol.), Ctes.; LEGAL, Aldo (Dirig. Pol.), Ctes.; MARTINEZ, Juan Domingo (Dirig. Pol.), Ctes.; PICCOLO, Marcelo (Dirig. Pol.), Bs. As.; RUFINO, Luis (Dirig. Pol.), Bs. As.; TELLO, Miguel (Dirig. Pol.), Bs. As.; ALVAREZ, Antonio (Dirig. Pol.), Bs. As.; INOCENZI, Enrique (Cjal. Tigre), Bs. As.

ADHESIONES: (0783-27148/24345) (0228-24069) (01-7650430/234522)

references

Abente, Diego. 1987. Venezuelan democracy revisited. *Latin American Research Review* 22:225–40.

———. 1990. The political economy of tax reform in Venezuela. *Comparative Politics* 22:199–216.

Acción Democrática. 1990. *Acción Democrática: Doctrina y programa.* Compiled by Horacio Zavala Medina. Caracas: Secretaría Nacional de Organización del Partido Acción Democrática and Instituto Latinoamericano de Investigaciones Sociales (ILDIS).

———. 1993. *Estatutos.* Sancionados por el Comité Directivo Nacional el 4, 5, y 6 de febrero de 1993. Caracas: Secretaría Nacional de Organización.

Acuña, Carlos H. 1994. Politics and economics in the Argentina of the nineties (or why the future no longer is what it used to be). In William C. Smith et al., eds., *Democracy, Markets, and Structural Reform in Latin America: Argentina, Bolivia, Brazil, Chile, and Mexico.* New Brunswick, N.J.: North-South Center and Transaction Books.

Acuña, Carlos H., and Catalina Smulovitz. 1995. Militares en la transición argentina: Del gobierno a la subordinación constitucional. In Carlos H. Acuña, ed., *La nueva matriz política Argentina.* Buenos Aires: Nueva Visión.

Adler Lomnitz, Larisa, Claudio Lomnitz-Adler, and Ilay Adler. 1990. El fondo de la forma: Actos públicos de la campaña presidencial del Partido Revolucionario Institucional, México, 1988. Working paper, Hellen Kellogg Institute for International Studies, Notre Dame, Ind., March.

Agüero, Felipe. 1993. Las fuerzas armadas y el debilitamiento de la democracia en Venezuela. In Andrés Serbín, Andrés Stambouli, Jennifer McCoy, and William C. Smith, eds., *Venezuela: La democracia bajo presión.* Caracas: Nueva Sociedad.

Alesina, Alberto, and Allan Drazen. 1991. Why are stabilizations delayed? *American Economic Review* 81:1170–88.

Alesina, Alberto, and Roberto Perotti. 1993. The political economy of growth: A critical survey of recent literature and some new results. The World Bank, Public Economic Division, Washington, D.C., September. Mimeographed.

Alexander, Myrna, and Carlos Corti. 1993. *Argentina's Privatization Program.* CFS Discussion Paper Series No. 103, August. Washington, D.C.: The World Bank.

Almond, Gabriel A. 1991. Capitalism and democracy. *PS: Political Science and Politics* 24:467–74.

Arias, Xosé Carlos. 1999. Reformas financieras en América Latina, 1990–1998. *Desarrollo Económico* (Buenos Aires) 39, no. 155 (October–December): 361–84.

Armijo, Leslie Elliott. 1998. Balance sheet or ballot box? Incentives to privatize in emerging democracies. In Phillip Oxhorn and Pamela K. Starr, eds., *Markets and Democracy in Latin America: Conflict or Convergence?* Boulder, Colo.: Lynne Rienner.

Arrieta A., José Ignacio. 1991. El sindicalismo adeco ante su encrucijada. *Revista SIC* 54:352–54.

Åslund, Anders. 1994. The case for radical reform. *Journal of Democracy* 5, no. 4 (October): 63–74.

Aznar, Luis. 1990. Las transiciones desde el autoritarismo en Venezuela: El proyecto de Acción Democrática y sus efectos sobre el sistema sociopolítico. *Desarrollo Económico* 30, no. 117: 55–83.

Baer, Delal. 1993. Mexico's second revolution: Pathways to liberalization. In Riordan Roett, ed., *Political and Economic Liberalization in Mexico: At a Critical Juncture?* Boulder, Colo.: Lynne Rienner.

Baptista, Asdrúbal. 1991. *Bases cuantitativas de la economía venezolana, 1930–1989.* Caracas: Ediciones María di Mase.

Barcia, Hugo, and Norberto Ivancich. 1991. *La carpa de Alí Baba: El Grupo de los Ocho contra la corrupción.* Buenos Aires: Editorial Legasa.

Bardhan, Pranab. 1999. Democracy and development: A complex relationship. In Ian Shapiro and Casiano Hacker-Cordon, eds., *Democracy's Value.* Cambridge: Cambridge University Press.

Bates, Robert H., and Anne O. Krueger. 1993. Introduction. In Robert H. Bates and Anne O. Krueger, eds., *Political and Economic Interactions in Economic Policy Reform: Evidence from Eight Countries.* Cambridge, Mass.: Basil Blackwell.

Benjamin, Roger, and Stephen L. Elkin, eds. 1985. *The Democratic State.* Lawrence: University Press of Kansas.

Bergquist, Charles. 1986. *Labor in Latin America: Comparative Essays on Chile, Argentina, Venezuela, and Colombia.* Stanford: Stanford University Press.

Berman, Sheri. 1997. The life of the party. *Comparative Politics* 30, no. 1 (October): 101–22.

Beroes, Agustín. 1990. *RECADI: La gran estafa.* Caracas: Planeta.

Betancourt, Rómulo. 1979. *Venezuela: Política y petróleo.* 3d ed. Caracas: Seix Barral, S.A.

Bevan, John. 1999. Review of Robert I. Rotberg, ed., *Haiti Renewed: Political and Economic Prospects. Journal of Latin American Studies* 31, no. 1 (February): 225–26.

Bhagwati, Jagdish. 1978. *Anatomy and Consequences of Exchange Control Regimes.* A Special Conference Series on Foreign Trade Regimes and Economic Development, Volume 11. New York: National Bureau of Economic Research; Cambridge: Ballinger.

———. 1994. Shock treatments. *New Republic,* March 28, pp. 39–43.

———. 1995. The new thinking on development. *Journal of Democracy* 6, no. 4 (October): 50–64.

Biersteker, Thomas J. 1995. The "triumph" of liberal economic ideas in the developing world. In Barbara Stallings, ed., *Global Change, Regional Response.* New York: Cambridge University Press.

Binder, Leonard, James S. Coleman, Joseph LaPalombara, Lucian W. Pye, Sidney Verba, and Myron Weiner, eds. 1971. *Crises and Sequences in Political Development.* Princeton: Princeton University Press.

Blank, David Eugene. 1973. *Politics in Venezuela.* Boston: Little, Brown.

Boix, Carles. 1998. *Political Parties, Growth and Equality: Conservative and Social Democratic Economic Strategies in the World Economy.* New York: Cambridge University Press.

Bond, Robert. 1992. Why Venezuela failed at economic reform. *Veneconomía* 10:1–2.
Borón, Atilio. 1996. Menem's neoliberal experiment. Paper presented at the International Congress of Americanists (ICA), 48th, Stockholm, Sweden, 1994. Problems of democracy in Latin America. Stockholm: Institute of Latin American Studies, Stockholm University.
Bouzas, Roberto. 1993. ¿Más allá de la estabilización y la reforma? Un ensayo sobre la economía argentina a comienzos de los '90. *Desarrollo Económico* 33:3–28.
Bresser Pereira, Luiz Carlos. 1993. Economic reforms and economic growth: Efficiency and politics in Latin America. In Luiz Carlos Bresser Pereira, José María Maravall, and Adam Przeworski, eds., *Economic Reforms in New Democracies: A Social-Democratic Approach*. Cambridge: Cambridge University Press.
———. 1995. Brazil. In John Williamson, ed., *The Political Economy of Policy Reform*. Washington, D.C.: Institute for International Economics.
Britez, Edwin, Ignacio Martínez, Carlos Peralta, and Néstor Escobar Franco. 1996. *El ocaso del jinete: Crónica de un intento de golpe de estado en el Paraguay*. Asunción: ABC Color.
Buendía, Jorge. 1996. Economic reform, public opinion, and presidential approval in Mexico, 1988–1993. *Comparative Political Studies* 29, no. 5 (October): 566–91.
Burgess, Katrina. 1995. Un divorcio a medias: Reforma económica y políticas laborales en España. *Política y Gobierno* 2:207–42.
———. 1999. Loyalty dilemmas and market reforms: Party-union alliances under stress in Mexico, Spain, and Venezuela. *World Politics*, 52, no. 1 (October): 105–34.
———. 2000. Loyalties under stress. Manuscript.
Burggraaff, Winfield J., and Richard L. Millet. 1995. More than failed coups: The crisis in Venezuelan civil-military relations. In Louis W. Goodman, Johanna Mendelson Forman, Moisés Naím, Joseph S. Tulchin, and Gary Bland, eds., *Lessons of the Venezuelan Experience*. Baltimore: Johns Hopkins University Press; Washington, D.C.: Woodrow Wilson Center Press.
Calvo, Guillermo A. 1989. Incredible reforms. In Guillermo Calvo, Ronald Findley, Pentti Kouri, and Jorge Braga de Macedo, eds., *Debt Stabilization and Development: Essays in Memory of Carlos Díaz-Alejandro*. Cambridge, Mass.: Basil Blackwell.
Cameron, Maxwell A. 1997. Political and economic origins of regime change in Peru: The Eighteenth Brumaire of Alberto Fujimori. In Maxwell A. Cameron and Philip Mauceri, eds., *The Peruvian Labyrinth: Polity, Society, Economy*. University Park: Pennsylvania State University Press.
Camp, Roderic A. 1999. *Politics in Mexico: The Decline of Authoritarianism*. 3d ed. New York: Oxford University Press.
Canache Mata, Carlos. 1991. ¿Qué partidos? ¿Qué proyecto? ¿Qué organización? *Revista SIC* 54:344–45.
Canitrot, Adolfo. 1994. Crisis and transformation of the Argentine state (1978–1992). In William C. Smith et al., eds., *Democracy, Markets, and Structural Reform in Latin America: Argentina, Bolivia, Brazil, Chile, and Mexico*. New Brunswick, N.J.: North-South Center and Transaction Books.
Cansino, César. 1995. Partidos políticos y gobernabilidad en América Latina. *Nueva Sociedad* 139 (September–October): 51–58.

Cardoso, Eliana A. 2000. Brazil's currency crisis: The shift from an exchange-rate anchor to a flexible regime. In Carol Wise and Riordan Roett, eds., *Exchange Rate Politics in Latin America*. Washington, D.C.: Brookings Institution.

Cardoso, Eliana A., and Ann Helwege. 1992. *Latin America's Economy: Diversity, Trends, and Conflicts*. Cambridge: MIT Press.

Carvallo, Gastón, and Margarita López Maya. 1987. Los interrogantes de Acción Democrática. *Revista SIC* 50:207–11.

Casas, Juan Carlos. 1991. *Nuevos políticos y nuevas políticas en América Latina*. Buenos Aires: Atlántida.

Castañeda, Jorge G. 2000. *Perpetuating Power: How Mexican Presidents Were Chosen*. New York: The New Press.

Castro, Jorge. 2000. *La gran década*. Buenos Aires: Editorial Sudamericana.

Catterberg, Edgardo. 1989. *Los argentinos frente a la política: Cultura política y opinión pública en al transición argentina a la democracia*. Buenos Aires: Editorial Planeta.

Cavallo, Domingo F. 1991. La financiación del crecimiento. Paper presented at the Segundas Jornadas Bancarias, Buenos Aires, Asociación de Bancos de la República Argentina, June 27.

———. 1997. *El peso de la verdad: Un impulso a la transparencia en la Argentina de los 90*. Buenos Aires: Planeta.

Cavallo, Domingo F., and Joaquín A. Cottani. 1997. Argentina's convertibility plan and the IMF. *AEA Papers and Proceedings* 87, no. 2 (May): 17–22.

Cavallo, Domingo F., Roberto Domenech, and Yair Mundalak. 1989. *La Argentina que pudo ser*. Buenos Aires: Ediciones Manantial.

Cavarozzi, Marcelo. 1984. El rol de los partidos gobernantes y las organizaciones públicas en la generación de políticas de industrialización. In Alfred H. Saulniers, ed., *The Public Sector in Latin America*. Austin: University of Texas Press.

———. 1986. Peronism and radicalism: Argentina's transitions in perspective. In Paul W. Drake and Eduardo Silva, eds., *Elections and Democratization in Latin America, 1980–1985*. San Diego: Center for Iberian and Latin American Studies, University of California, San Diego.

———. 1994. Politics: A key for the long term in South America. In William C. Smith et al., eds., *Latin American Political Economy in the Age of Neoliberal Reforms: Theoretical and Comparative Perspectives for the 1990s*. New Brunswick, N.J.: Transaction.

Cavarozzi, Marcelo, and María Grossi. 1992. Argentine parties under Alfonsín: From democratic reinvention to political decline and hyperinflation. In Edward C. Epstein, ed., *The New Argentine Democracy: The Search for a Successful Formula*. Westport, Conn.: Praeger.

Cavarozzi, Marcelo, and Oscar Landi. 1992. Political parties under Alfonsín and Menem: The effects of state shrinking and the devaluation of democratic politics. In Edward C. Epstein, ed., *The New Argentine Democracy: The Search for a Successful Formula*. Westport, Conn.: Praeger.

Celli, Humberto. 1993. *Dos discursos y un pensamiento*. Caracas: Tipografía Lucena, C.A.

Centeno, Miguel Ángel. 1994. *Democracy Within Reason: Technocratic Revolution in Mexico*. University Park: Pennsylvania State University Press.

Centeno, Miguel Ángel, and Mauricio Font. 1997. *Toward a New Cuba? Legacies of a Revolution*. Boulder, Colo.: Lynne Rienner.

Centro de Estudios Unión para la Nueva Mayoría. Various years. Conflictos laborales. Buenos Aires: Centro de Estudios Unión para la Nueva Mayoría.

CEPAL (Comisión Económica para América Latina). 1994. *Panorama social de América Latina.* Santiago: CEPAL.

Cerruti, Gabriela. 1993. *El Jefe: Vida y obra de Carlos Saúl Menem.* Buenos Aires: Editorial Planeta.

Chand, Vikram K. 2001. *Mexico's Political Awakening.* Notre Dame: University of Notre Dame Press.

Cheresky, Isidoro. 1991. El proceso de democratización: Creencias políticas, partidos y elecciones. Serie Cuadernos. Buenos Aires: Instituto de Investigaciones, Facultad de Ciencias Sociales, Universidad de Buenos Aires.

Chisari, Omar, José M. Fanelli, Roberto Frenkel, and Guillermo Rozenwurcel. 1993. Argentina and the role of fiscal accounts. In Edmar L. Bacha, ed., *Savings and Investment Requirements for the Resumption of Growth in Latin America.* Washington, D.C.: Inter-American Development Bank, distributed by the Johns Hopkins University Press.

Cicioni, Antonio. 1996. *Informe sobre el Presupuesto Nacional, 1996.* Buenos Aires: Grupo Sophia.

———. 1997. *Informe sobre el Presupuesto Nacional, 1997.* Buenos Aires: Grupo Sophia.

Cohen, Youssef, Brian R. Brown, and A.F.K. Organski. 1981. The paradoxical nature of state making: The violent creation of order. *American Political Science Review* 75:901–10.

Collier, David, and Ruth Berins Collier. 1977. Who does what, to whom, and how: Toward a comparative analysis of Latin American corporatism. In James M. Malloy, ed., *Authoritarianism and Corporatism in Latin America.* Pittsburgh: University of Pittsburgh Press.

Collier, Ruth Berins, and David Collier. 1991. *Shaping the Political Arena: Critical Junctures, the Labor Movement, and Regime Dynamics in Latin America.* Princeton: Princeton University Press.

Colosio, Luis Donaldo. 1993. Why the PRI won the 1991 elections. In Riordan Roett, ed., *Political and Economic Liberalization in Mexico: At a Critical Juncture?* Boulder, Colo.: Lynne Rienner.

Conaghan, Catherine M. 1996. A deficit of democratic authenticity: Political linkage and the public in Andean polities. *Studies in Comparative International Development* 31, no. 3 (Fall): 32–55.

Conaghan, Catherine M., and James M. Malloy. 1994. *Unsettling Statecraft: Democracy and Neoliberalism in the Central Andes.* Pittsburgh: University of Pittsburgh Press.

Congreso de la República. 1999. Informe de coyuntura primer trimestre de 1999. Caracas: Congreso de la República, Oficina de Asesoría Económica y Financiera, Serie Informes 99-005.

Consultores 21. 1994. *Estudio trimestral de temas económicos. Serie 1989–1993.* Caracas. Mimeographed.

Coppedge, Michael. 1988. La política interna de Acción Democrática durante la crisis económica. *Cuadernos del CENDES* 7, no. 2 (January–April): 159–80.

———. 1993. Mexican democracy: You can't get there from here. In Riordan Roett, ed., *Political and Economic Liberalization in Mexico: At a Critical Juncture?* Boulder, Colo.: Lynne Rienner.

———. 1994a. Prospects for democratic governability in Venezuela. *Journal of Interamerican Studies and World Affairs* 36:39–64.

————. 1994b. *Strong Parties and Lame Ducks: Presidential Partyarchy and Factionalism in Venezuela.* Stanford: Stanford University Press.

————. 1994c. Venezuela: Democratic despite presidentialism. In Juan J. Linz, and Arturo Valenzuela, eds., *The Crisis of Presidential Democracy: The Latin American Evidence.* Baltimore: Johns Hopkins University Press.

————. 1998. Latin American parties: Political Darwinism in the lost decade. Hellen Kellogg Institute for International Studies, Notre Dame, Ind. Mimeographed.

Coppedge, Michael, and Wolfgang H. Reinicke. 1990. Measuring polyarchy. *Studies in Comparative International Development* 25:51–72.

Corden, W. Max. 2000. Exchange rate regimes and policies: An overview. In Carol Wise and Riordan Roett, eds., *Exchange Rate Politics in Latin America.* Washington, D.C.: Brookings Institution.

Cornelius, Wayne A. 1996. *Mexican Politics in Transition: The Breakdown of a One-Party Dominant Regime.* San Diego: Center for U.S.-Mexican Studies, University of California.

Coronil, Fernando. 1997. *The Magical State: Nature, Money and Modernity in Venezuela.* Chicago: University of Chicago Press.

Corrales, Javier. 1997. Why Argentines followed Cavallo: A technopol between democracy and economic reforms. In Jorge I. Domínguez, ed., *Technopols: Ideas and Leaders in Freeing Politics and Markets in Latin America in the 1990s.* University Park: Pennsylvania State University Press.

————. 1997–98. Do economic crises contribute to economic reforms? Argentina and Venezuela in the 1990s. *Political Science Quarterly* 112 (Winter): 617–44.

————. 1998. Coalitions and corporate choices in Argentina, 1976–1994: The recent private sector support of privatization. *Studies in Comparative International Development* 32, no. 4 (Winter): 24–51.

————. 1999a. Venezuela in the 1980s, the 1990s and beyond: Why citizen-detached parties imperil economic governance. *David Rockefeller Center for Latin American Studies Newsletter* (Harvard University), Fall: 26–29.

————. 1999b. Respuesta. *Desarrollo Económico* 155, no. 39 (October–December): 468–70.

————. 2000a. Presidents, ruling parties and party rules: A theory on the politics of economic reform in Latin America. *Comparative Politics* 32, no. 2 (January): 127–50.

————. 2000b. Reform-lagging states and the question of devaluation: Venezuela's response to the exogenous shocks of 1997–1998. In Carol Wise and Riordan Roett, eds., *Exchange Rate Politics in Latin America.* Washington, D.C.: Brookings Institution.

Corrales, Javier, and Imelda Cisneros. 1999. Corporatism, trade liberalization, and sectoral responses: The case of Venezuela, 1989–1999. *World Development* 27, no. 12 (December): 2099–122.

Cortés, Rosalía, and Adriana Marshall. 1999. Estrategia económica, instituciones y negociación política en la reforma social de los '90. *Desarrollo Económico* 154, no. 39 (July–September): 195–212.

Cortés Conde, Roberto. 1992. Growth and stagnation in Argentina. In Simón Teitel, ed., *Towards a New Development Strategy for Latin America: Pathways from Hirschman's Thought.* Washington, D.C.: Inter-American Development Bank.

Crisp, Brian. 1994. Limitations to democracy in developing capitalist societies: The case of Venezuela. *World Development* 22 (October): 1491–509.

―――. 2000. *Democratic Institutional Design: The Powers and Incentives of Venezuelan Politicians and Interest Groups.* Stanford: Stanford University Press.

Crouch, Colin. 1985. Conditions for trade union wage restraint. In Leon N. Lindberg and Charles S. Maier, eds., *The Politics of Inflation and Economic Stagnation: Theoretical Approaches and International Case Studies.* Washington, D.C.: Brookings Institution.

Cukierman, A., and Mariano Tommasi. 1998. When does it take a Nixon to go to China? *American Economic Review* 88, no. 1 (March): 180–97.

Curia, Eduardo. 1999. *La trampa de la Convertibilidad.* Buenos Aires: Ediciones Realidad Argentina.

Dahl, Robert A. 1998. *On Democracy.* New Haven: Yale University Press.

Damill, Mario, and Roberto Frenkel. 1993. Restauración democrática y política económica: Argentina, 1984–1991. In Juan Antonio Morales and Gary McMahon, eds., *La política económica en la transición a la democracia: Lecciones de Argentina, Bolivia, Chile, y Uruguay.* Santiago: CIEPLAN.

de Ípola, Emilio. 1987. La difícil apuesta del peronismo democrático. In José Nun and Juan Carlos Portantiero, eds., *Ensayos sobre la transición democrática en la Argentina.* Buenos Aires: Ediciones Puntosur.

de la Balze, Felipe A.M. 1995. *Remaking the Argentine Economy.* New York: Council of Foreign Relations Press.

de Melo, Martha, Cavdet Denizer, and Alan Gelb. 1996. Patterns of transition from plan to market. *World Bank Economic Review* 10, no. 3 (September): 397–424.

de Pablo, Juan Carlos. 1990. Argentina. In John Williamson, ed., *Latin American Adjustment: How Much Has Happened?* Washington, D.C.: Institute for International Economics.

―――. 1994. *¿Quién hubiera dicho? La transformación que lideraron Menem y Cavallo.* Buenos Aires: Editorial Planeta.

Degregori, Carlos Iván. Forthcoming. Peru. In Jorge I. Domínguez and Michael Shifter, eds., *Constructing Democratic Governance in Latin America.*

Diamant, Rut. 2000. Militares y democracia en Argentina. In Peter Birle, ed., *Argentinien nach zehn Jahren Menem—Bilanz und Perspektiven.* Berlin: Das Ibero-Amerikanische Institut, Preußischer Kulturbesitz.

Domínguez, Jorge I. 1985. The foreign policies of Latin American states in the 1980s: Retreat or refocus? In Samuel P. Huntington, and Joseph S. Nye Jr., eds., *Global Dilemmas.* Lanham, Md.: University Press of America.

―――, ed. 1997. *Technopols: Ideas and Leaders in Freeing Politics and Markets in Latin America in the 1990s.* University Park: Pennsylvania State University Press.

Domínguez, Jorge I., and Jeanne K. Giraldo. 1996. Conclusion: Parties, institutions, and market reforms in constructing democracies. In Jorge I. Domínguez and Abraham F. Lowenthal, eds., *Constructing Democratic Governance: Latin America and the Caribbean, Themes and Issues.* Baltimore: Johns Hopkins University Press.

Domínguez, Jorge I., and Susan Kaufman Purcell. 1999. Political evolution in the hemisphere. In Albert Fishlow and James Jones, eds., *The United States and the Americas: A Twenty-first Century View.* New York: Norton.

Downs, Anthony. 1957. *An Economic Theory of Democracy.* New York: Harper and Row.

Drazen, Allan, and Vittorio Grilli. 1993. The benefit of crises for economic reforms. *American Economic Review* 83 (June): 598–607.

Dresser, Denise. 1991. Bringing the poor back in: National solidarity as a strategy of regime legitimation. In Wayne A. Cornelius, Ann L. Craig, and Jonathan Fox, eds., *Transforming State-Society Relations in Mexico: The National Solidarity Strategy*. San Diego: Center for U.S.-Mexican Studies, University of California.

ECLAC (Economic Commission for Latin America and the Caribbean). Various years. *Economic Panorama of Latin America*. Santiago: United Nations.

———. Various years. *Economic Survey of Latin America and the Caribbean*. Santiago: United Nations.

———. 1995. *Preliminary Overview of the Latin American and Caribbean Economy, 1995*. Santiago: United Nations.

The Economist Intelligence Unit. Various issues. *Argentina: Country Report*.

Edwards, Sebastian. 1995. *Crisis and Reform in Latin America: From Despair to Hope*. New York: Oxford University Press.

Epstein, Edward C. 1992a. Democracy in Argentina. In Edward C. Epstein, ed., *The New Argentine Democracy: The Search for a Successful Formula*. Westport, Conn.: Praeger.

———. 1992b. Labor-state conflict in the new Argentine democracy: Parties, union factions, and power maximizing. In Edward C. Epstein, ed., *The New Argentine Democracy: The Search for a Successful Formula*. Westport, Conn.: Praeger.

Escudé, Carlos. 1992. *Realismo periférico: Fundamentos para la nueva política exterior argentina*. Buenos Aires: Planeta.

Etchemendy, Sebastián, and Vicente Palermo. 1998. Conflicto y concertación: Gobierno, Congreso y organizaciones de interés en la reforma laboral del primer gobierno de Menem (1989–1995). *Desarrollo Económico* 37, no. 148 (January–March): 559–90.

Evans, Peter B. 1992. The state as problem and solution: Predation, embedded autonomy, and structural change. In Stephan Haggard, and Robert R. Kaufman, eds., *The Politics of Economic Adjustment*. Princeton: Princeton University Press.

———. 1995. *Embedded Autonomy: States and Industrial Transformation*. Princeton: Princeton University Press.

Evans, Peter, Dietrich Rueschemeyer, and Theda Skocpol, eds. 1985. *Bringing the State Back In*. Cambridge: Cambridge University Press.

Fajardo Cortez, Víctor. 1992. El colapso del paquete económico: Causas, efectos y perspectivas, Venezuela 1989–1992. *Cuadernos del CENDES*: 27–52.

Fanelli, José María, and Roberto Frenkel. 1995. Stability and structure: Interactions in economic growth. *CEPAL Review* 56 (August): 25–41.

Faucher, Philippe. 1999. Restoring governance: Has Brazil got it right (at last)? In Philip Oxhorn and Pamela K. Starr, eds., *Markets and Democracy in Latin America: Conflict or Convergence?* Boulder, Colo.: Lynne Rienner.

Fawcett, Louise, and Andrew Hurrell, eds. 1995. *Regionalism in World Politics: Regional Organization and International Order*. New York: Oxford University Press.

Feletti, Roberto, and Claudio Lozano. 1994. La etapa Menem: Cambio estructural, crisis recurrentes, y destino político. *IDEP (Instituto de Estudios Sobre Estado y Participación)*, no. 14 (March): 7–37.

Fernández, Eduardo. 1989. Declaración oficial de la dirección nacional del Partido Social Cristiano COPEI presentado por el Secretario General Doctor Eduardo Fernández. Caracas, 25 February. Mimeographed.

Fernández, Raquel, and Dani Rodrik. 1991. Resistance to reform: Status quo bias in the presence of individual-specific uncertainty. *American Economic Review* 81, no. 5 (December): 1146–55.

Fernández, Roque B. 1991. What have populists learned from hyperinflation? In Rudiger Dornbusch and Sebastian Edwards, eds., *The Macroeconomics of Populism in Latin America*. Chicago: University of Chicago Press.

Ferreira Rubio, Delia, and Matteo Goretti. 1998. Menem's decretazo (1989–1998). Paper prepared for the meeting of the Latin American Studies Association, Chicago, Ill., September.

FIEL (Fundación de Investigaciones Económicas Latinoamericanas). 1990. *Argentina: Hacia una economía de mercado*. Buenos Aires: Ediciones Manantial.

FIEL and CEA (Consejo Empresario Argentino). 1990. *El gasto público en la Argentina 1960–1988*. Buenos Aires: FIEL.

Fontana, A. 1986. Armed forces and neoconservative ideology: State shrinking in Argentina, 1976–1981. In William P. Glade, ed., *State Shrinking: A Comparative Inquiry into Privatization*. Austin: Institute of Latin American Studies, University of Texas at Austin.

Fraga, Rosendo. 1989. *Claves de la campaña electoral, 1989*. Buenos Aires: Editorial Centro de Estudios Unión para la Nueva Mayoría.

Francés, Antonio, et al. 1993. *¡Aló Venezuela! Apertura y privatización de las telecomunicaciones*. Caracas: Ediciones IESA.

Freedom House. 2001. *Freedom in the World Survey: All Countries' Ratings: 1972–73 – 2000–01*. www.freedomhouse.org/research/freeworld/FHSCORES.xls

Frenkel, Roberto, and Guillermo O'Donnell. 1994. The "stabilization programs" of the International Monetary Fund and their internal impacts. In Paul W. Drake, ed., *Money Doctors, Foreign Debts, and Economic Reforms in Latin America from the 1890s to the Present*. Wilmington, Del.: Scholarly Resources.

Friedman, Milton (with the assistance of Rose D. Friedman). 1962. *Capitalism and Freedom*. Chicago: University of Chicago Press.

Gamarra, Eduardo A. 1994. Market-oriented reforms and democratization in Latin America: Challenges of the 1990s. In William C. Smith et al., eds., *Democracy, Markets, and Structural Reform in Latin America: Theoretical and Comparative Perspectives for the 1990s*. New Brunswick, N.J.: North-South Center and Transaction Books.

Gamble, Andrew, and Anthony Payne, eds. 1996. *Regionalism and World Order*. London: Macmillan.

García, Gustavo. 1993. Fiscal issues and non-oil taxation in Venezuela. The World Bank, Washington, D.C. Mimeographed.

García, Gustavo, with Rafael Rodríguez and Silvia Salvato. 1998. *Lecciones de la crisis bancaria de Venezuela*. Caracas: Ediciones IESA.

García-Herrero, Alicia. 1997. Banking Crises in Latin America in the 1990s: Lessons from Argentina, Paraguay, and Venezuela. Working paper, International Monetary Fund, Washington, D.C., October.

Gaudio, Ricardo, and Andrés Thompson. 1990. *Sindicalismo peronista, gobierno Radical. Los años de Alfonsín*. Buenos Aires, Fundación Friedrich Ebert, Folios Ediciones.

Geddes, Barbara. 1994. *Politician's Dilemma: Building State Capacity in Latin America*. Los Angeles: University of California Press.

————. 1995. The politics of economic liberalization. *Latin American Research Review* 30, no. 2: 195–214.

Gente. 1976. *Fotos, hechos, testimonios de 1035 dramáticos días: 25 de mayo de 1973–24 de marzo de 1976.* 2d ed. Buenos Aires: Revista Gente y la Actualidad, Editorial Atlántida.

Gereffi, Gary. 1990. Paths of industrialization: An overview. In Gary Gereffi and Donald L. Wyman, eds., *Manufacturing Miracles: Paths of Industrialization in Latin America and East Asia.* Princeton: Princeton University Press.

Gerschenkron, Alexander. 1962. *Economic Backwardness in Historical Perspective.* Cambridge: The Belknap Press of Harvard University Press.

Gervasoni, Carlos. 1998. Del distribucionismo al neoliberalismo: Los cambios en la coalición electoral peronista durante el gobierno de Menem. Paper presented at the Latin American Studies Association Congress, Chicago, Ill., September.

Gibson, Edward L. 1997. The populist road to market reform: Policy and electoral coalitions in Mexico and Argentina. *World Politics* 49 (April): 339–70.

Gibson, Edward L., and Ernesto Calvo. 2000. Federalism and low-maintenance constituencies: Territorial dimensions of economic reform in Argentina. *Studies in Comparative International Development* 35, no. 3 (Fall): 32–55.

Gil Yepes, José Antonio. 1981. *The Challenge of Venezuelan Democracy.* New Brunswick, N.J.: Transaction.

Giraldo, Jeanne Kinney. 1997. Development and democracy in Chile: Finance Minister Alejandro Foxley and the Concertación's project for the 1990s. In Jorge I. Domínguez, eds., *Technopols: Freeing Politics and Markets in Latin America in the 1990s.* University Park: Pennsylvania State University Press.

Glade, William P. 1998. The Latin American economies restructure, again. In Jan Knippers Black, ed., *Latin America: Its Problems and Its Promise.* 3d ed. Boulder, Colo.: Westview Press.

————, ed. 1986. *State Shrinking: A Comparative Inquiry into Privatization.* Austin: Institute of Latin American Studies, University of Texas at Austin.

Godio, Julio. 1986. *50 Años de la C.T.V. (1936–1986): Historia, doctrina y acción.* Caracas, Instituto Latinoamericano de Investigaciones Sociales/Editorial Nueva Sociedad.

Golob, Stephanie R. 1997. "Making possible what is necessary": Pedro Aspe, the Salinas Team and the next Mexican "miracle." In Jorge I. Domínguez, ed., *Technopols: Ideas and Leaders in Freeing Politics and Markets in Latin America in the 1990s.* University Park: Pennsylvania State University Press.

Gómez Calcaño, Luis, and Margarita López Maya. 1990. *El tejido de Penélope: La reforma del estado en Venezuela (1984–1988).* Caracas: CENDES.

González, Rosa Amelia. 1995. La reforma impositiva en Venezuela: La fuerza de la necesidad. Presented at the Latin American Studies Association Congress, Washington, D.C., September 28–30.

Gourevitch, Peter A. 1986. *Politics in Hard Times: Comparative Responses to International Economic Crises.* Ithaca: Cornell University Press.

Grindle, Merilee S. 1996. *Challenging the State.* New York: Cambridge University Press.

Grupo Roraima. 1985. *A Proposal to the Nation: The Roraima Project, Plan of Action.* Caracas: Grupo Roraima.

Guerchunoff, Pablo, ed. 1992. *Las privatizaciones en la Argentina: Primera etapa.* Buenos Aires: Instituto Torcuato di Tella.

Guerchunoff, Pablo, and Lucas Llach. 1998. *El ciclo de la ilusión y el desencanto.* Buenos Aires: Ariel Sociedad Económica.

Guerrero Gutiérrez, Eduardo. 1999. Inestabilidad y crimen en el nuevo régimen. *Nexos* 262 (October): 57–66.

Haggard, Stephan, and Robert R. Kaufman. 1992. The political economy of inflation and stabilization in middle-income countries. In Stephan Haggard, and Robert R. Kaufman, eds., *The Politics of Economic Adjustment.* Princeton: Princeton University Press.

———. 1995. *The Political Economy of Democratic Transitions.* Princeton: Princeton University Press.

Haggard, Stephan, and Steven B. Webb. 1994. *Voting for Reform: Democracy, Political Liberalization, and Economic Adjustment.* New York: Oxford University Press.

Haggard, Stephan, and Tun-jen Cheng. 1987. State and foreign capital in the East Asian NICs. In Frederic C. Deyo, ed., *The Political Economy of the New Asian Industrialism.* Ithaca: Cornell University Press.

Hagopian, Frances. 1998. Democracy and political representation in Latin America in the 1990s: Pause, reorganization, or decline? In Felipe Agüero and Jeffrey Stark, eds., *Fault Lines of Democracy in Post-Transition Latin America.* Miami: North-South Center Press at the University of Miami.

Hall, Peter A. 1989. *The Political Power of Economic Ideas: Keynesianism Across Nations.* Princeton: Princeton University Press.

Halperín Donghi, Tulio. 1994. *La larga agonía de la Argentina peronista.* Buenos Aires: Ariel.

Harberger, Arnold C. 1993. The other side of tax reform. In Rudiger Dornbusch, ed., *Policymaking in the Open Economy. Concepts and Case Studies in Economic Performance.* New York: Oxford University Press for the World Bank / EDI Series in Economic Development.

Harmel, Robert, U. K. Heo, Alexander Tan, and Kenneth Janda. 1995. Performance, leadership, factions, and party change: An empirical analysis. *West European Politics* 18, no. 1 (January): 1–33.

Hausmann, Ricardo. 1990. Venezuela. In John Williamson, ed., *Latin American Adjustment: How Much Has Happened?* Washington, D.C.: Institute for International Economics.

———. 1995. Quitting populism cold turkey: The "big bang" approach to macroeconomic balance. In Louis W. Goodman, Johanna Mendelson Forman, Moisés Naím, Joseph Tulchin, and Gary Bland, eds., *Lessons of the Venezuelan Experience.* Washington, D.C.: Woodrow Wilson Press; Baltimore: Johns Hopkins University Press.

Hausmann, Ricardo, and Gustavo Márquez. 1993. La crisis económica venezolana: Origen, mecanismos y encadenamientos. *Investigación Económica* 165:117–54.

Held, David. 1987. Pluralism, corporate capitalism, and the state. In David Held, ed., *Models of Democracy.* Stanford: Stanford University Press.

Hellman, Joel. 1998. Winners take all: The politics of partial reform in postcommunist transitions. *World Politics* 50 (January): 203–34.

Heredia, Blanca. 1994. Making economic reform politically viable: The Mexican experience. In William C. Smith et al., eds., *Democracy, Markets, and Structural Reform in Latin America: Argentina, Bolivia, Brazil, Chile, and Mexico.* New Brunswick, N.J.: North-South Center and Transaction Books.

Heritage Foundation. Various years. *Index of Economic Freedom.* www.heritage.org

Hernández, Carlos Raúl. 1990. AD y el programa económico: La clave del éxito electoral. *Veneconomía* 8 (December): 21–23.

Hillman, Richard S. 1994. *Democracy for the Privileged: Crisis and Transition in Venezuela.* Boulder, Colo.: Lynne Rienner.

Hirschman, Albert O. 1970. *Exit, Voice, and Loyalty; Response to Decline in Firms, Organizations, and States.* Cambridge: Harvard University Press.

———. 1979. The turn to authoritarianism in Latin America and the search for its economic determinants. In David Collier, ed., *The New Authoritarianism in Latin America.* Princeton: Princeton University Press.

———. 1981. The changing tolerance for income inequality in the course of economic development. In Albert O. Hirschman, *Essays in Trespassing: Economics to Politics and Beyond.* Cambridge: Cambridge University Press.

Horcasitas, Juan Molinar, and Jeffrey A. Weldon. 1994. Electoral determinants and consequences of National Solidarity. In Wayne A. Cornelius, Ann L. Craig, and Jonathan Fox, eds., *Transforming State-Society Relations in Mexico.* San Diego: University of California Center for U.S.-Mexican Studies.

Huber, Evelyne. 1995. Assessments of state strength. In Peter H. Smith, ed., *Latin America in Comparative Perspective: New Approaches to Methods and Analysis.* Boulder, Colo.: Westview Press.

Huber, John D. 1998. How does cabinet instability affect political performance? Portfolio volatility and health care cost containment in parliamentary democracies. *American Political Science Review* 92, no. 3 (September): 577–92.

Huntington, Samuel P. 1968. *Political Order in Changing Societies.* New Haven: Yale University Press.

INDEC (Instituto Nacional de Estadística y Censos). Various years. *Anuario Estadístico de la República Argentina.* Buenos Aires: INDEC.

Inter-American Development Bank. Various years. *Economic and Social Progress in Latin America.* Washington, D.C.: Inter-American Development Bank.

Inter-American Dialogue Task Force on Cuba. 1995. *Cuba in the Americas: Breaking the Policy Deadlock.* The Second Report. Washington, D.C.: Inter-American Dialogue, September.

International Finance Corporation. 2000. Trends in privatization in developing countries, 1970–1998. Washington, D.C.

International Monetary Fund (IMF). 1988. *Government Finance Statistics Yearbook.* Washington, D.C.: International Monetary Fund.

———. 1995. Argentina—Recent Economic Developments. Washington, D.C.: IMF Staff Country Report No. 95/110, November.

———. 1996. *World Economic Outlook, October 1996.* Washington, D.C.: International Monetary Fund.

———. 1999. Argentina policy memorandum. www.imf.og/external/np/loi/199/011199.htm.

———. 2000. Argentina: Selected issues and statistical analysis. Washington, D.C.: IMF Staff Country Report No. 00/160, December.

———. 2001. Argentina: Third review under the stand-by arrangement. Washington, D.C.: IMF Country Report No. 01/90.

Iturrieta, Aníbal. 1994. Apuntes sobre el largo recorrido del pensamiento peronista. In Aníbal Iturrieta, ed., *El pensamiento político argentino contemporáneo.* Buenos Aires: Grupo Editor Latinoamericano, S.R.L.

Jatar-Hausmann, Ana Julia. 1999. *The Cuban Way: Capitalism, Communism and Confrontation*. West Hartford, Conn.: Kumarian Press.

Johnson, Chalmers. 1982. *MITI and the Japanese Miracle*. Stanford: Stanford University Press.

Jones, Mark P., Sebastian Saiegh, Pablo Spiller, and Mariano Tommasi. 2000. Professional politicians, amateur legislators: The Argentine congress in the twentieth century. Paper presented at the Annual Conference of the International Society of New Institutional Economics, Tübingen, Germany, September 22–24.

Kahler, Miles. 1992. External influence, conditionality, and the politics of adjustment. In Stephan Haggard and Robert R. Kaufman, eds., *The Politics of Economic Adjustment*. Princeton: Princeton University Press.

———. 1994. External actors and adjustment: The role of the IMF. In Paul W. Drake, ed., *Money Doctors, Foreign Debts, and Economic Reforms in Latin America from the 1890s to the Present*. Wilmington, Del.: Scholarly Resources.

Karl, Terry Lynn. 1987. Petroleum and political pacts: The transition to democracy in Venezuela. *Latin American Research Review* 22, no. 1: 63–94.

———. 1997. *The Paradox of Plenty: Oil-booms and Petro-states*. Berkeley and Los Angeles: University of California Press.

Katznelson, Ira, and Mark Kesselman. 1987. *The Politics of Power: A Critical Introduction to American Government*. 3d ed. Orlando, Fla.: Harcourt Brace Jovanovich.

Kaufman, Robert R. 1977. Corporatism, clientelism, and partisan conflict: A study of seven Latin American countries. In James M. Malloy, ed., *Authoritarianism and Corporatism in Latin America*. Pittsburgh: University of Pittsburgh Press.

———. 1990. Stabilization and adjustment in Argentina, Brazil and Mexico. In Joan M. Nelson, ed., *Economic Crisis and Policy Choice: The Politics of Adjustment in the Third World*. Princeton: Princeton University Press.

Kaufman, Robert R., and Barbara Stallings. 1991. The political economy of Latin American populism. In Rudiger Dornbusch and Sebastian Edwards, eds., *The Macroeconomics of Populism in Latin America*. Chicago: University of Chicago Press.

Kavanagh, Dennis. 1980. Political leadership: The labours of Sisyphous. In Richard Rose, ed., *Challenge to Governance: Studies in Overloaded Polities*. Beverly Hills, Calif.: Sage Publications.

Kay, Bruce H. 1996. "Fujipopulism" and the liberal state in Peru, 1990–95. *Journal of Interamerican Studies and World Affairs* 38, no. 4 (January): 55–99.

Keeler, John T.S. 1993. Opening the window for reform: Mandates, crises and extraordinary policy-making. *Comparative Political Studies* 25, no. 4 (Winter): 433–86.

Kelly, Janet. 1986. Reform without pain: The Commission on State Reform in the Lusinchi administration. Paper presented at the Latin American Studies Association Congress, Boston, October.

Kesselman, Mark. 1973. Order or movement? The literature of political development as ideology. *World Politics* 26, no. 1 (October): 139–54.

Kessler, Timothy. 1998. Political capital: Mexican financial policy under Salinas. *World Politics* 51, no. 1 (October): 36–66.

———. 2000. The Mexican peso crash: Causes, consequences, and comeback. In Carol Wise and Riordan Roett, eds., *Exchange Rate Politics in Latin America*. Washington, D.C.: Brookings Institution.

King, Gary, Robert A. Keohane, and Sidney Verba. 1994. *Designing Social Inquiry: Scientific Inference in Qualitative Research*. Princeton: Princeton University Press.

Kingstone, Peter R. 1999a. Constitutional reform and macroeconomic stability: Implications for democratic consolidation in Brazil. In Philip Oxhorn and Pamela K. Starr, eds., *Markets and Democracy in Latin America: Conflict or Convergence?* Boulder, Colo.: Lynne Rienner.

———. 1999b. *Crafting Coalitions for Reform: Business Preferences, Political Institutions, and Neoliberal Reform in Brazil.* University Park: Pennsylvania State University Press.

Kitschelt, Herbert. 1994. *The Transformation of European Social Democracy.* New York: Cambridge University Press.

———. 1999. European social democracy between political economy and electoral competition. In Herbert Kitschelt, Peter Lange, and Gary Marks, eds., *Continuity and Change in Contemporary Capitalism.* New York: Cambridge Studies in Comparative Politics, Cambridge University Press.

Kohan, Alberto. 1991. *Me llamo Alberto Kohan.* Buenos Aires: Editorial América Edita.

Kohli, Atul. 1986. Democracy and development. In John P. Lewis and Valeriana Kallab, eds., *Development Strategies Reconsidered.* New Brunswick, N.J.: Transaction.

Kohli, Atul, and Vivienne Shue. 1994. State power and social forces: On political contention and accommodation in the Third World. In Joel S. Migdal, Atul Kohli, and Vivienne Shue, eds., *State Power and Social Forces: Domination and Transformation in the Third World.* Cambridge: Cambridge University Press.

Kornblith, Miriam. 1989. Deuda y democracia en Venezuela: Los sucesos del 27 y 28 de febrero. *Cuadernos del CENDES* 10:17–34.

Kornblith, Miriam, and Daniel H. Levine. 1995. Venezuela: The life and times of the party system. In Scott Mainwaring and Timothy R. Scully, eds., *Building Democratic Institutions: Party Systems in Latin America.* Stanford: Stanford University Press.

Korzeniewicz, Roberto Patricio, and William C. Smith. 2000. Growth, poverty and inequality in Latin America: Searching for the high road. *Latin American Research Review* 35, no. 3: 7–56.

Krasner, Stephen. 1978. *Defending the National Interest: Raw Materials Investments and U.S. Foreign Policy.* Princeton: Princeton University Press.

Krueger, Anne. O. 1974. The political economy of the rent-seeking society. *American Economic Review* 64, no. 3 (June): 291–303.

———. 1978. *Liberalization Attempts and Its Consequences.* A Special Conference Series on Foreign Trade Regimes and Economic Development, Vol. 10. New York: National Bureau of Economic Research; Cambridge, Mass.: Ballinger.

———. 1992. *Economic Policy Reform in Developing Countries: The Kuznets Memorial Lectures at the Economic Growth Center, Yale University.* Cambridge, Mass.: Basil Blackwell.

———. 1993. Virtuous and vicious circles in economic development. AEA Papers and Proceedings of the 105th Annual Meeting, Anaheim, Calif., January 5–7: 351–55.

Lal, Deepak. 1987. The political economy of economic liberalization. *World Bank Economic Review* 1:273–99.

Larraín, Felipe. 1990. Comment [on the Venezuela chapter]. In John Williamson, ed., *Latin American Adjustment: How Much Has Happened?* Washington, D.C.: Institute for International Economics.

Lepage, Octavio. 1991. *Política, democracia, partidos.* Caracas: Ediciones Centauro.

Levi, Margaret. 1999. Death and taxes: Extractive equality and the development of democratic institutions. In Ian Shapiro and Casiano Hacker-Cordon, eds., *Democracy's Value*. Cambridge: Cambridge University Press.

Levine, Daniel H. 1978. Venezuela since 1958: The consolidation of democratic politics. In Juan J. Linz and Alfred C. Stepan, eds., *The Breakdown of Democratic Regimes, Latin America*. Baltimore: Johns Hopkins University Press.

Levitsky, Steven. 1998. Institutionalization and peronism. *Party Politics* 4, no. 1: 77–92.

———. 1999a. From laborism to liberalism: Institutionalization and labor-based party adaptation in Argentina (1983–1997). Ph.D. diss., University of California, Berkeley.

———. 1999b. Fujimori and post-party politics. *Journal of Democracy* 10, no. 3 (July): 78–92.

———. 2000. The "normalization" of Argentine politics. *Journal of Democracy* 11, no. 2 (April): 56–69

Lewis-Beck, Michael S., and Mary Stegmaier. 2000. Economic determinants of electoral outcomes. *Annual Review of Political Science* 3:183–219.

Lindblom, Charles E. 1977. *Politics and Markets*. New York: Basic Books.

———. 1982. The market as prison. *Journal of Politics* 44:324–36.

Lipset, Seymour Martin. 2000. The indispensability of political parties. *Journal of Democracy* 11, no. 1: 48–56.

Llach, Juan J. 1997. *Otro siglo, otra Argentina*. Buenos Aires: Ariel Sociedad Económica.

Llanos, Mariana. 1998. El presidente, el Congreso y la política de privatizaciones en la Argentina (1989–1997). *Desarrollo Económico* 151, no. 38: 743–70.

López Maya, Margarita, Luis Gómez Calcaño, and Thais Maingón. 1989. *De Punto Fijo al Pacto Social: Desarrollo y hegemonía en Venezuela (1958–1985)*. Caracas: Fondo Editorial Acta Científica Venezolana.

Lynch, Menéndez, Nivel y Asoc. N.d. Approval rating of economic program among respondents who voted for the PJ in the 1989 elections. Buenos Aires. Mimeographed.

Machinea, José Luis. 1993. Stabilisation under Alfonsín. In Colin M. Lewis and Nissa Torrents, eds., *Argentina in the Crisis Years (1983–1990): From Alfonsín to Menem*. London: Institute of Latin American Studies, University of London.

Magallanes, Manuel Vicente. 1993. *Acción Democrática: Partido del Pueblo*. Caracas: Ediciones Adeven.

Maingón, Thais. 1993. Agenda Social de los '90: Proposiciones para una política de salud y nutrición para Venezuela. Instituto Latinoamericano de Investigaciones Sociales (ILDIS) / Comisión Presidencial para la Reforma del Estado (COPRE), Caracas, September. Mimeographed.

Mainwaring, Scott. 1992. Brazilian party underdevelopment in comparative perspective. *Political Science Quarterly* 107:677–707.

———. 1995. Democracy in Brazil and the Southern Cone: Achievements and problems. *Journal of Interamerican Studies and World Affairs* 37:113–79.

Mainwaring, Scott, and Timothy R. Scully, eds. 1995. *Building Democratic Institutions: Party Systems in Latin America*. Stanford: Stanford University Press.

Malloy, James M. 1977. Authoritarianism and corporatism in Latin America: The modal pattern. In James M. Malloy, ed., *Authoritarianism and Corporatism in Latin America*. Pittsburgh: University of Pittsburgh Press.

Mamalakis, Markos J., 1969. The theory of sectoral clashes. *Latin American Research Review* 4, no. 3: 9–46.

Márquez, Gustavo. 1993. Poverty and social policies in Venezuela. IESA, Caracas, April. Mimeographed.

Márquez, Gustavo, et al. 1993. Fiscal policy and income distribution in Venezuela. In Ricardo Hausmann and Roberto Rigobón, eds., *Government Spending and Income Distribution in Latin America*. Washington, D.C.: Inter-American Development Bank, distributed by the Johns Hopkins University Press.

Martz, John D. 1966. *Acción Democrática: Evolution of a Modern Political Party in Venezuela*. Princeton: Princeton University Press.

———. 1992. Party elites and leadership in Colombia and Venezuela. *Journal of Latin American Studies* 24:87–121.

———. 1998. Deconstruction versus reconstruction: The challenge to Venezuelan parties. In Damarys Canache and Michael R. Kulisheck, eds., *Reinventing Legitimacy: Democracy and Political Change in Venezuela*. Westport, Conn.: Greenwood Press.

———. 1999–2000. Political parties and candidate selection in Venezuela and Colombia. *Political Science Quarterly* 114, no. 4 (Winter): 639–59.

Mauceri, Philip. 1995. State reform, coalitions, and the neoliberal *autogolpe* in Peru. *Latin American Research Review* 30, no. 1: 7–38.

McConnell, Shelley A. 2001. Ecuador's centrifugal politics. *Current History* 100, no. 643 (February): 73–79.

McCoy, Jennifer. 1989. Labor and the state in a party-mediated democracy: Institutional change in Venezuela. *Latin American Research Review* 24, no. 2 (May): 35–67.

McCoy, Jennifer, and William C. Smith. 1995. From deconsolidation to reequilibration? Prospects for democratic renewal in Venezuela. In Jennifer McCoy, Andrés Serbín, William C. Smith, and Andrés Stambouli, eds., *Venezuelan Democracy under Stress*. New Brunswick, N.J.: Transaction.

McGuire, James W. 1997. *Peronism without Perón: Unions, Parties, and Democracy in Argentina*. Stanford: Stanford University Press.

Memorando relacionado con las políticas económicas de Venezuela al FMI del 28 de febrero de 1989. 1989. *Revista venezolana de ciencia política* 2 (December): 451–67.

Menem, Carlos S. 1991. Movilización peronista para la actualización política y doctrinaria. Mensaje de Carlos Menem. Buenos Aires, Consejo Nacional Justicialista, March 16.

Merkx, Gilbert W. 1969. Sectoral clashes and political change: The Argentine experience. *Latin American Research Review* 4, no. 3: 89–114.

Mesa Lago, Carmelo. 1994. *Are Economic Reforms Propelling Cuba to the Market?* Coral Gables, Fla.: University of Miami North-South Center.

Migdal, Joel S. 1987. Strong states, weak states: Power and accommodation. In Myron Weiner and Samuel P. Huntington, eds., *Understanding Political Development: An Analytic Study*. Boston: Little, Brown.

Migdal, Joel S., Atul Kohli, and Vivienne Shue, eds. 1994. *State Power and Social Forces: Domination and Transformation in the Third World*. Cambridge: Cambridge University Press.

Mill, John Stuart. 1965. *A System of Logic: Ratiocinative and Inductive*. 8th ed. New York and London: Longmans.

Ministerio de Economía. 1992. Consejo Nacional Económico para la Producción, la Inversión, y el Crecimiento: Antecedentes y bibliografía. Ministerio de Economía y Obras y Servicios Públicos, Secretaría de Relaciones Institucionales, Buenos Aires. Mimeographed.

———. 1994. Volumen y respuestas a pedidos de informes. Buenos Aires: Ministerio de Economía y Obras y Servicios Públicos, Secretaría de Relaciones Institucionales.

———. 1999. *Caracterización y evolución del gasto público social.* Buenos Aires: Ministerio de Economía, Secretaría de Programación Económica y Regional.

———. Various issues. *Informe Económico Trimestral.* Buenos Aires.

Ministerio del Trabajo. Various years. *Memorias del Ministerio del Trabajo.* Caracas: Venezuela.

Ministry of the Economy. 1994. *Argentina: A Country for Investment and Growth.* Buenos Aires.

———. 2000. *Economic Report, Year 1999.* Buenos Aires, Ministry of the Economy, Secretariat of Economic and Regional Programming.

Minsburg, Naúm. 1991. Políticas económicas en torno al papel del estado. In Arnaldo Bocco and Naúm Minsburg, eds., *Privatizaciones: Reestructuración del Estado y de la Sociedad.* Buenos Aires: Ediciones Letra Buena.

Molano, Walter T. 1997. *The Logic of Privatization: The Case of Telecommunications in the Southern Cone of Latin America.* Westport, Conn.: Greenwood Press.

Molinelli, N. Guillermo, M. Valeria Palanza, and Gisela Sin. 1999. *Congreso, Presidencia y Justicia en Argentina.* Buenos Aires: Grupo Editorial Temas.

Montesinos, Verónica. 1997. El valor simbólico de los economistas en la democratización de la política chilena. *Nueva Sociedad* 152 (November–December): 108–26.

Moore, Barrington. 1966. *The Social Origins of Dictatorship and Democracy: Lord and Peasant in the Making of the Modern World.* Boston: Beacon Press.

Morales Solá, Joaquín. 1990. *Asalto a la ilusión: Historia secreta del poder en la Argentina desde 1983.* Buenos Aires: Editorial Planeta.

Mora y Araujo, Noguera y Asociados. 1994. Las demandas sociales y la legitimidad de la política de ajuste (second draft). Buenos Aires. Mimeographed.

Morley, Samuel A., Roberto Machado, and Stefano Pettinato. 1999. Indexes of structural reform in Latin America. Santiago. ECLAC. Mimeographed.

Morrell, James R., Rachel Neild, and Hugh Byrne. 1999. Haiti and the limits to nation-building. *Current History* 98, no. 626 (March): 127–32.

Morris, Stephen D. 1995. *Political Reformism in Mexico: An Overview of Contemporary Mexican Politics.* Boulder, Colo.: Lynne Rienner.

Munck, Gerardo L., and Jay Verkuilen. 2000. Measuring democracy: Evaluating alternative indices. Paper presented at the 2000 Annual Meeting of the American Political Science Association, Washington, D.C.

Murillo, M. Victoria. 1994. Union response to economic reform in Argentina. Paper presented at the Conference on Inequality and New Forms of Popular Representation, Columbia University, New York, March 3–5.

———. 2000. From Populism to neoliberalism: Labor unions and market reforms in Latin America. *World Politics* 52, no. 2 (January): 135–74.

Mustapic, Ana María. 2000. Oficialistas y diputados: Las relaciones ejecutivo-legislativo en la Argentina. *Desarrollo Económico* 39, no. 156 (January–March): 571–98.

Mustapic, Ana María, and Matteo Goretti. 1991. Gobierno y oposición en el Congreso: La práctica de la cohabitación durante la Presidencia de Alfonsín (1983–1989). Instituto Torcuato di Tella, Serie Documentos de Trabajo 117, Buenos Aires, September.

Naím, Moisés. 1993a. The launching of radical policy changes, 1989–1991. In Joseph S. Tulchin with Gary Bland, eds., *Venezuela in the Wake of Radical Reform*. Boulder, Colo.: Lynne Rienner.

———. 1993b. *Paper Tigers and Minotaurs: The Politics of Venezuela's Economic Reforms*. Washington, D.C.: Carnegie Endowment for International Peace.

Naím, Moisés, and Antonio Francés. 1995. The Venezuelan private sector: From courting the state to courting the market. In Louis W. Goodman et al., eds., *Lessons of the Venezuelan Experience*. Washington, D.C.: Woodrow Wilson Center Press; Baltimore: Johns Hopkins University Press.

Naím, Moisés, and Ramón Piñango, eds. 1985. *El caso Venezuela: Una ilusión de armonía*. Caracas: Ediciones IESA.

Navarro, Juan Carlos. 1993. En busca del pacto perdido: La fallida búsqueda del consenso en la Venezuela de los ochenta y los noventa. In Andrés Serbín, Andrés Stambouli, Jennifer McCoy, and William Smith, eds., *Venezuela: La democracia bajo presión*. Caracas: Nueva Sociedad.

———. 1994. Reversal of fortune: The ephemeral success of adjustment in Venezuela between 1989 and 1993. In *Caracas: Project on Governance and Successful Adjustment*, The World Bank, November.

Nelson, Joan M. 1988. The political economy of stabilization: Commitment, capacity, and public response. In Robert H. Bates, ed., *Toward a Political Economy of Development: A Rational Choice Perspective*. Berkeley and Los Angeles: University of California Press.

———. 1992. Poverty, equity, and the politics of adjustment. In Stephan Haggard and Robert R. Kaufman, eds., *The Politics of Economic Adjustment*. Princeton: Princeton University Press.

———, ed. 1989. *Fragile Coalitions: The Politics of Economic Adjustment*. New Brunswick, N.J.: Transaction Press.

———, ed. 1990. *Economic Crisis and Policy Change*. Princeton: Princeton University Press.

Niño, Carlos Santiago. 1996. Hyperpresidentialism and constitutional reform in Argentina. In Arend Lijphart and Carlos H. Waisman, eds., *Institutional Design in New Democracies: Eastern Europe and Latin America*. Boulder, Colo.: Westview.

Norden, Deborah. 1996. The rise of the lieutenant colonels: Rebellion in Argentina and Venezuela. *Latin American Perspectives* 23, no. 3 (Summer): 74–86.

Nordlinger, Eric A. 1981. *On the Autonomy of the Democratic State*. Cambridge: Harvard University Press.

North, Douglass C., and Barry R. Weingast. 1989. Constitutions and commitment: The evolution of institutions governing public choice in seventeenth-century England. *Journal of Economic History* 49, no. 4: 803–32.

Novaro, Marcos. 1994. *Pilotos de tormentas: Crisis de representación y personalización de la política en Argentina (1989–1993)*. Buenos Aires: Ediciones Letra Buena.

———. 1999a. Crisis y renovación de los partidos: Una perspectiva comparada sobre los años del menemismo. In Juan Carlos Torre, Marcos Novaro, Vicente Palermo, and Isidoro Cheresky, eds., *Entre el abismo y la ilusión: Peronismo, democracia y mercado*. Buenos Aires: Grupo Editorial Norma.

————. 1999b. Presentación: La década del menemismo. In Juan Carlos Torre, Marcos Novaro, Vicente Palermo, and Isidoro Cheresky, eds., *Entre el abismo y la ilusión: Peronismo, democracia y mercado*. Buenos Aires: Grupo Editorial Norma.

OCEI (Oficina Central de Estadística e Informática). Various years. *Anuario Estadístico de Venezuela*. Caracas: OCEI / Presidencia de la República.

O'Donnell, Guillermo A. 1973. *Modernization and Bureaucratic-Authoritarianism: Studies in South American Politics*. Berkeley: University of California, Institute of International Studies.

————. 1978a. Permanent crisis and the failure to create a democratic regime: Argentina, 1955–66. In Juan J. Linz, and Alfred Stepan, eds., *The Breakdown of Democratic Regimes, Latin America*. Baltimore: Johns Hopkins University Press.

————. 1978b. State and alliances in Argentina, 1956–1976. *Journal of Development Studies* 15:3–33.

————. 1992. Delegative democracy. Working Paper No. 172, Hellen Kellogg Institute for International Studies, Notre Dame, Ind.

————. 1994. The state, democratization, and some conceptual problems (a Latin American view with glances at some post-communist countries). In William C. Smith, Carlos H. Acuña, and Eduardo A. Gamarra, eds., *Latin American Political Economy in the Age of Neoliberal Reforms: Theoretical and Comparative Perspectives for the 1990s*. New Brunswick, N.J.: Transaction.

O'Donnell, Guillermo, Philippe C. Schmitter, and Lawrence Whitehead, eds. 1986. *Transitions from Authoritarian Rule: Tentative Conclusions about Uncertain Democracies*. Baltimore: Johns Hopkins University Press.

Offe, Claus. 1983. Competitive party democracy and the Keynesian welfare state. *Policy Sciences* 15:225–46.

————. 1984. *Contradictions of the Welfare State*. Cambridge: MIT Press.

Olson, Mancur. 1965. *The Logic of Collective Action: Public Goods and the Theory of Groups*. Cambridge: Harvard University Press.

————. 1982. *The Rise and Decline of Nations*. New Haven: Yale University Press.

————. 1993. Dictatorship, democracy, and development. *American Political Science Review* 87:567–76.

————. 2000. *Power and Prosperity: Outgrowing Communist and Capitalist Dictatorships*. New York: Basic Books.

Oropeza, Luis J. 1983. *Tutelary Pluralism: A Critical Approach to Venezuelan Democracy*. Cambridge: Harvard University Center for International Affairs.

Oxhorn, Philip, and Graciela Ducatenzeiler. 1999. The problematic relationship between economic and political liberalization: Some theoretical considerations. In Philip Oxhorn and Pamela K. Starr, eds., *Markets and Democracy in Latin America. Conflict or Convergence*. Boulder, Colo.: Lynne Rienner.

Palermo, Vicente. 1992. El menemismo, ¿perdurará? In Aníbal Iturrieta, ed., *El pensamiento político argentino contemporáneo*. Buenos Aires: Grupo Editor Latinoamericano S.R.L.

————. 1999. Crisis económicas y reformas de mercado. Comentario. *Desarrollo Económico* 39, no. 155 (October–December): 459–70.

Palermo, Vicente, and Marcos Novaro. 1996. *Política y poder en el gobierno de Menem*. Buenos Aires: Grupo Editorial Norma.

Panebianco, Angelo. 1988. *Political Parties: Organization and Power*. Trans. Marc Silver. Cambridge: Cambridge University Press.

Pastor Jr., Manuel. 2000. After the deluge? Cuba's potential as a market economy. In Susan Kaufman Purcell and David Rothkopf, eds., *Cuba: The Contours of Change*. Boulder, Colo.: Lynne Rienner.

Pastor Jr., Manuel, and Carol Wise. 1999a. The politics of second-generation reform. *Journal of Democracy* 10, no. 3 (July): 34–48.

———. 1999b. Stabilization and its discontents: Argentina's economic restructuring in the 1990s. *World Development* 27, no. 3 (1999): 477–503.

Penfold, Michael. 1998. Decentralization in Venezuela and Colombia. Paper presented at the Public Policy Brown Bag Breakfast, Caracas, IESA, July.

Pérez, Carlos A. 1991. *Discurso ante el Congreso*. Caracas, Venezuela.

———. 1993. *Discurso ante el Congreso*. Caracas, Venezuela.

Pérez-Stable, Marifeli. 1999. Caught in a contradiction: Cuban socialism between mobilization and normalization. *Comparative Politics* 32, no. 1 (October): 63–82.

Perry, William. 1993. Venezuela local elections. December 6, 1992, post-election report. Center for Strategic and International Studies, Latin American Election Study Series, vol. 11, study 1, Washington, D.C.

Peters, B. Guy. 1998. *Comparative Politics: Theory and Methods*. New York: New York University Press.

Pierson, Paul. 1994. *Dismantling the Welfare State? Reagan, Thatcher, and the Politics of Retrenchment*. New York: Cambridge University Press.

———. 2000. Increasing returns, path dependence and the study of politics. *American Political Science Review* 94, no. 2 (June): 251–67.

Pirker, Elizabeth. 1991. Participación de las empresas estatales en la economía. In Arnaldo Bocco and Naúm Minsburg, eds., *Privatizaciones: Reestructuración del estado y de la sociedad*. Buenos Aires: Ediciones Letra Buena.

Poggi, Gianfranco. 1990. *The State: Its Nature, Development and Prospects*. Stanford: Stanford University Press.

Powers, Nancy. 1995. The politics of poverty in Argentina in the 1990s. *Journal of Interamerican Studies and World Affairs* 37 (Winter): 89–137.

Prieto, Hugo. 1998. La defenestración de CAP. www.el-nacional.com/aniversario/3er/cap.htm.

PROVEA. Various years. *Informe anual: Situación de los derechos humanos*. Caracas: Provea.

———. Various issues. *Boletín mensual de derechos humanos y coyuntura*. Caracas.

Przeworski, Adam. 1991. *Democracy and the Market: Political and Economic Reforms in Eastern Europe and Latin America*. New York: Cambridge University Press.

———. 1993. Economic reforms, public opinion, and political institutions: Poland in the Eastern European perspective. In Bresser Pereira, Luiz Carlos et al., eds., *Economic Reforms in New Democracies: A Social-Democratic Approach*. Cambridge: Cambridge University Press.

Przeworski, Adam, et al. 1995. *Sustainable Democracy*. New York: Cambridge University Press.

Przeworski, Adam, and Henry Teune. 1970. *The Logic of Comparative Social Inquiry*. New York: Wiley-Interscience.

Putnam, Robert D. 1993. *Making Democracy Work: Civic Traditions in Italy*. Princeton: Princeton University Press.

Quirós Corradi, Alberto. 1992. *La desaceleración del entusiasmo*. Caracas: Editorial Futuro.

Remmer, Karen L. 1991a. New wine or old bottlenecks? The study of Latin American democracy. *Comparative Politics* 23 (July): 479–95.

———. 1991b. The political impact of economic crisis in Latin America in the 1980s. *American Political Science Review* 85 (September): 777–800.

———. 1998. The politics of neoliberal economic reform in South America, 1980–1994. *Studies in Comparative International Development* 33, no. 2 (Summer): 3–29.

Resende-Santos, João. 1997. Fernando Henrique Cardoso: Social and institutional building in Brazil. In Jorge I. Domínguez, ed., *Technopols: Ideas and Leaders in Freeing Politics and Markets in Latin America in the 1990s*. University Park: Pennsylvania State University Press.

Rey, Juan Carlos. 1989. *El futuro de la democracia en Venezuela*. Caracas: Instituto Internacional de Estudios Avanzados.

Rivarola, Domingo. 1991. Recomposición interna del Partido Colorado. In Domingo Rivarola, Marcelo Cavarozzi, and Manuel A. Garretón, eds., *Militares y políticos en una transición atípica*. Buenos Aires: CLACSO

Roberts, Kenneth M. 1995. Neoliberalism and the transformation of populism in Latin America: The Peruvian Case. *World Politics* 48 (October): 282–116.

Rodríguez, Miguel. 1991. Public sector behavior in Venezuela. In Felipe Larraín and Marcelo Selowsky, eds., *The Public Sector and the Latin American Crisis*. San Francisco: ICS Press.

Rodríguez Balza, Rafael Antonio. 1993. La economía política de la reforma tributaria en Venezuela. Master's thesis, Instituto de Estudios Superiores de Administración (IESA), Caracas.

Rodrik, Dani. 1989. Promises, promises: Credible policy reform via signalling. *Economic Journal* 99:756–72.

———. 1994. Comment [on Chapter 4]. In John Williamson, ed., *The Political Economy of Policy Reform*. Washington, D.C.: Institute for International Economics.

———. 1996. Understanding economic policy reform. *Journal of Economic Literature* 34, no. 1: 9–41.

Romero, Aníbal. 1986. *La miseria del populismo: Mitos y realidades de la democracia en Venezuela*. Caracas: Ediciones Centauro.

———. 1994. *Decadencia y crisis de la democracia. ¿A dónde va la democracia venezolana?* Caracas: Editorial Panapo.

———. 1997. Rearranging the deck chairs on the Titanic: The agony of democracy in Venezuela. *Latin American Research Review* 21, no. 1: 7–36.

Rose, Richard. 1980. The nature of the challenge. In Richard Rose, ed., *Challenge to Governance: Studies in Overloaded Polities*. Beverly Hills, Calif.: Sage Publications.

Rueschemeyer, Dietrich, Evelyne Huber Stephens, and John D. Stephens. 1992. *Capitalist Development and Democracy*. Chicago: University of Chicago Press.

Sachs, Jeffrey. 1994. Life in the economic emergency room. In John Williamson, ed., *The Political Economy of Policy Reform*. Washington, D.C.: Institute for International Economics.

———. 1995. Keynote address. In *Credible Signals of Reforming Governments: What to Believe?* Rapporteur's report by Karissa Price. Conference sponsored by Baring Asset Management and the Center for International Affairs, Harvard University, Cambridge, Mass., February 6.

Santoro, Daniel. 1994. *El hacedor: Una biografía política de Domingo Cavallo*. Buenos Aires: Planeta.

Sartori, Giovanni. 1976. *Parties and Party System: A Framework for Analysis.* Vol. 1. Cambridge: Cambridge University Press.

Schamis, Héctor E. 1999. Distributional coalitions and the politics of economic reform in Latin America. *World Politics* 51 (January): 236–68.

Schattschneider, E. E. 1942. *Party Government.* New York: Holt, Rinehart and Winston.

Schmitter, Philippe C. 1974. Still the century of corporatism? *Review of Politics* 36:85–131.

———. 1981. Interest intermediation and regime governability in contemporary Western Europe and North America. In Suzanne Berger, ed., *Organizing Interests in Western Europe: Pluralism, Corporatism, and the Transformation of Politics.* New York: Cambridge University Press.

Schmitter, Philippe C., and Terry Lynn Karl. 1991. What democracy is . . . and is not. *Journal of Democracy* 2, no. 3 (Summer): 75–88.

Schneider, Ben Ross. 1998. Elusive synergy: Business-government relations and development [review article]. *Comparative Politics* 31, no. 1: 101–22.

Schoultz, Lars. 1983. *The Populist Challenge: Argentine Electoral Behavior in the Postwar Era.* Chapel Hill: University of North Carolina Press.

Schumpeter, Joseph A. 1950. *Capitalism, Socialism and Democracy.* 3d ed. New York: Harper.

Schvarzer, Jorge. 1993. Expansión, maduración y perspectivas de las ramas básicas de procesos en la industria argentina: Una mirada expost desde la economía política. *Desarrollo Económico* 33:377–402.

Sheahan, John. 1987. *Patterns of Development in Latin America: Poverty, Repression, and Economic Strategy.* Princeton: Princeton University Press.

Silva, Patricio. 1997. Ascenso tecnocrático y democracia en América Latina. *Nueva Sociedad* 152 (November–December): 68–77.

Siqueira Wiarda, Iêda. 1990. Brazil: The politics of order and progress? In Howard J. Wiarda and Harvey F. Kline, eds., *Latin American Politics and Development.* 3d ed. Boulder, Colo.: Westview.

Skocpol, Theda. 1985. Bringing the state back in: Strategies of analysis in current research. In Peter B. Evans, Dietrich Rueschemeyer, and Theda Skocpol, eds., *Bringing the State Back In.* New York: Cambridge University Press.

Smith, William C. 1991. *Authoritarianism and the Crisis of the Argentine Political Economy.* Stanford: Stanford University Press.

———. 1992. Hyperinflation, macroeconomic instability, and neoliberal restructuring in democratic Argentina. In Edward C. Epstein, ed., *The New Argentine Democracy: The Search for a Successful Formula.* Westport, Conn.: Praeger.

Smith, William C., and Carlos H Acuña. 1994. Future politico-economic scenarios for Latin America. In William C. Smith, Carlos H. Acuña, and Eduardo A. Gamarra, eds., *Latin American Political Economy in the Age of Neoliberal Reforms: Theoretical and Comparative Perspectives for the 1990s.* New Brunswick, N.J.: Transaction.

Smith, W. Rand. 1995. Industrial crisis and the left: Adjustment strategies in socialist France and Spain. *Comparative Politics* 28:1–24.

Snow, Peter G., and Luigi Manzetti. 1993. *Political Forces in Argentina.* 3d ed. Westport, Conn.: Praeger.

SOFRES. Various years. Public Opinion Polls. Buenos Aires, Argentina.

Sola, Lourdes. 1994. The state, structural reform, and democratization in Brazil. In William C. Smith, Carlos H. Acuña, and Eduardo A. Gamarra, eds., *Latin American Political Economy in the Age of Neoliberal Reforms: Theoretical and Comparative Perspectives for the 1990s.* New Brunswick, N.J.: Transaction.

Sonntag, Heinz R., and Thais Maingón, with the collaboration of Xavier Biardeau. 1992. *Venezuela: 4-F. Un análasis sociopolítico.* Caracas: Nueva Sociedad.

Stallings, Barbara. 1990. Politics and economic crisis: A comparative study of Chile, Peru and Colombia. In Joan M. Nelson, ed., *Economic Crisis and Policy Choice.* Princeton: Princeton University Press.

———. 1992. International influence on economic policy: Debt, stabilization, and structural reform. In Stephan Haggard and Robert R. Kaufman, eds., *The Politics of Economic Adjustment.* Princeton: Princeton University Press.

———. 1995. The new international context of development. In Barbara Stallings, ed., *Global Change, Regional Response.* New York: Cambridge University Press.

Stallings, Barbara, and Wilson Peres. 2000. *Growth, Employment, and Equity: The Impact of the Economic Reforms in Latin America and the Caribbean.* Washington, D.C.: Brookings Institution.

Starr, Pamela K. 1997. Government coalitions and the viability of currency boards: Argentina under the Cavallo Plan. *Journal of Interamerican Studies and World Affairs* 39, no. 2 (Summer): 83–134.

———. 1999. Capital flows, fixed exchange rates, and political survival: Mexico and Argentina. In Philip Oxhorn and Pamela K. Starr, eds., *Markets and Democracy in Latin America: Conflict or Convergence.* Boulder, Colo.: Lynne Rienner.

Stempel París, Antonio. 1981. *Venezuela, Apuntes para el estudio del desarrollo político venezolano: Una democracia enferma.* Caracas: Editorial Ateneo de Caracas.

Stiglitz, Joseph E. 1996. Some lessons from the East Asian miracle. *World Bank Research Observer* 11, no. 2 (August): 151–77.

Stokes, Susan C. 1999. What do policy switches tell us about democracy? In Bernard Manin, Adam Przeworski, and Susan C. Stokes, eds., *Democracy, Accountability, and Representation.* New York: Cambridge University Press.

Sweeney, John. 1990. Acción Democrática: Un partido a la deriva. *Veneconomía,* March, 15–18.

Teichman, Judith A. 1995. *Privatization and Political Change in Mexico.* Pittsburgh: University of Pittsburgh Press.

Templeton, Andrew. 1995. The evolution of popular opinion. In Louis W. Goodman et al., eds., *Lessons of the Venezuelan Experience.* Washington, D.C.: Woodrow Wilson Center Press; Baltimore: Johns Hopkins University Press.

Tilly, Charles. 1975. Reflections on the history of European state-making. In Charles Tilly, ed., *The Formation of National States in Western Europe.* Princeton: Princeton University Press.

———. 1985. War-making and state-making as organized crime. In Peter B. Evans, Dietrich Rueschemeyer, and Theda Skocpol, eds., *Bringing the State Back In.* New York: Cambridge University Press.

———. 1992. *Coercion, Capital, and European States, AD 990–1990.* Oxford: Basil Blackwell.

Tinoco, Pedro R., Jr., Eglée Iturbe de Blanco, and Miguel F. Rodríguez. 1989. Carta de intención del gobierno venezolano al FMI del 24 de mayo de 1989. *Revista venezolana de ciencia política* 2:469–90.

Tommasi, Mariano, and Andrés Velasco. 1995. Where are we in the political economy of reform? Presented at the Conference on Economic Reform and Transitional Economies, Columbia University, May 12. Mimeographed.

Tornell, Aaron. 1995. Are economic crises necessary for trade liberalization and fiscal reform? In Rudiger Dornbusch and Sebastian Edwards, eds., *Reform, Recovery, and Growth*. Chicago: University of Chicago Press.

Torre, Juan Carlos. 1989. Interpretando (una vez más) los orígenes del peronismo. Buenos Aires: Instituto Torcuato di Tella, Centro de Investigaciones Sociales, Serie Documentos de Trabajo No. 107, May.

———. 1993. Conflict and cooperation in governing the economic emergency: The Alfonsín years. In Colin M. Lewis and Nissa Torrents, eds., *Argentina in the Crisis Years (1983–1990)*. London: Institute of Latin American Studies, University of London.

———. 1994. América Latina, el gobierno de la democracia en tiempos difíciles. Buenos Aires: Instituto Torcuato di Tella, Centro de Investigaciones Sociales, Serie Documentos de Trabajo No. 122, July.

———. 1999. Los desafíos de la oposición en un gobierno peronista. In Juan Carlos Torre, Marcos Novaro, Vicente Palermo, and Isidoro Cheresky, eds., *Entre el abismo y la ilusión: Peronismo, democracia y mercado*. Buenos Aires: Grupo Editorial Norma.

Torres, Gerver. 1993. La economía que podemos construir. In Carlos Blanco, ed., *Venezuela del siglo XX al siglo XXI: Un proyecto para construirla*. Caracas: COPRE and PUND.

Trimberger, Ellen Kay. 1978. *Revolution from Above: Military Bureaucrats in Development in Japan, Turkey, Egypt and Peru*. New Brunswick, N.J.: Transaction.

Tugwell, Franklin. 1975. *The Politics of Oil in Venezuela*. Stanford: Stanford University Press.

Tulchin, Joseph S. 1990. *Argentina and the United States: A Conflicted Relationship*. Boston: Twayne.

Tullock, Gordon. 1990. The costs of special privilege. In James E. Alt and Kenneth A. Shepsle, eds., *Perspectives on Positive Political Economy*. New York: Cambridge University Press.

UBS (Union de Banques Suisses). Various years. *Prices and Earnings Around the Globe*. Zurich: Union de Banques Suisses, Economic Research Department.

U.S. Department of Labor / Labor Department of International Affairs Bureau. 1991. *Foreign Labor Trends*. Washington, D.C.

Valecillos, Héctor. 1992. *El reajuste neoliberal en Venezuela*. Caracas: Monte Ávila Editores.

Van der Gaag, Makonnen, et al. 1991. Trends in social indicators and social financing. Washington, D.C.: World Bank Report No. WPS662.

Varas, Augusto. 1995. Latin America: Toward a new reliance on the market. In Barbara Stallings, ed., *Global Change, Regional Response*. New York: Cambridge University Press.

Virtuoso, José. 1992. ¿Hacia dónde nos lleva el Presidente Pérez? *Revista SIC*, April, 110–12.

Wade, John. 1993. Back to business. *Business Venezuela* 147:39–43.

Waisman, Carlos H. 1987. *Reversal of Development in Argentina*. Princeton: Princeton University Press.

Walt, Stephen M. 1987. *The Origins of Alliances*. Ithaca: Cornell University Press.

Waterbury, John. 1992. The heart of the matter? Public enterprise and the adjustment process. In Stephan Haggard, and Robert R. Kaufman, eds., *The Politics of Economic Adjustment*. Princeton: Princeton University Press.

Weber, Max. 1968. *Economy and Society: An Outline of Interpretive Sociology.* Vol. 2. Edited by Guenther Roth and Claus Wittich. New York: Bedminster Press.

Werlau, Maria C. 1997. Foreign investment in Cuba: The limits of commercial engagement. *World Affairs* 160, no. 2 (Fall): 51–69.

Weyland, Kurt. 1996a. Neopopulism and neoliberalism in Latin America. *Studies in Comparative International Development* 31, no. 3 (Fall): 3–31.

——. 1996b. Risk taking in Latin American economic restructuring: Lessons from prospect theory. *International Studies Quarterly* 40 (June): 185–208.

Williamson, John. 1994. In search of a manual for technopols. In John Williamson, ed., *The Political Economy of Policy Reform*. Washington, D.C.: Institute for International Economics.

——, ed. 1990. *Latin American Adjustment: How Much Has Happened?* Washington, D.C.: Institute for International Economics.

Williamson, John, and Stephan Haggard. 1994. The political conditions for economic reform. In John Williamson, ed., *The Political Economy of Policy Reform*. Washington, D.C.: Institute for International Economics.

Wilson, Frank L. 1980. Sources of party transformation: The case of France. In Peter H. Merkl, ed., *Western European Party Systems: Trends and Prospects*. New York: The Free Press.

World Bank. 1987. *World Development Report, 1987*. Washington, D.C.: The World Bank.

——. 1990a. Report and recommendation of the president of the I.B.R.D. to the executive directors on a proposed financial sector adjustment loan in an amount equivalent to US$—to the Republic of Venezuela for financial sector adjustment. Washington, D.C.: The World Bank [Quoted with permission].

——. 1990b. *World Development Report, 1990*. New York: Oxford University Press.

——. 1993. Venezuela: Structural and macroeconomic reforms—the new regime. Report No. 10404-VE, Washington, D.C. [Quoted with permission].

——. 1994. *World Tables, 1994*. Baltimore: Johns Hopkins University Press.

——. 1996a. Argentina: Country assistance review. www.worldbank.org/html/oed/ 15844.htm#/introduction.

——. 1996b. Argentina: Country overview. In *Trends in Developing Economies, 1996*. Washington, D.C. www.worldbank.org/html/extdr/offrep/lac/argentin.htm>

——. 1996c. Venezuela: Country overview. In *Trends in Developing Economies, 1996*. Washington, D.C. www.worldbank.org/html/extdr/offrep/lac/venezuel.htm>

——. 1996d. *World Development Report, 1996: From Plan to Market*. New York: Oxford University Press.

——. 2001. Argentina: Provincial finances, Update 4. Washington, D.C.: World Bank, Argentina, Chile, Paraguay, and Uruguay Country Dept. [Quoted with permission.]

Wynia, Gary W. 1992. *Argentina: Illusions and Realities*. 2d ed. New York: Holmes and Meier.

Yergin, Daniel, and Joseph Stanislaw. 1998. *The Commanding Heights*. New York: Simon and Schuster.

Zago, Angela. 1998. *La rebelión de los ángeles*. 4th ed. Caracas: WARP Editores.

Dailies and Newsletters

Venezuela:
El Diario de Caracas
Economía Hoy
Gerente
El Nacional
Revista SIC
El Universal
Veneconomía

Argentina:
Ámbito Financiero
Carta Económica
Clarín
El Cronista Comercial
La Nación
Página/12
La Prensa
Primicia
Review of the River Plate

Others:
Análisis del Mes (Asunción)
Cambio 16
The Economist
Latin American Regional Reports
Latin American Regional Reports: Andean Group
Latin American Regional Reports: Southern Cone
Latin Finance
Latin Trade (formerly *U.S./Latin Trade*)
Miami Herald
La Nación (Asunción)
New York Times
Notisur

index